The VINEYARDS of CENTRAL OTAGO

The VINEYARDS of CENTRAL OTAGO

A Passion for Winemaking on the Edge

TEXT BY **VIV MILSOM**   PHOTOGRAPHY BY **MIKE WILKINSON**

GODWIT

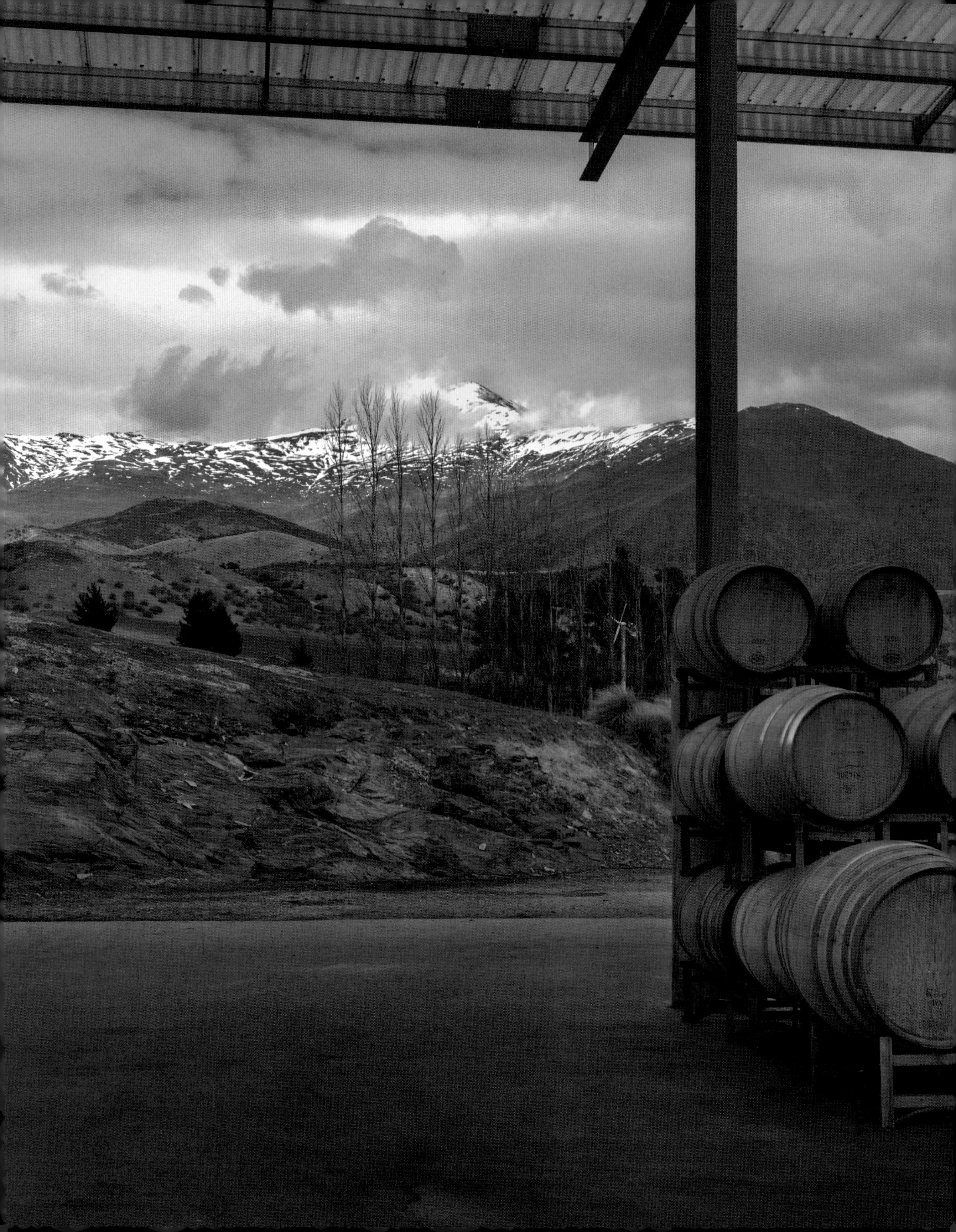

FOREWORDS	**6**
INTRODUCTION	**8**
GIBBSTON	**19**
Gibbston Valley	22
Chard Farm	34
Valli	46
Peregrine	56
Brennan Wines	68
ALEXANDRA	**77**
Two Paddocks	80
Judge Rock	92
Grasshopper Rock	102
BANNOCKBURN	**113**
Felton Road	116
Mt Difficulty	128
Carrick	142
Akarua	154
LOWBURN–PISA	**167**
Amisfield	170
Aurum	182
Burn Cottage	194
BENDIGO	**207**
Quartz Reef	210
Mondillo	222
Prophet's Rock	232
WANAKA	**243**
Rippon	246
Maude Wines	258
GLOSSARY	**270**

Forewords

FOR A COUNTRY THAT PRODUCES less than 1 per cent of the world's wine, New Zealand is blessed with more than its fair share of beautiful wine regions. Most wine lovers would agree the jewel in New Zealand's crown is Central Otago.

Central's landscape is awe-inspiring, full of deep, winding, river-tumbled gorges and soaring majestic peaks cutting through the region. Sloping hillsides provided the first intrepid pioneers with ideal geography to establish vineyards. The impact of bracing, crystal clear mountain air and intense piercing sunlight enable the production of wines of precision and detail.

Local winemakers are always keen to take advantage of the physical environment and the wealth of outdoor pursuits on their doorstep and go mountain biking, skiing or hiking. But Otago winemakers are also a thoughtful, inquisitive, contemplative group. A desire to explore all possibilities, to push boundaries and seek the fullest expression and potential from their vineyards is a thread that runs through them all. The result? Wines that display a true sense of place, that are beguiling in their youth, but which have the potential to develop and mature into something very special.

Every person who visits Central Otago cannot fail to be struck by the sheer splendour of the landscape and the warmth of its people. Most will leave with an appreciation of the region and its wines. In this book, Viv Milsom has done a truly wonderful job of conveying the magic of Central and its proud, talented winemakers.

JANE SKILTON MW
New Zealand School of Wines and Spirits

IT WAS AN INCREDIBLE RISK when they started. Central Otago is further south than any other vine-growing region in the world. It was the late 1970s—early 1980s; there were no supplies, little knowledge of the area's growing conditions, and no vines nearby. The pioneers of Central Otago wine had little more than determined vision, a leap of faith, and each other. Experts advised against it — the region was surely too cold and the seasons too short to ripen grapes. But together a handful of people spearheaded what, within just two decades, would become one of the most admired Pinot Noir regions in the world.

Through her steady look at Central Otago's sub-regions and leading producers, Viv Milsom has outlined the growth and character that has helped bring the area to the world stage. Photographs by Mike Wilkinson illustrate the dedication and dogged hard work that still define the heart of Central Otago wine — the people themselves. As the region has expanded, so has its sense of community, its winegrowers and winemakers working together to understand one of wine's most unusual landscapes.

The outstanding features of New Zealand's southern-most wine region are part of what make its wines distinctive. Incredible sunshine with still cold nights bring impressive flavour with brightening acidity. A dry climate with four distinct seasons encourages wines of concentration and clear focus. The extreme southern latitude brings marked vintage variation and winemakers who earn their stripes with every season. It is not easy making wine in Central Otago. Yet those featured in this book have found the opportunity to make hallmark wines in the challenges of the place. Together, they swiftly raised a region of quality wine out of what not so long ago the experts said would be impossible.

ELAINE CHUKAN BROWN
Writer, speaker, illustrator — Hawk Wakawaka Wine Reviews

INTRODUCTION

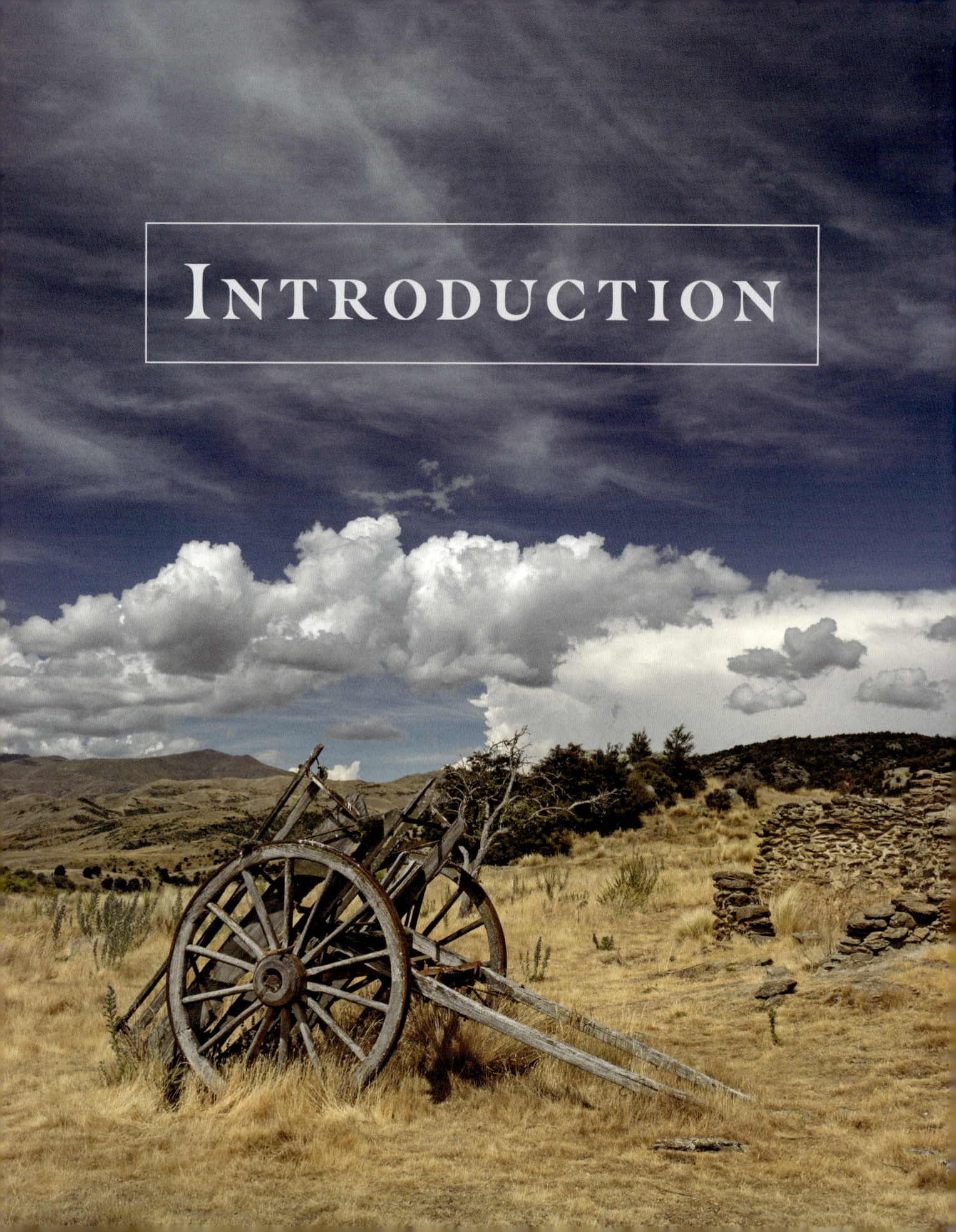

CENTRAL OTAGO has enjoyed three gold rushes: in the nineteenth century, gold was discovered in its wild rivers; in the twentieth century, its spectacular scenery was discovered by the tourism industry; and in the twenty-first century, Central Otago Pinot Noir was discovered by the world.

THE LAND

Covering 10,000 square kilometres, Central Otago is the southernmost wine region in the world and the highest and most inland region in New Zealand. Lying at latitude 45 degrees south, most of its vineyards are between 200 and 400 metres above sea level.

As a winegrowing region, Central Otago naturally divides into six sub-regions: Gibbston Valley, Alexandra and Wanaka; and, in the Cromwell Basin, Bannockburn, Lowburn–Pisa and Bendigo. While all differ in terms of their climate and rainfall, their geography and soil types, the Cromwell Basin sub-regions are the most consistently warm and account now for over 75 per cent of vineyards in Central Otago.

Central Otago is a region of rugged landscapes, stark beauty and climatic extremes. The winters bring snow and freezing temperatures, while the summers are hot and dry, regularly reaching 30 degrees Celsius. The diurnal shifts in temperature are also marked, especially during the growing season, with often as much as a 20-degree difference between day and night. This semi-continental climate, combined with the region's schist-based soils, has proved to be ideal for growing Pinot Noir. Cool-climate white wines, such as Pinot Gris, Riesling and Chardonnay, like it here too.

Formed by glaciers over millions of years, the free-draining soils are mostly low in organic matter, and with a low annual rainfall of between 350 and 660 millimetres the grape vines are forced to struggle — but out of this struggle comes the glory of high-quality grapes and wines of exceptional purity, intensity and vibrancy.

In Burgundy (Bourgogne) in central eastern France, the home of Pinot Noir, the wine industry has been developed over the course of 1000 years, while in Central Otago the first wines were produced commercially just over 30 years ago. Already, though, Central Otago Pinot Noir has achieved a global reputation for excellence, and the region is now recognised as one of the New World's outstanding wine producers.

THE PIONEERS

So how did a handful of pioneers set the stage for this remarkable and surprising success story? Remarkable because it has happened so quickly; and surprising because, 40 years ago, there was much scepticism about Central Otago's potential to become a winegrowing region. It was generally believed that Central Otago was too far south, too cold, and the frosts in spring and autumn were too severe. 'Don't be crazy', 'Forget it', 'You'll never do it' the pioneers were told. But these pioneers were people with vision, tenacity and energy, and working together they would overcome the daunting challenges that lay ahead.

Ann Pinckney had been brought up on a Southland farm and studied horticulture at Lincoln College, as it then was. Keen to grow grapes and make wine in Central Otago, she believed it could be done. She had already gained experience working in the wine industry in

Australia and Europe and planted her first grapes in 1976 on family land at Dalefield, near Queenstown. She was the first to plant with the express purpose of producing wine in commercial quantities, and the first to plant Pinot Noir grapes, although her main interest was in producing cool-climate white wines.

Meanwhile, 60 kilometres away, over the Crown Range, Rolfe and Lois Mills had left their city lives to come and live on the shores of Lake Wanaka at Rippon, on family land Mills was keen to develop. They started experimenting with different grape varieties in 1975. Then, in 1978, a fortuitous meeting at a winegrowing seminar at Lincoln led to Rolfe and Ann becoming friends. Four years later, in 1982, Mills started planting vines with a commercial outlook.

'Don't be crazy', 'Forget it', 'You'll never do it' the pioneers were told.

Back towards Queenstown, near the Kawarau Gorge at Gibbston, Alan Brady and his wife Denise had also abandoned city life for a new start in Central Otago. They, too, were interested in growing grapes, but knew nothing about the industry. When, however, Denise had her first baby, in 1979, a second fortuitous meeting with Ann, who was also working as a Karitane nurse, led to a new friendship. With Ann's help and advice the first Gibbston Valley grapes were planted in 1981.

These fortuitous encounters led to Pinckney establishing the first winery in Central Otago, at Taramea, on Speargrass Flat Road, the site where she had replanted her vineyard. Pinckney provided the building, and Mills and Brady the equipment.

A hundred kilometres away, near Alexandra, Verdun Burgess and his partner Sue Edwards bought land in 1981, and were developing a vineyard, which they called Black Ridge. A builder by trade, Verdun was a beer drinker who by his own admission had 'only drunk about seven bottles of wine' in his life, and the locals thought he was a 'nutter' to be setting up a vineyard. But, as determined as he was stubborn, Verdun was not giving up. He read up all he could about vines and made contact with Bill and Gill Grant, who were growing grapes in the Alexandra Basin, near Clyde, and who, like the other pioneers, had planted different varieties to see what would grow best.

The region had a bright future in vine-growing.

Clyde was close to Monte Christo, where Jean Desire Feraud, a Frenchman who had made his money gold-mining, had planted the first vineyard in Central Otago back in the mid-1860s. His 'Burgundy' wine, which was possibly Pinot Noir, had won awards in Dunedin and Australia between 1879 and 1881. However, Feraud left Clyde in 1882, sold his land in 1886 and wine production there ceased. A decade later, in 1895, the Austro-Hungarian viticulturist Romeo Bragato, having been invited by the New Zealand government to investigate the country's winegrowing potential, reported that the region had a bright future in vine-growing and suggested that both Pinot Noir and Riesling would be suitable grape varieties for Central Otago. Some 60 years later, however, in 1958, a Department of Agriculture report suggested the opposite, stating that the economics of grapegrowing in Central Otago were not very favourable. And this remained the popular belief until the pioneers proved that Feraud and Bragato had been right in their thinking all along. Very right indeed.

International Cool Climate Wine Symposium, Auckland, 1988. From left to right: Alan Brady, Tony Bish, Lois Mills, Jancis Robinson MW, Verdun Burgess, Ann Pinckney, Sue Edwards and Rolfe Mills. *Photo courtesy of Ann Pinckney*

It was not just negative public thinking that challenged the pioneers. There were the rabbits that treated Central Otago as their personal dining table, the birds that loved nothing better than a grape breakfast, lunch or dinner, and the wasps that came in behind the birds to clean up. Then there was the weather: frosts, especially in late spring and early autumn; strong winds; and little rainfall. Not to mention thin soils, geographic isolation, and bankers wary of lending to a fledgling industry yet to prove itself.

The culture of collegiality which developed from helping each other to get started and overcome these daunting challenges has since characterised the Central Otago wine industry and led to the setting up of the Central Otago Winegrowers Association (COWA) in 1986. As the first president, Rolfe Mills further encouraged this culture, and advised all in the nascent industry to work together to promote Central Otago first and their own vineyards second. His motto: 'There's only one boat we're rowing — Central Otago.'

This spirit of working in unison to develop and then promote the region has led to Central Otago becoming, after Marlborough, the best-known of New Zealand's wine regions on the world stage — and this despite the fact that it produces only 5 per cent of the country's wine. Central Otago exports over 60 per cent of its production, with Australia and the UK being the biggest markets. The US is also an important market and smaller amounts are sold into Europe and Asia.

In 2000, the first Central Otago Pinot Noir Celebration was held in Queenstown. The success of this event, which attracted writers, merchants and Pinot Noir enthusiasts from all over the world, led to the establishment of Central Otago Pinot Noir Limited (COPNL), an organisation charged with promoting and marketing the Central Otago wine brand. The first COPNL offshore event was held in 2003 in London and drew a large number of influential UK wine writers to Peter Gordon's Sugar Club restaurant. Central Otago had well and truly arrived on the world stage, and its reputation as a premium Pinot Noir producer has grown steadily ever since.

Alan Brady says of the pioneers, 'We were peasant grapegrowers, not making great wine, but we showed it could be done.' Following the trail they had blazed, in 1991 John Olssen planted 9 hectares at Bannockburn in the Cromwell Basin, closely followed by others like Robin Dicey from Mt Difficulty and Stewart Elms at Felton Road. The collective capital and expertise of this second wave of investors really kicked off the winegrowing industry in Central Otago. On their arrival in the early 1990s, there were about 25 hectares planted, with six winegrowers producing 71 tonnes of grapes; a decade later, by 2002, this had become 534 hectares and 46 producers. Fast-forward to 2018 and there are close to 2000 hectares planted, over 130 wineries, and 33 grapegrowers producing nearly 8500 tonnes. Although this output is still tiny, Central Otago in recent years has been one of the fastest-growing wine regions in New Zealand.

THE WINES

Pinot Noir accounts for 78 per cent of production in Central Otago and is the wine that has earned the region its global reputation for excellence. In the early days, when the pioneers had planted up to 30 different varieties to see what would do well, Pinot Noir had soon put its hand up and said, 'I like it here.' It was not too long before Central Otago's Pinots started to win gold medals, and the region was on its way to becoming a Pinot-centric region.

Grown in Burgundy since AD 400, Pinot Noir is considered the holy grail of wines. As Alan Brady explains, 'The perfect Pinot remains just out of reach, mysterious and elusive, a capricious and complex enigma that is always at least one more vintage away.'

Notoriously fickle and difficult to grow, Pinot Noir does not thrive everywhere. It needs a relatively cool climate to avoid ripening too quickly, before it has had time to develop flavour. Growing conditions in Central Otago can be challenging and yields low, and if anything can go wrong, it will. But the fruit quality and flavour intensity in Central Otago grapes is exceptionally high. The secret seems to lie in a combination of factors: intense summer heat, long warm autumns

Pinot Noir is a chameleon, reflecting its site more than other varieties.

with cool nights, low rainfall, and free-draining soils which are low in organic matter but rich in minerals, including calcium. Added to these environmental factors has been a bunch of talented and committed viticulturists and winemakers, well supported by investors with deep pockets, who together have believed in Central Otago's potential to produce some of the best wines in the world.

Pinot Noir is a chameleon, reflecting its site more than other varieties, and now that the Central Otago vines are ageing, the Pinots are starting to reflect their different sites across the sub-regions. Central Otago is known for producing a fruit-forward style of Pinot Noir, but with this ageing of the vines, the wines have been starting to show more complexity too. In general, the wines coming from the cooler sub-regions of Gibbston, Alexandra and Wanaka tend to be lighter in colour, and their flavour profile is strawberries and raspberries — red berries, or blueberries; while the wines coming from the Cromwell Basin sub-regions tend to be darker, with flavours of dark cherries and plums.

White wines, which account for just over 20 per cent of production in Central Otago, have achieved success too, winning national and international recognition. Pinot Gris has been the most popular white variety grown over the last decade, but Riesling, Chardonnay and Sauvignon Blanc, while they are grown in smaller quantities, have all done well too. Chardonnay is used, along with Pinot Noir, to make sparkling wine, but has been making a comeback in its own right, and Rosé too is becoming more popular.

In New Zealand there has been a strong movement towards organics in the wine industry, with a national goal of 20 per cent of vineyards and wineries becoming certified organic by 2020. Central Otago is already well ahead of other regions with over 20 per cent of its winegrowers either certified or in the process of becoming certified organic or biodynamic.

Central Otago winegrowers have found it easier to convert to organics because of the region's low rainfall and winter frosts; fewer weeds grow and fewer pests and diseases thrive, meaning fewer herbicides and pesticides are required. The use of sheep to eat the grass in vineyards has further eliminated the need for herbicides and has helped enrich the soil naturally.

A small number of vineyards have gone beyond organics and adopted biodynamics. Based on the philosophy and teachings of Rudolf Steiner, some biodynamic practices seem to be more about hocus-pocus than good science, but even the sceptics cannot dispute the quality of the wines being produced from these vineyards. As Nigel Greening from Felton Road says, 'Steiner had some pretty weird beliefs, but he had two incredibly powerful ideas: you must take the whole farm and see it as a single living ecosystem, and you must recognise that there is no natural hierarchy — everything is equally valuable and interconnected.'

THE BURGUNDY CONNECTION

There are only a few places outside of Burgundy where Pinot Noir has been grown successfully. Central Otago is one of them, along with Oregon in the United States, and it is a well-established custom now for young winemakers learning their craft to travel to France, the US or New Zealand to work the different harvests. The Central Otago Burgundy Exchange programme was initiated in 2006 by Nick Mills from Wanaka's Rippon vineyard. He had lived in France as a child, and later as a young man returned to study and work in Burgundy. Through the programme, each year around harvest time a small group of young

New Zealanders travel to Burgundy, where they study for a week, before being hosted at a domaine (vineyard/winery) over vintage to learn about French culture and winemaking practices and traditions. Then, when it is harvest time in Central Otago, a small group of French students (or 'stagiaires') are hosted at local vineyards to learn how Pinot Noir is being made in the New World. They also spend a week studying at Cromwell Polytechnic before going out into the vineyards.

Over the last decade, this programme has helped forge a strong bond between these two winemaking regions, and in 2017 its tenth anniversary was celebrated in Burgundy with a special lunch and tasting of Central Otago wines in the Chambre du Roy (King's Bedroom) at the historic Hospices de Beaune. Ten Central Otago wineries were involved: Aurum, Domaine Rewa, Domaine Thomson, Felton Road, Gibbston Valley, Mt Difficulty, Prophet's Rock, Quartz Reef, Rippon and Wooing Tree.

WINE TOURISM

Well over two million international visitors a year come to Queenstown, and although they do not all want to do a wine tour, the tourism and wine industries have always made happy bedfellows. What better way to spend a day off from skiing or mountain-biking than by visiting a few local wineries to sample their best wine and food? In fact, why not combine the two — in the Gibbston Valley, cycling through the vineyards is always an option. But if that seems too active, tourists can opt for a helicopter wine tour and get flown from one vineyard to the next. In reality, most overseas visitors to Central Otago opt for a half-day guided wine tour in a vehicle. Such a tour is likely to include wine-tasting at up to four wineries and a vineyard lunch.

Whatever the season, Central Otago never disappoints, and with plenty of vineyards and winery restaurants to choose from, local and overseas visitors alike are spoilt for choice in what, according to *Decanter* magazine, 'may just be the most visually spectacular wine region in the world'.

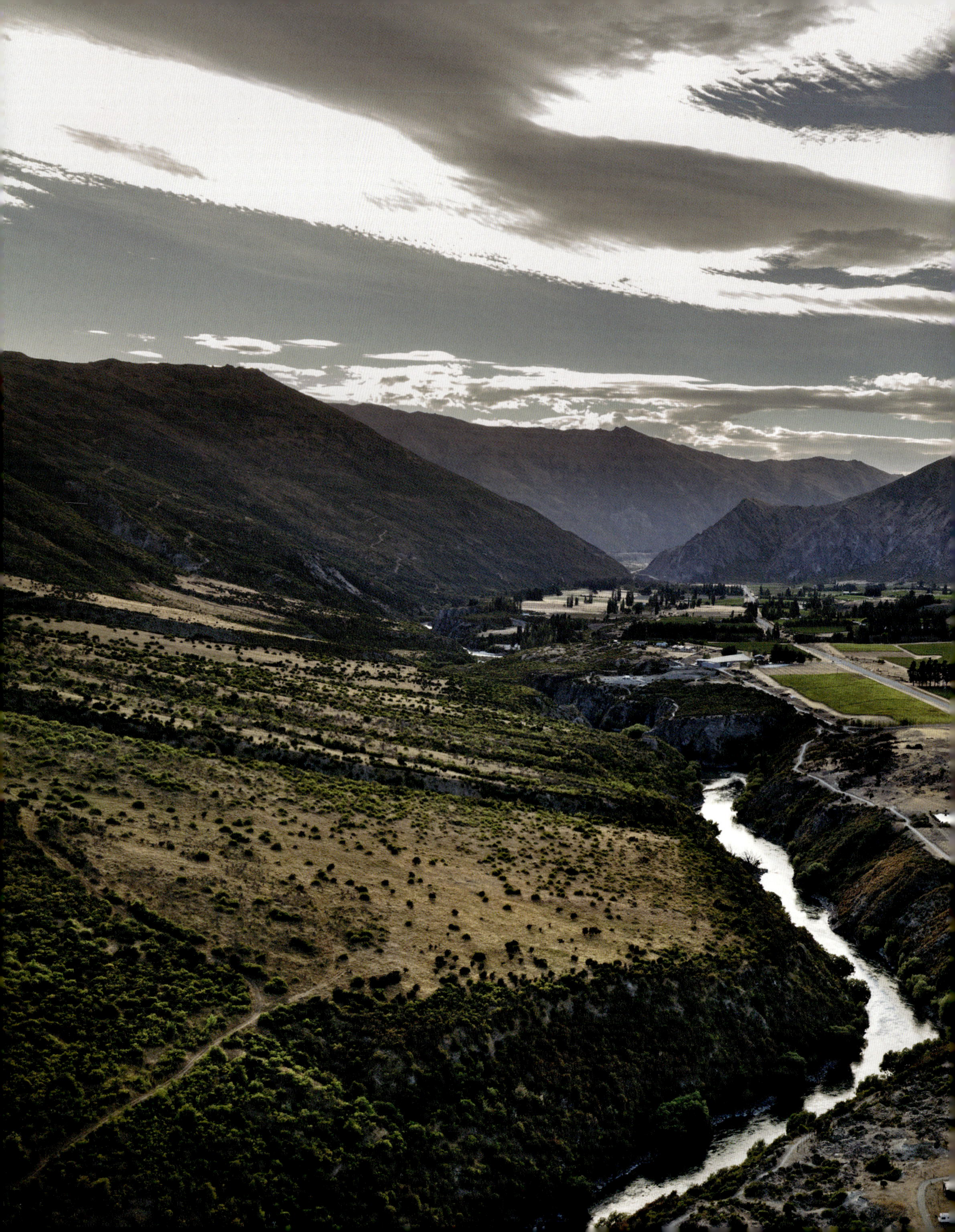

GIBBSTON

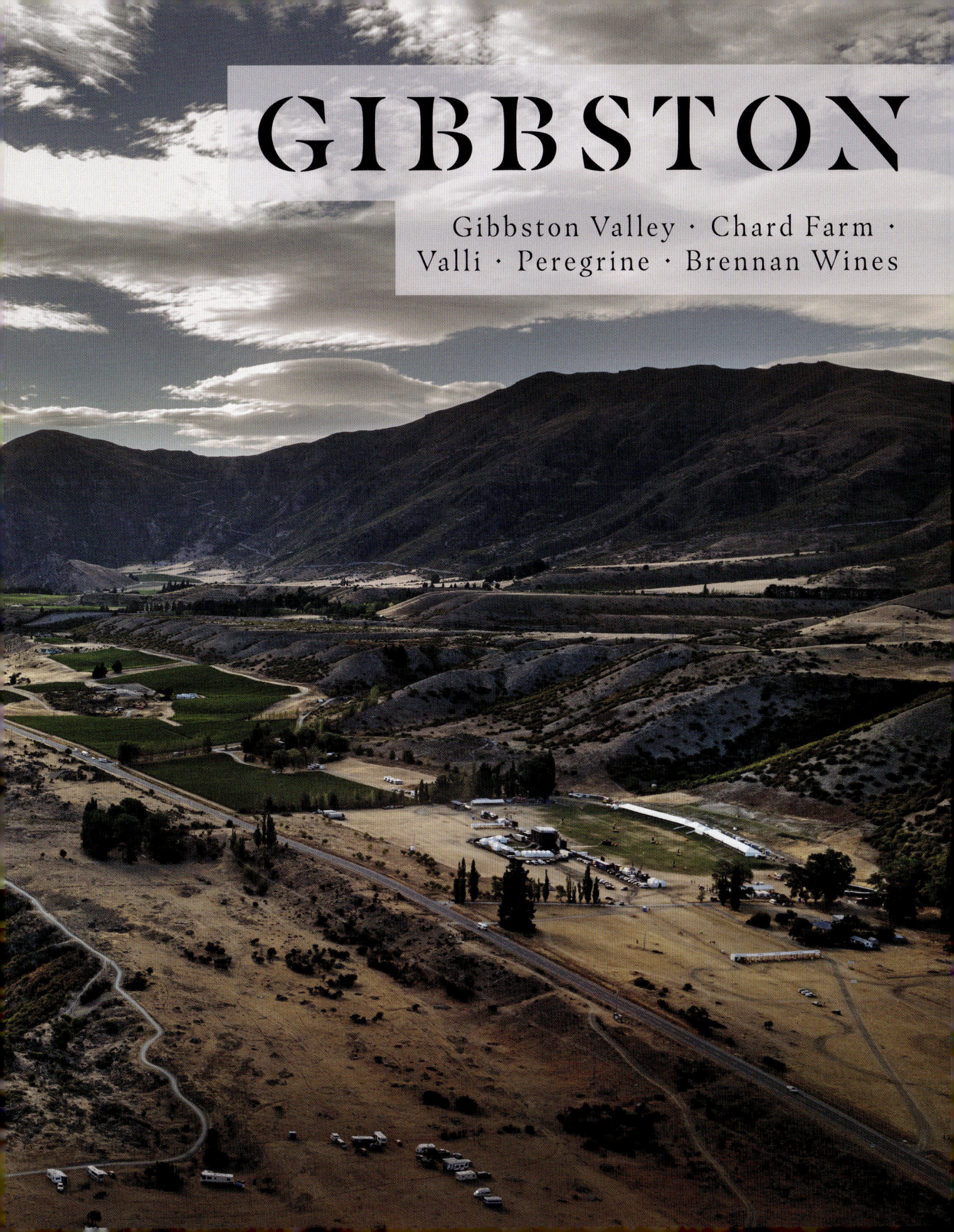

Gibbston Valley · Chard Farm ·
Valli · Peregrine · Brennan Wines

GIBBSTON is the highest and coolest sub-region in Central Otago and with an annual rainfall of 600 millimetres is considerably wetter than Alexandra and the Cromwell Basin. The narrow strip of land beside the Kawarau River starts at 320 metres above sea level and the vineyards in the valley rise up to over 400 metres. The long hot days and cool nights over the growing season provide perfect conditions for developing flavour and colour intensity in the grapes, while retaining natural acidity. However, because it is cooler and wetter, the grapes can take longer to ripen, with harvest often not happening until late April or early May. This means more risk of insufficient ripeness, as well as frost damage in late spring and early autumn.

The first vines were planted in Gibbston in 1981 by Alan Brady at Gibbston Valley, and these are now the oldest continuously producing vines in Central Otago. Five years later, Rob Hay and his brother Greg started planting their Chard Farm vineyard, just down the road. Today there are about 250 hectares of vines in Gibbston. The silty loams and free-draining gravels of this sub-region produce Pinot Noirs that are often lighter in colour, less powerful, but more perfumed than those grown in the Cromwell Basin.

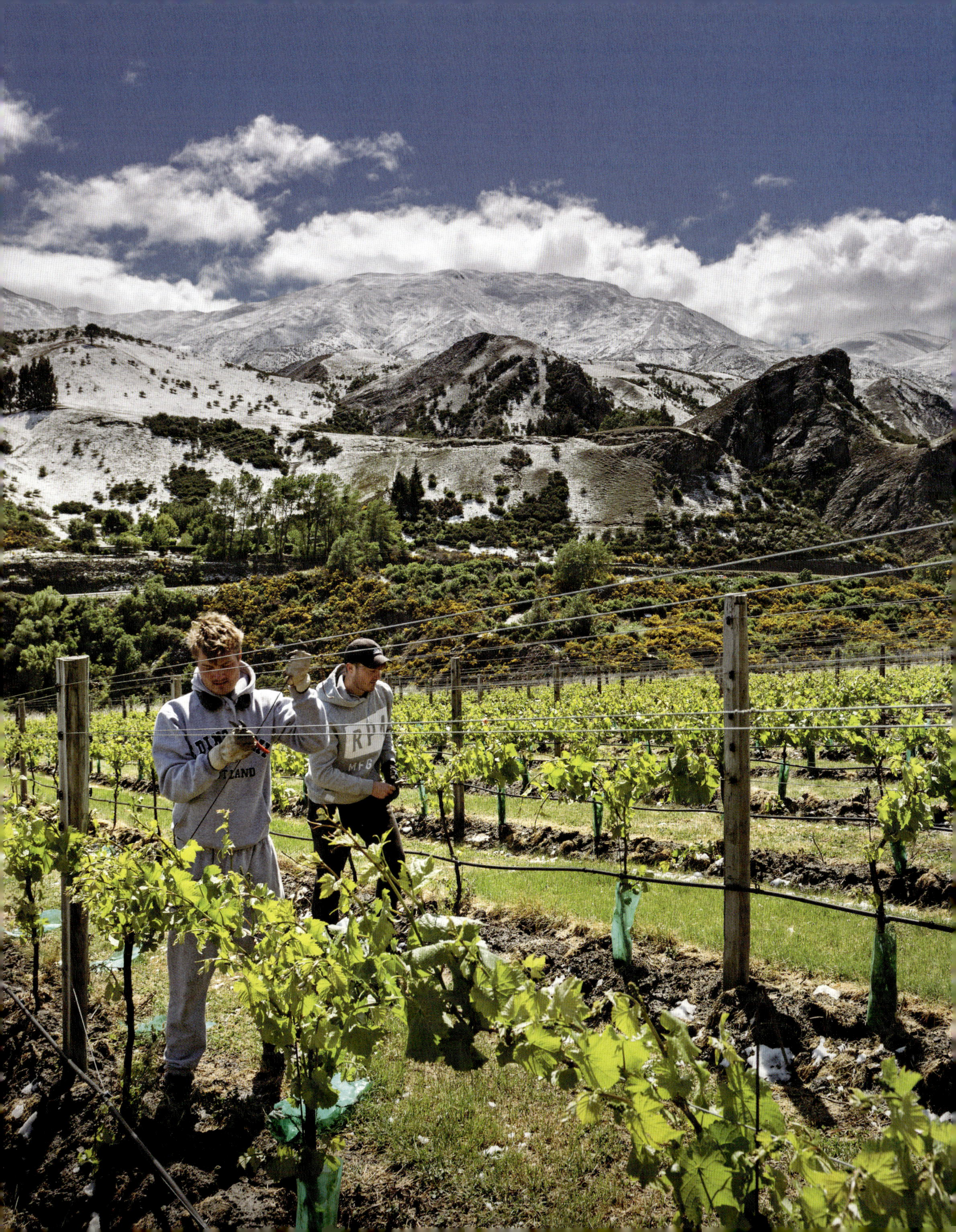

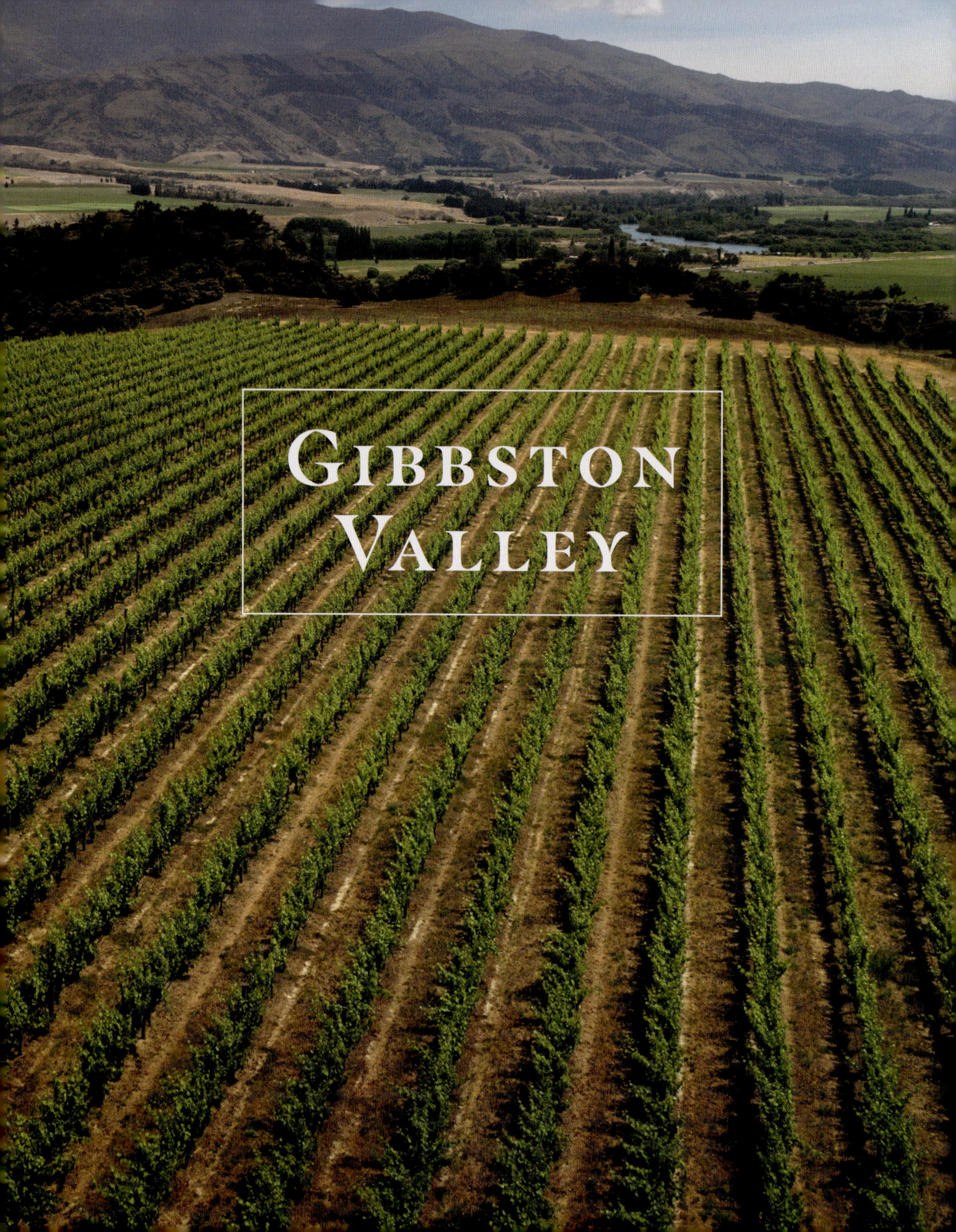

Gibbston Valley

'Pinot kept me awake at night and got me out of bed in the morning. Pinot challenges you all the way.'

Alan Brady and his wife Denise bought land in Gibbston and built a home there in the late 1970s. Like many now involved in the wine industry in Central Otago, they had fallen in love with the place: the rugged mountains, the wild rivers and the clear blue skies. When they planted their first grape vines in 1981, they adopted a 'fruit salad' approach, planting 12 different varieties to see what would do well. 'It wasn't long before Pinot Noir put its hand up and said, "I like it here",' says Brady. In 1987, using Ann Pinckney's Taramea winery, Brady's friend and adviser Rob Hay from nearby Chard Farm made Gibbston Valley's and Central Otago's first small commercial vintage.

Three years later, in 1990, and with a group of investors now involved, Brady built the Gibbston Valley winery and restaurant, having seen the opportunity to capture the tourist traffic that drove past his gate every day. Five years later, in a brave move, he persuaded his fellow investors to build a wine cave. It was to be New Zealand's largest underground barrel cellar and proved to be a great success. Not only did it provide the perfect storage area for Gibbston Valley's wines but it became so popular that soon there were 50,000 people a year visiting the cave. And everyone was happy.

Working with the local tourism industry to promote Gibbston Valley and the Central Otago wine industry, Brady paved the way for the win–win situation of today, which sees both industries working together for the good of the region. What better way to spend a day than sipping a glass of glorious Central Otago wine while enjoying the spectacular Central Otago landscape?

At the 1991 Royal Easter Show Wine Awards in Auckland, Gibbston Valley's 1990 Pinot Noir was awarded a silver medal, and the Top Pinot Noir trophy. It went on to win the Champion Pinot Noir trophy at the Air New Zealand Wine Awards in 1991. This was a stunning result for a winery at such an early stage of development, and the start of a journey that has seen Gibbston Valley wines go on to regularly win awards and accolades, not just in New Zealand but around the world. Brady attributes much of the success of Central Otago's wines to the young winemakers who were 'ensnared by Pinot Noir, and by the beauty of the landscape it grows in'. Grant Taylor became the Gibbston Valley winemaker in 1993 and brought new energy and rigour to the winery. His Gibbston Valley Reserve Pinot Noir 2000 won the trophy at the London International Wine Competition, and in 2003 when UK wine writer Jancis Robinson MW highly rated just 10 New Zealand Pinot Noirs, five were from Central Otago and two were Gibbston Valley Pinot Noirs.

By the time Brady resigned as managing director of Gibbston Valley in 1997, he had become known in the industry as the 'godfather'. Others had played their part, but Brady, who had extensive media experience and contacts from his previous career, had, more than anyone else, helped put Central Otago on the map as a winegrowing region. 'Pinot kept me awake at night and got me out of bed in the morning. Pinot challenges you all the way,' he says. 'You know you'll never create the perfect wine, but you're always trying to get as close as you can. I'm driven by the passion of it.'

Over the following two decades, Gibbston Valley's reputation has

Gibbston Valley winemaker Christopher Keys, with his son.

continued to flourish and today the company is under the ownership of American Phil Griffith and his family. In 1999, Gibbston Valley started planting 40 hectares of vineyards at Bendigo to ensure its supply of fruit. A second, 6-hectare vineyard, called Glenlee, was also bought in Gibbston and a Lowburn vineyard is on long-term lease, bringing Gibbston Valley's total vineyard area to nearly 60 hectares.

For him, making wine is a constant and irresistible challenge.

While Gibbston still produces some of the winery's finest wines, Le Maitre and Glenlee Pinot Noirs, it can be more challenging than other places and most of the wineries based in Gibbston have acquired vineyards in other sub-regions. This allows them to spread their risk in difficult years and affords their winemakers more blending opportunities. They can choose to make single-vineyard wines, expressive of the individual sites, or blend the grapes from different sites.

In 2006, Christopher Keys took over as chief winemaker. He sees Gibbston Valley's first 30 years as the foundation of a process extending hundreds of years into the future, as the vines continue to mature. For him, making wine is a constant and irresistible challenge as he teases out the character of each individual site. Keys is responsible for making more than 25 different wines, often in small, single-vineyard lots. The grapes are still hand-picked and traditional winemaking methods are used, and while Gibbston is not yet fully organic, it is moving in this direction, with the original Home Block vineyard now certified organic.

Pinot Noir, which accounts for 70 per cent of production at Gibbston Valley, 'shows place in a way that gives distinct flashes of character', according to Keys. Gibbston's acclaimed single-vineyard Pinots come from the Home Block (Le Maitre) and Glenlee vineyards in Gibbston and the School House and China Terrace vineyards at Bendigo. Coming from differing altitudes, aspects, soil types and clones, these wines all have distinct characteristics and flavours.

Keys is excited, too, about making Chardonnay in Central Otago. He describes it as having its own unique character here: 'flinty, linear, pure — it dances across the tongue'. His Gibbston Valley Reserve Chardonnay 2009 won gold at the Air New Zealand Wine Awards. Since 2010, Keys has been using Chardonnay to make sparkling wines too, including a Blanc de Blancs and a Pinot Noir/Chardonnay blend. Gibbston Valley's wine portfolio also includes Pinot Gris, Riesling, Pinot Blanc, Sauvignon Blanc, Gewürztraminer and Rosé, and the quality of these wines is further evidence of Keys' and his colleagues' commitment to excellence. At the 2014 New Zealand International Wine Show, the Champion Rosé was from Gibbston Valley.

Gibbston Valley produces between 20,000 and 25,000 cases of wine. From the start, when Brady saw the opportunity to capture the tourist traffic driving past the vineyard, Gibbston Valley has sold over half of its production through the cellar door and through its wine club. This has meant there has been less emphasis on exporting Gibbston Valley wines.

As one of the oldest vineyards in Central Otago, Gibbston Valley already has a proud history, and with the quality of its vineyards and people, the next 30 years and beyond look like they will produce plenty more premium wines.

ABOVE RIGHT Wine Cave, Gibbston Valley. RIGHT China Terrace vineyard, Bendigo.

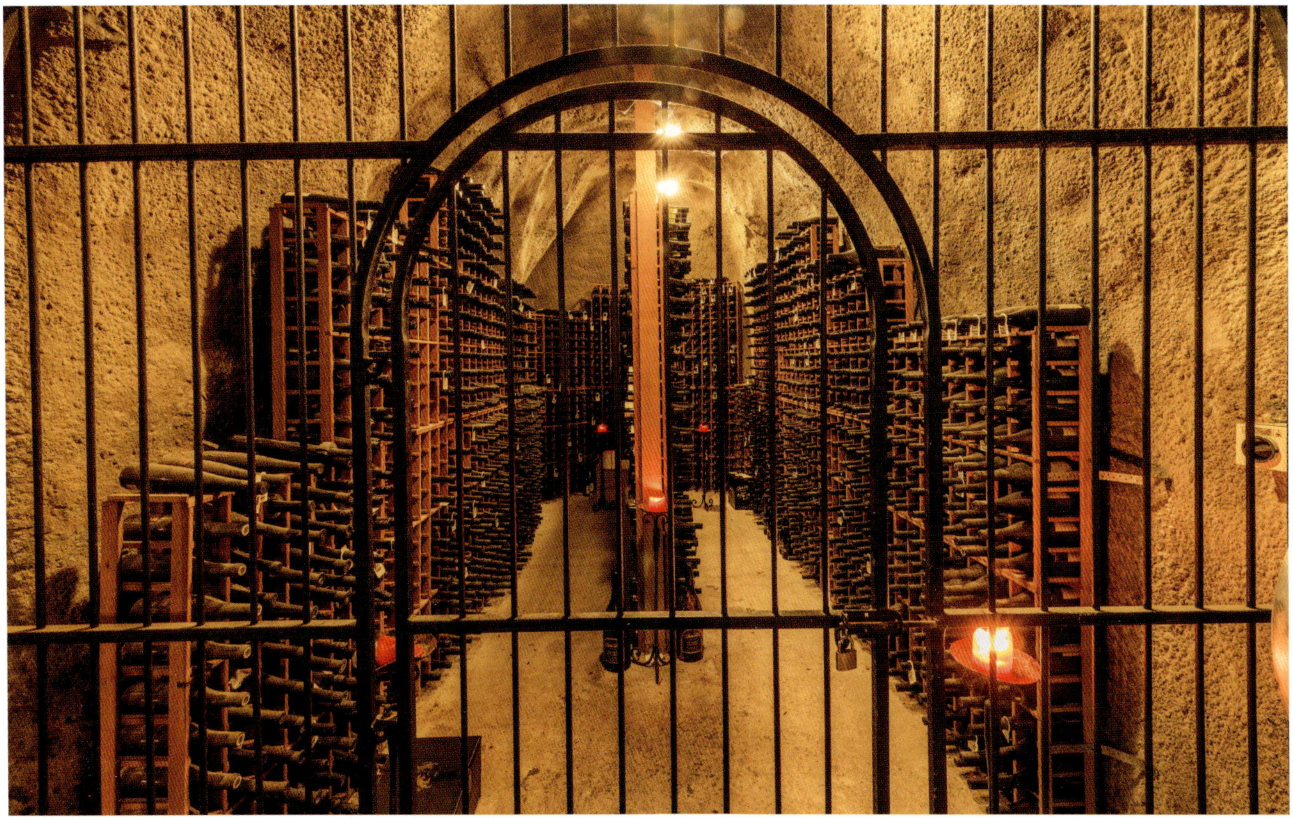

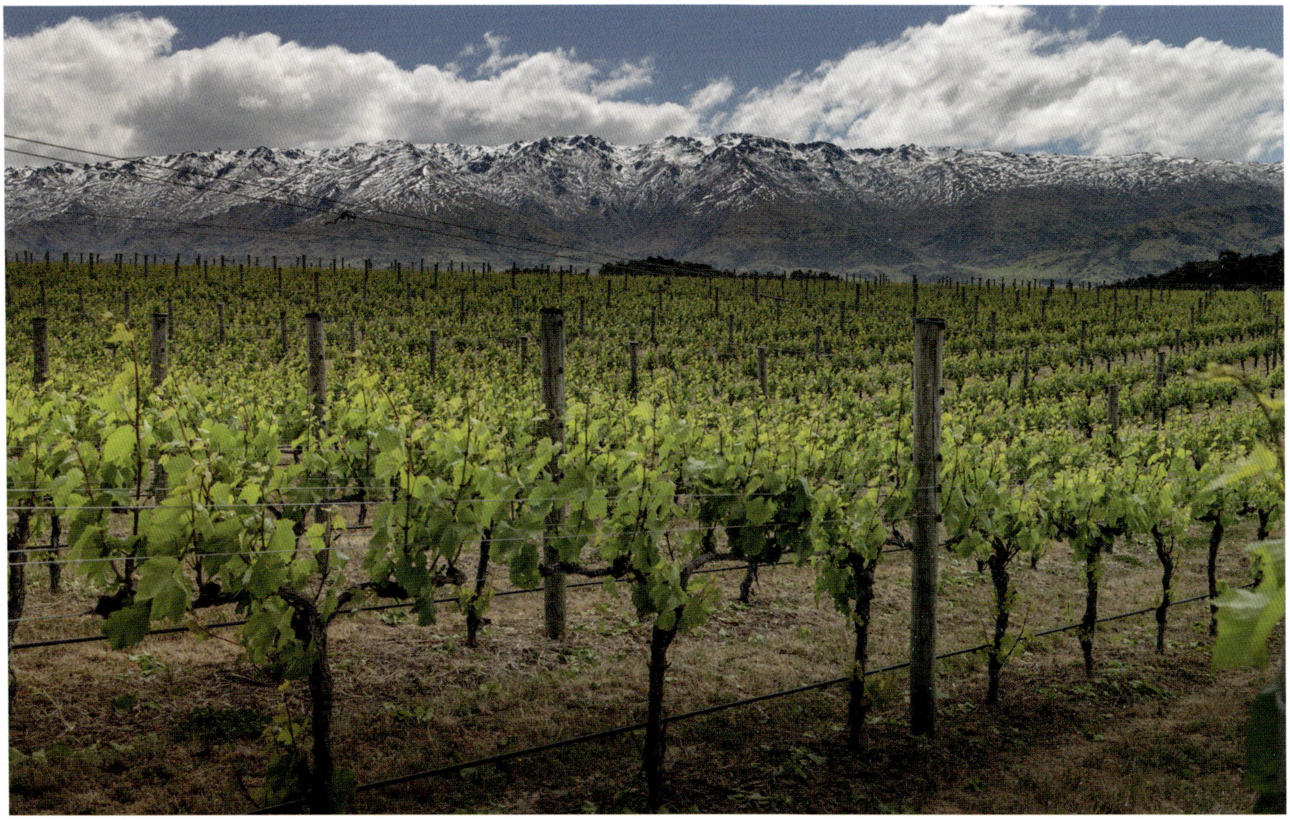

ABOVE Wire lifting at Red Shed vineyard, Bendigo. ABOVE RIGHT Harvesting at China Terrace vineyard, Bendigo. RIGHT Winemaker Sascha Herbert topping up Pinot Noir barrels.

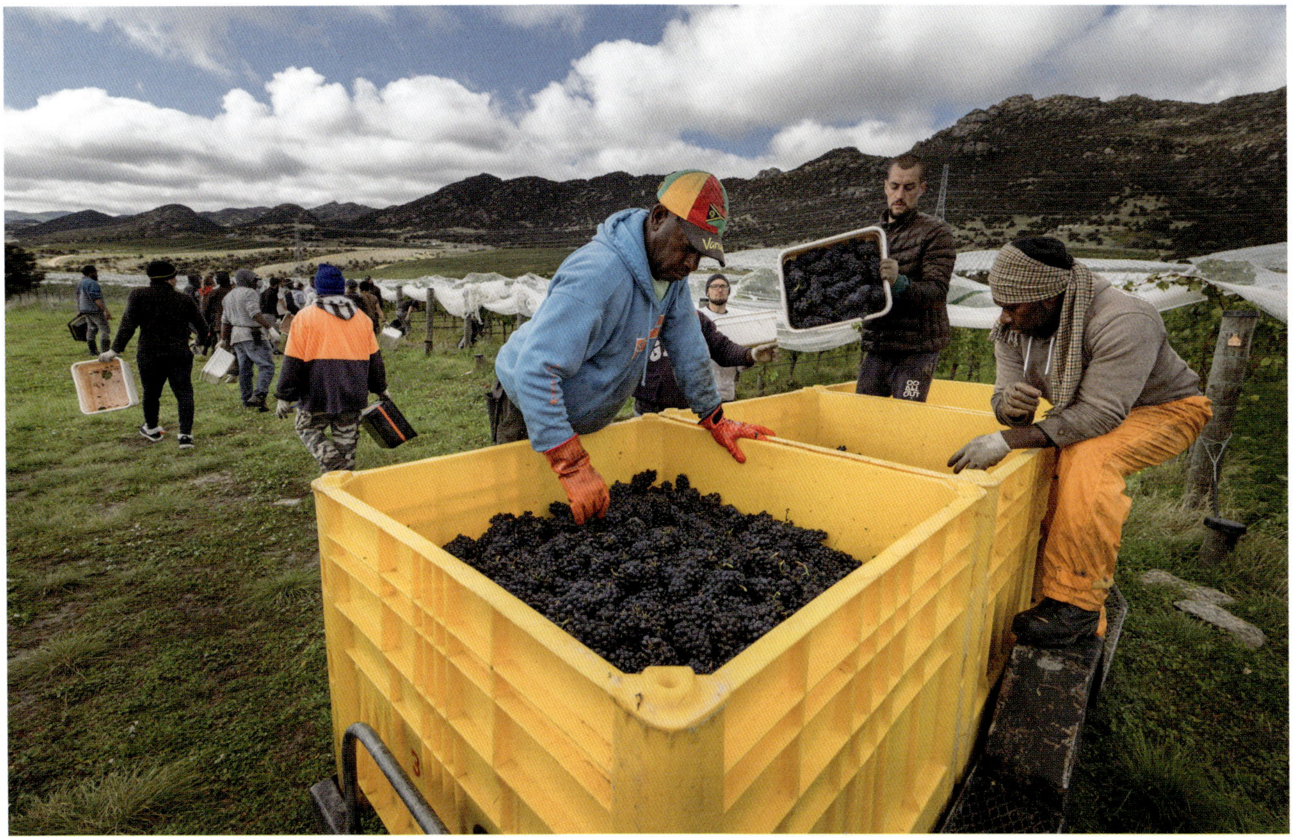

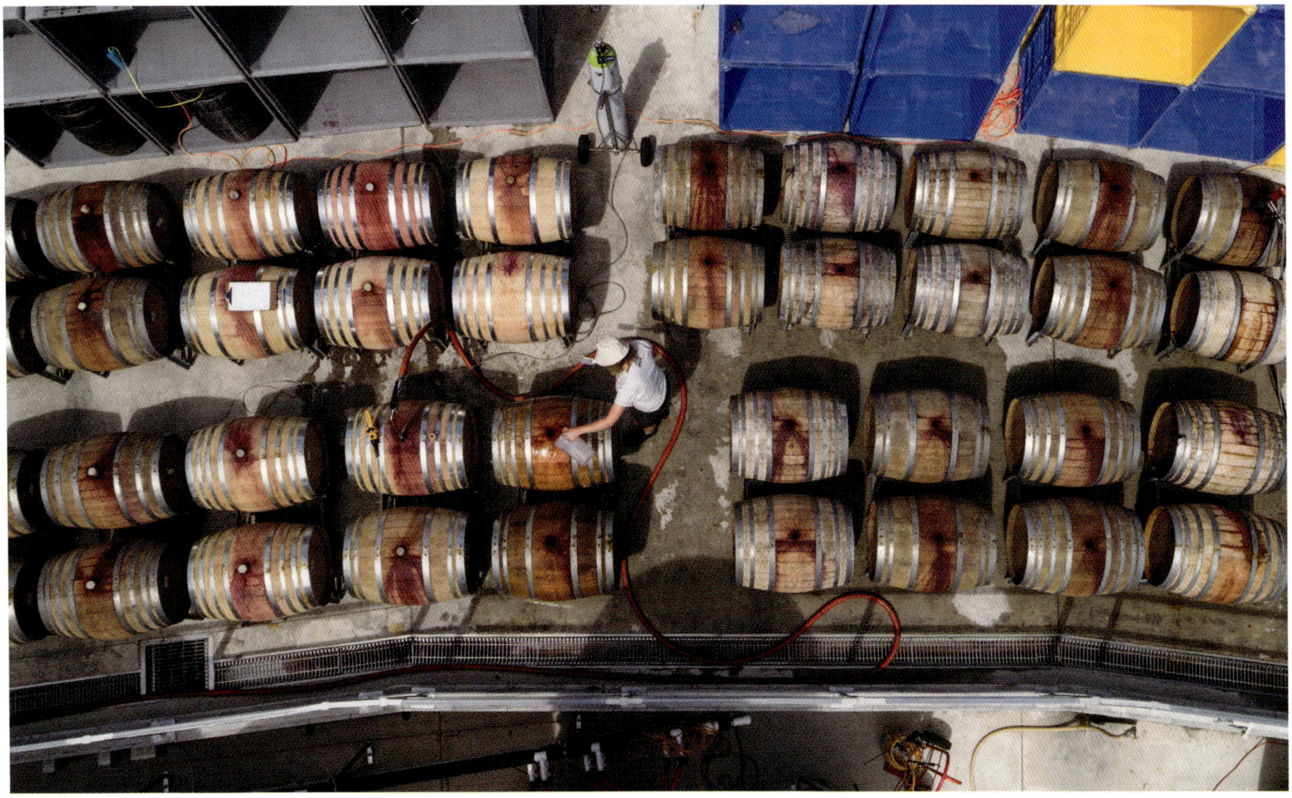

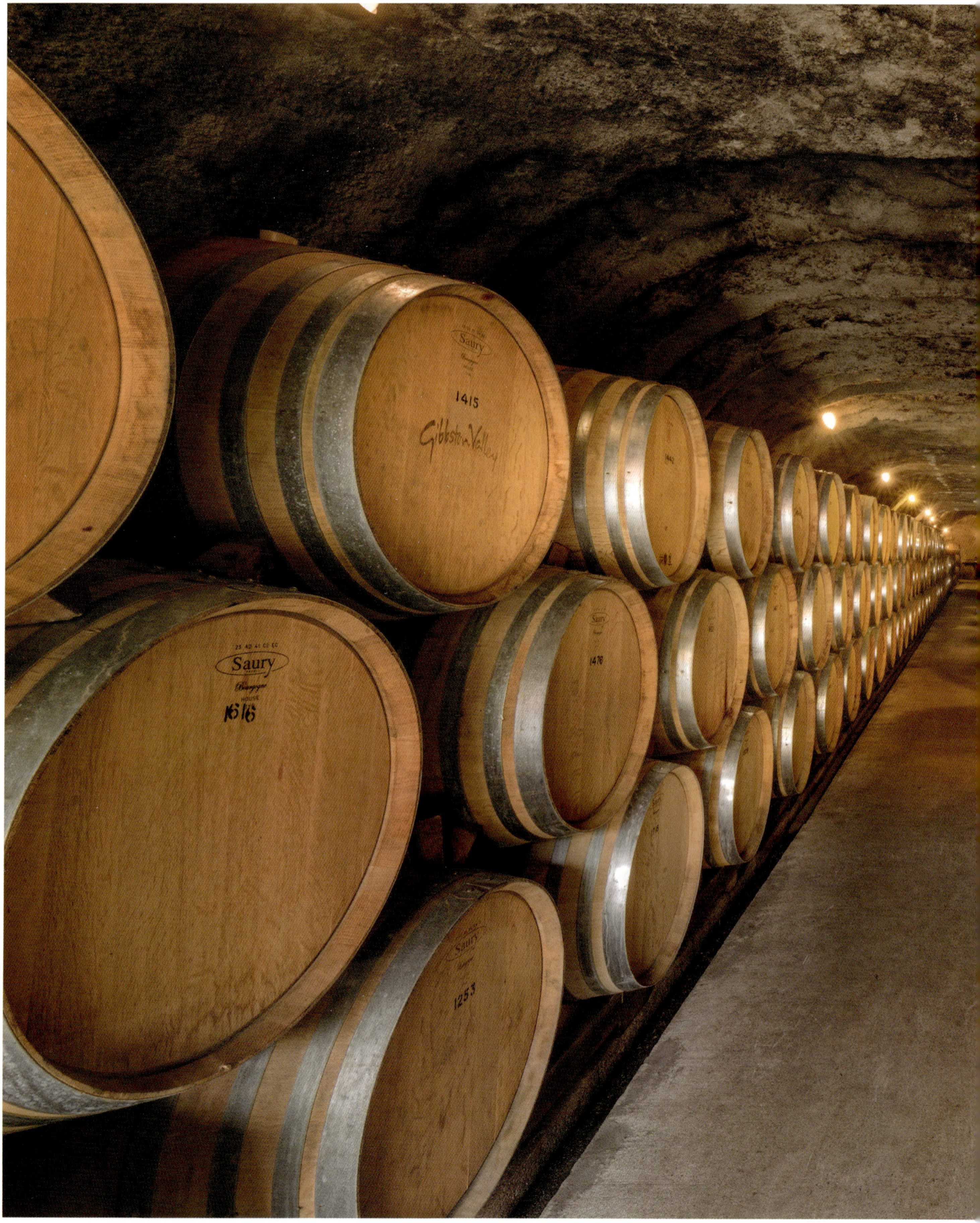
Saury
1415
Gibbston Valley
Saury
1253

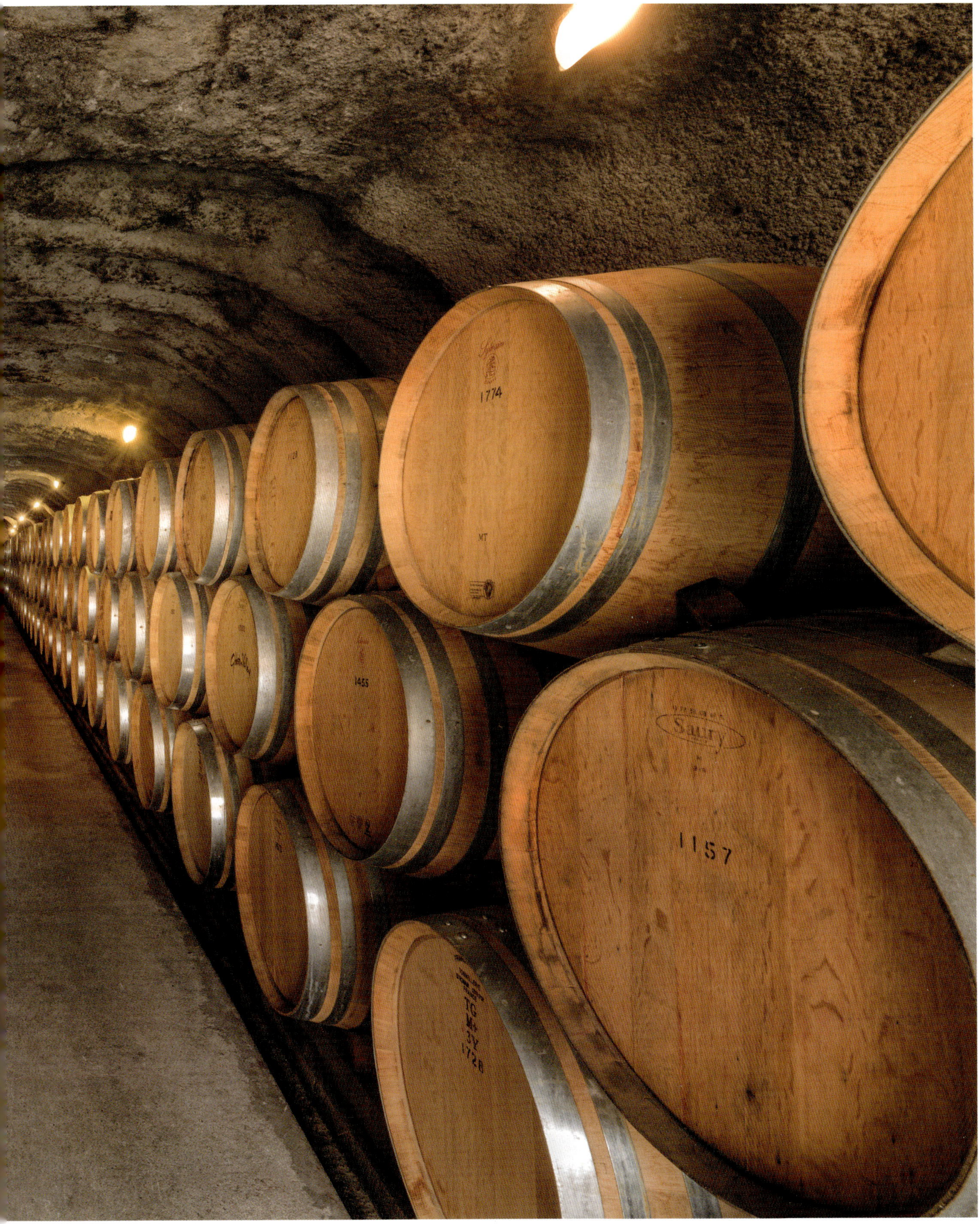
1774
MT
1455
Saury
1157

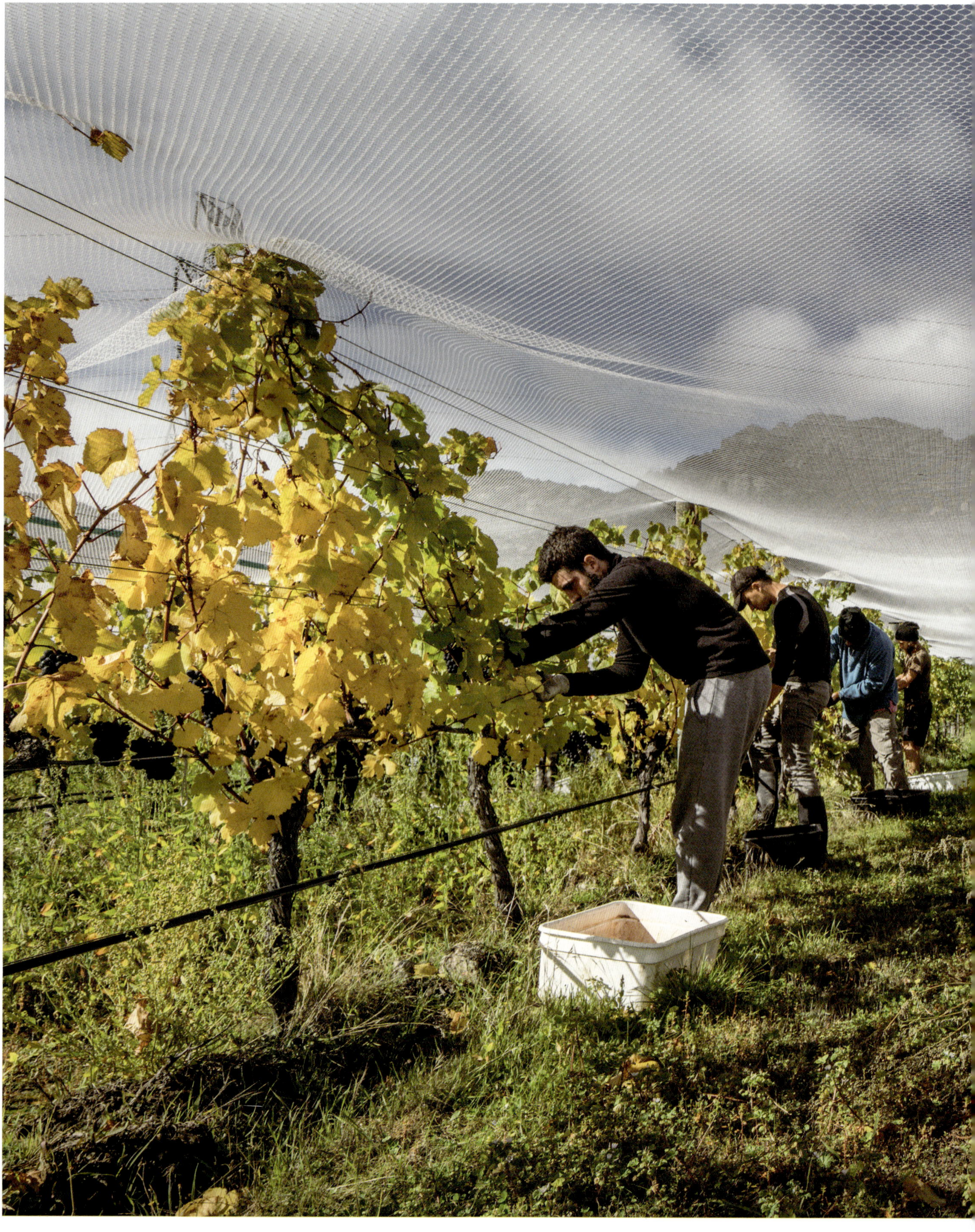

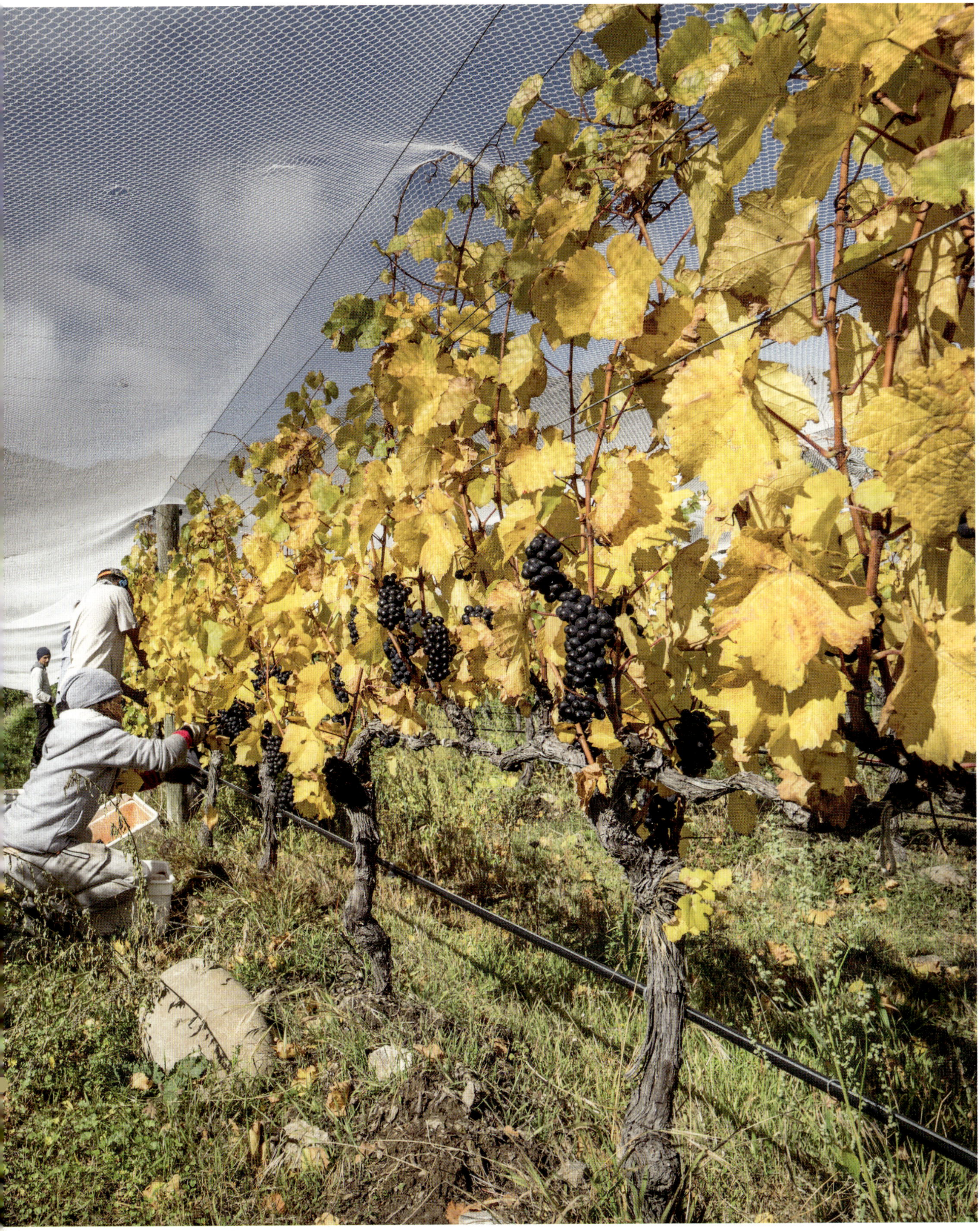

CHARD FARM

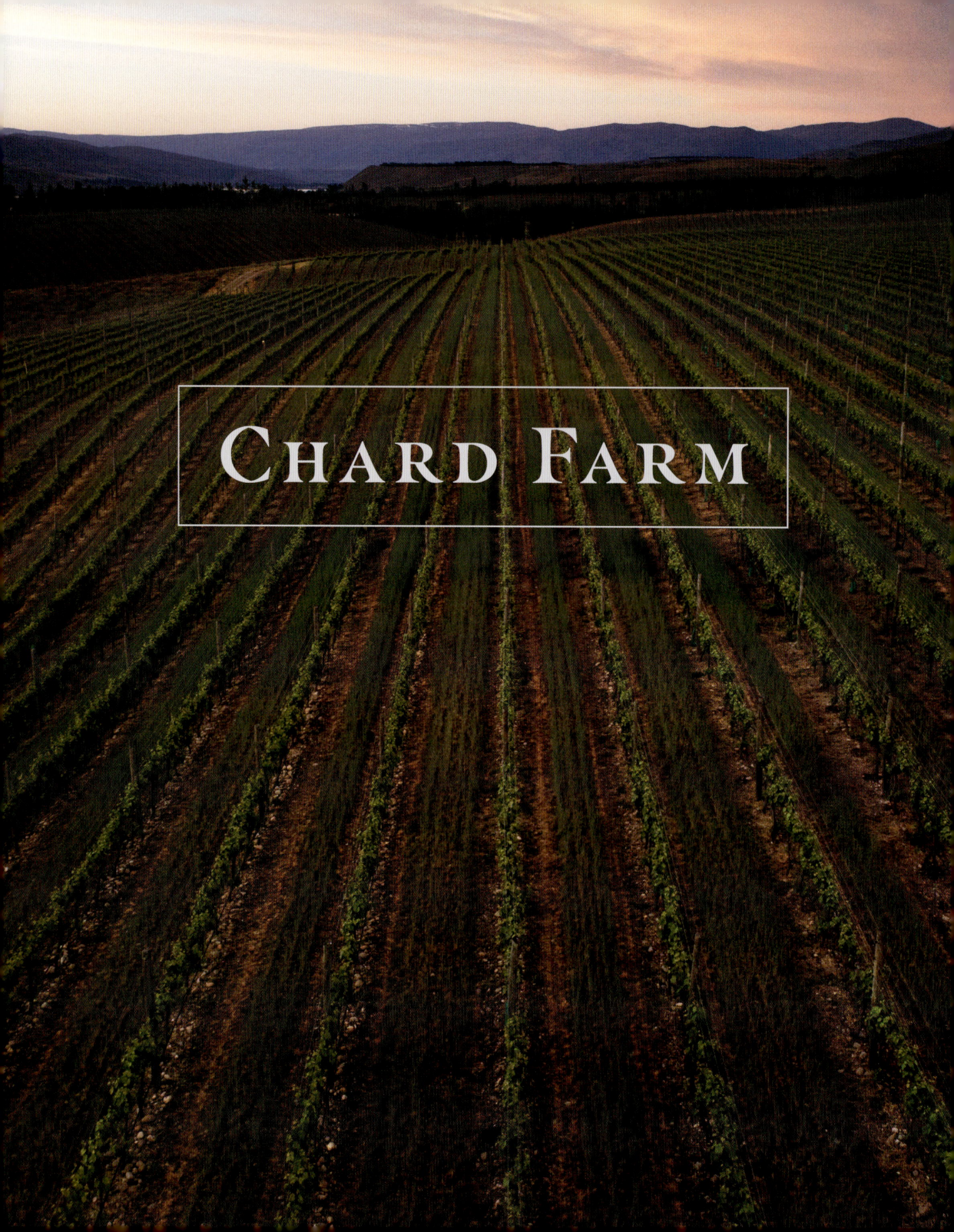

'It's the most revered grape variety in the world.'

Rob Hay describes Central Otago as 'drop-dead gorgeous'. As a young man, he fell in love with the place and the outdoors lifestyle it offered. Having gained valuable experience and training in viticulture and winemaking in Germany, on his return he became the first fully qualified winemaker in the region. Rob's wife Gerda comes from Germany too, but met her future husband back in New Zealand.

The general belief in the 1980s was that Central Otago was too far south and too cold to grow grapes. 'Don't plant down there, but if you are stupid enough, plant early-ripening varieties,' Hay was told, and he grins when he remembers another warning: 'If Central Otago producers think they can produce premium wine, they're seriously deluding themselves.'

When he became the manager at Chard Farm, which was being run as an orchard, Hay soon got to know Alan Brady, who had by now planted grapes down the road at Gibbston Valley. A local farmer had told Hay that the first daffodils in the valley came out at Chard Farm, and further research convinced him it would be possible to grow grapes and develop a vineyard there. When he learned that Chard Farm could be for sale, he made his move.

His intention was to set up a commercial vineyard, and in 1987, with the help of his brother Greg, he started to develop the 12-hectare home block, planting Pinot Noir, Pinot Gris, Chardonnay, Riesling and

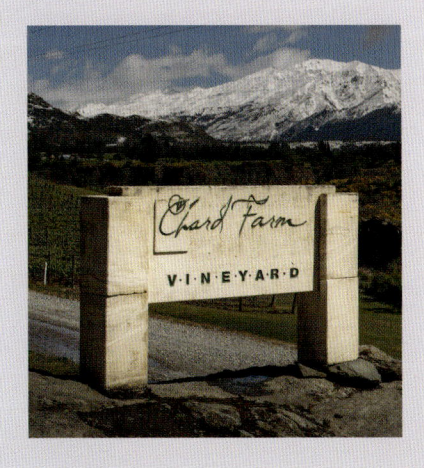

Gewürztraminer. In these early days nobody knew which grapes would do well in Central Otago and Hay planted other varieties too, but it did not take long to realise they were not going to thrive in these new vineyards at the end of the world.

Five years later, in 1993, the distinctive, 'drop-dead gorgeous' Chard Farm winery was completed and Hay became the first winemaker there. He had previously been making Brady's Gibbston Valley wines from 1987 to 1991. The early years were tough, even with family financial support, and the banks told them that vineyards and ski fields could not exist together — it was a dangerous idea. But in 1991 Gibbston Valley's 1990 Pinot Noir, made by Hay, won the Champion Pinot Noir trophy at the Air New Zealand Wine Awards and the Top Pinot Noir trophy in the Royal Easter Show. The sceptics were proved wrong, and these days, 70 per cent of Chard Farm's production is Pinot Noir. 'It's the most revered grape variety in the world,' says Hay.

One of the most visually spectacular vineyards in Central Otago, at 360 metres above sea level Chard Farm is also one of the highest. Hay's purchase of 60 hectares in the Lowburn–Pisa sub-region, in the Cromwell Basin, which is 100 metres lower and 1 to 2 degrees warmer, has provided Chard Farm with a 'safe haven'. A further 25 hectares is leased in the area, and together these Lowburn vineyards have become the 'engine room' of the business, which is one of the biggest in Central Otago. It either owns or leases close to 100 hectares and buys grapes in from other growers.

In 1997, Rob's brother Greg left Chard Farm to help set up Peregrine, another vineyard development in the Gibbston Valley. Then, in 2003, in a joint venture with growers mostly from the Cromwell Basin and with Chard Farm as production partners, the Rabbit Ranch label was launched to offer the market a range of more affordable wines. Described as 'a bright-eyed red with hints of briar patch and a whiff of gun smoke', Rabbit Ranch Pinot Noir was to be the first of a new style of early-drinking, fruit-driven Pinot Noirs, which have proved popular in the marketplace.

Rob Hay.

At the top end of the market, Chard Farm continues to produce elegant single-vineyard Pinot Noirs, including two from different sites in the Lowburn–Pisa sub-region: the Tiger Single Vineyard Pinot Noir, from the vineyard named after the late 'Tiger' Thompson, cellar-door host at Chard Farm for over a decade; and the Viper Single Vineyard Pinot Noir. Chard Farm's signature Pinot Noir is called Mata-Au and is made from a barrel selection of Lowburn grapes.

As a grape variety that expresses its origins very clearly, Pinot Noir is very much about provenance. It is also a grape that is both fickle and unforgiving and after veraison (the onset of ripening) needs a long, slow ripening period. Hay believes that the semi-continental climate is

It is also a grape that is both fickle and unforgiving.

the most significant factor in creating Central Otago's distinctive Pinot Noirs. Over late summer and into autumn, the days are often warm, but at night the temperature can drop by 20 degrees or more, and it is this high diurnal temperature range which, by slowing down and extending the ripening process, is considered critical for developing flavour and colour in the fruit.

Chard Farm's white-wine portfolio includes Pinot Gris, and small amounts of Chardonnay, Riesling, Gewürztraminer and Sauvignon Blanc. Recently, Chard Farm has planted more Chardonnay, and Hay believes that with the right sites and clones it could be the next big thing for the region. The Central Otago style of Chardonnay, he says, 'requires minimal oak, is citrusy with wonderful mineral acidity and is great with food'. A Rosé completes the Chard Farm line-up, and with its growing popularity as a white-wine alternative, Chard Farm will soon be making more Rosé too.

In 2015, Chard Farm celebrated its twenty-fifth anniversary. Since the early days, there have been just three winemakers at Chard Farm: Rob Hay, Duncan Forsyth and John Wallace, who has been with the company since the early 2000s. As a real foodie, Wallace brings a well-honed palate to his winemaking, and Hay says this is essential when it comes to high-end winemaking, which requires making the fine calls in the vineyard and winery to get the absolute best out of your grapes.

When it comes to selling their wines, around 15 per cent of Chard Farm wine sales are at the cellar door and to private customers, and together New Zealand and Australia are their biggest markets, representing 75 per cent of sales. A small amount is also sold in the US.

Chard Farm may be a drop-dead gorgeous vineyard in a drop-dead gorgeous region, but it is also a thriving business, thanks to Rob Hay and his family and their refusal to believe grapes could not be grown successfully in Central Otago.

ABOVE RIGHT 'Punching the cap' at Chard Farm winery. RIGHT Harvest at Chard Farm.

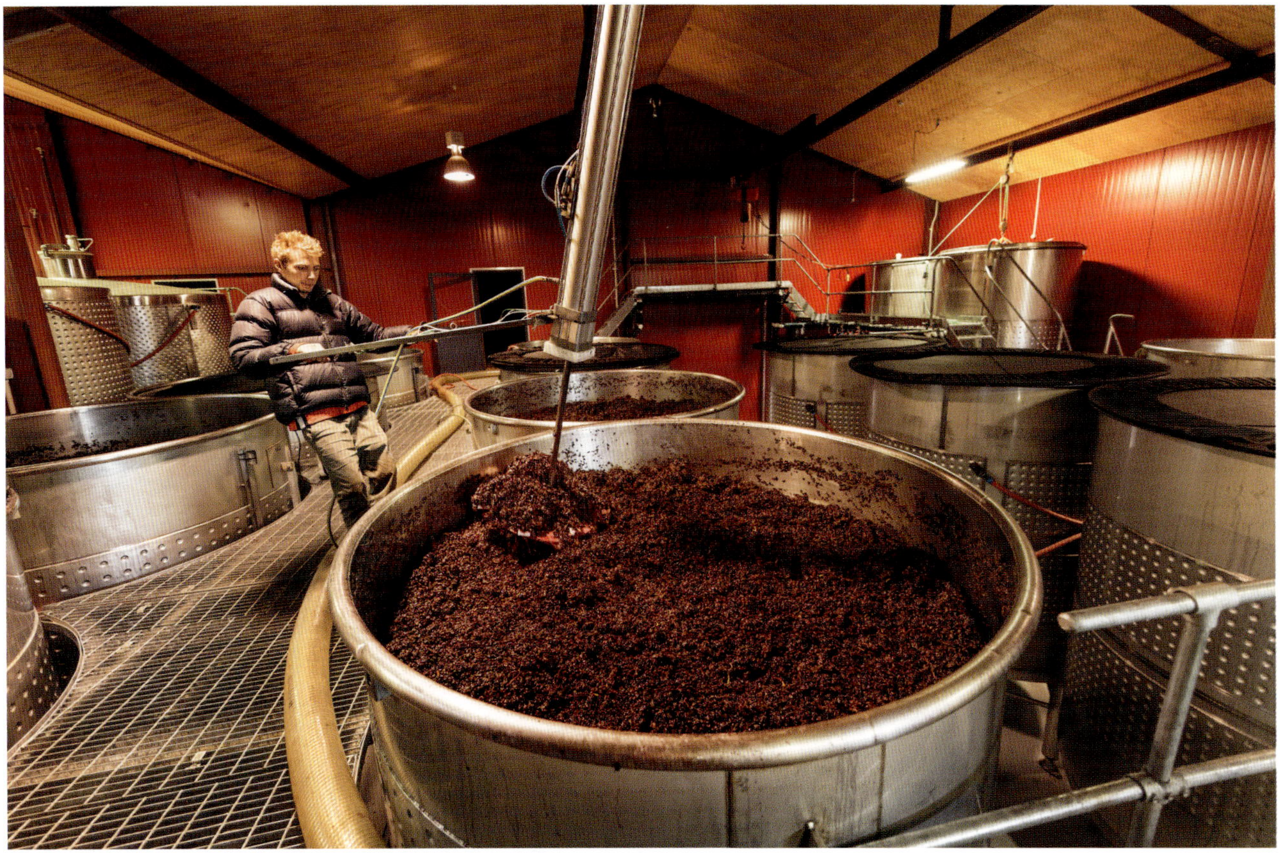

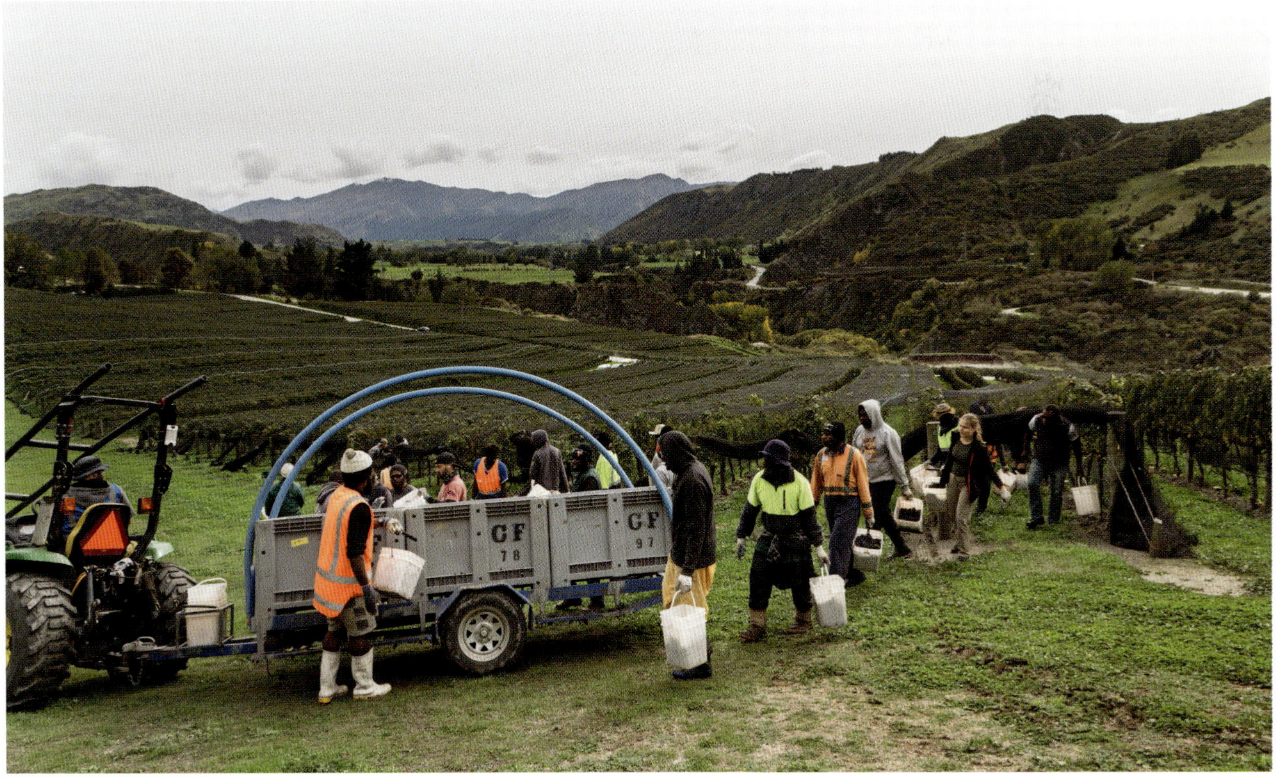
GF
78
GF
97

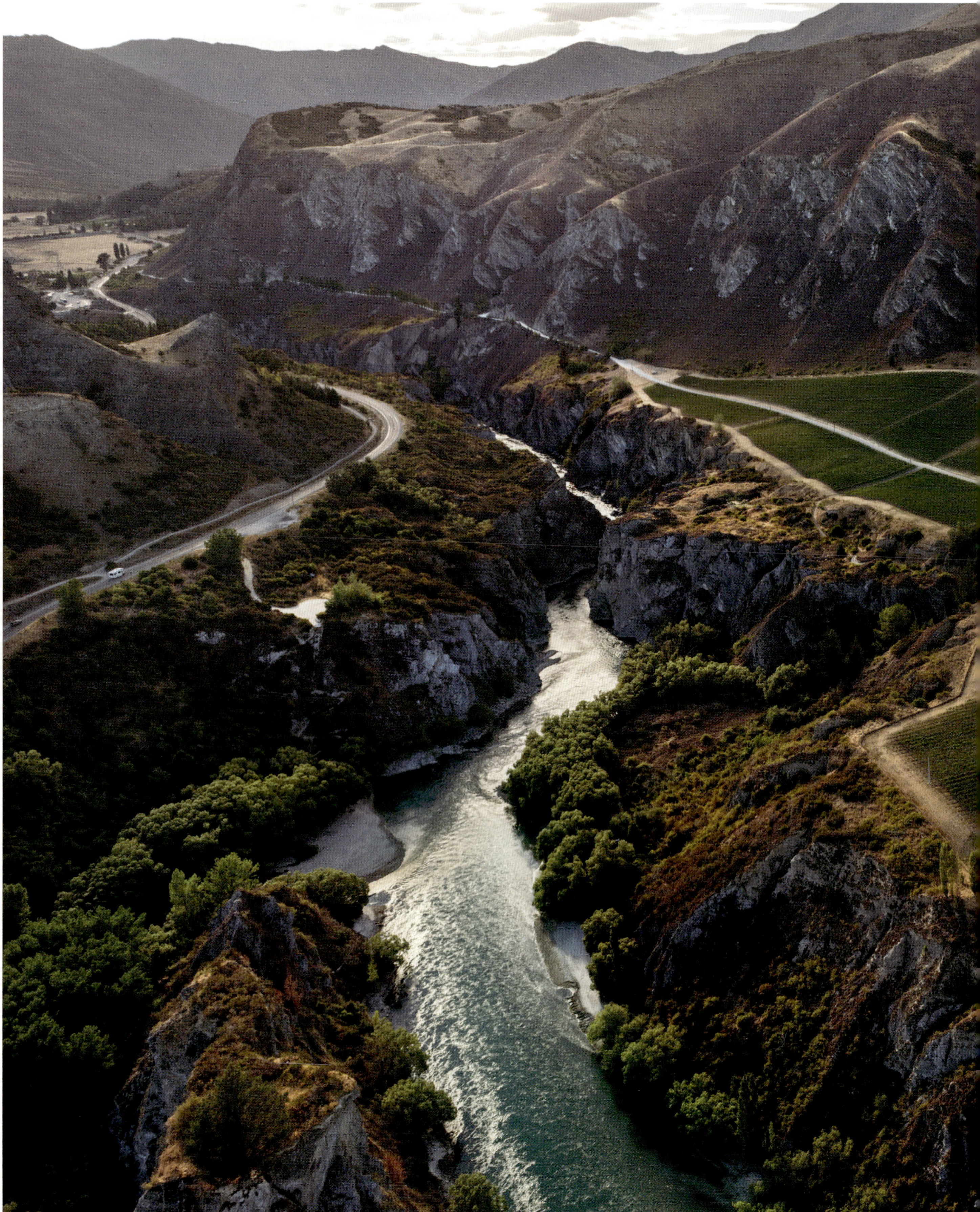

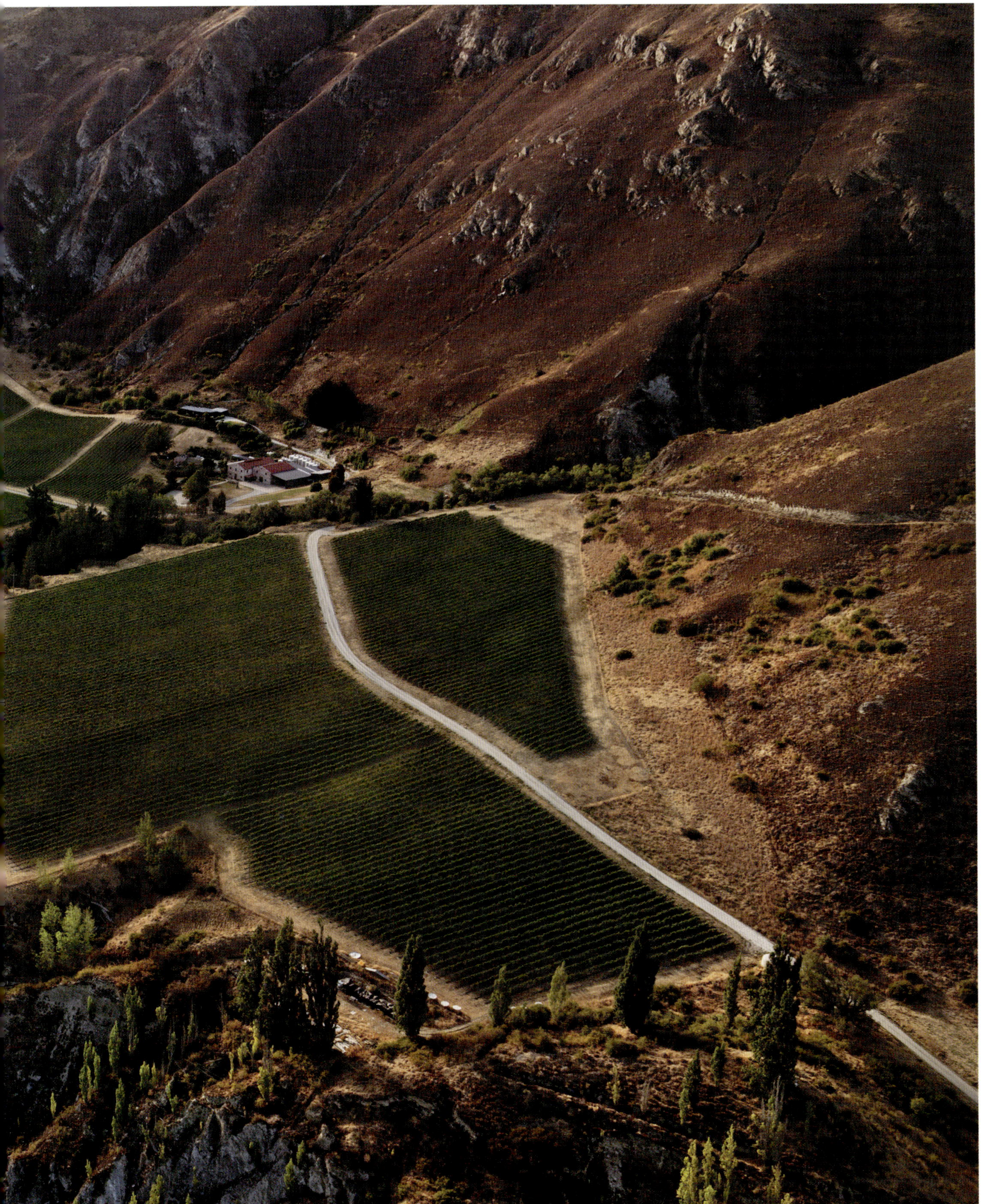

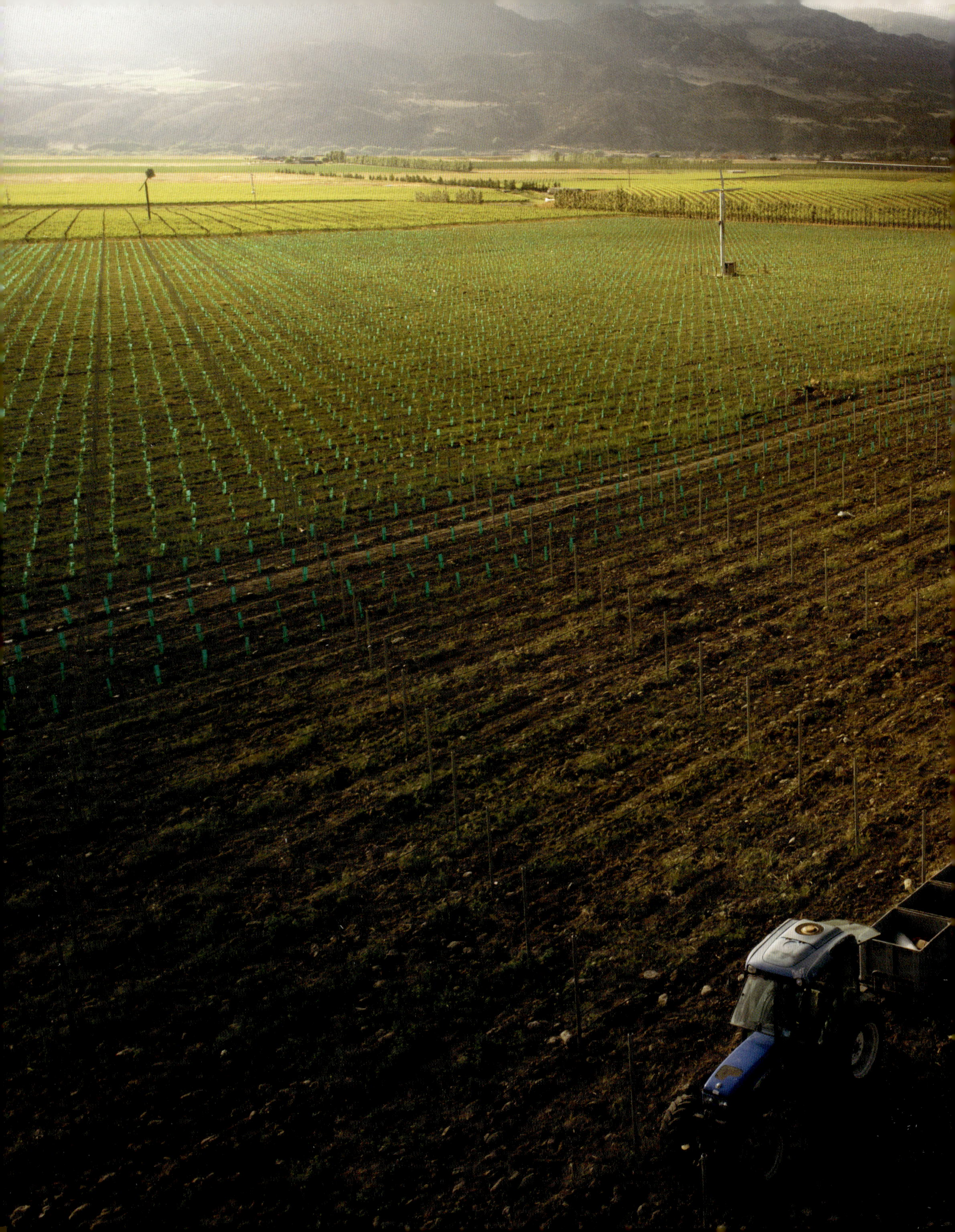

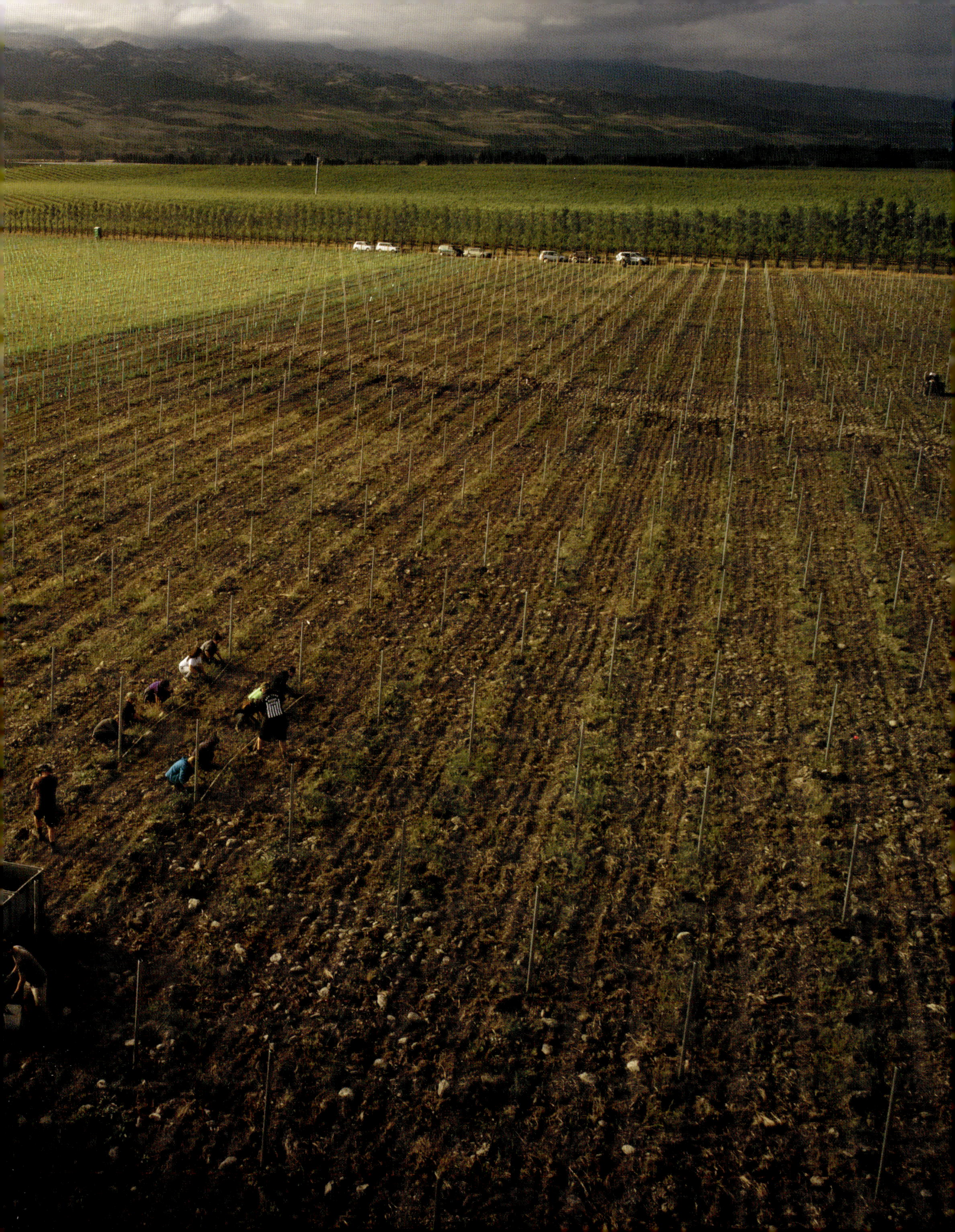

Top Sunset through the vines. Above New plantings. Right Shoot thinning, Viper Block.

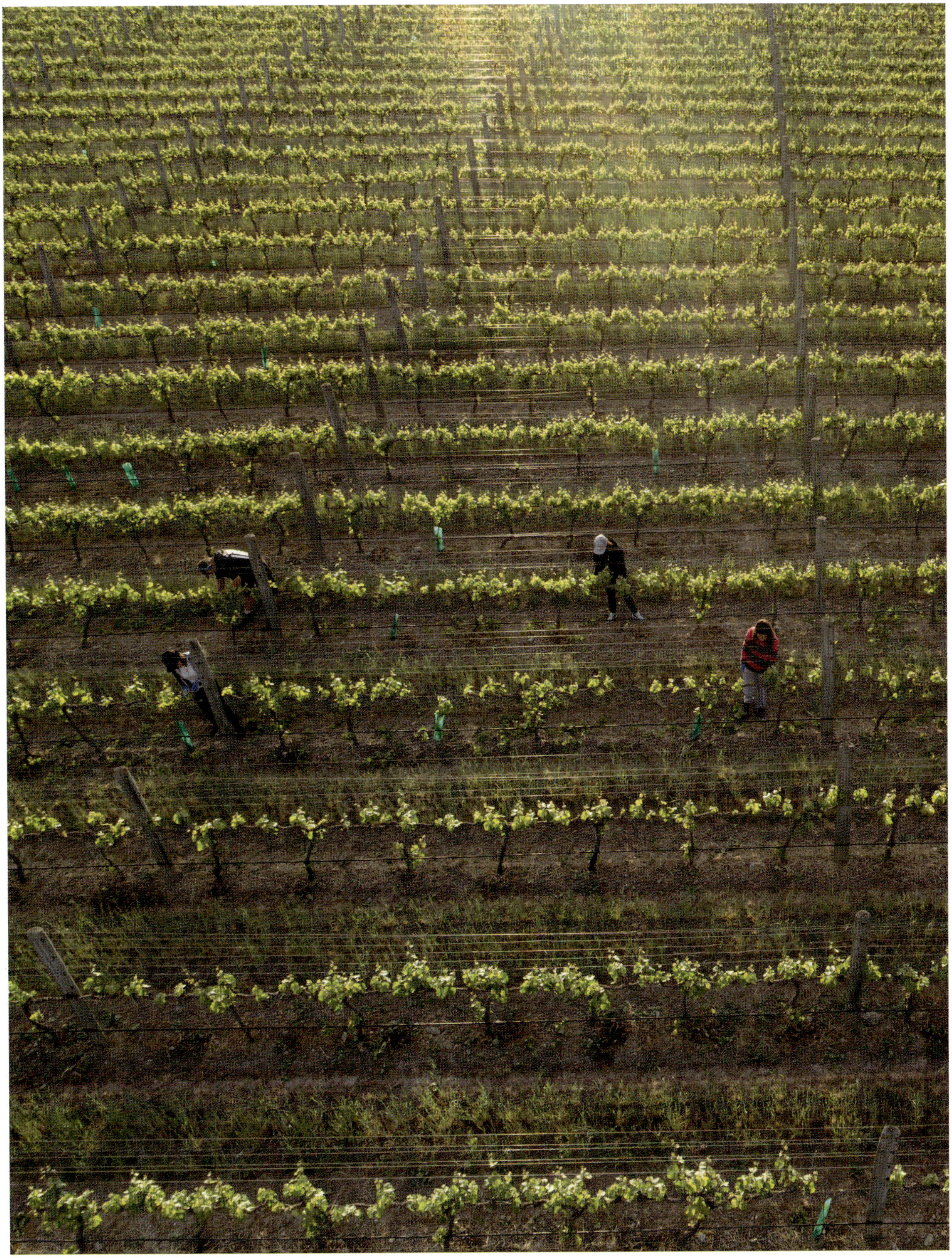

VALLI

'I just want to put Central Otago in a bottle.'

Grant Taylor is the quintessential Central Otago winemaker — a free spirit and innovator, he brought an intelligence and knowledge to winemaking in Central Otago which he has willingly shared with others. Educated at Lincoln College, Taylor worked in Australia, France and the US, before returning to New Zealand in 1993. When he arrived back, lured by the promise of the plentiful large trout, the clean air and the potential he saw for Central Otago wines, there were only about 25 hectares of grapes planted. Twenty-five years later there are close to 2000 hectares.

Taylor had come to work as the winemaker at Gibbston Valley and remained there until 2006, playing a pivotal role in helping to establish Central Otago as a winegrowing region. While at Gibbston Valley, he also made the first vintages for a number of other well-known Central Otago labels, including Bald Hills, Carrick, Felton Road, Mt Difficulty and Peregrine, and has continued to consult in Oregon in the US; he helped set up Archery Summit there in 1995, a winery renowned for its Pinot Noir.

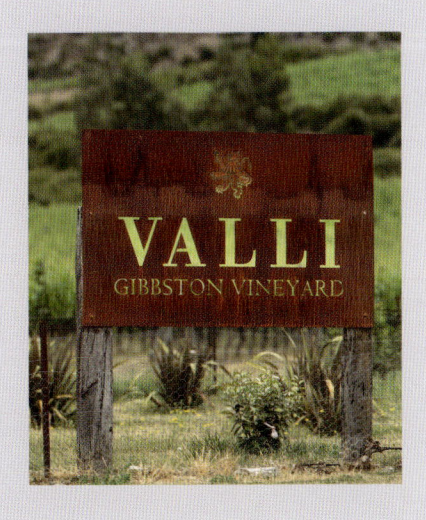

With his valuable knowledge and experience, Taylor was soon winning accolades for his wines both at home and abroad. His Gibbston Valley Reserve Pinot Noir 2000 won the trophy for Best Pinot Noir at the International Wine Challenge in 2001 — the first ever non-French wine to win. Taylor went on to win the Best Pinot Noir trophy at the International Wine & Spirit Competition a staggering three times, and he remains the only winemaker in the world to have won four times across these two competitions. Out of all these wins, Taylor says his proudest moment was when his Valli Gibbston Pinot Noir 2010 won the trophy in 2012.

In 1998, Taylor launched his own Valli label, which he named after his great-great-grandfather, Giuseppe Valli, who immigrated to New Zealand and came from a winemaking background in Italy. At Valli, Taylor was the first in Central Otago to commit to making single-vineyard Pinot Noirs, wines that would reflect their vintage and site with 'honesty and purity'. He had realised, as he was making wine for others, that the fruit from different areas displayed different characteristics and he found pleasure in discovering what wines could come from different areas. He believed, too, that what happened in the vineyard was all-important: 'When you treat it well in the vineyard, Pinot Noir says "thank you".'

Taylor sources his grapes from vineyards in three of Central Otago's sub-regions — Gibbston Valley, Bannockburn and Bendigo — and from a vineyard in the Waitaki Valley in North Otago. In Gibbston, where he lives, he owns 3.6 hectares and leases another 4 hectares, and in the Waitaki Valley he owns another 4 hectares, and he buys grapes under contract from vineyards at Bendigo and Bannockburn. While 80 per cent of his production is Pinot Noir, Taylor also makes a Riesling and a Chardonnay from the Waitaki Valley, a dry Pinot Gris from Gibbston, and in recent years, together with accomplished winemaker and wine judge Jen Parr, has started making a Pinot Gris Orange Wine ('The Real McCoy'), which derives its colour from fermenting the grapes on their skins, a technique generally used for red wine.

Gibbston is one of the coolest sub-regions in Central Otago, but Valli's estate vineyard maximises the sunlight hours the vines receive, assisting the uniform ripening of the fruit, a factor critical in producing quality Pinot Noir. The Gibbston grapes are sometimes not picked until early May, and while this means risking early frost damage, the longer hang time helps the fruit develop more elegance and complexity

Grant Taylor.

of flavour. Gibbston Pinot Noirs are not so much about the fruit, but are more floral, spicy and earthy. Lighter-bodied, the best show fine tannins and length of flavour.

Over in the Cromwell Basin, Valli's Bannockburn vineyard is warmer than Gibbston and produces darker, denser and more powerful fruit, with cherry flavours and higher tannins. While Bendigo, also in the Cromwell Basin, is one of the warmest sub-regions, Valli's grapes come from the Zebra vineyard, high up on Chinaman's Terrace. At close to 400 metres above sea level, this higher elevation means slightly cooler temperatures and good air flow. From the Bendigo fruit, Taylor makes what he describes as 'dark, rich, lush wines — big friendly beasts'.

'As the vines age they will do their job better — their best wines have yet to be made.'

The Waitaki soils are limestone-based, as in Burgundy, and because the region is cooler than Central Otago, early-ripening clones have been planted. Taylor, who was born in the Waitaki Valley, is already, after only a few commercial vintages, excited by what he describes as 'the consistency in the perfume and minerality of these wines'. So far there are only about 100 hectares planted in grapes in North Otago, but Taylor believes the region has great winemaking potential and says the best sites are hardly planted yet.

The winemaking culture in Central Otago has been characterised by a hunger to find out more, to share ideas and compare terroirs, and after 56 vintages Taylor says he is still always playing, experimenting. 'There's still a lot more to see and learn and discover. As the vines age they will do their job better — their best wines have yet to be made.' Valli has not converted to organics or biodynamics. 'I don't want to see your philosophy or religion, I want to see great wine,' he says. However, in recent years he has been collaborating with his old friends and colleagues Ted Lemon and Claire Mulholland from Burn Cottage, a biodynamic vineyard in Lowburn. Exchanging a small quantity of grapes, he has made a Valli Burn Cottage Pinot Noir and they have made a Burn Cottage Valli Pinot Noir. As well as having the pleasure of working together again, they are gaining further understanding of their own sites. 'I just want to put Central Otago in a bottle,' says Taylor.

Production is small for this boutique winery — about 4000 cases — but for Taylor winemaking has always been about quality not quantity. Over time, Valli wines have built up a loyal local following, with between 35 to 40 per cent of production sold in Central Otago. Most of Queenstown's top restaurants sell his wine and Taylor believes the best market is always local. However, some of his wine finds its way to the rest of the South Island and a small amount even makes it up north. This leaves about 35 per cent to be exported, mostly to Australia.

Taylor has been one of a handful of iconic winemakers who have helped unlock the potential of winegrowing in Central Otago, helped establish Pinot Noir as the region's signature wine, and helped put Central Otago on the global wine map. His journey is not finished yet, though. When the ultimate goal in your life is to make the most truthful wines possible, your journey is a long one.

And the trout? 'Fishing washes your mind clear, so you can approach the issues feeling fresh again.'

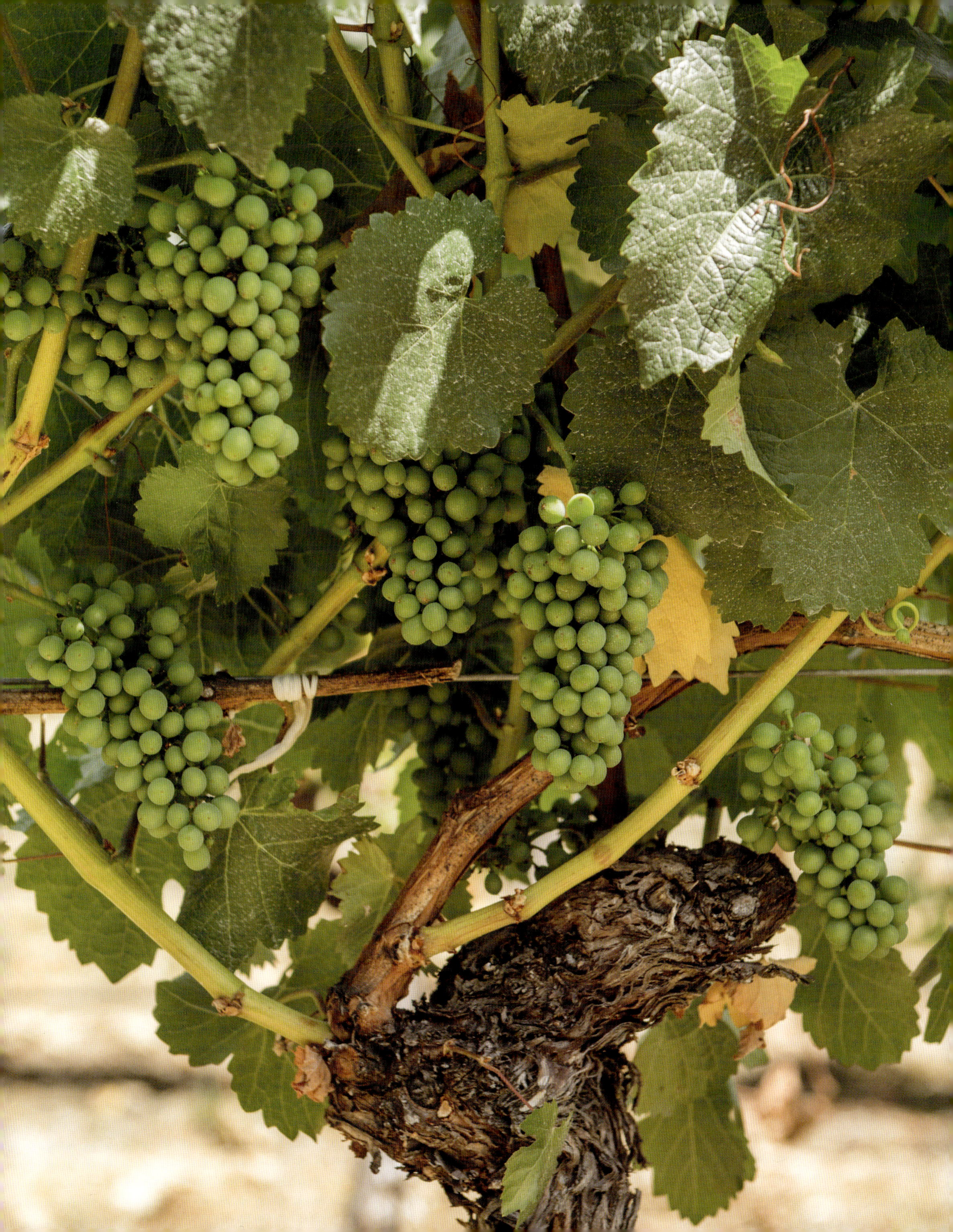

TOP Waitaki Valley. ABOVE Grant Taylor with vineyard manager Murray Turner, Waitaki Valley. RIGHT Ripe Pinot Noir.

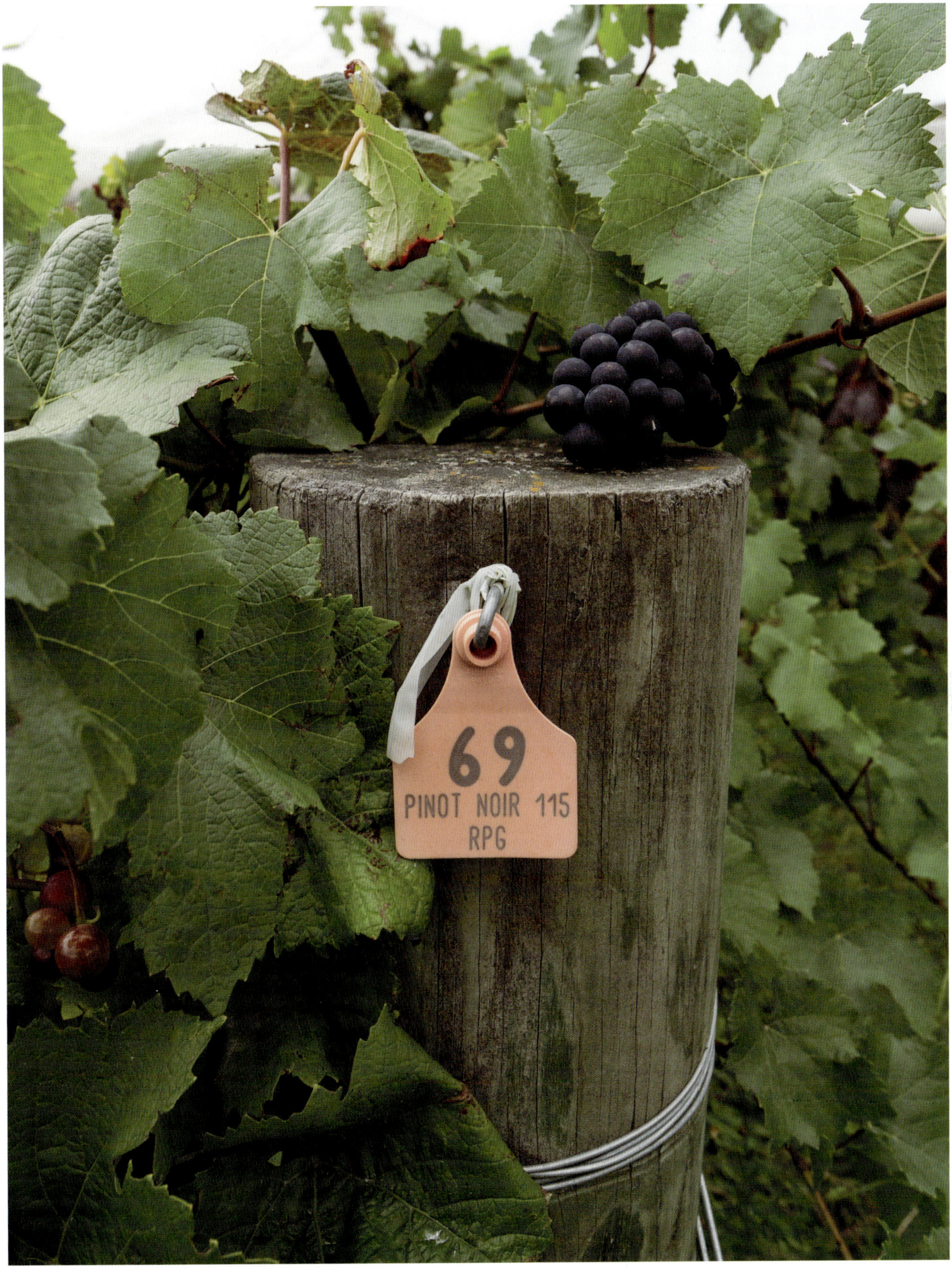
69
PINOT NOIR 115
RPG

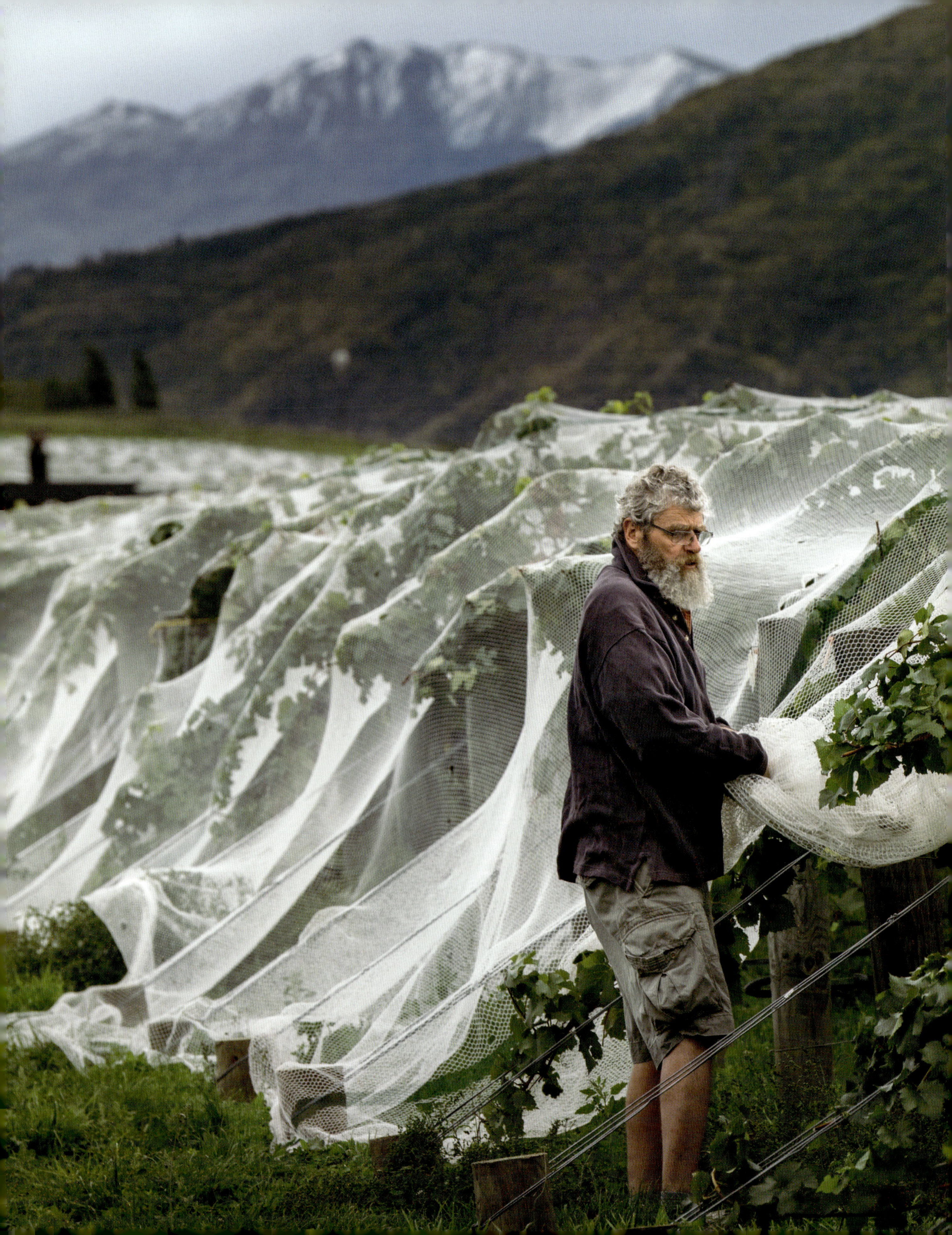

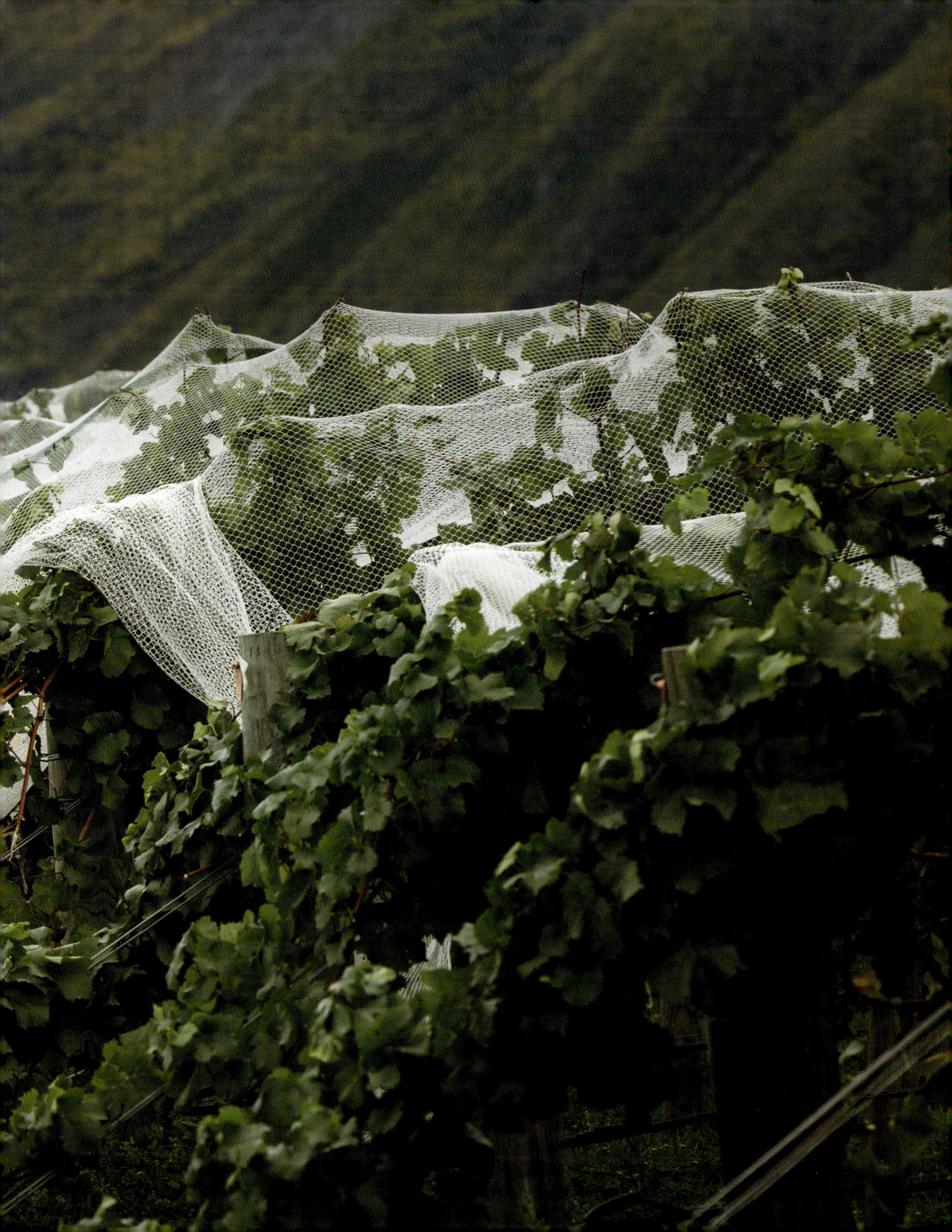

PEREGRINE

'What happens in the vineyard has to make sense in the marketplace at the other end.'

When it was first set up in 1998, Peregrine was a 'virtual' winery, buying in fruit from 14 different growers and getting its wine made at a contract facility in Cromwell. Then, in 2003, the Peregrine winery, with its distinctive bird's-wing roof, was opened in Gibbston. Greg Hay, who was one of the group of investors who developed Peregrine, became the sales and marketing director. He remained with the company until 2015, when Lindsay McLachlan, who had been a majority shareholder since 2007, bought him out.

McLachlan says he spent 25 years 'pretending to be an accountant' before he and his wife Jude bought land at Bendigo and started planting their Lamont vineyard in 1998. Buying in to Peregrine and combining the two operations has meant that Peregrine is now what McLachlan describes as 'a big small business'. It is also very much a family affair. Lindsay is the owner and chairman, Jude is a director, their son Fraser, who joined Peregrine in 2012, is a director and CEO, and their younger son Blair is involved too, working in the vineyard. Peregrine's base remains in Gibbston, but McLachlan has 30 hectares of vineyards planted, with plans to plant another 15 hectares at Bendigo, and Peregrine also has long-term contracts to buy grapes from different vineyards in the Lowburn–Pisa sub-region.

the balance is exported to the US, UK, Canada, Japan and Belgium. The US is an important growth market for Peregrine, with national distributor Vineyard Brands, which has taken on board their full range of wines, recently making Peregrine their sole New Zealand producer.

Peregrine has been in an expansion phase in recent years, buying more land and planting 7 hectares of vines, but in the future, McLachlan says the size of their winery will dictate how much the business can grow. Because of their different sites at Gibbston, Bendigo and Lowburn, their fruit ripens at different times over a six- to seven-week period, allowing the winery to process more fruit. 'To be successful you need a balance between how much your vineyards produce, how much your winery can handle and how much you can sell.'

ABOVE RIGHT Home Vineyard, Gibbston. RIGHT New plantings at Bendigo.

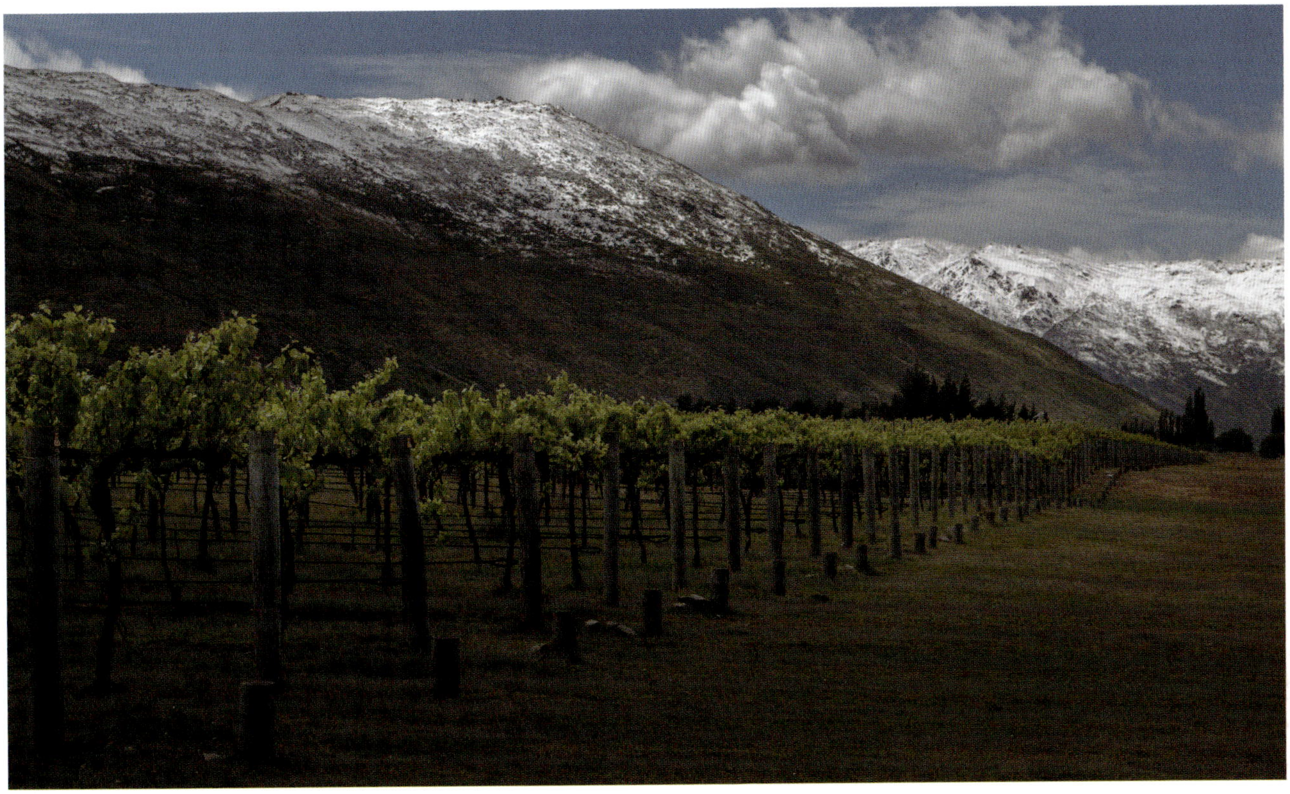

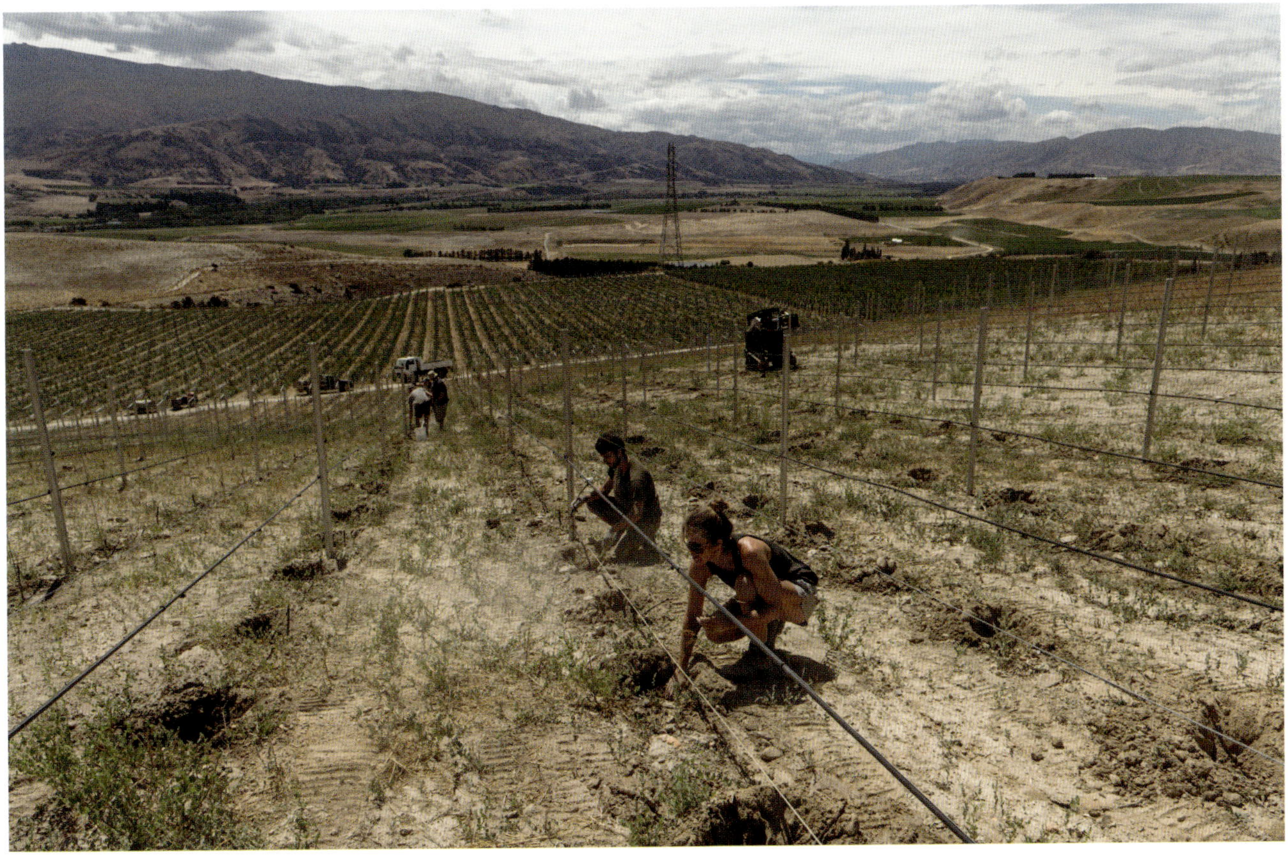

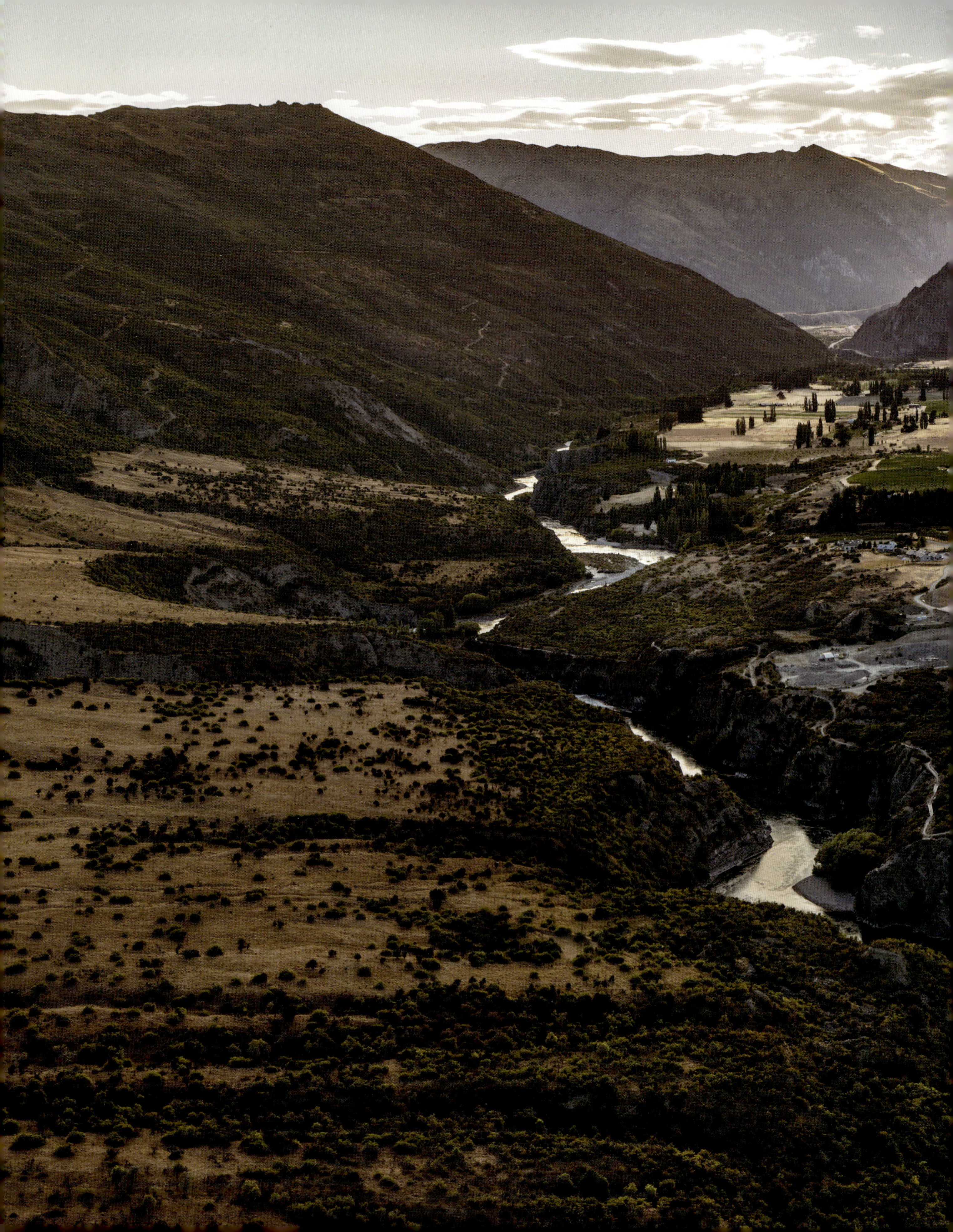

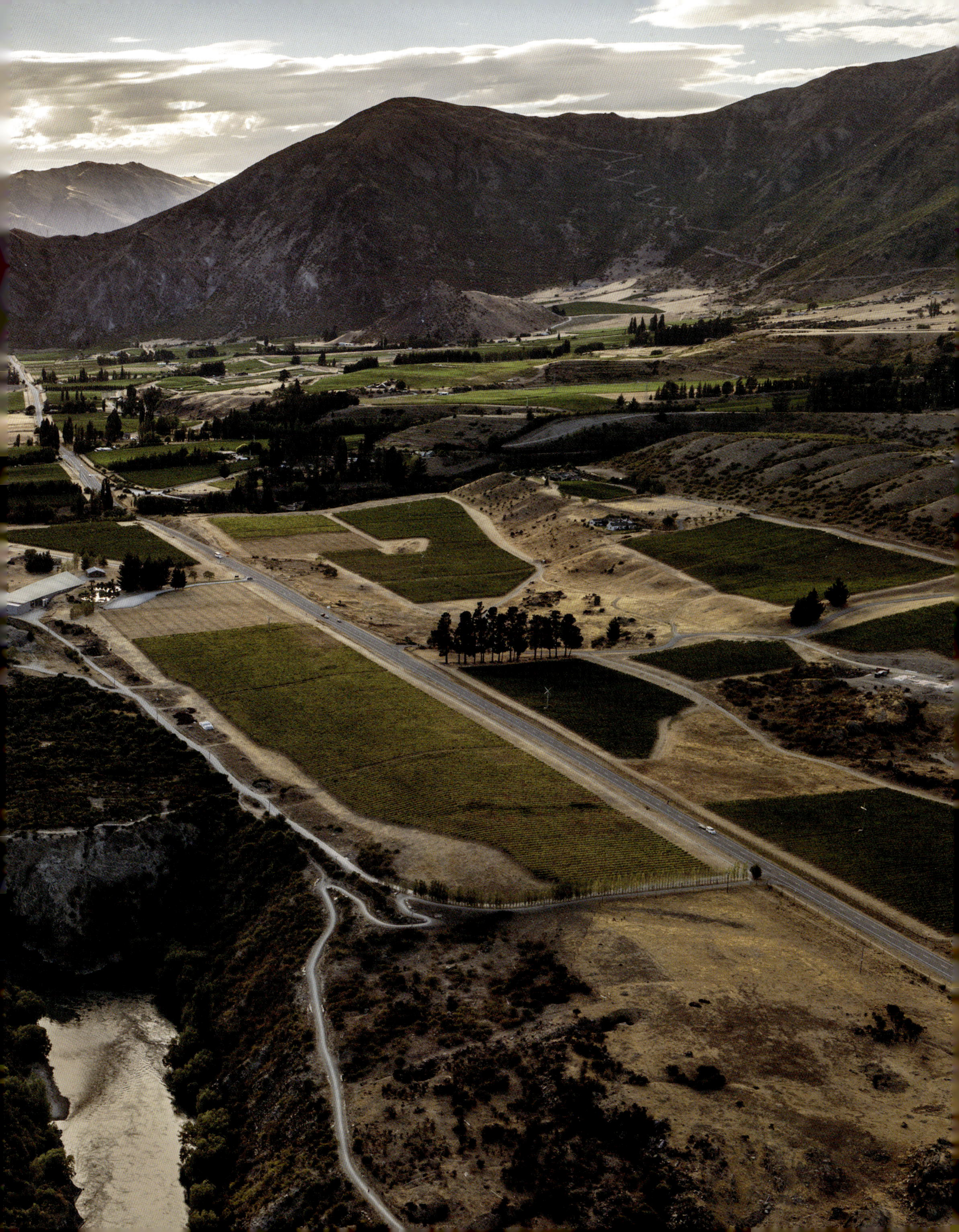

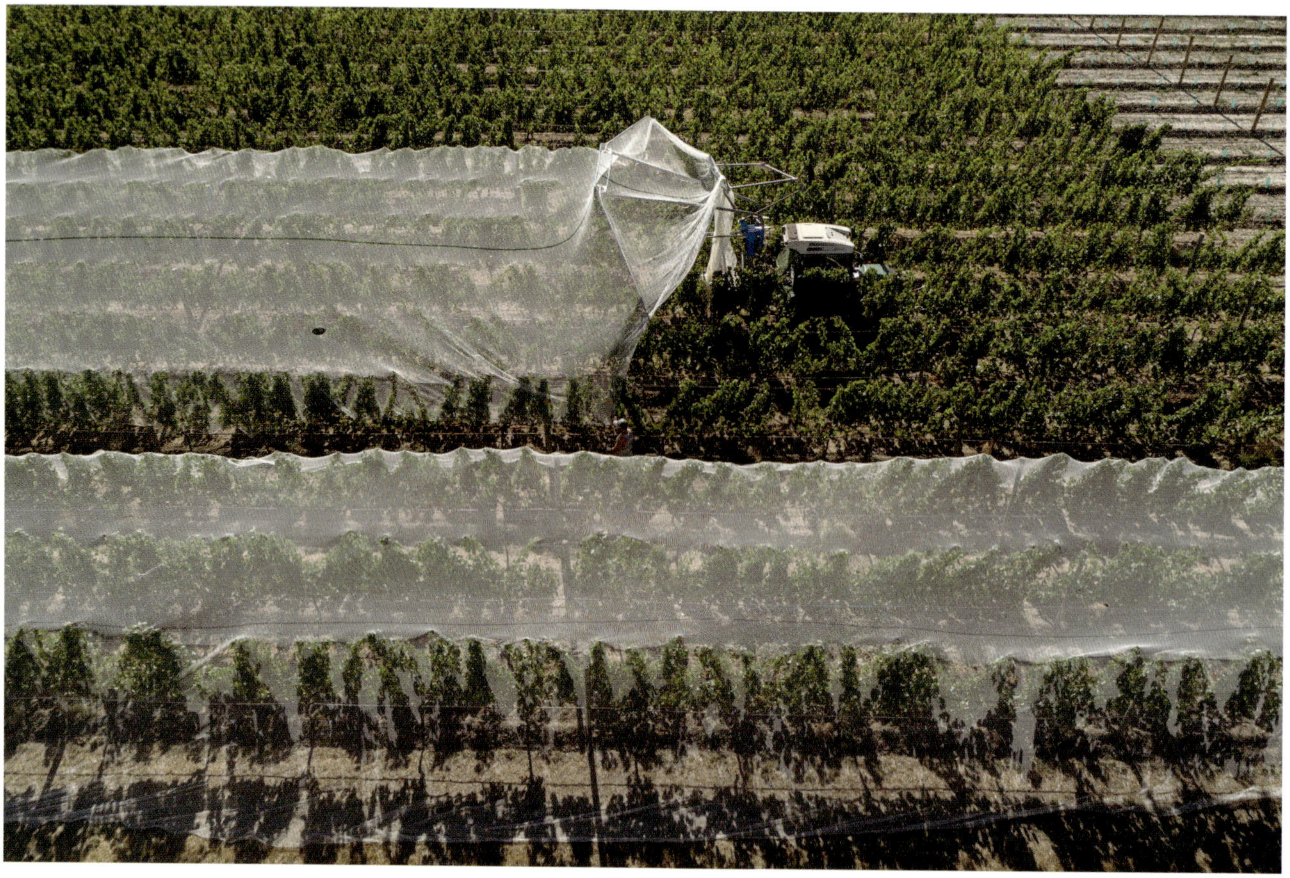

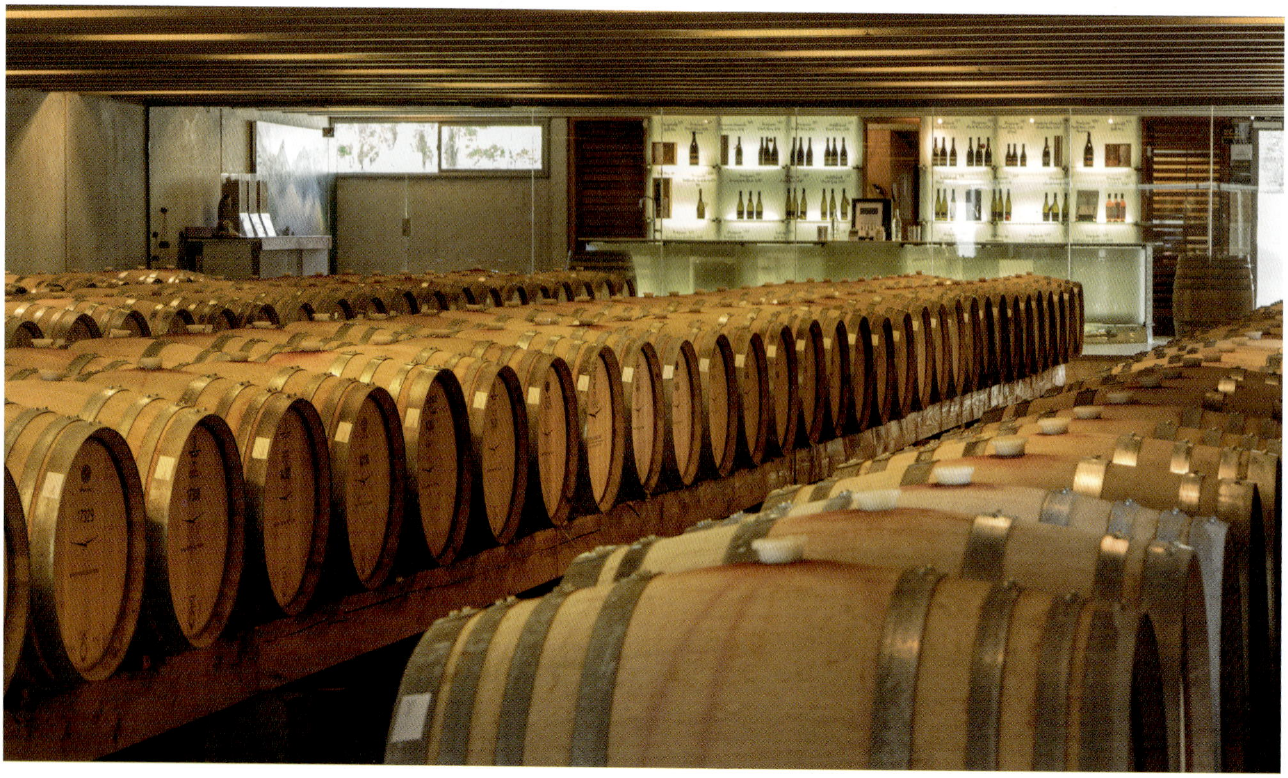

ABOVE LEFT Installing bird netting, Bendigo. LEFT Barrel room looking towards wine shop. TOP Lindsay McLachlan turning organic compost.
ABOVE Organic compost.

TOP Pinot harvest, Bendigo. ABOVE AND RIGHT A wedding in the historic 1860s woolshed at Peregrine, Gibbston.

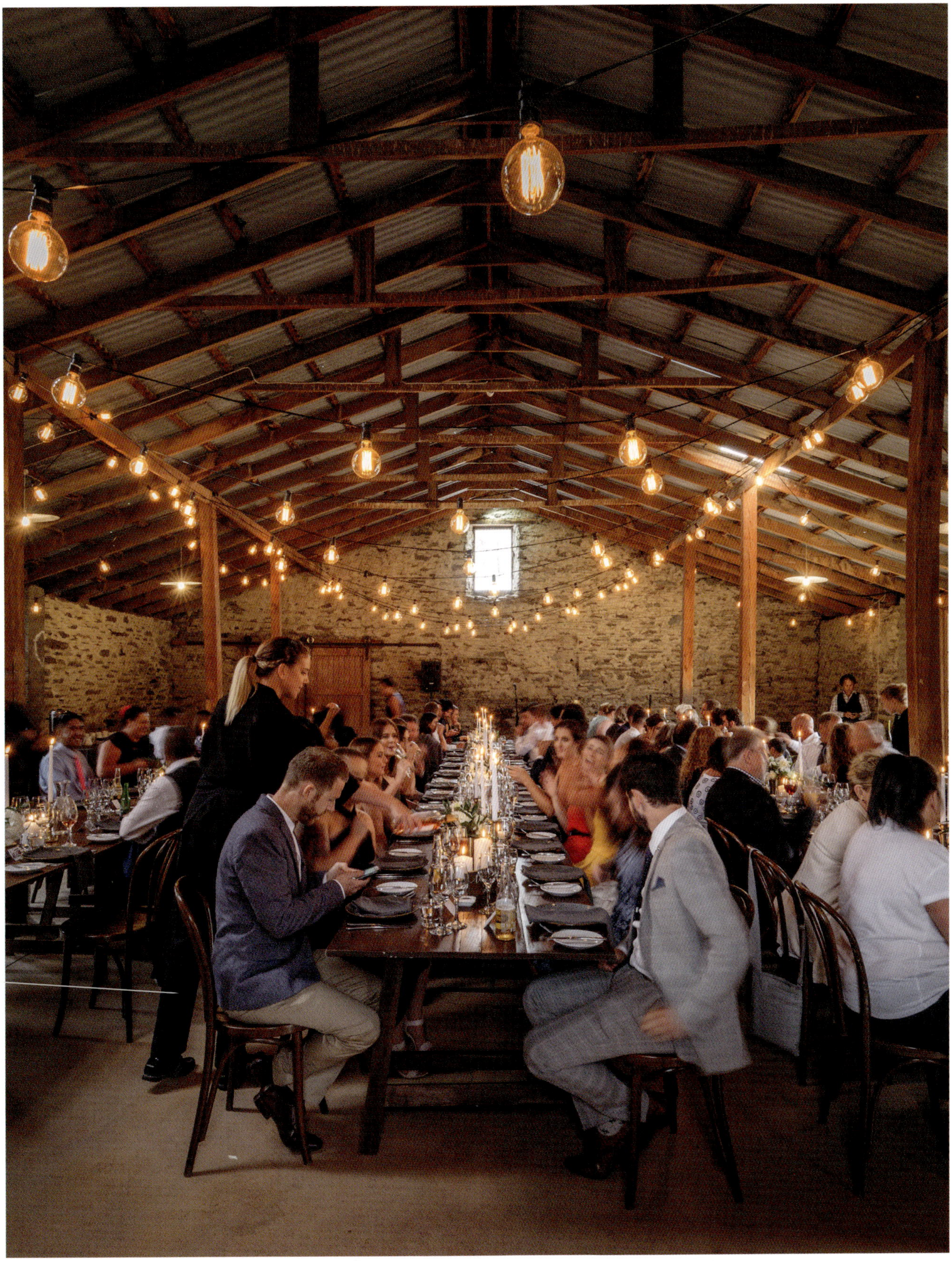

BRENNAN WINES

'What about in fifty or one hundred years' time?'

Brennan is a boutique, 13-hectare family-owned and -run vineyard in Gibbston. Murray Brennan fell for Central Otago while studying medicine at Otago University in the 1960s, and although his career took him to the US, he retained his love for the region. In 1994 he bought 6 hectares in Gibbston. He soon began planting a vineyard, but for the next decade the grapes were sold to Peregrine. So it was not until 2006, when Murray's son Sean returned with his wife and family to take over the vineyard, that the Brennan label was finally launched.

While growing up in the US, Sean had regularly visited Central Otago with his family. Then as a young man he worked vintages in New Zealand, the US and Australia, and studied viticulture and winemaking at Roseworthy (the former agricultural college now part of the University of Adelaide). It was during his time there that he was introduced to 'decent Pinot Noir'. His goal at Brennan has been to produce 'limited quantities of iconic, aged wines' — wines that truly represent the potential of their sites.

Like the vignerons of France, Brennan works as both viticulturist and winemaker. He says the thing that excites him the most about making wine in Central Otago is that if, after only 30 years, the region is already producing world-class wines, 'what about in fifty or one hundred years' time?' A year after he took over, Brennan bought a neighbouring 4-hectare mature vineyard, and in 2014 the purchase

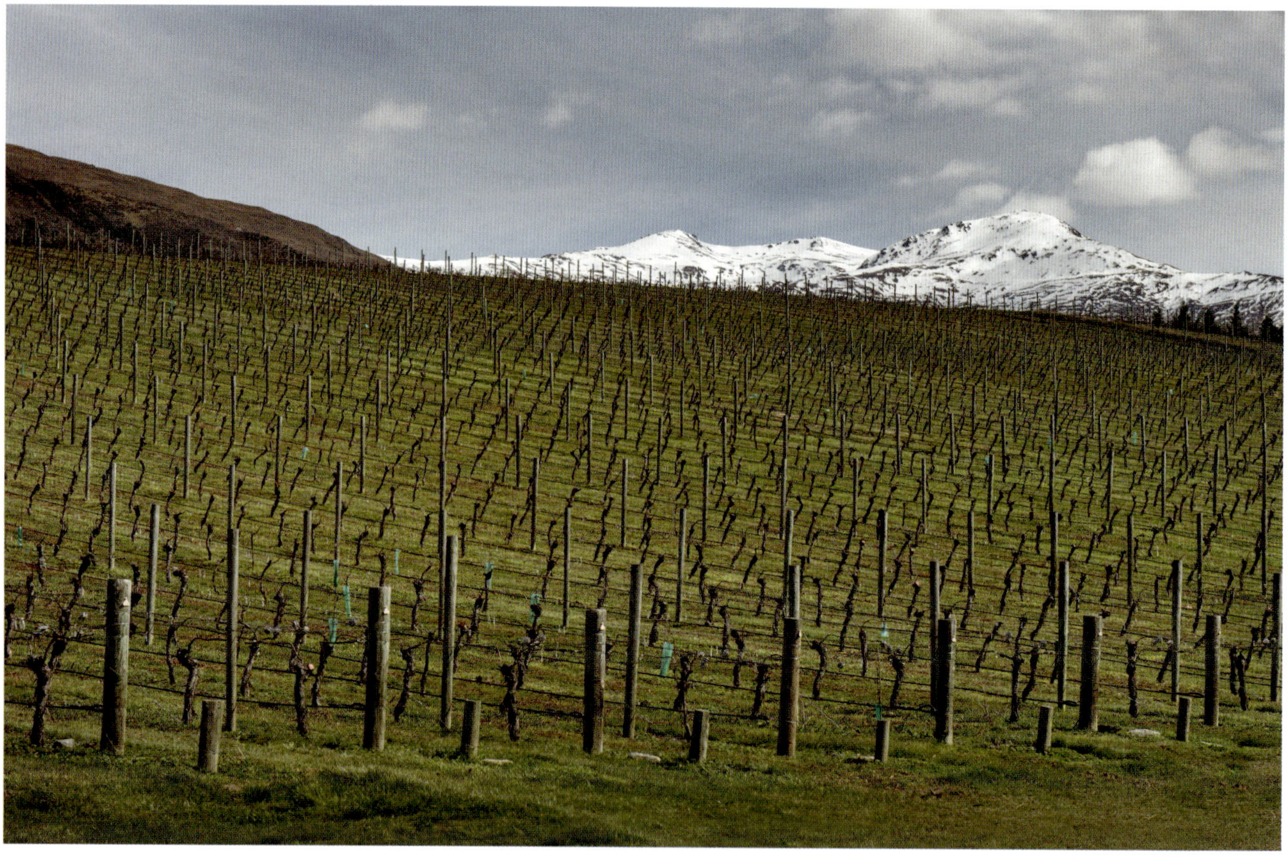

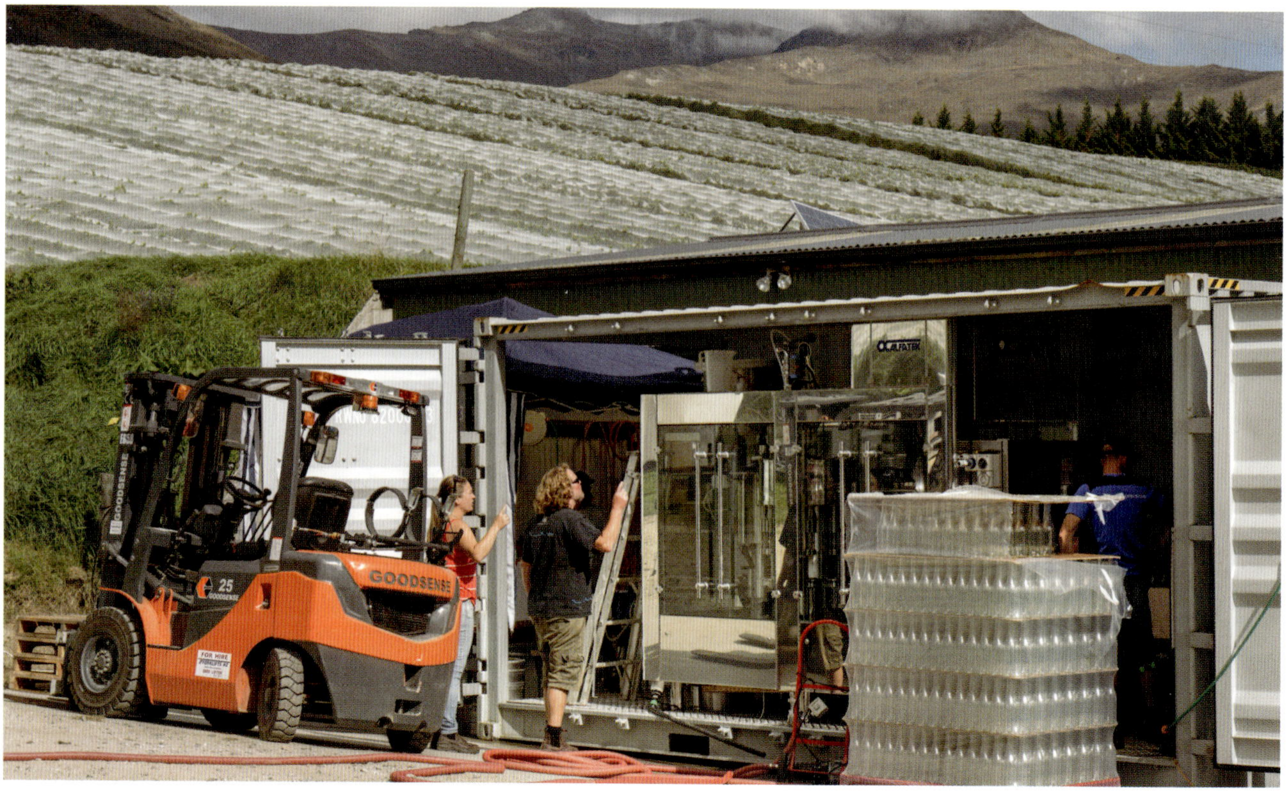
GOODSENSE
25
FOR HIRE

ABOVE LEFT Vineyard in winter. LEFT On-site bottling plant. TOP Bird netting in place. ABOVE Vineyard turkeys.

THIS SPREAD Muscat harvest.

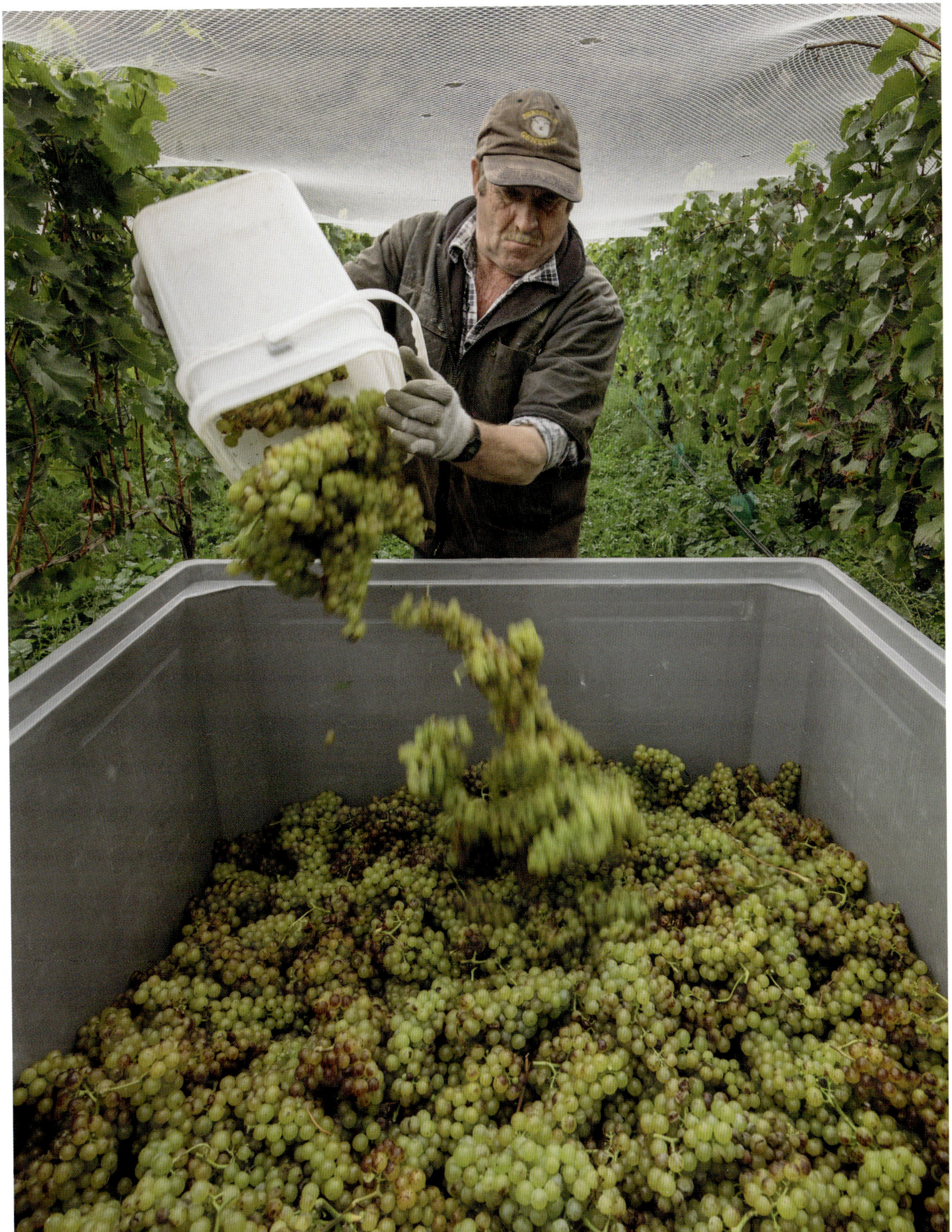

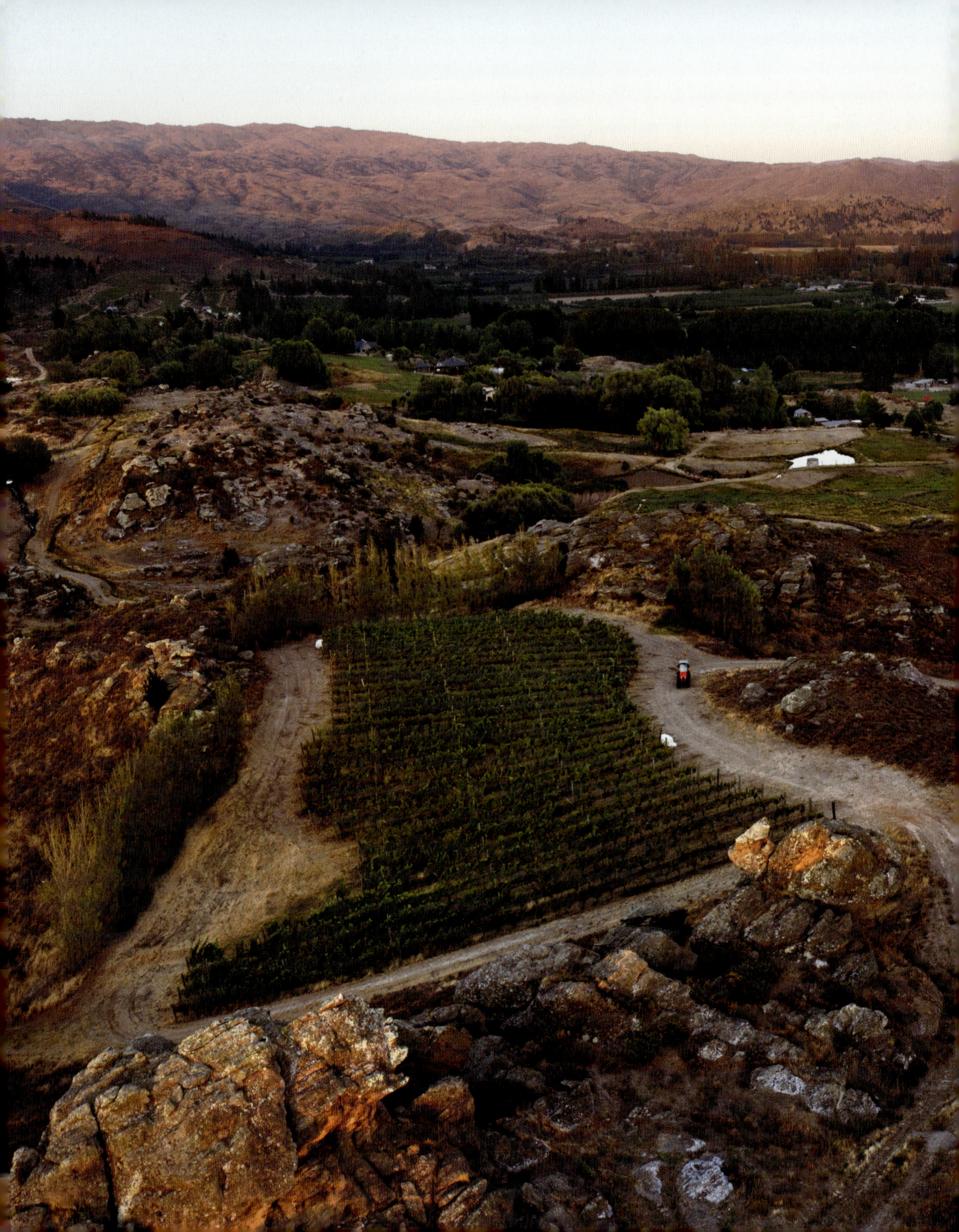

ALEXANDRA

Two Paddocks · Judge Rock
· Grasshopper Rock

THE ALEXANDRA BASIN, at between 140 and 180 metres above sea level, is the lowest and most southern sub-region in Central Otago. It also has the most extreme climate. It is very hot and dry, with an annual rainfall of just 350 millimetres, but it can also be very cold. Often, especially over the growing season, it can have the hottest days and coolest nights. This greater diurnal shift in temperature helps to slow down the ripening process, allowing the Pinot Noir fruit to develop greater complexity of flavour and more perfume.

There have not been many larger blocks of land available for vineyard development in the Alexandra Basin, and a lot of suitable sites were already planted in fruit trees. This has resulted in a number of small and very small vineyards being planted, with the grand exception of McArthur Ridge which, with 174 hectares of vineyards and multiple owners, is the biggest vineyard development in Central Otago. In total, there are about 240 hectares of vines planted across the Alexandra Basin.

Winegrowers in Alexandra have established their own association and each year at Easter they hold a Wine and Food Harvest Festival in the small and historic town of Clyde, giving the sub-region's smaller boutique vineyards a chance to showcase their wines.

The style of Pinot Noir here is generally lighter in colour, more delicate and softer than Pinots from other Central Otago sub-regions. Phil Handford from Grasshopper Rock vineyard describes them as 'elegant with red-fruit flavours, a bit more savoury, spicy, and perfumed'.

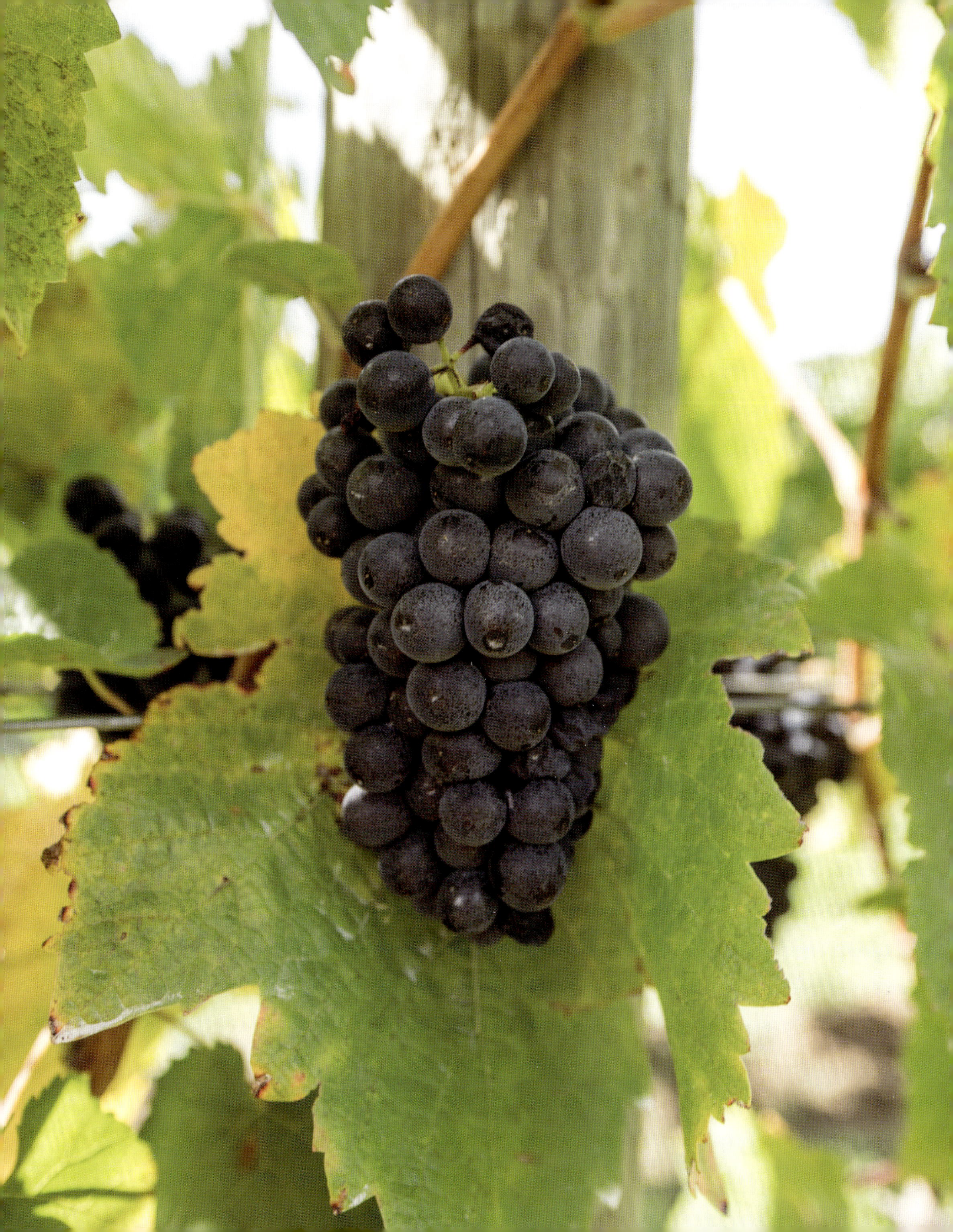

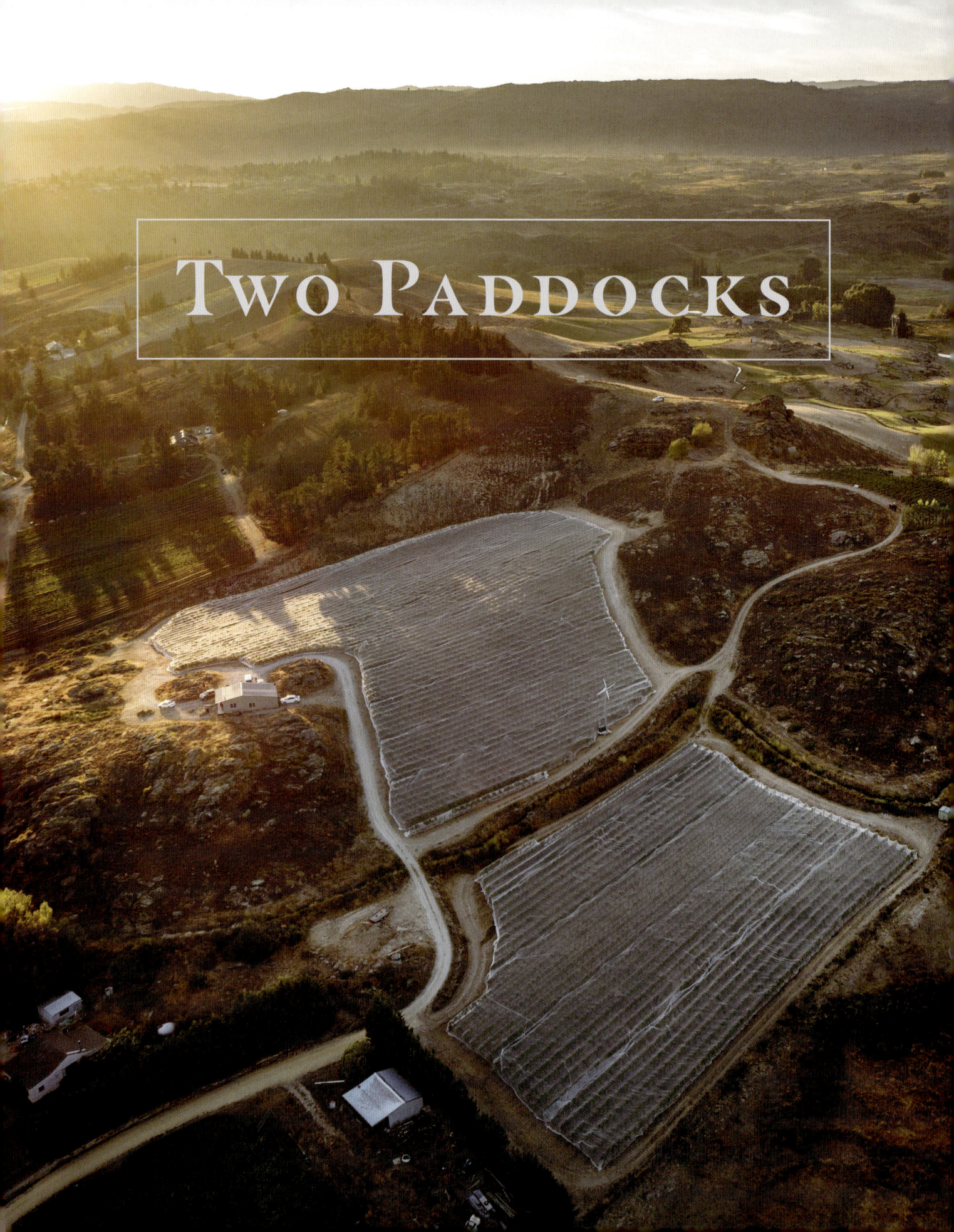

Two Paddocks

'It's not a sane person's business — Pinot.'

In the beginning, in 1993, there was The First Paddock vineyard in Gibbston. Then, five years later, The Last Chance vineyard was planted in the Alexandra Basin, and soon after, Red Bank Farm, near Clyde, at the other end of the Alexandra Basin, was bought and planted. Twenty years on, in 2013, The Fusilier vineyard on Felton Road in Bannockburn was bought. Two Paddocks now had four vineyards in three sub-regions, with a total of 20 hectares of grape vines. Since 1999, Red Bank Farm, which had been a government research station, has been the engine room for Two Paddocks, and is now also the home of the Two Paddocks Wine Club.

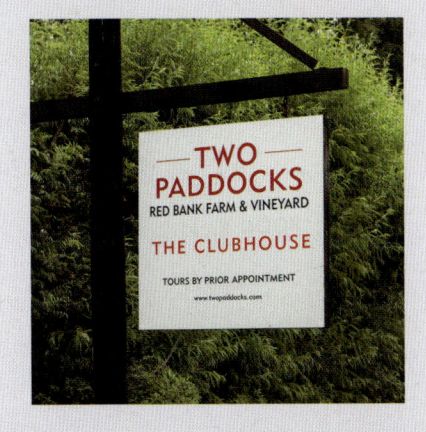

Sam Neill's twin love affair with Central Otago and Pinot Noir goes back to childhood days when he camped in the region with his family and 'fell in love with the big empty hills'. The Pinot bug came a bit later. His father had seen the potential for growing grapes in Central Otago back in the 1950s and was excited when his friend Rolfe Mills started planting grape vines in the 1970s at Rippon, in Wanaka. Then, when he was living in London in the 1980s, the best French wine Neill could afford to buy was Burgundy. 'You could get a really good Burgundy back then for about twenty quid.' Once he had enough money to invest in Central Otago, 'Pinot rang like a bell', and from the start Two Paddocks has been all about Pinot Noir. However, Neill has also planted 2 hectares of Riesling at Red Bank Farm to extend his portfolio to include two different Rieslings as well as five different Pinot Noirs.

Two Paddocks is certified organic, and alongside the vineyard at Red Bank Farm, Neill also has a cherry orchard, lavender, saffron, chickens, ducks, pigs, sheep and cattle, and he has planted natives to encourage the native bird population to return. The cattle and sheep provide compost for the vineyards, and the sheep are also winter lawnmowers and provide the odd roast of lamb. The chickens lay free-range eggs and the pigs are there because Neill 'likes pigs', and he has named them after friends. Angelica, the kunekune pig, actually turned out to be a boy, while Charlie Pickering, the white duck, who swims with Neill in his pond, is in fact a girl. Well, Sam Neill is an actor as well as a farmer, so a little poetic licence is probably allowed. Being organic is more work and more expensive, but Neill believes in providing a healthy place for the people working with him, and in making healthy wine.

Neill spends about four months a year in Central Otago and describes Pinot as an obsession. 'You can't make good Pinot on the cheap. It's hand-crafted from beginning to end.' His talented viticulturist Mike Wing has been with him for 12 years now, taking good organic care of all the Two Paddocks vineyards. The work is hard and ongoing — the vines are visited up to 14 times a year. It starts with winter pruning and ends with the harvest. In between, it includes bud rubbing, shoot thinning, leaf plucking, wire lifting and fruit thinning. Not to mention putting on and taking off nets in late summer and early autumn. Pinot is a naturally low-yielding grape vine anyway, but to get the desired concentration of flavour inevitably some fruit has to be dropped, making for even lower cropping levels and making it even more expensive to produce.

In 2016, Two Paddocks celebrated its twentieth Pinot Noir vintage. Winemaker Dean Shaw makes three single-vineyard Pinot Noirs, a blended Pinot, which is Two Paddocks' flagship wine, and then, under the Picnic label, a second blended Pinot Noir and a small quantity of Riesling. He has been working with Neill for nearly 20 years and both are shareholders in the Central Otago Wine Company (COWCo), which Neill co-founded back in 1997.

Sam Neill with Charlie Pickering.

Shaw says of winemaking that 80 per cent of the final result depends on the vineyard and what happens there, 15 per cent is down to luck, and 5 per cent is about the winemaking process. 'Winemakers prefer to work with good material and not do too much. But you have to have the confidence to not do too much. You only get one shot a year.' However, in a poor year, he does acknowledge that winemakers need much more skill and knowledge. 'Very good winemakers can make something ordinary pretty bloody good.'

Both Pinot Noir and Riesling are very much soil-based wines, and in their single-vineyard Pinot Noirs, Shaw is trying to reflect the different Two Paddocks sites, as well as the particular vintage. With three single-vineyard Pinots from three different sub-regions, Gibbston, Bannockburn and Alexandra, fans have plenty of Pinots to choose from, but if they are unable to decide where to start, the Two Paddocks flagship blended Pinot Noir 'ticks all the boxes', in the words of New Zealand Master Sommelier Cameron Douglas.

Gibbston is higher and colder than the other Central Otago sub-regions, and so more frost-prone, but Neill says in a good year the wine is superb. His Last Chance vineyard, near Alexandra, is not so high, but is 'possibly the southernmost vineyard in the world'. His 2015 Pinot Noir from this vineyard was described by Frank Wilden in *Business Insider Australia* as being 'as good as any Pinot I've seen out of NZ. Outstanding.'

'Some places have magic; some don't,' says Neill modestly.

The latest offering from Two Paddocks is a 'natural' Pinot Noir, made from grapes from The Fusilier vineyard at Bannockburn. A natural wine is not built to age as it has no preservatives, but 'it's entirely different and very delicious'. Just 40 cases were made and these are for sale only to members of the Two Paddocks Wine Club.

Neill wants to leave a 'wine legacy' — a legacy in which he takes quiet pride and which gives him ultimate satisfaction. 'When my films are all dead and gone, there will still be the great vineyards.' It may not be 'a sane person's business', but thanks Sam — for your films *and* your wine.

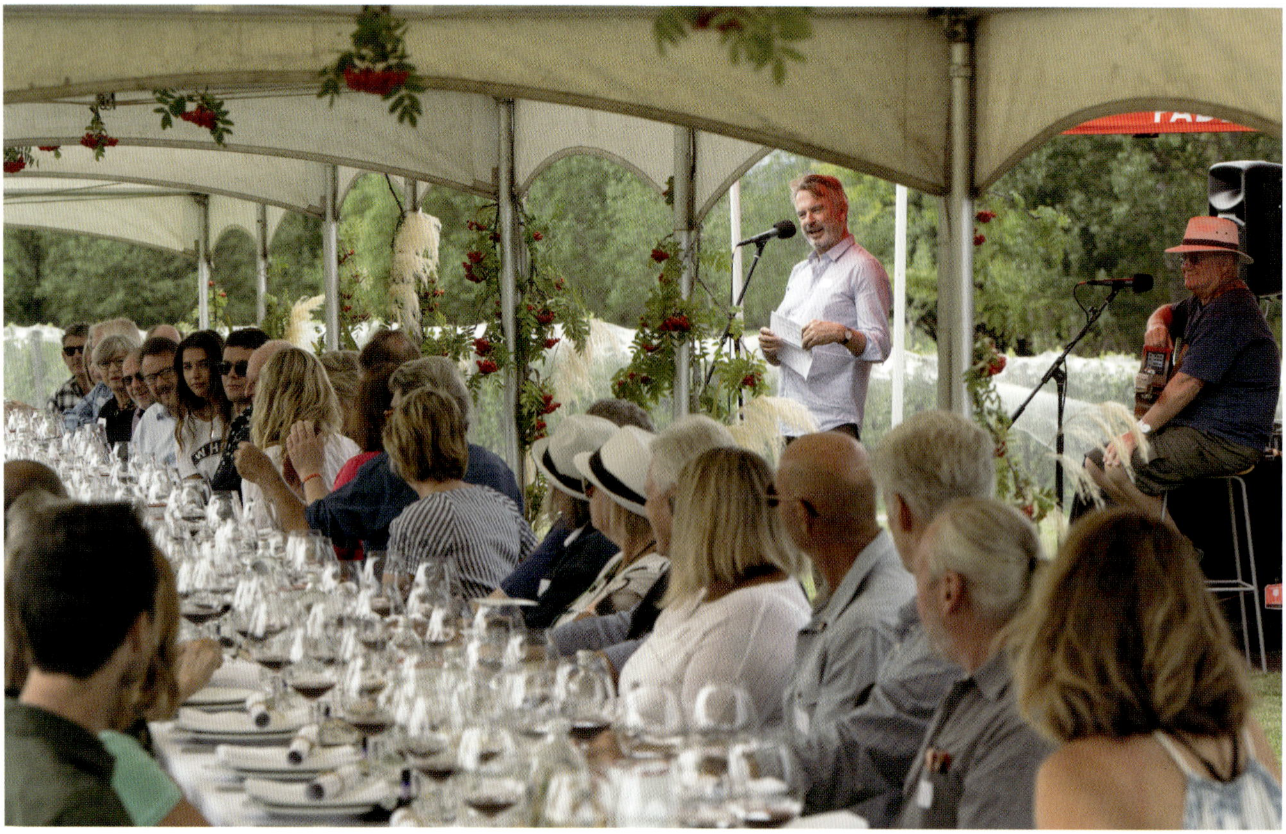

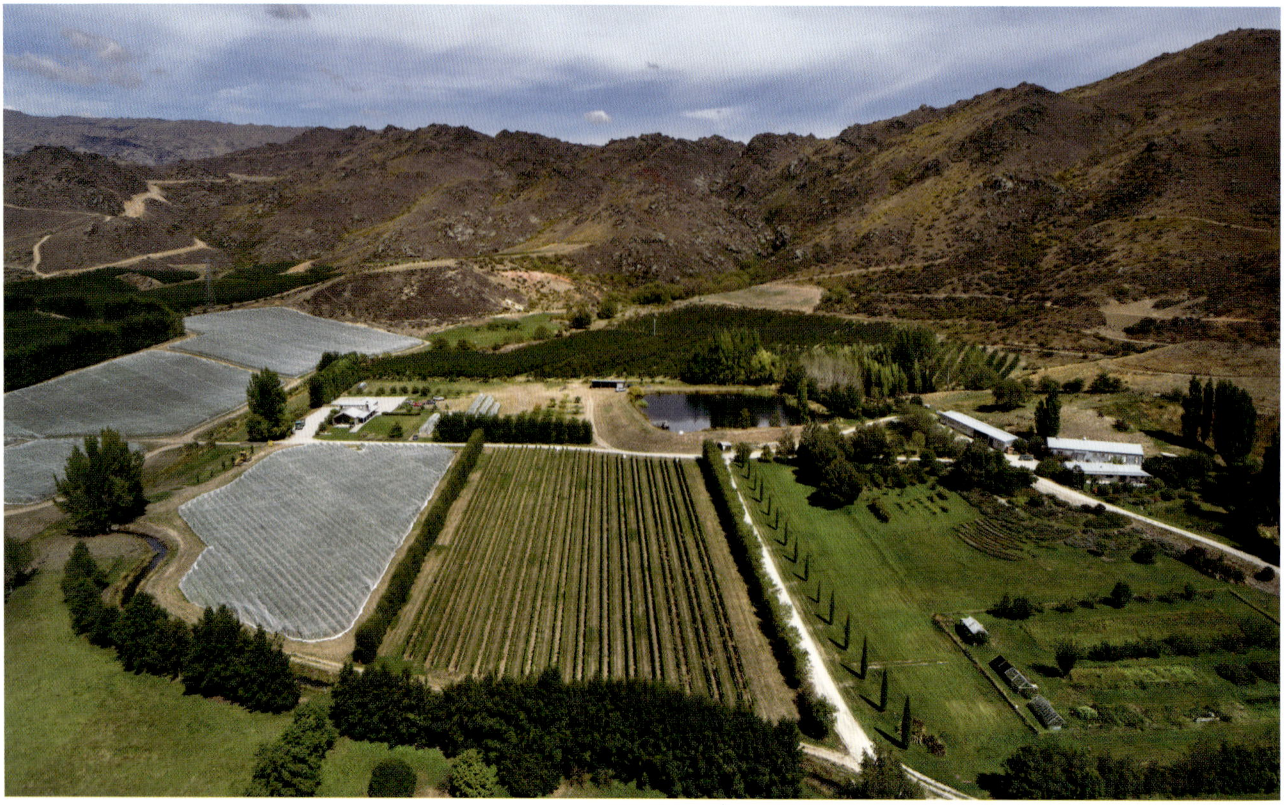

ABOVE LEFT Annual long lunch at the Private Paddock Club House. **LEFT** Red Bank Farm vineyard. **TOP** Highland cow.
ABOVE Leaf thinning, Red Bank Farm.

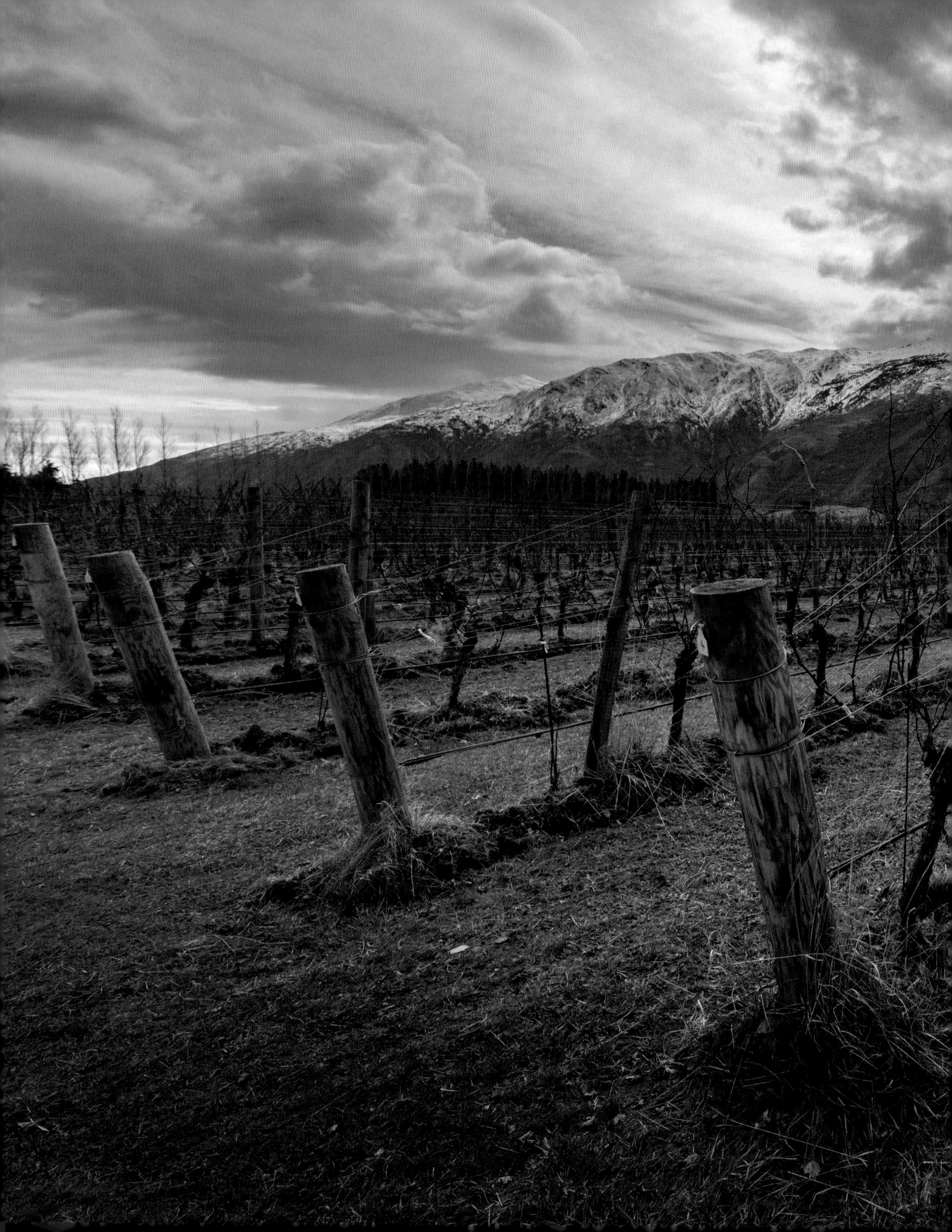

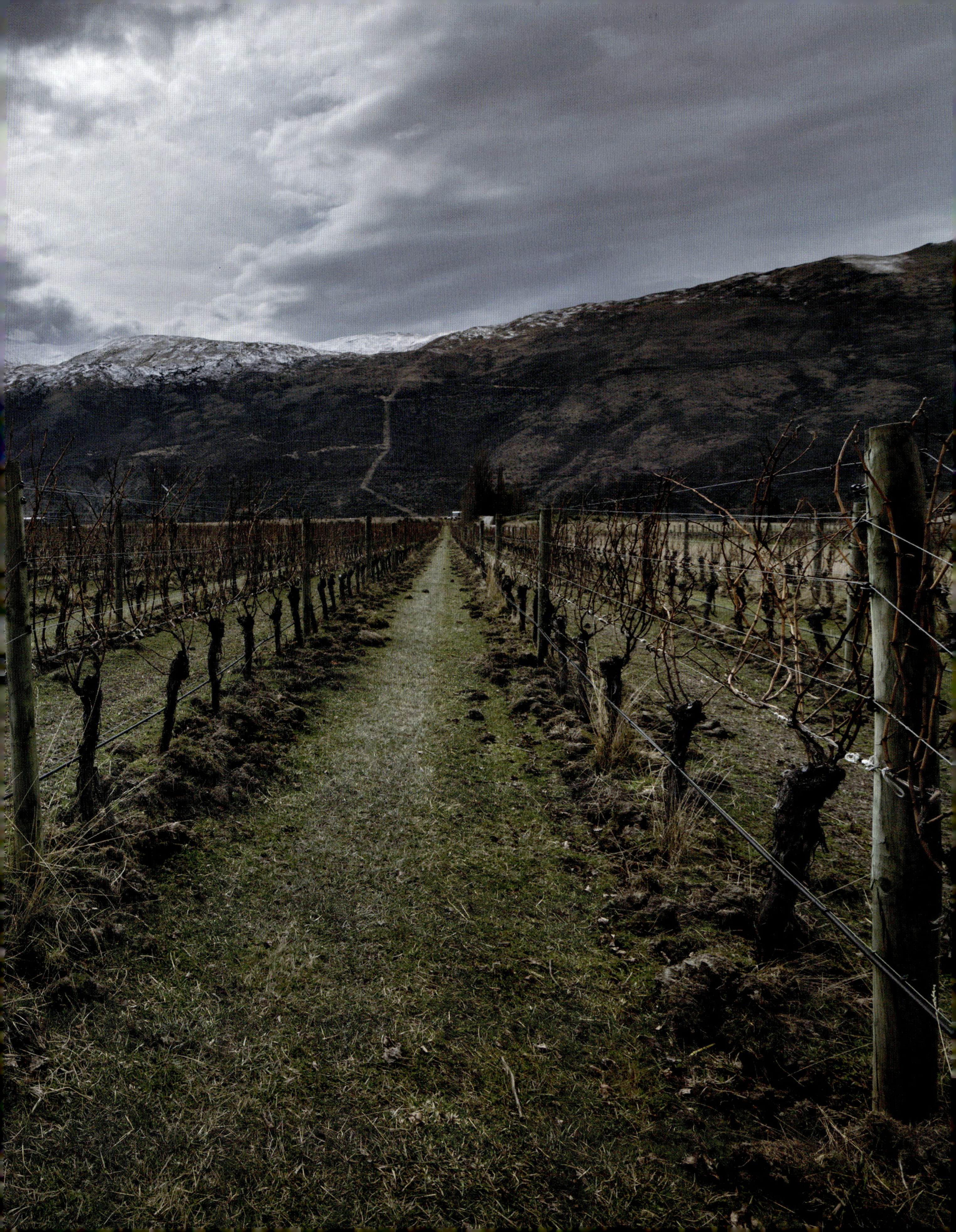

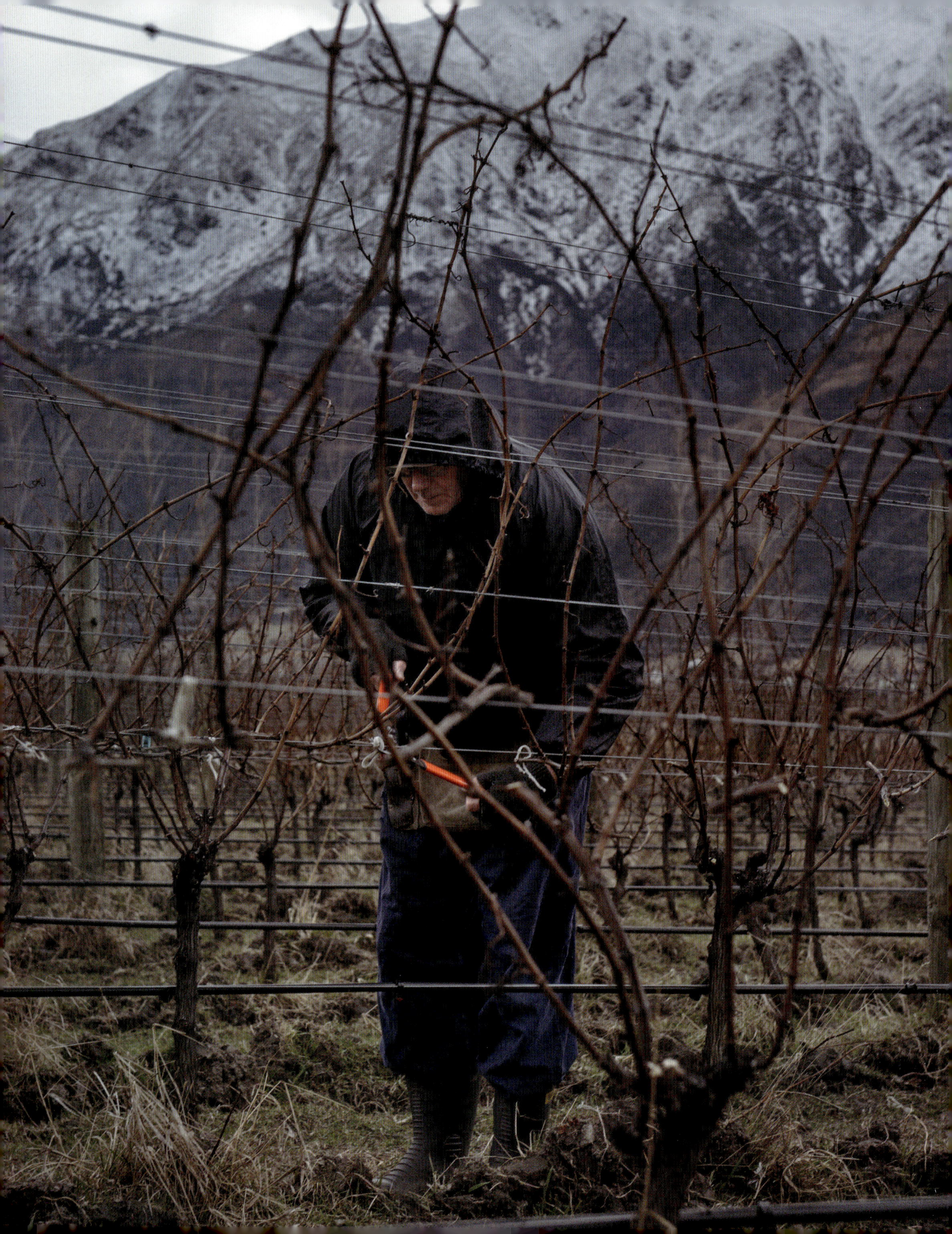

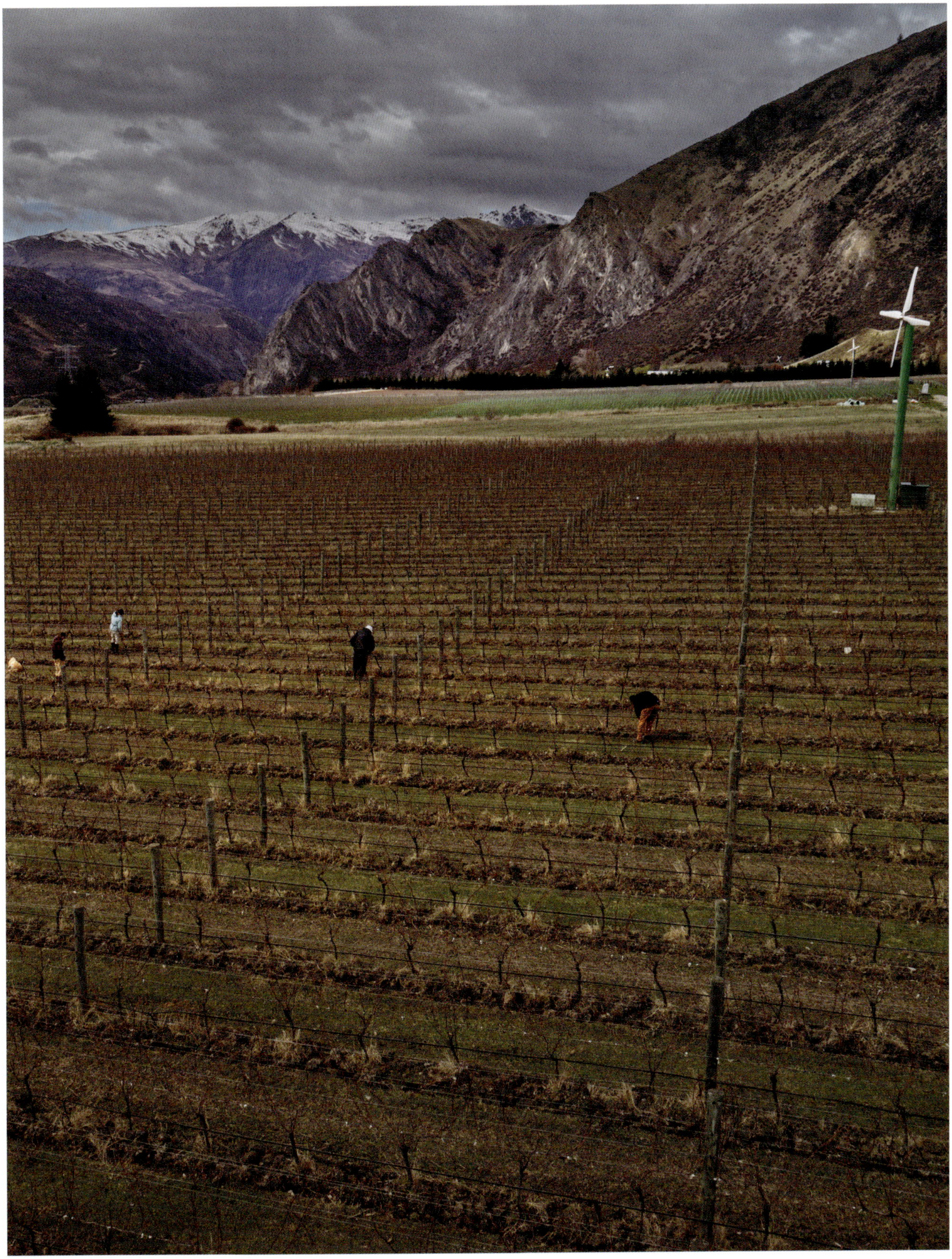

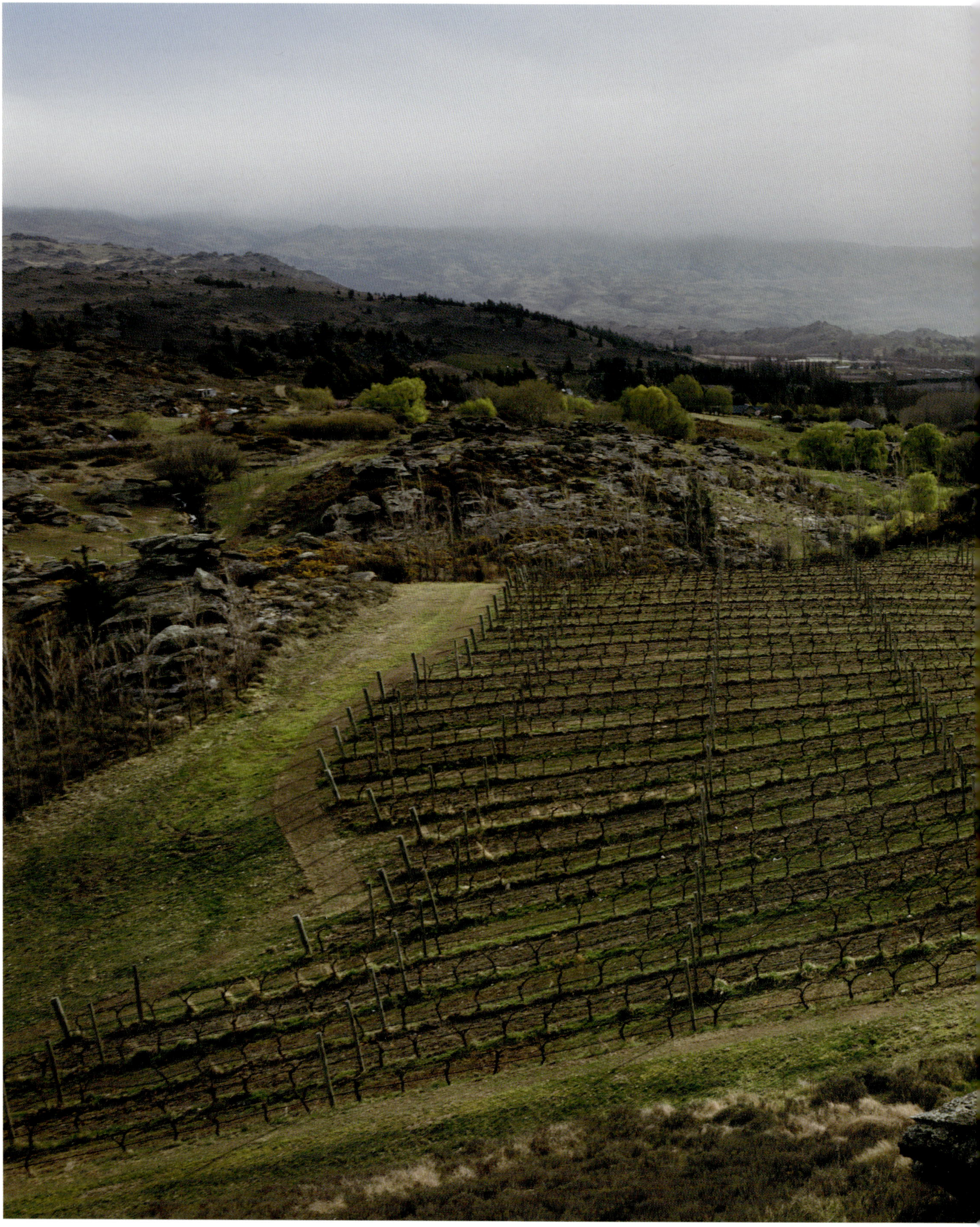

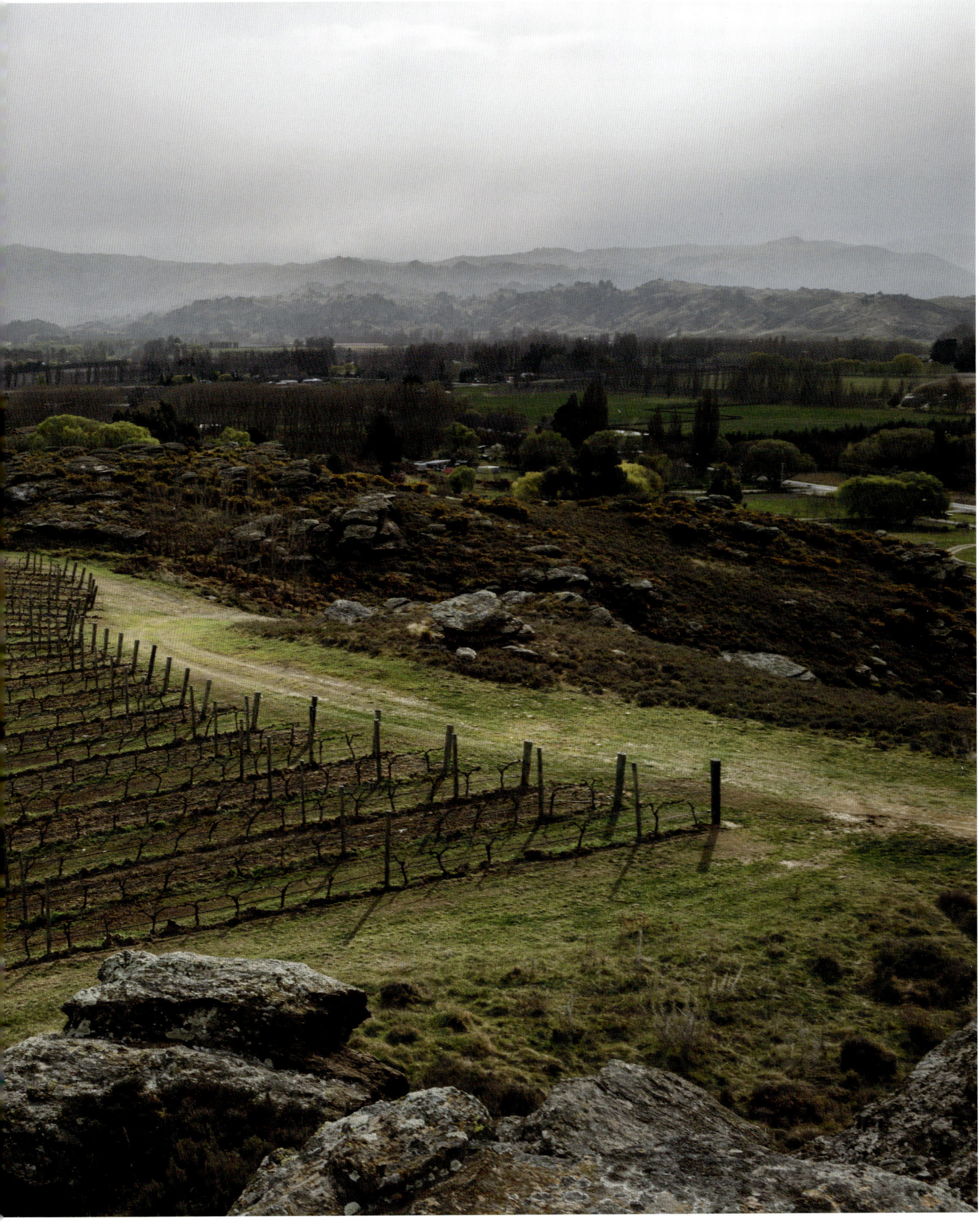

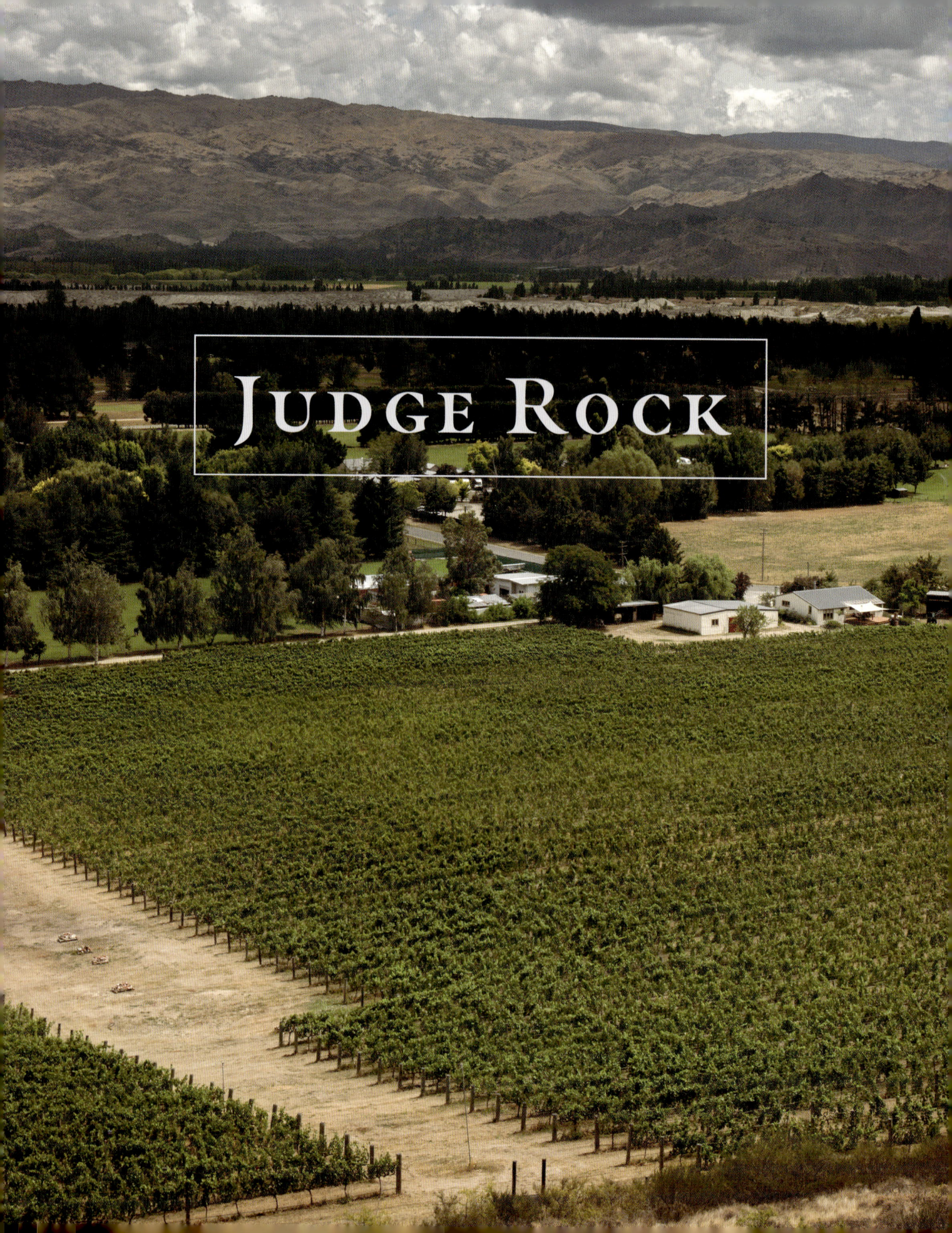

Judge Rock

'We had a bathtub full of grapes and googled "How to make a barrel of Pinot Noir".'

Run by Angela Chiaroni and her husband Paul Jacobson, Judge Rock is a family-owned boutique vineyard, close to Alexandra, with just 4 hectares in grape vines. Being super-small, though, has proved to be no barrier to making top Pinot Noir.

Originally two neglected orchards, transforming it into a vineyard entailed pulling out all the old trees, clearing the land, and repositioning all the frost-fighting irrigators to fit the grape rows. Planting of the vineyard, which is on a gently sloping alluvial fan, finally started in 1998 and took over three years. It was a family affair with the couple's three sons helping; everything was done by hand. Because of the site's northwest aspect, the vines were planted across the slope, allowing a more even spread of sunlight across the vineyard. Twenty years on, most of the work in the vineyard is still done by hand, and is still a family affair.

Chiaroni is the viticulturist and responsible for bookkeeping, marketing, dispatching, and hosting wine-tastings at the vineyard. Not to mention looking after the garden and running a B&B on the property. Jacobson, who has continued to work as a civil engineer, does the tractor work in the vineyard. Before they bought their Alexandra property, the family lived in Blenheim, where they had made fruit wine as a hobby. 'We decided to make some real wine for fun,' says Chiaroni. 'We had a bathtub full of grapes and googled "How to make a barrel of Pinot Noir".'

This early interest and enthusiasm for winemaking has translated into two decades of dedication and hard work. Deciding to commit to organics has meant even more work, with the conversion process taking three years, but Chiaroni believes being organic is better for the general health of the vineyard.

Small, even by boutique standards, Judge Rock produces about 18 tonnes of fruit in a good year. In the industry, any vineyard that produces under 240 tonnes qualifies for the Australian & New Zealand Boutique Wine Show. So it was a proud moment when, in 2016, Judge Rock Pinot Noir 2014 took out both the Best Pinot Noir and Best Red Wine trophies at the show. Not bad for a 4-hectare vineyard. At home, Judge Rock Pinot Noir 2007 and 2010 had already won Elite Gold medals at the Air New Zealand Wine Awards. But it is not just in Australasia that Judge Rock has gained recognition. In the *Decanter World Wine Awards*, which is considered the Olympics of wine competitions, they have been awarded no less than three gold medals for their 2010, 2012 and 2013 Pinot Noirs.

Alongside their Pinot Noir, Jacobson has planted a small quantity of St Laurent vines, an ancient French cool-climate grape variety, grown mostly in Austria, with one known parent being Pinot Noir. The only grower in Central Otago, they imported 180 tissue cultures in 2001 and in 2009 Judge Rock produced New Zealand's first St Laurent wine. Described as Pinot Noir on steroids, it is darker than Pinot Noir and has its own distinctive character and taste. 'If you have to be crazy to grow Pinot Noir, you have to be almost insane to grow St Laurent,' reckons Jacobson. You only get a small crop, but Judge Rock's St Laurent has proved to be an award winner both locally and internationally; the 2011 vintage took silver at both the Air New Zealand Wine Awards and the International Wine & Spirit Competition.

Peter Bartle from the VinPro contract winemaking facility is

Paul Jacobson and Angela Chiaroni.

responsible for making Judge Rock's wines. He visits the vineyard throughout the season and makes two crucial decisions: when to pick the fruit and when to separate the wine from the skins. Because Pinot is more fickle, more delicate, it cannot be overworked. As a hands-off winemaker, Bartle knows this well. Coming from the Alexandra sub-region, Judge Rock Pinot Noir is often lighter in colour than other Central Otago Pinots, with earthy, forest-floor aromas, silky tannins and fresh acidity giving it a long, persistent finish. Bartle also makes Judge Rock's perfumed, dry-style Rosé, which in 2017 featured in the top 20 in *Cuisine* magazine's annual Rosé tasting, and he also makes an off-dry Riesling for them, using grapes bought from the Lowburn–Pisa sub-region.

When it comes to selling their wine, Chiaroni is enthusiastic about the fantastic things wine tourism has done for Central Otago. In recent years, up to 25 per cent of Judge Rock sales have been through the vineyard cellar door, which is open seven days a week. People love the personal experience of kicking back in the cottage garden and tasting the wines, while Chiaroni herself explains their history and shares her knowledge of the different vintages. At weekends, Jacobson helps sell their wine too. 'We are so small, we are almost invisible,' he says. 'The only place we are visible is once a week at the Otago Farmers Market in Dunedin, on a Saturday morning, at the beautiful, historic railway station. This has become our cellar door to the world.'

Judge Rock wines are also exported to Australia, the UK, and more recently to China. Which all goes to show just where a bathtub full of grapes can lead.

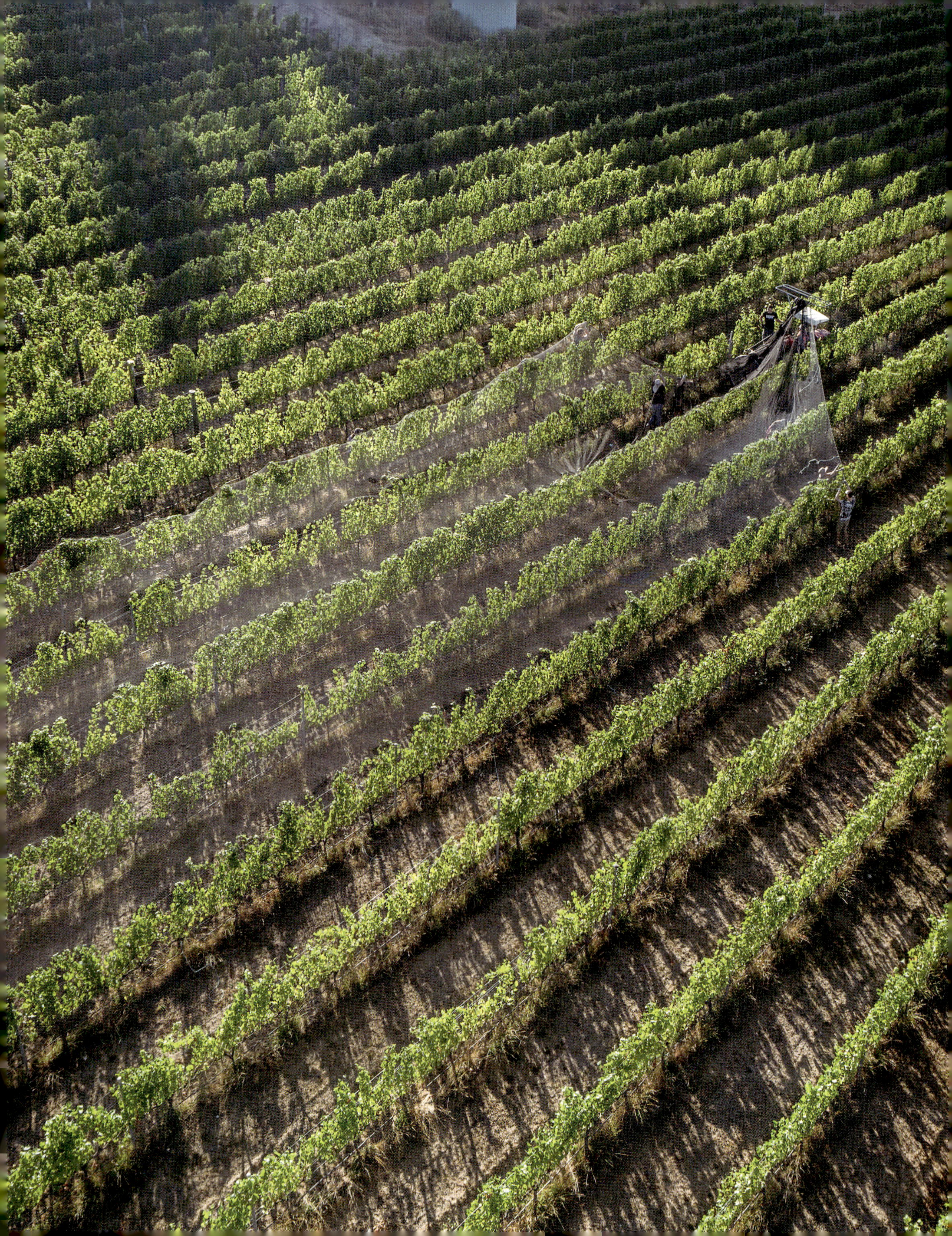

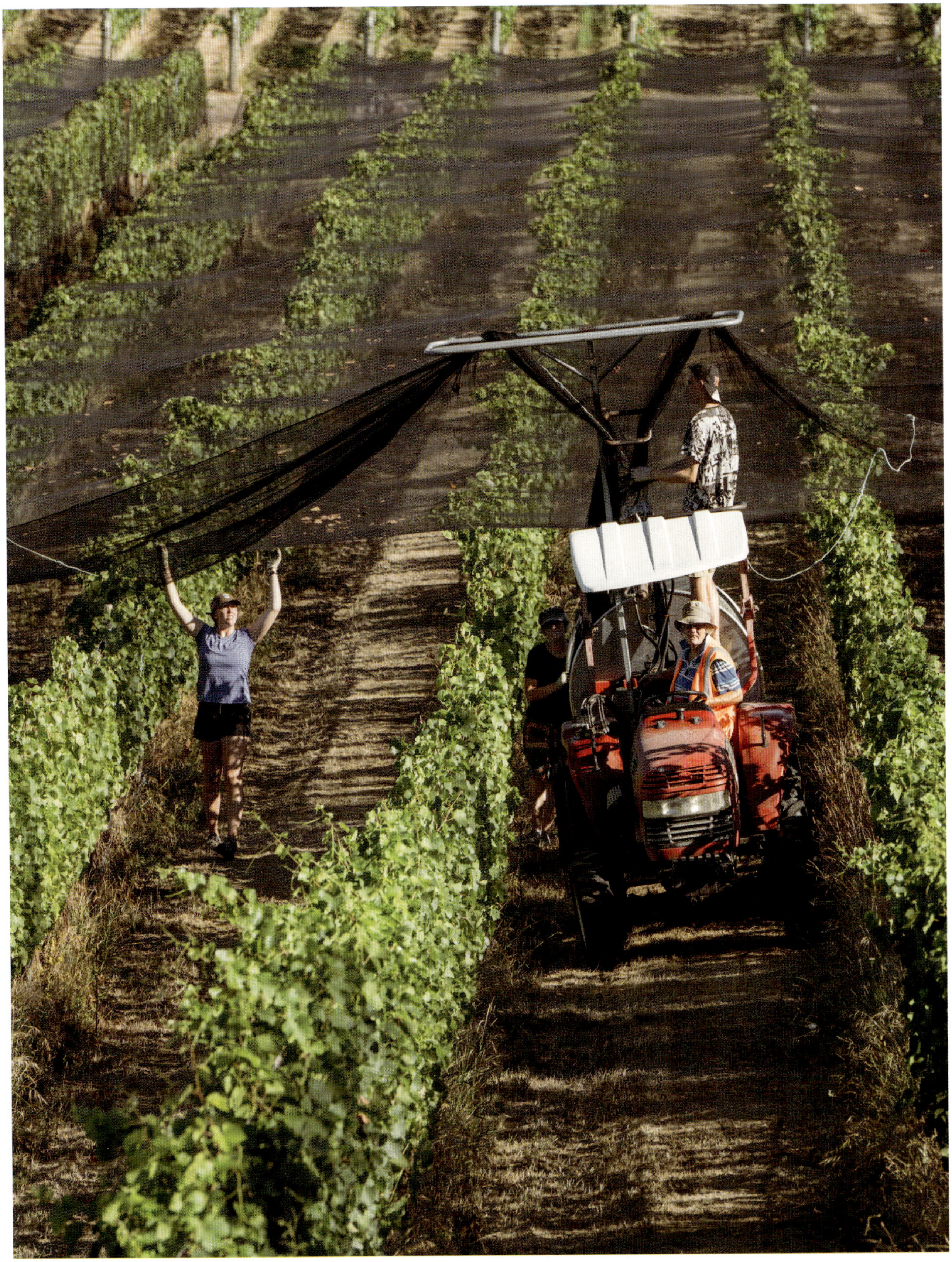

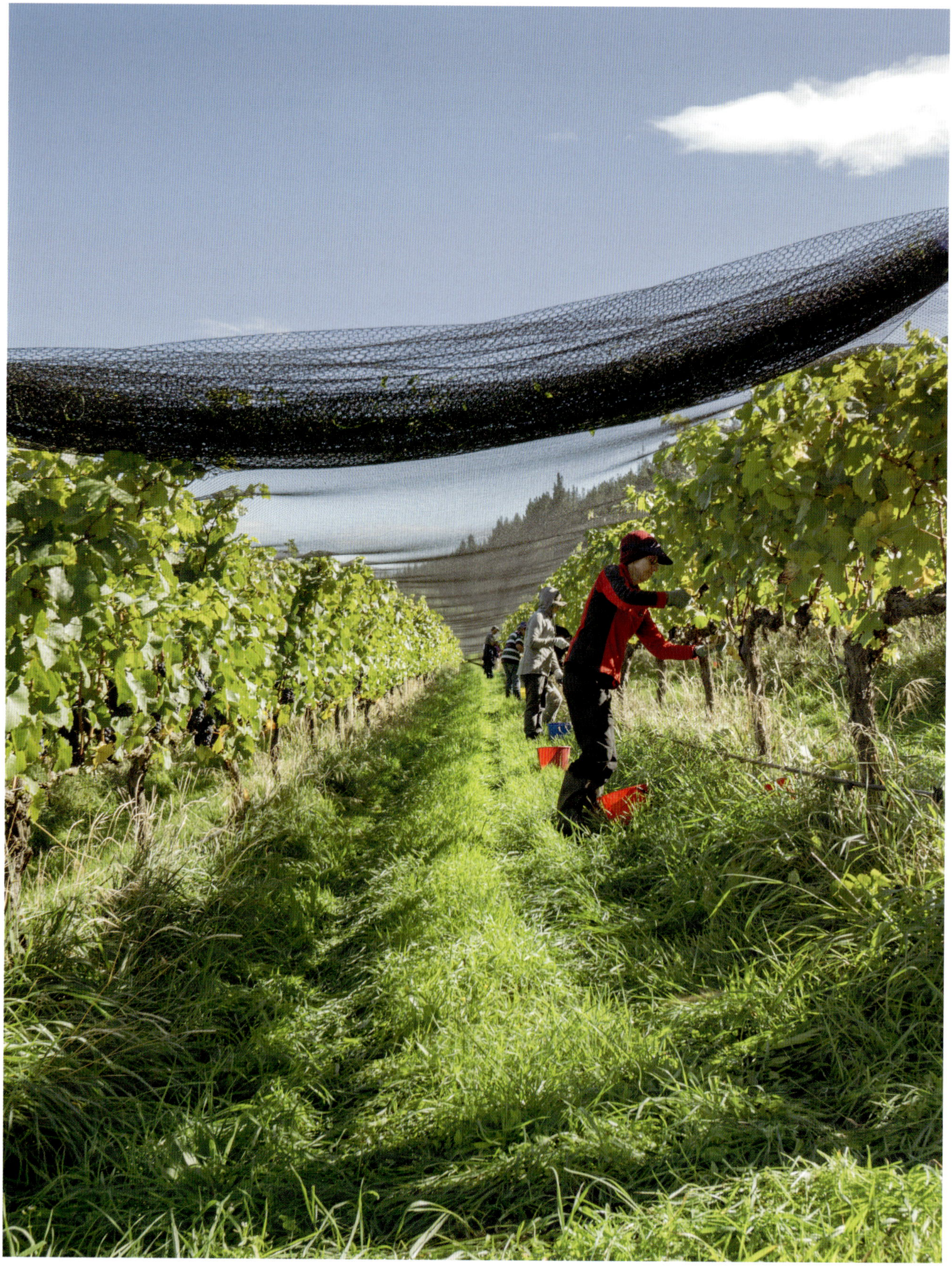

LEFT AND TOP Pinot harvest. ABOVE Clyde Wine and Food Festival.

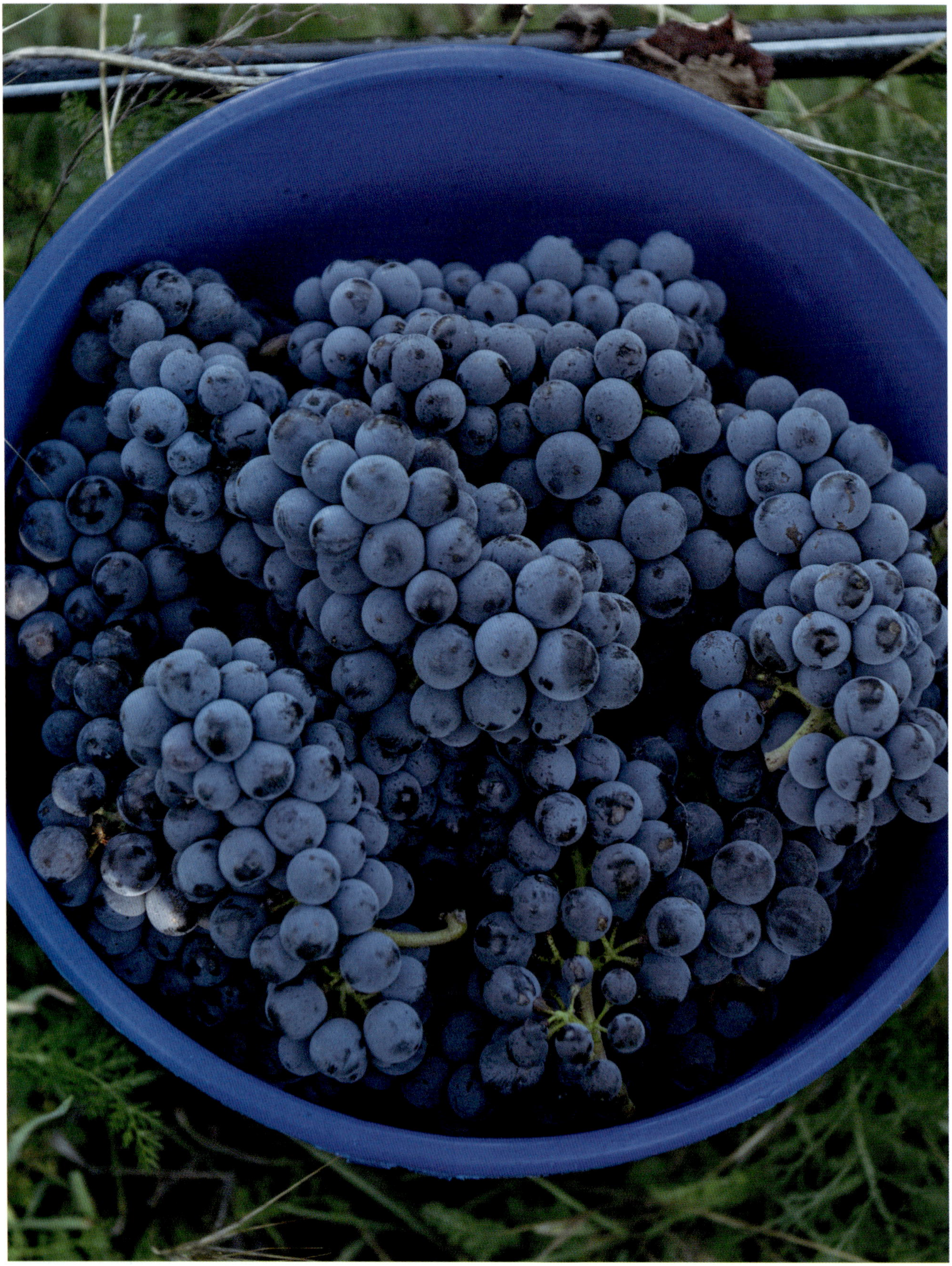

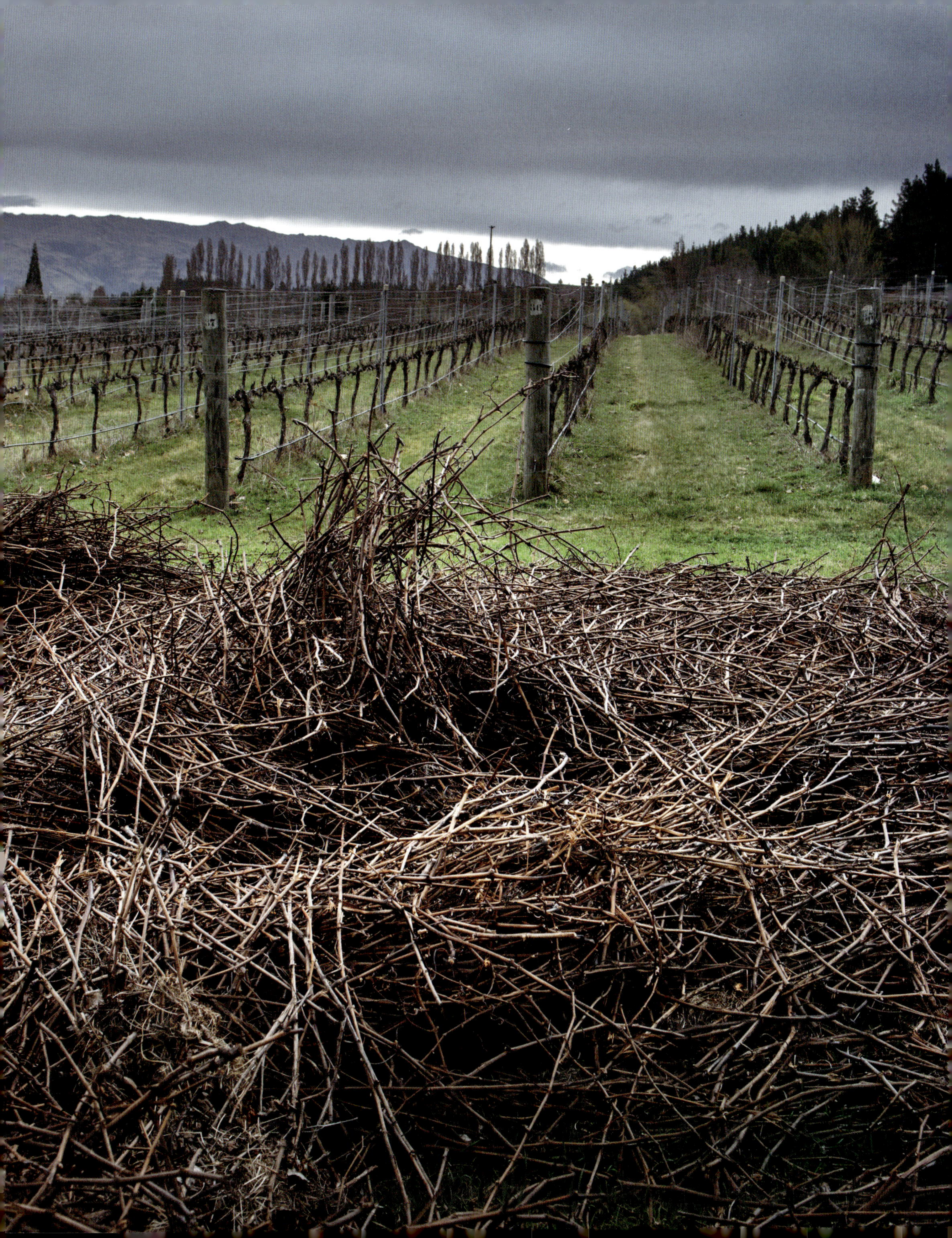

Grasshopper Rock

'We wanted to do something really, really well — produce something world class off the land.'

Owned by a group of five Kiwi families, with backgrounds in rural banking and agriculture, Grasshopper Rock is named after the endangered native grasshopper, *Sigaus childi,* found in the rocky gold-mining tailings near the vineyard. Lying to the southeast of Alexandra, on Earnscleugh Road, the north-facing site, which had previously been an orchard, is gently sloping with free-draining soils and has a reliable water source, thanks to the old gold-mining Last Chance water race. In short, it is a really good site for growing world-class Pinot Noir grapes.

The 7.8-hectare vineyard was planted in 2003 and is totally dedicated to producing Pinot Noir, and from the get-go has been all about having a single focus on producing one outstanding Central Otago wine. 'We wanted to do something really, really well — produce something world class off the land,' says co-owner and managing director Phil Handford.

Mike Moffitt is the vineyard manager for Grasshopper Rock and lives close by. 'It's a good way to live your life,' he says. But making world-class Pinot Noir is not for the faint-hearted. It is risky and hard

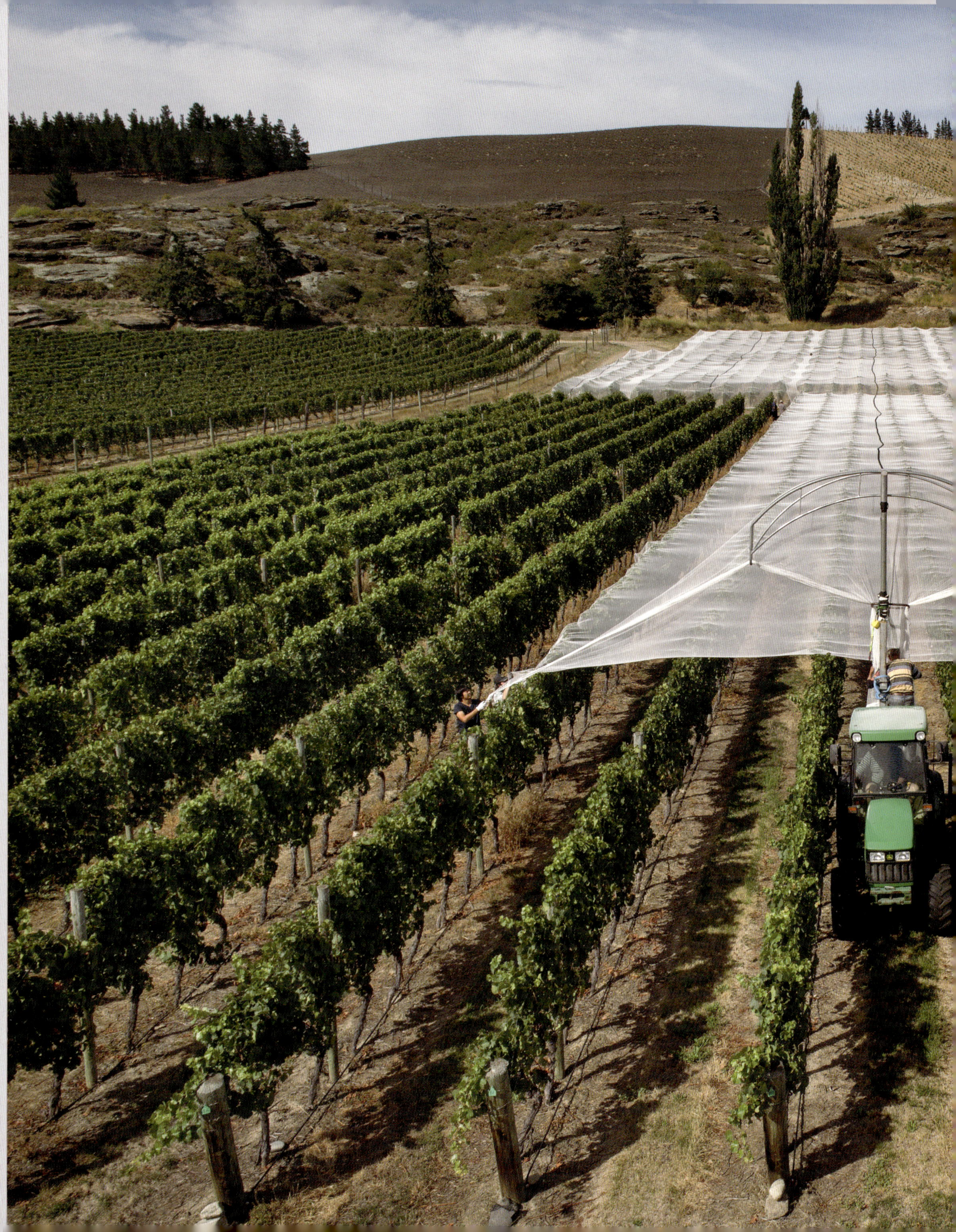

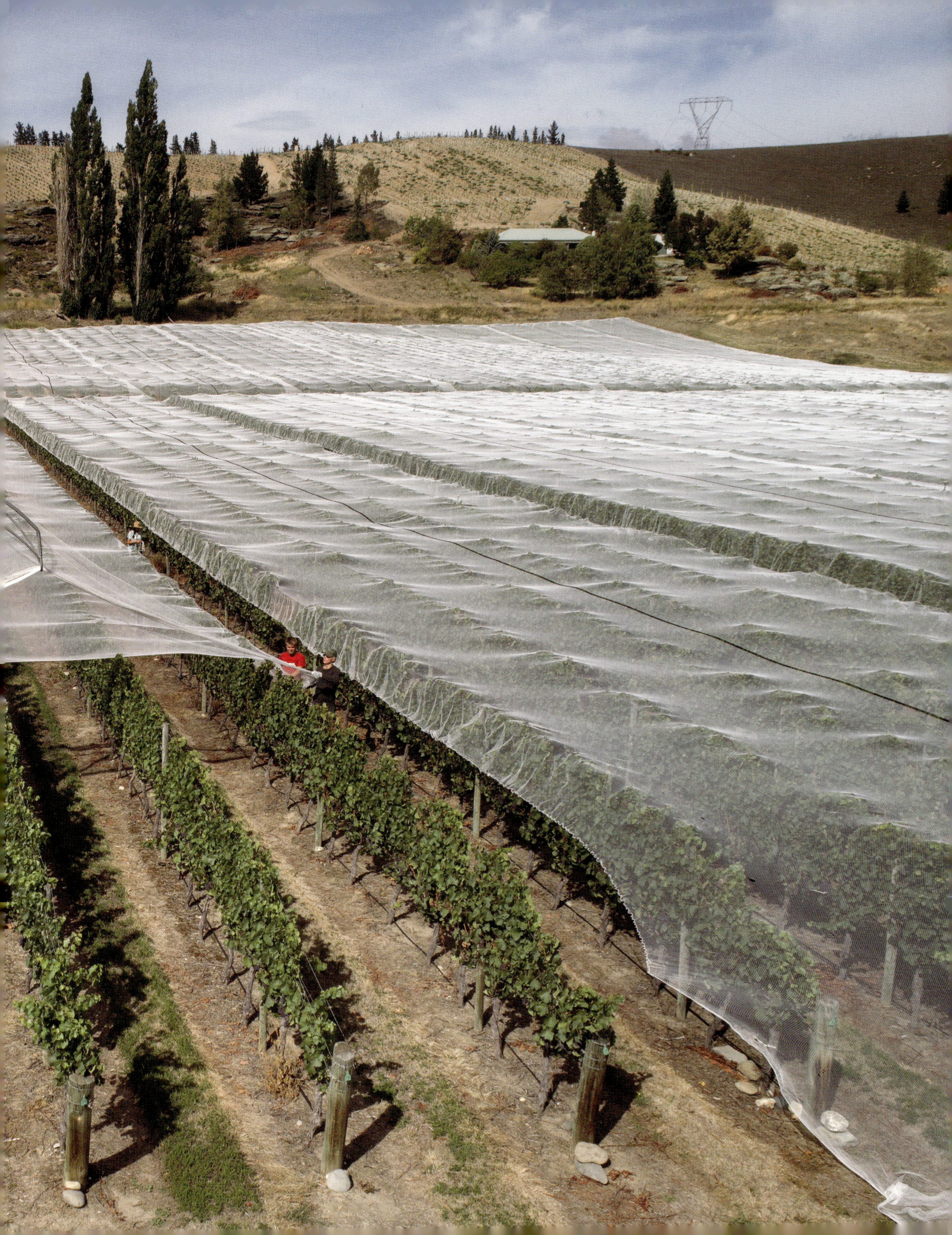

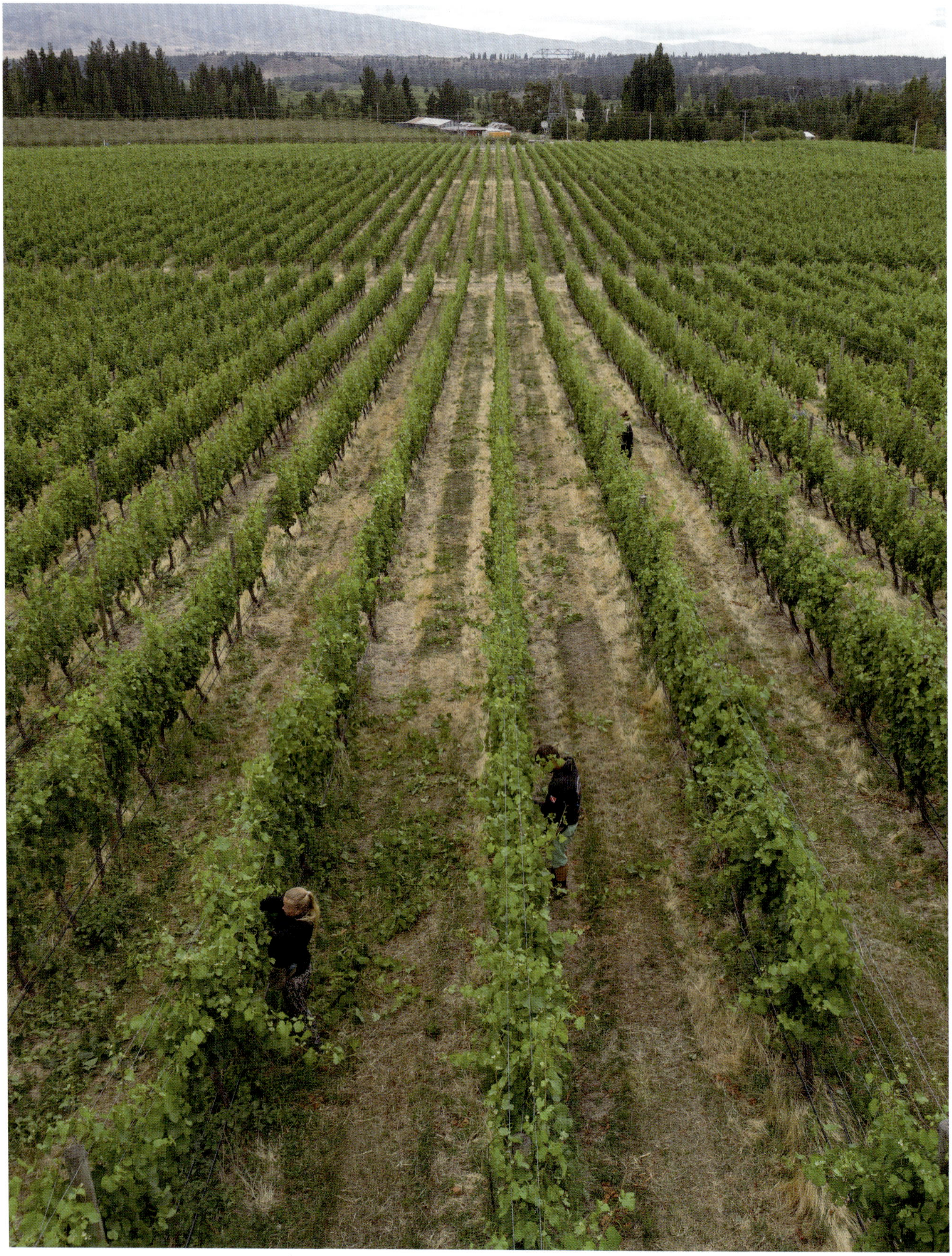

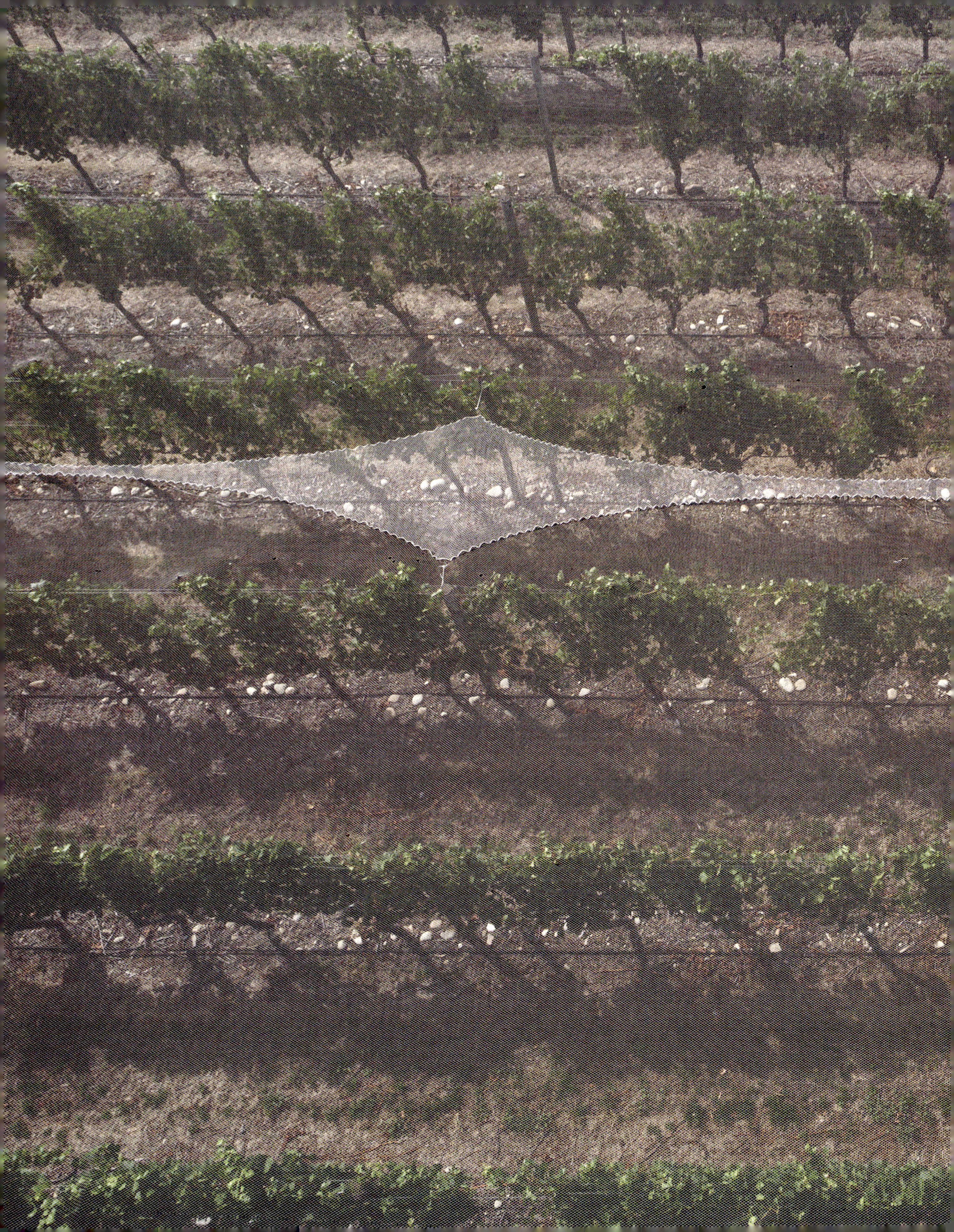

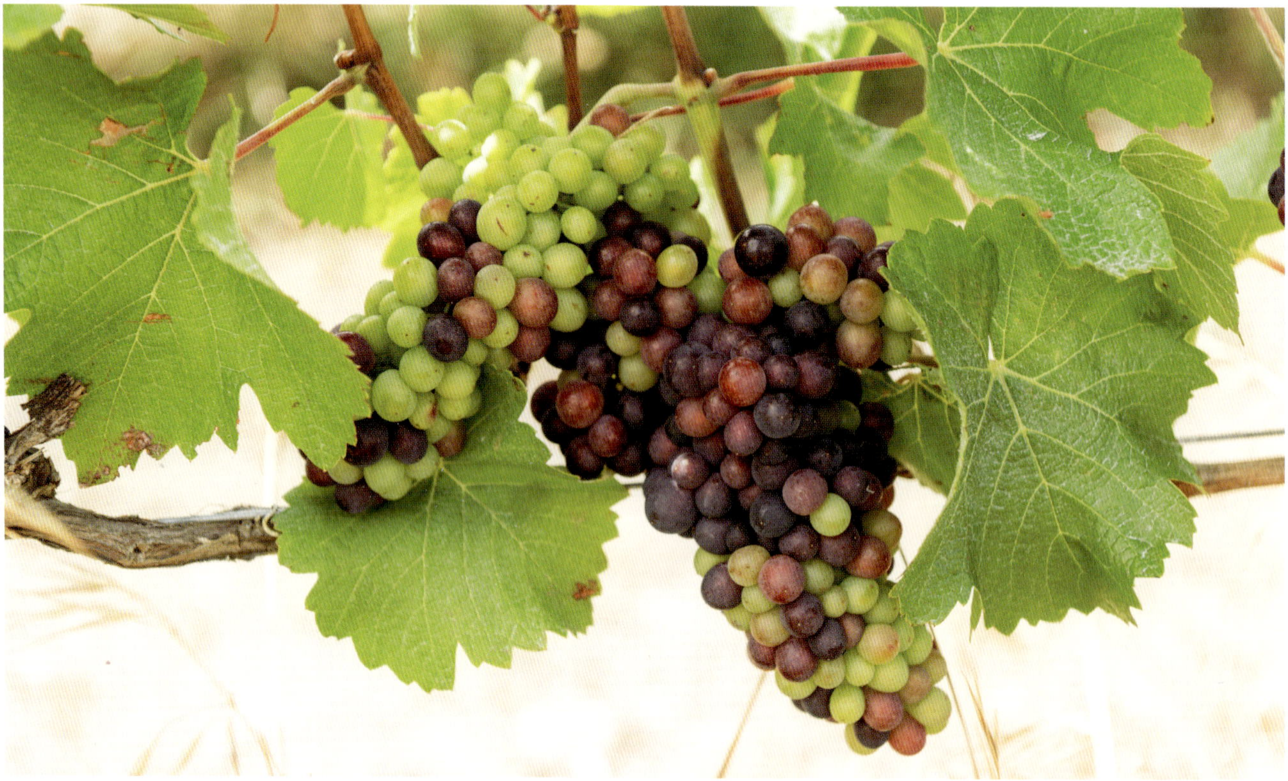
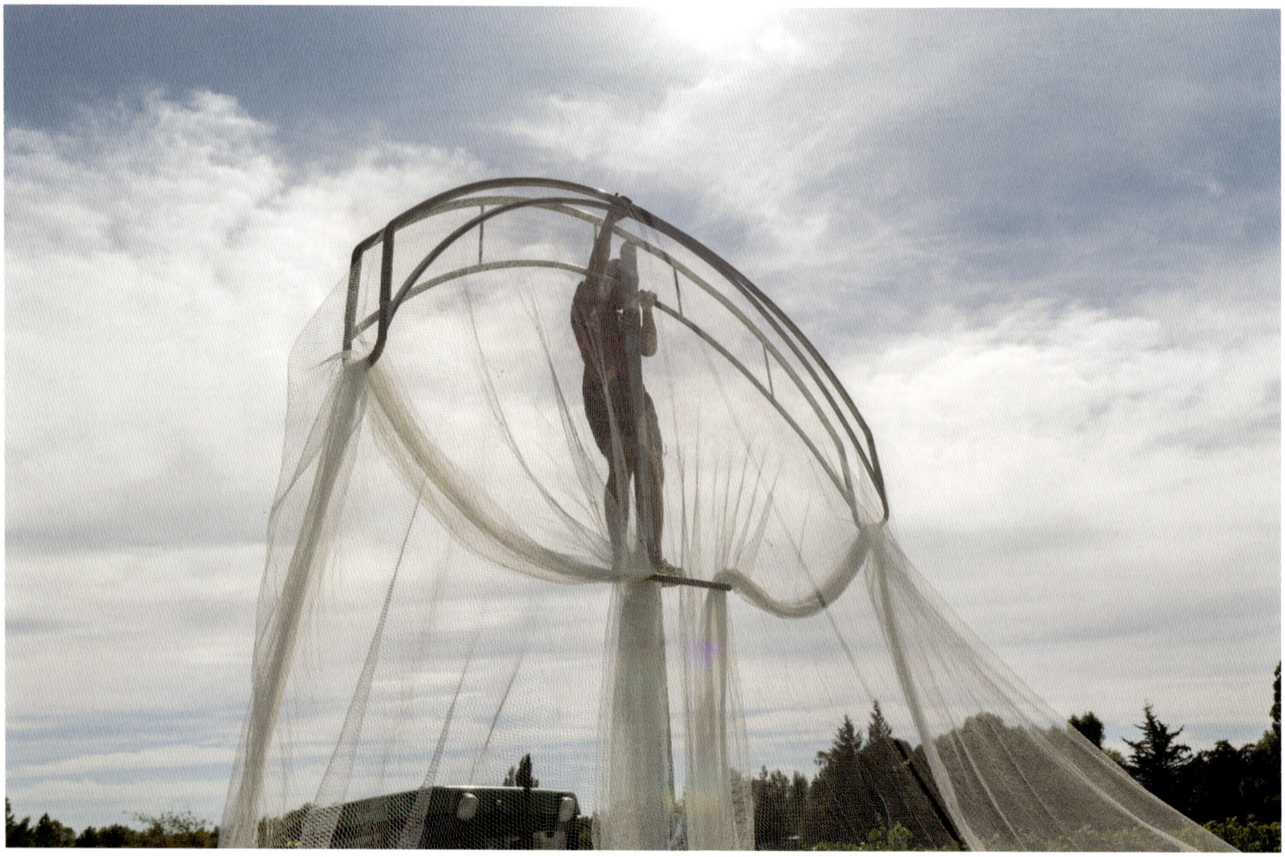

Above left Veraison. **Left** Rigging the tractor with bird netting. **Top** Tour of wine writers. **Above** Jane Skilton and Elaine Chukan Brown.

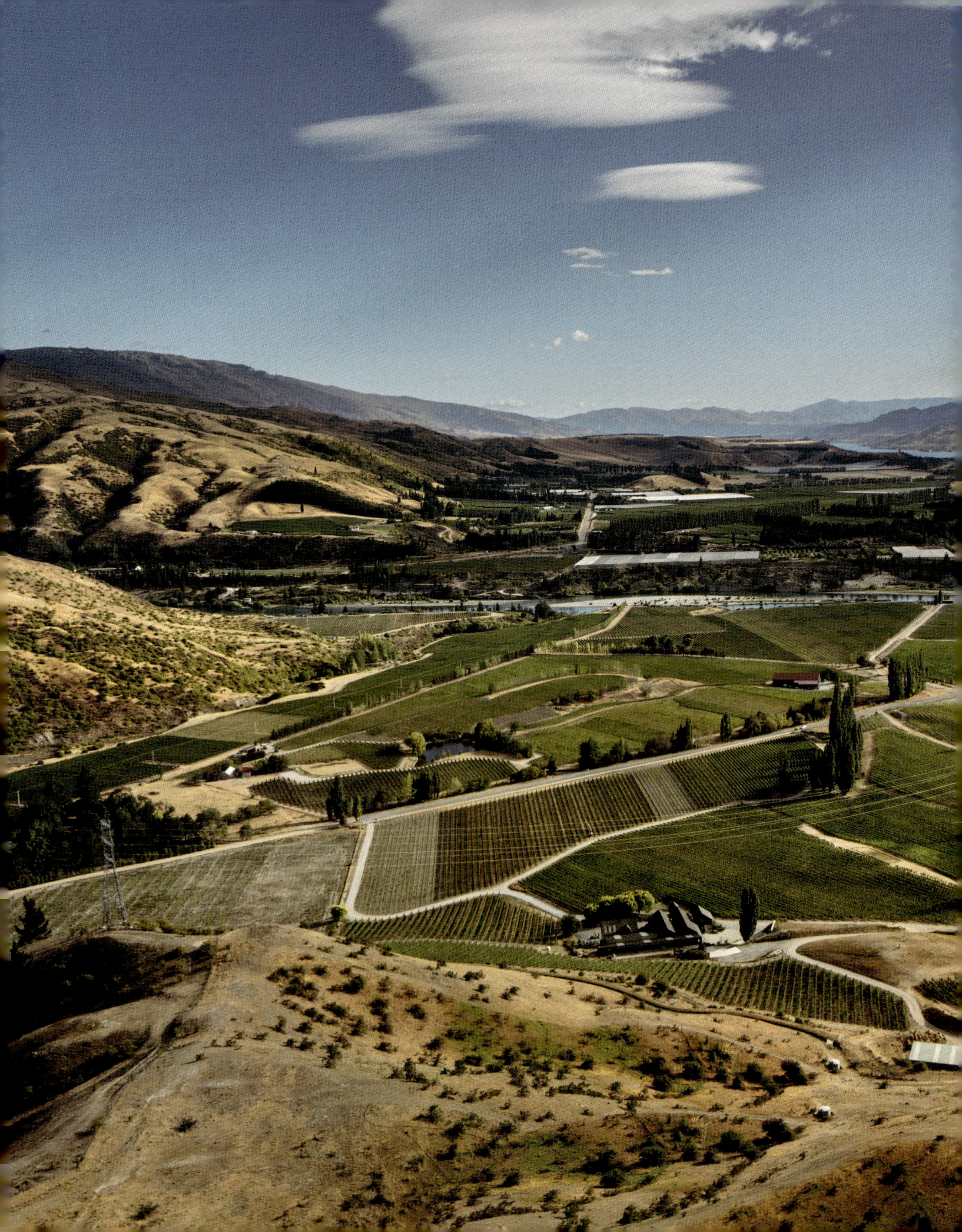

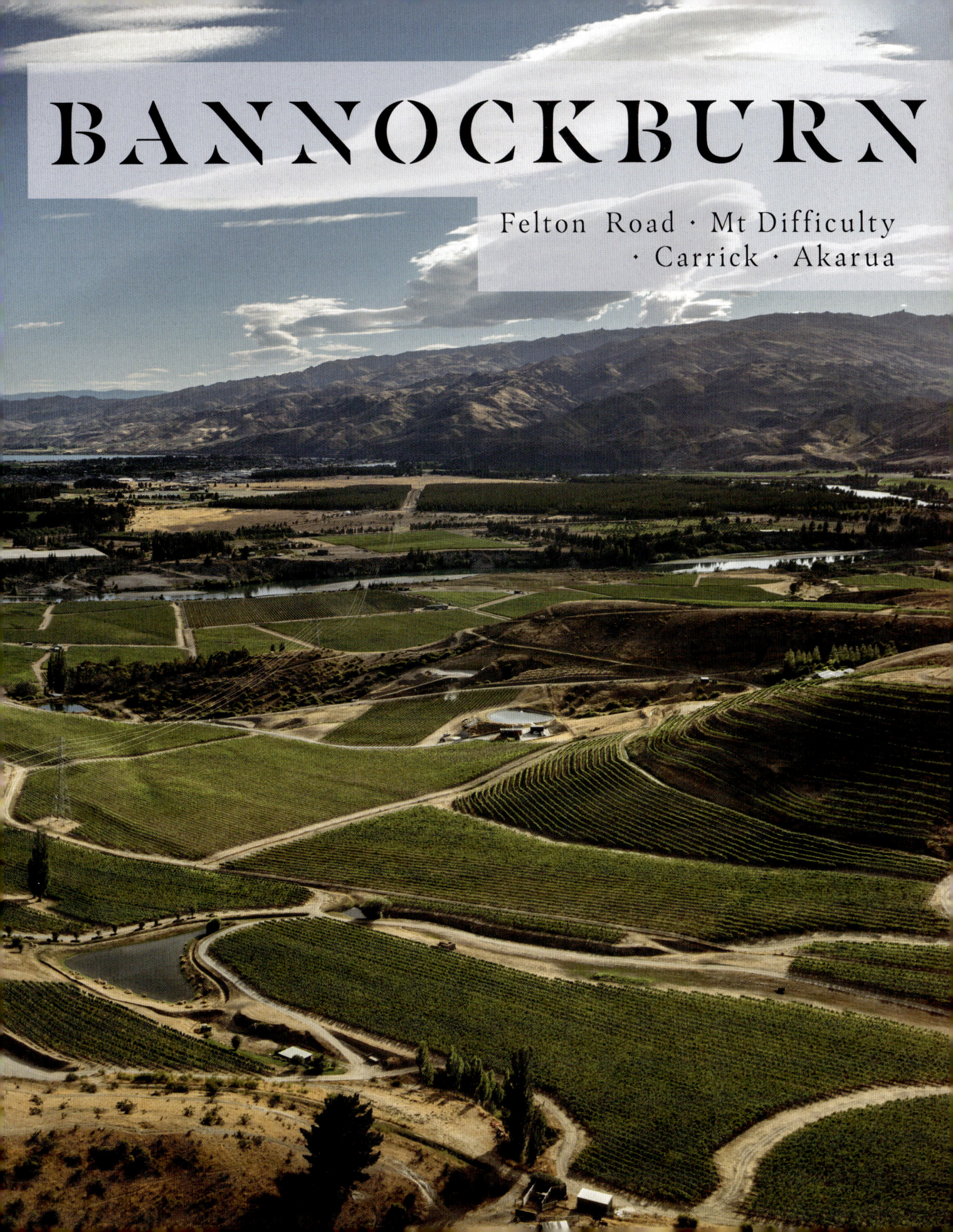

BANNOCKBURN

Felton Road · Mt Difficulty
· Carrick · Akarua

BANNOCKBURN, with its north-facing slopes rising from 220 to 370 metres above sea level, has some of the warmest sites in Central Otago and a lower risk of frost than other sub-regions. Temperatures in February and March are often over 30 degrees Celsius and harvest is usually a month earlier than at Gibbston.

With the planting of Olssen's vineyard in 1991, closely followed by Felton Road and Robin Dicey's Full Circle vineyard in 1992, Bannockburn's vineyards were the first to be developed in the Cromwell Basin.

The soils in Bannockburn, as in the other sub-regions, vary considerably. They include lighter, stonier, schist-based soils that are well suited to growing Chardonnay and Riesling, and heavier, more clay-based soils, where Pinot Noir does well.

Seen as the jewel in the crown of Central Otago, Bannockburn is the most densely planted sub-region with around 325 hectares of vines.

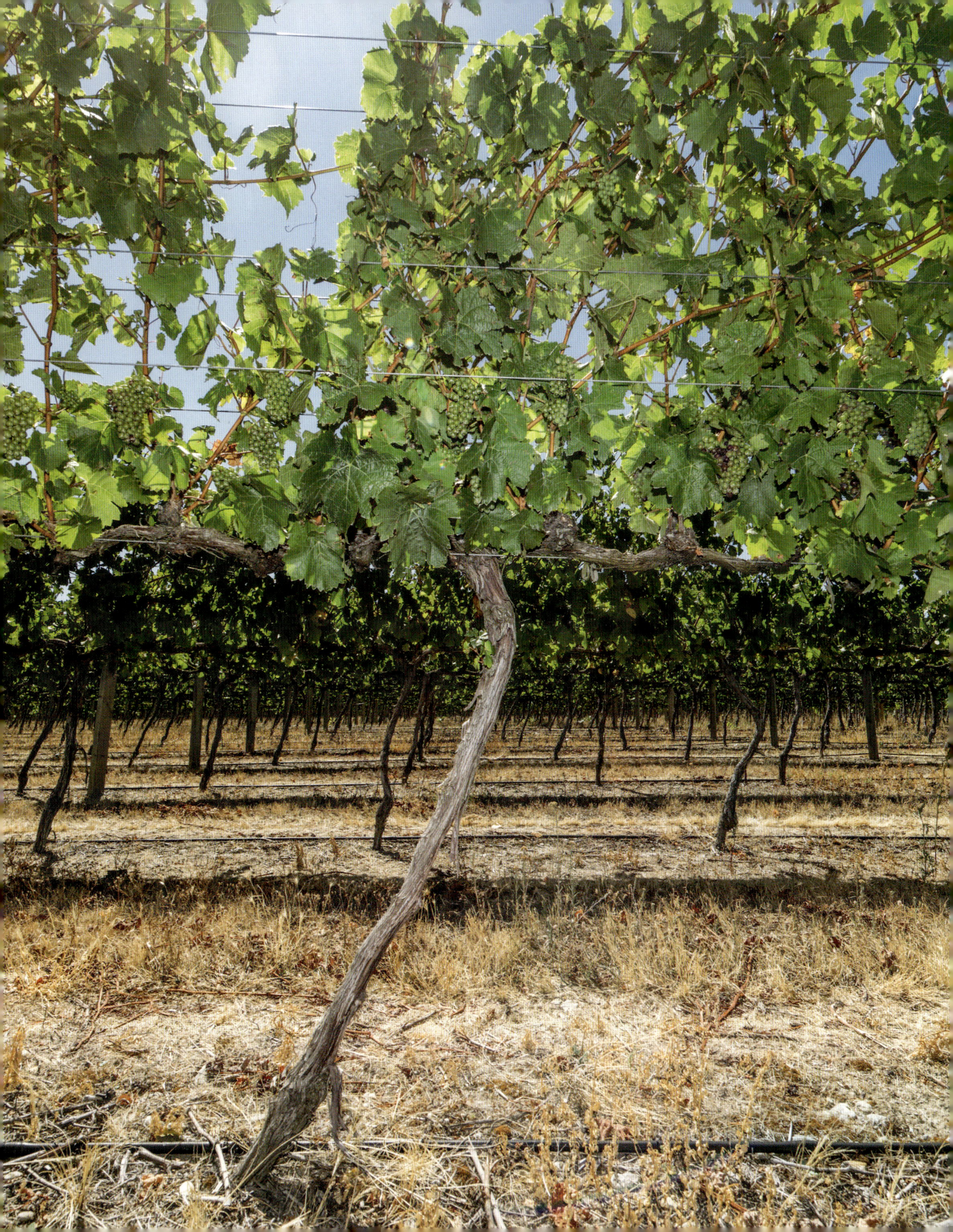

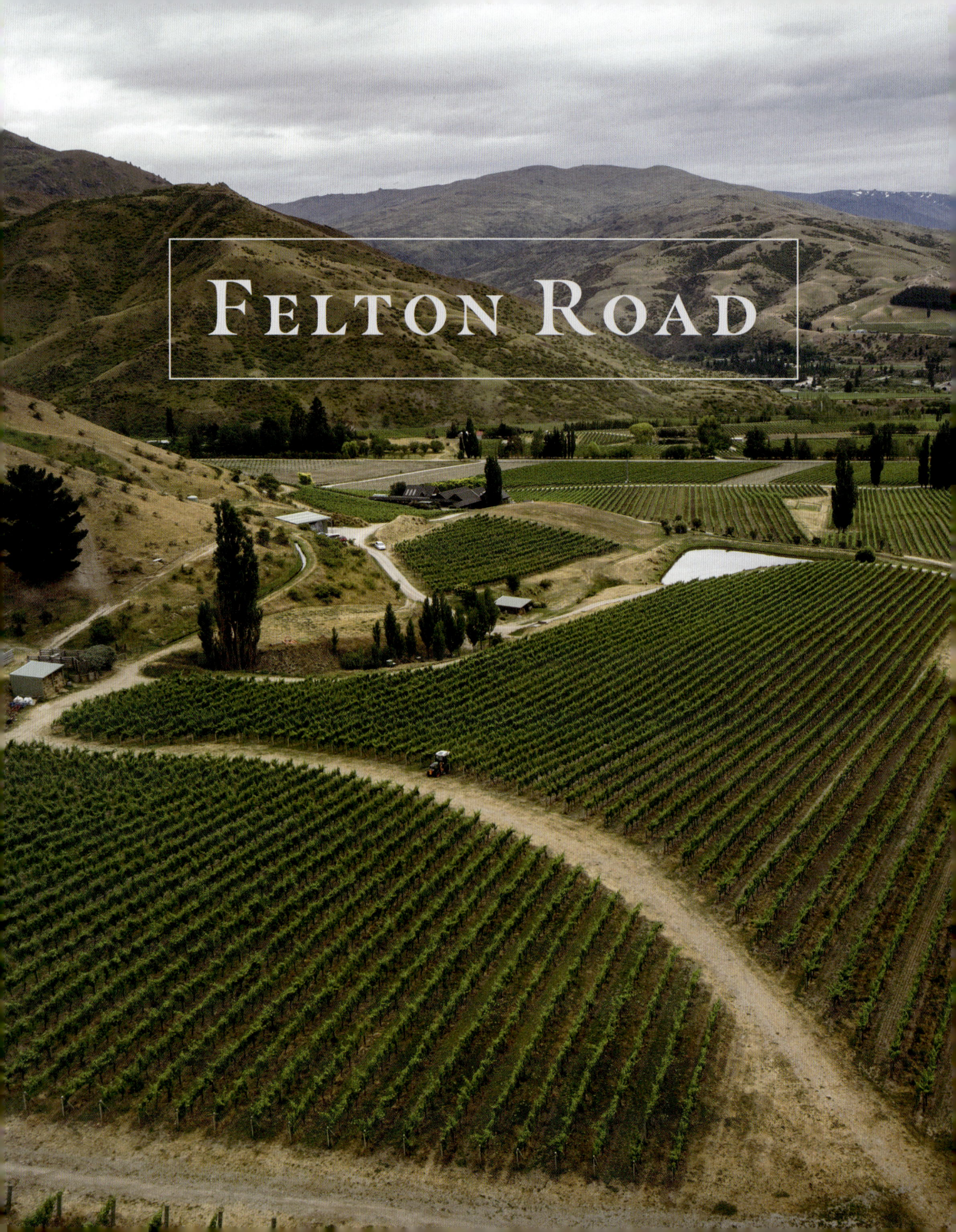

Felton Road

'If a thing's worth doing, it's worth doing fanatically.'

One of Bannockburn's original vineyards, Felton Road today has 32 hectares of vines planted across four properties: The Elms, Cornish Point, Calvert and MacMuir. Growing 70 per cent Pinot Noir, 20 per cent Chardonnay and 10 per cent Riesling, it is one of only a few vineyards in Central Otago where all the grapes are estate grown and all the wines are made and bottled on site.

The man who developed Felton Road, Stewart Elms, had been a hotel owner and farmer when he bought land at the end of Felton Road in Bannockburn in 1991. Having 'drunk it and sold it', he now wanted to grow grapes and make wine too — one of the first to do so in Bannockburn. He began planting part of his 44-hectare site in 1992, mostly in Pinot Noir, but also in Chardonnay and some Riesling. 'The land was covered in tussocks, rabbits and briar. We kept pretty quiet about it, in case people thought we were nuts.'

Elms knew what he was looking for, though, and had chosen the Felton Road site with great care: 'Site selection is everything.' In Central Otago, frost is a major downside, but sloping land allows more air movement and minimises the frost problem. Elms also knew that the soils, while different from Burgundy, had similar characteristics, and he had secured water rights, essential for establishing grape vines. He was aware, too, of the need for so many growing degree days, or GDD, to ripen the grapes. Temperatures vary across Central

makes three different Rieslings. One that is picked earlier is a slightly sweet Riesling with a vibrant fruit flavour and dry finish. The others are an off-dry and dry style.

Felton Road produces between 10,000 and 12,000 cases of highly sought-after wine. Around 75 per cent of production is exported — mainly to Australia and the UK, but to over 35 different countries in all. The remaining 25 per cent is sold within New Zealand to fine wine retailers, restaurants, lodges and private customers. Despite a waiting list for some of their wines, Walter says there are no plans to grow the business. 'We want to focus our energy on quality, rather than increasing production.'

In 2005, Felton Road joined New Zealand's 'Family of Twelve', a group of the most prestigious family-owned wine producers from across the country. Family of Twelve works together to share information and best practice at home and to promote what they consider to be the best New Zealand wines around the world. To join you have to be family-owned, making great wine, 'be a good bugger', and be able to make decisions within 24 hours. Given that Nigel Greening bought Felton Road in about 24 hours, his team makes great wine, and although he's a somewhat fanatical Englishman, he still probably rates as 'a good bugger', it is easy to see how Felton Road got to be a member.

To celebrate its twentieth vintage in 2017, a newly renovated tasting room and cellar door and extra barrel cellar were officially opened, and Walter offered invited guests a vertical wine-tasting of some of Felton Road's best vintages. One of the most respected vineyards in Central Otago, Felton Road has helped set the standard for the region's Pinot Noir, Chardonnay and Riesling wines and continues to lead the country with its best vintages.

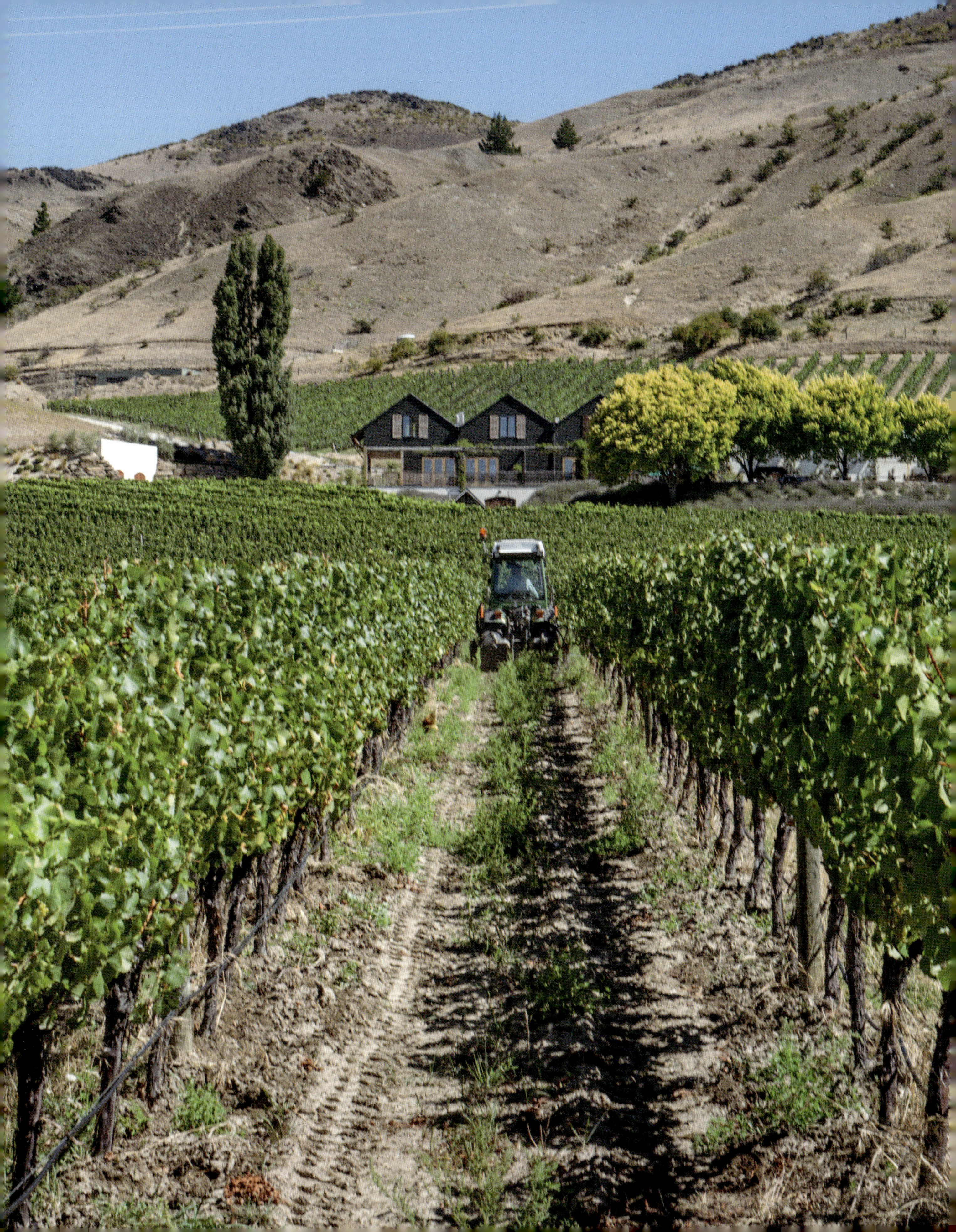

TOP Opening of cellar-door renovations and new barrel cellar. ABOVE Blair Walter hosts vertical wine tasting.
RIGHT Nigel Greening and Blair Walter.

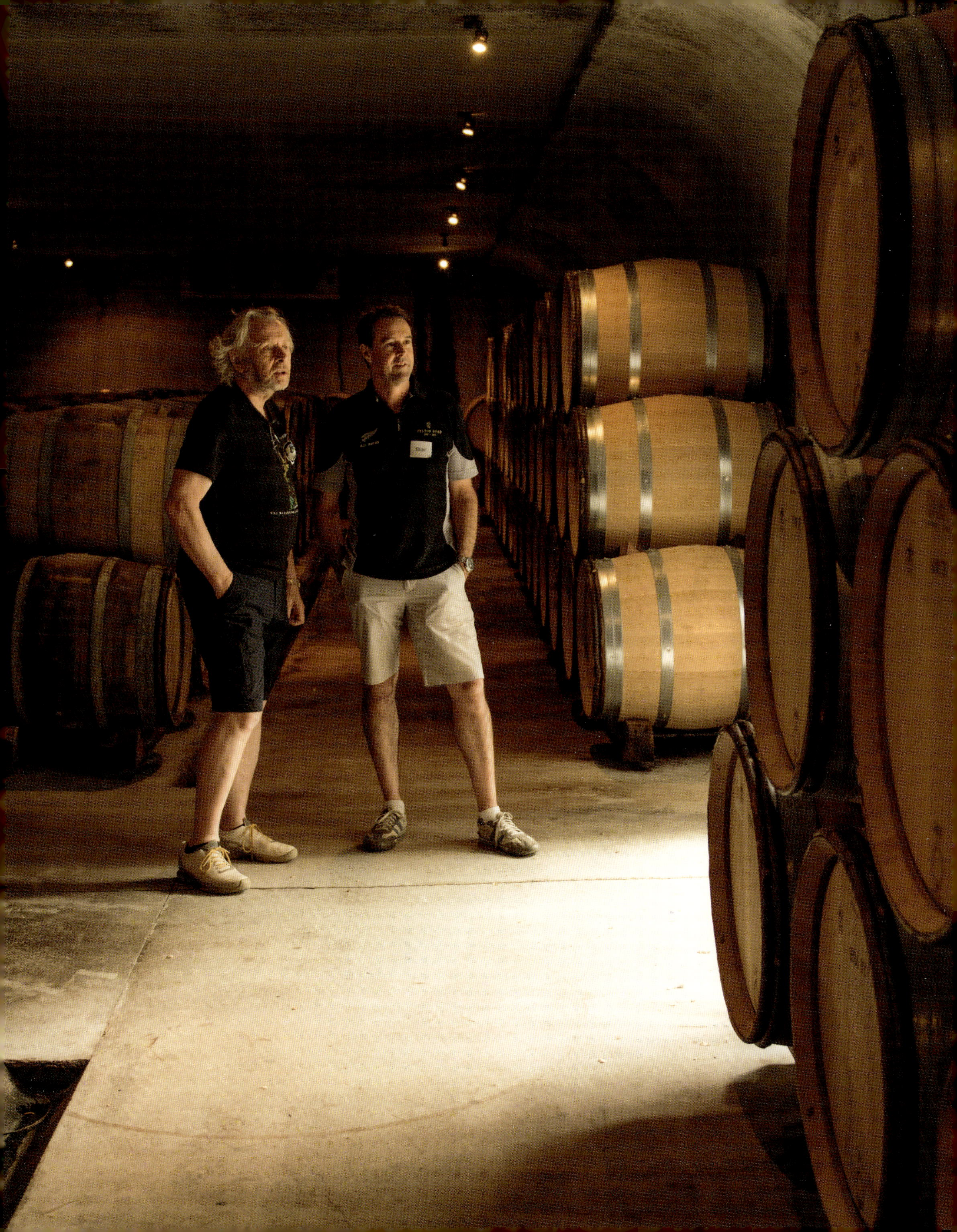

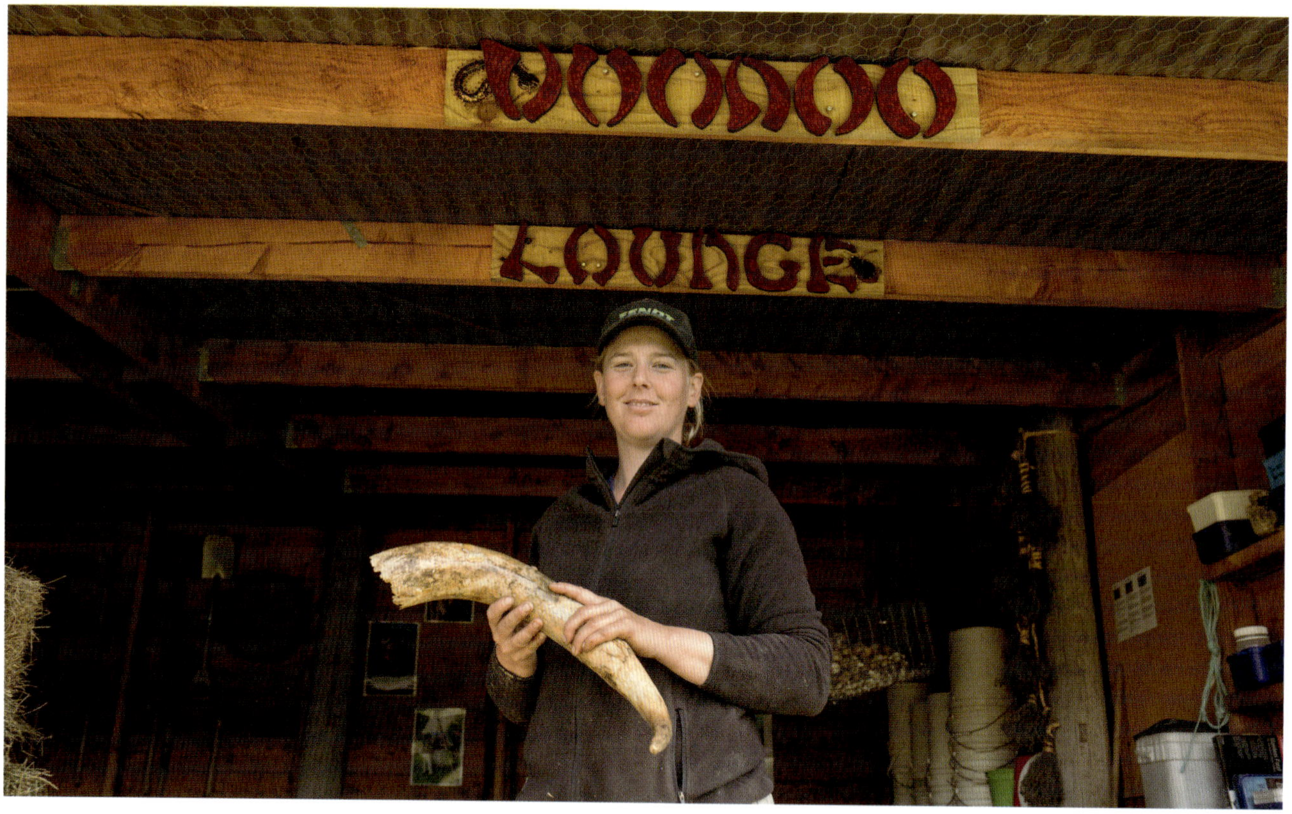
LOUNGE

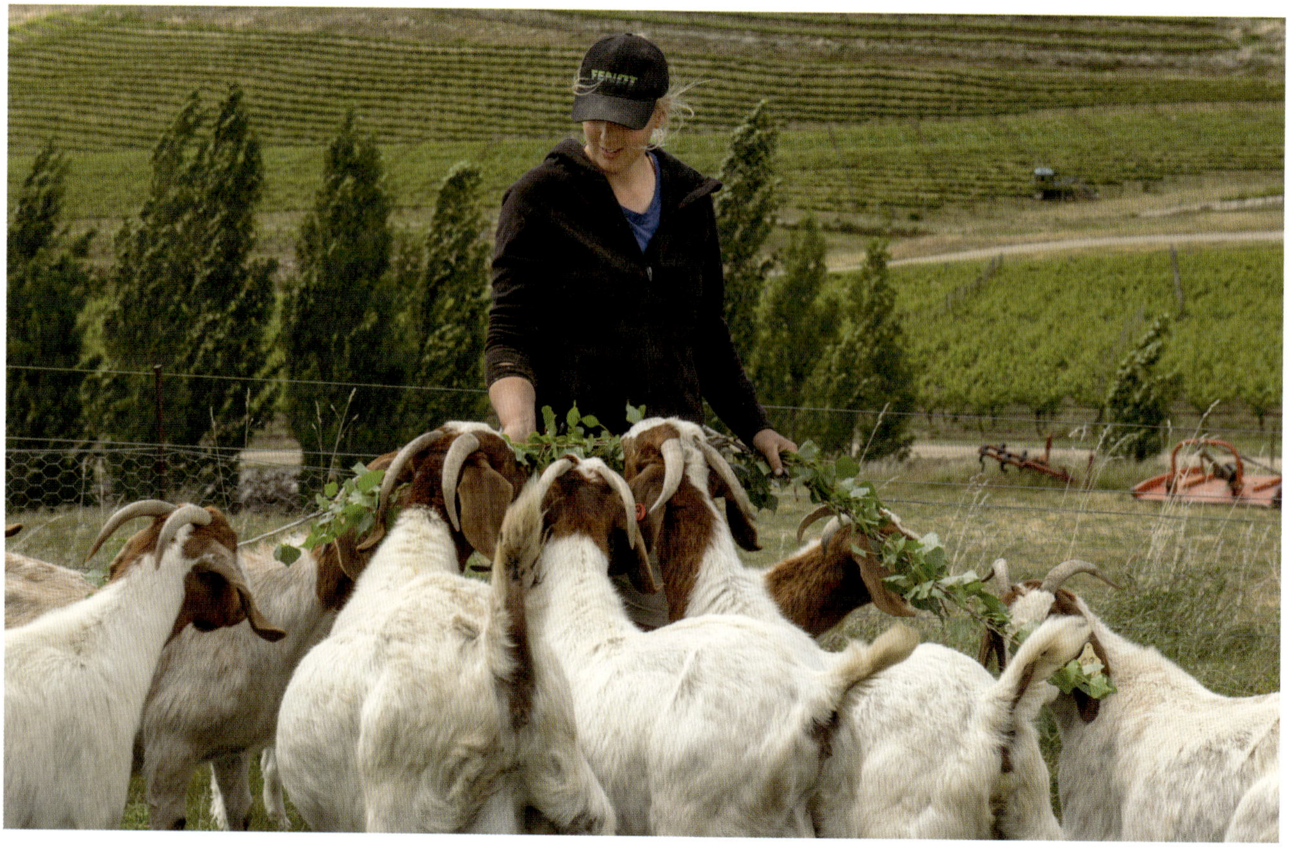

ABOVE LEFT Annabel Bulk in the Voodoo Lounge. LEFT Annabel with the Boer goats. ABOVE Leaf thinning.

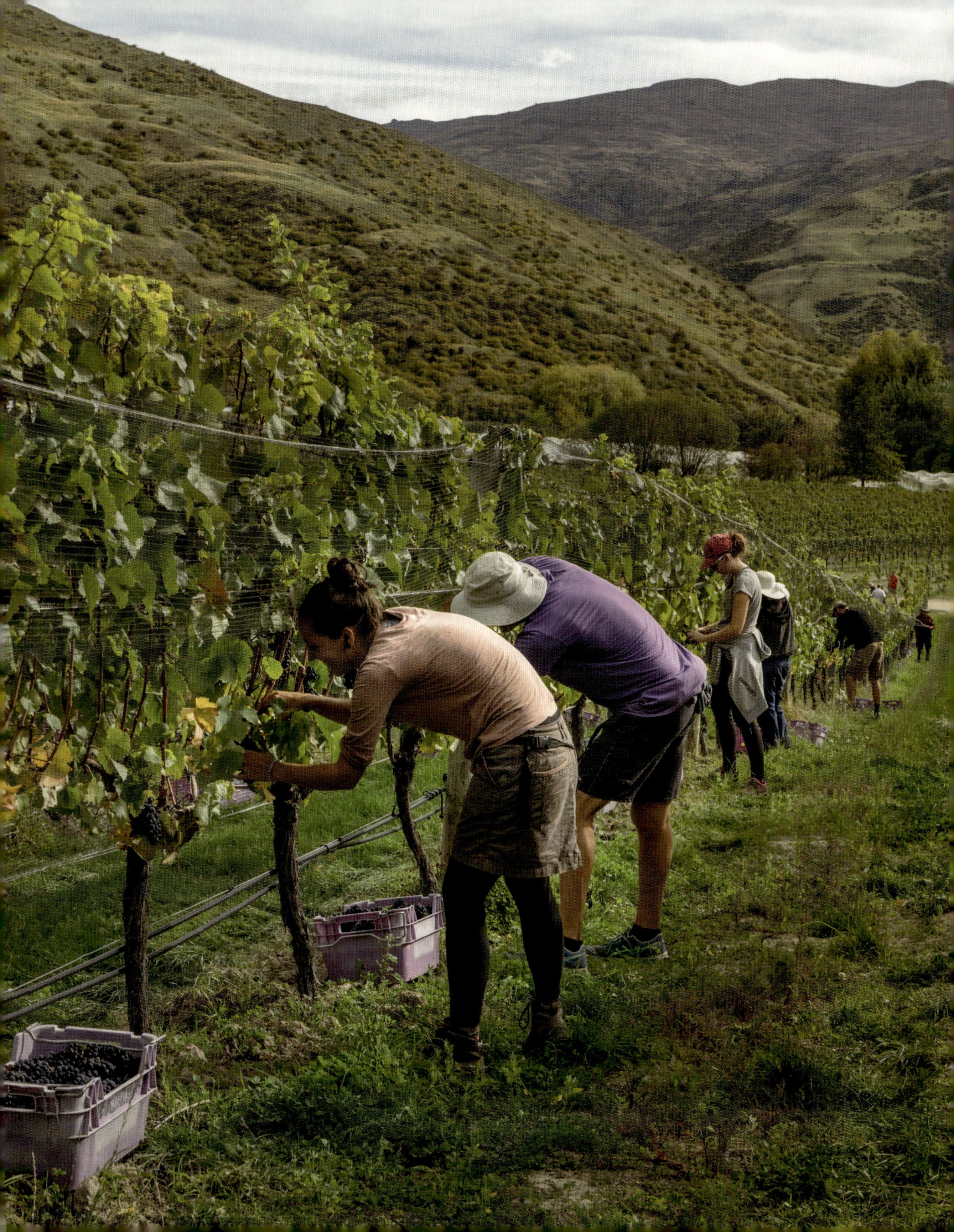

Left Pinot Noir harvest. Top right Sorting Pinot grapes. Middle right Blair Walter processing Pinot. Bottom right Pinot in fermentation vats.

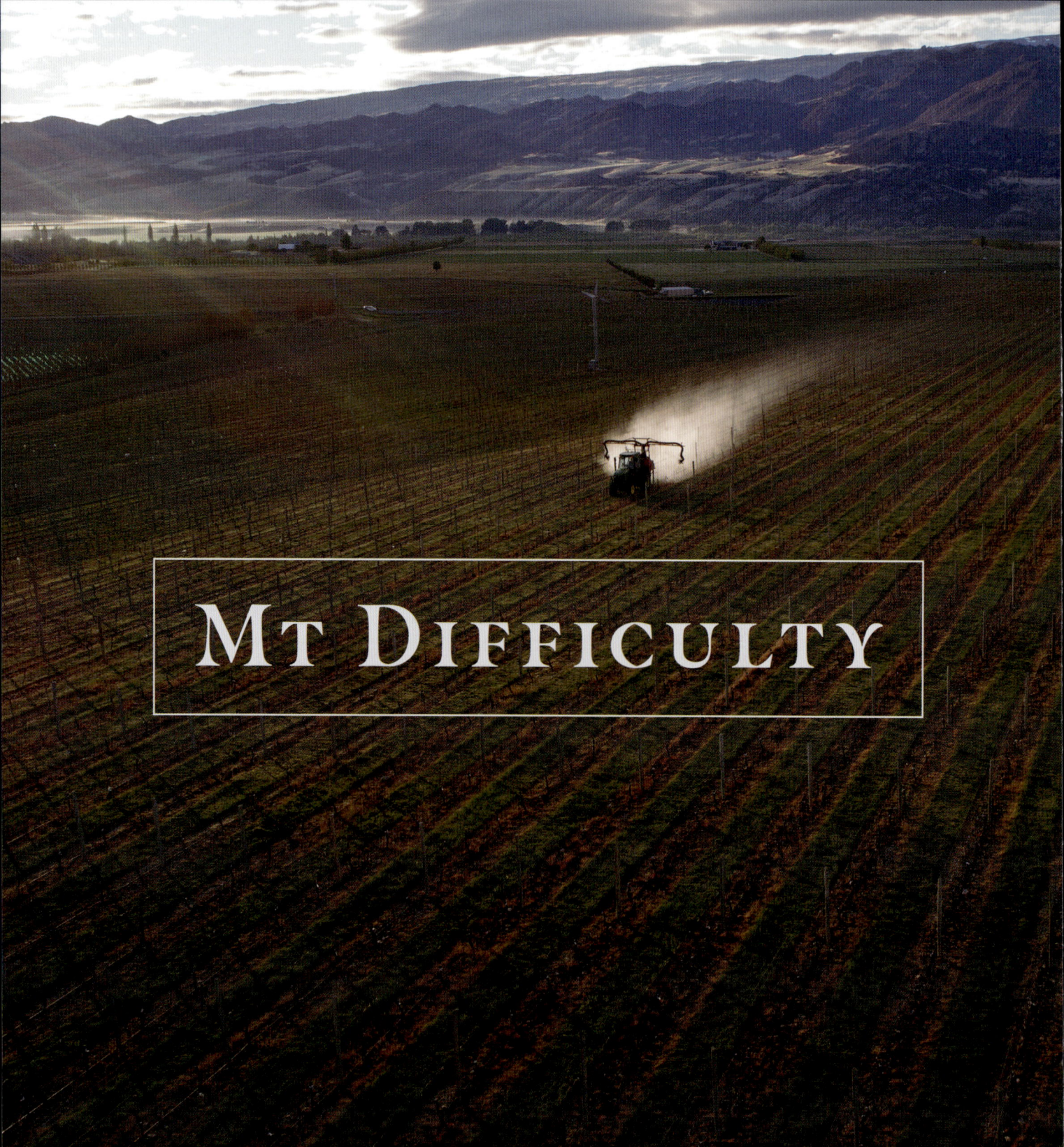

Mt Difficulty

'I've been involved in horticulture and grapes my whole life.'

Mt Difficulty has been one of the stand-out success stories in the Central Otago winegrowing industry. At the time of printing, it had been sold for $55 million, but was awaiting approval of the sale from the Overseas Investment Office (OIO). Mt Difficulty has also been one of the biggest players, with 150 hectares of vineyards either owned, leased or under management, and a winery processing up to 1200 tonnes of grapes. Based in Bannockburn, the company takes its name from the nearby 1285-metre Mt Difficulty, which rises steeply above Bannockburn's vineyards and orchards to the northwest.

The driving force behind Mt Difficulty, and one of its co-founders, is Robin Dicey. Originally from South Africa, Dicey studied viticulture and oenology at Stellenbosch University: 'I've been involved in horticulture and grapes my whole life.' He came to New Zealand in the late 1970s and worked at first in the North Island's fledgling wine industry. However, Dicey and his family soon discovered and fell in love with Central Otago. They used to come down on family holidays, and in 1988 were renting a house in Wanaka when Dicey spied Rippon vineyard from the lake, then met Rolfe Mills and got talking. Two years later, he and wife Margie bought land in Bannockburn.

Overall, Pinot Noir accounts for 65 per cent of production, and Pinot Gris, the most popular of Mt Difficulty's white wines, accounts for a further 25 per cent. Riesling, Rosé, Sauvignon Blanc, Chardonnay, Gewürztraminer and Chenin Blanc also feature in Mt Difficulty's diverse range.

In 2004, Dicey's second son, James, joined the Mt Difficulty team, taking over from his father as viticulturist. Trained as an accountant as well as in viticulture and winemaking, James, like his father before him, also works as a consultant and was president of COWA for six years up until 2016. Robin Dicey says wine quality can only come from the vineyard. 'The winemaker finishes what the grower starts. But if the wine is good, it's the winemaker who gets the praise.' He pauses. 'But if it's bad, the grower gets the blame.'

Dicey says it can take up to 16 years before you start making a true profit in the wine industry. He compares it to a three-legged Zulu pot: production, process and marketing must all be in balance, but 'marketing is the most critical'. Mt Difficulty has always had a strong domestic market base, selling over 60 per cent of its wines locally. The distinctive cellar door and winery restaurant, opened in 2003, caters for 45,000 visitors a year and allows Mt Difficulty to showcase what ideal partners wine and food can be.

When it comes to exporting, Matt Dicey says Central Otago has done this collectively and that there has been strength in numbers. He makes the point that because Central Otago is so small in the world market, it is not standing on anyone's toes. Australia has been a good export market for Mt Difficulty, followed by the US and UK, and it has small pockets in Europe and Asia as well.

Although Mt Difficulty has been sold, both Matt and James Dicey will continue working for the company as winemaker and viticulturist — and don't be surprised if before too long you see the next generation of Diceys working in the Mt Difficulty vineyards and winery. Wine just seems to be in their blood.

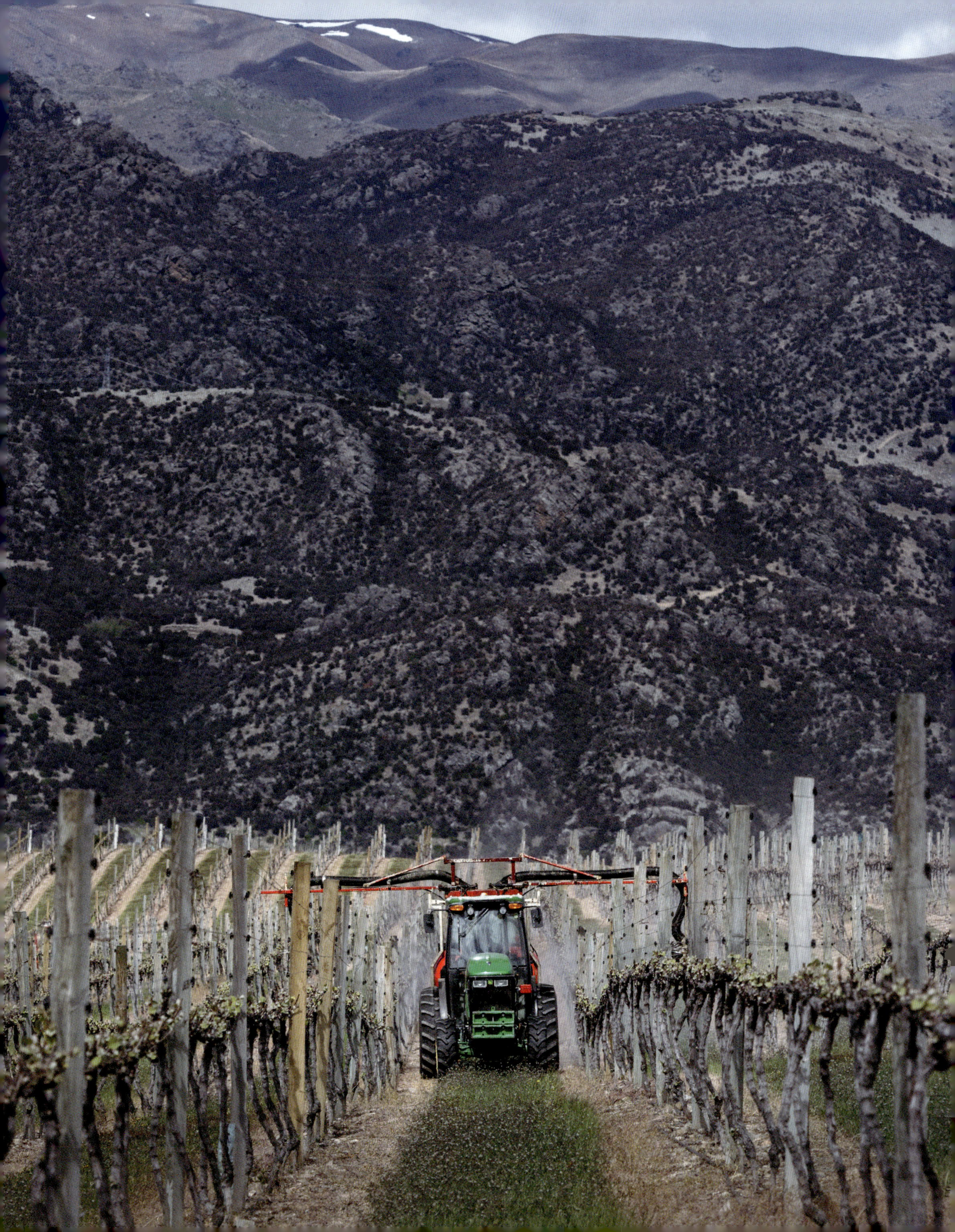

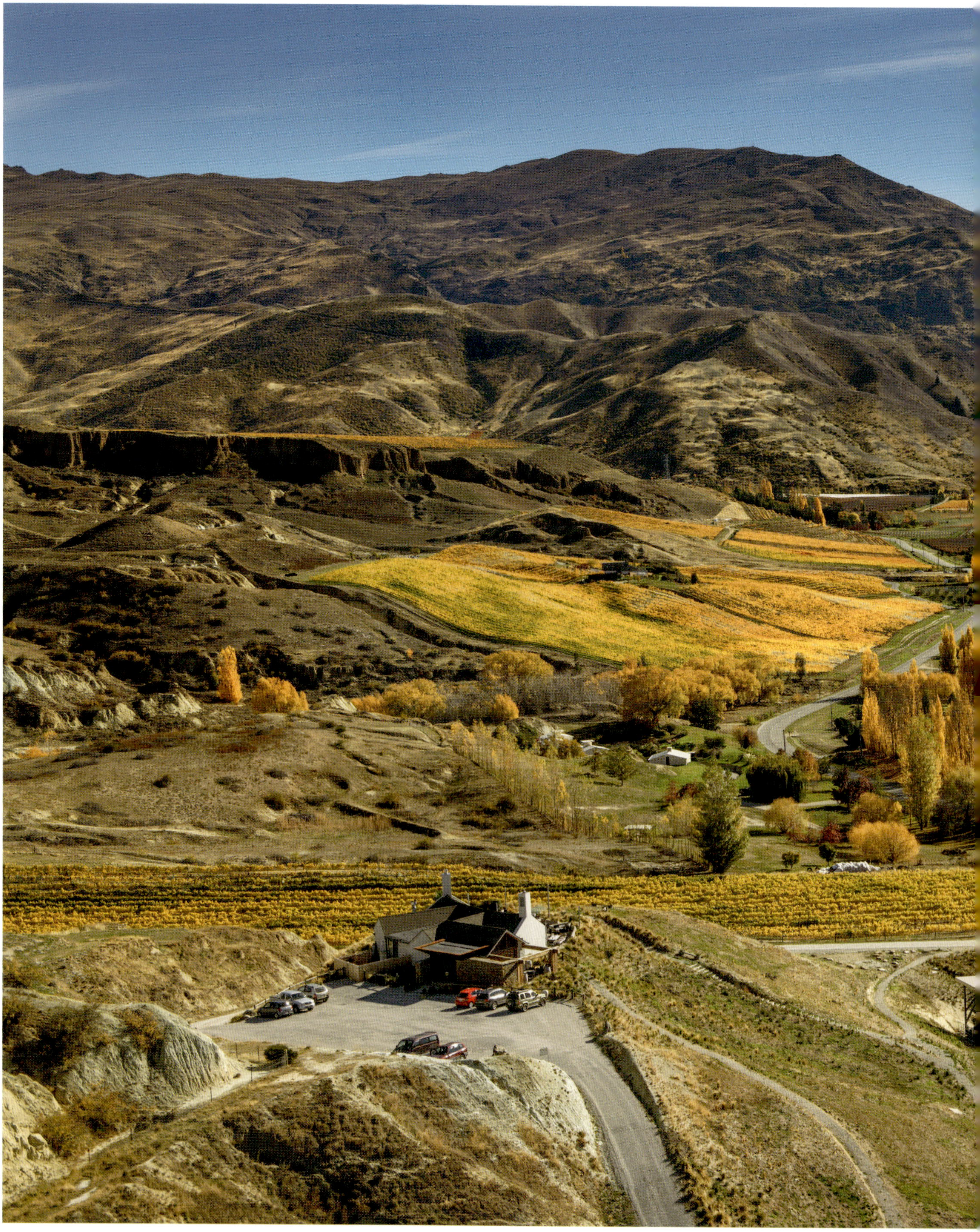

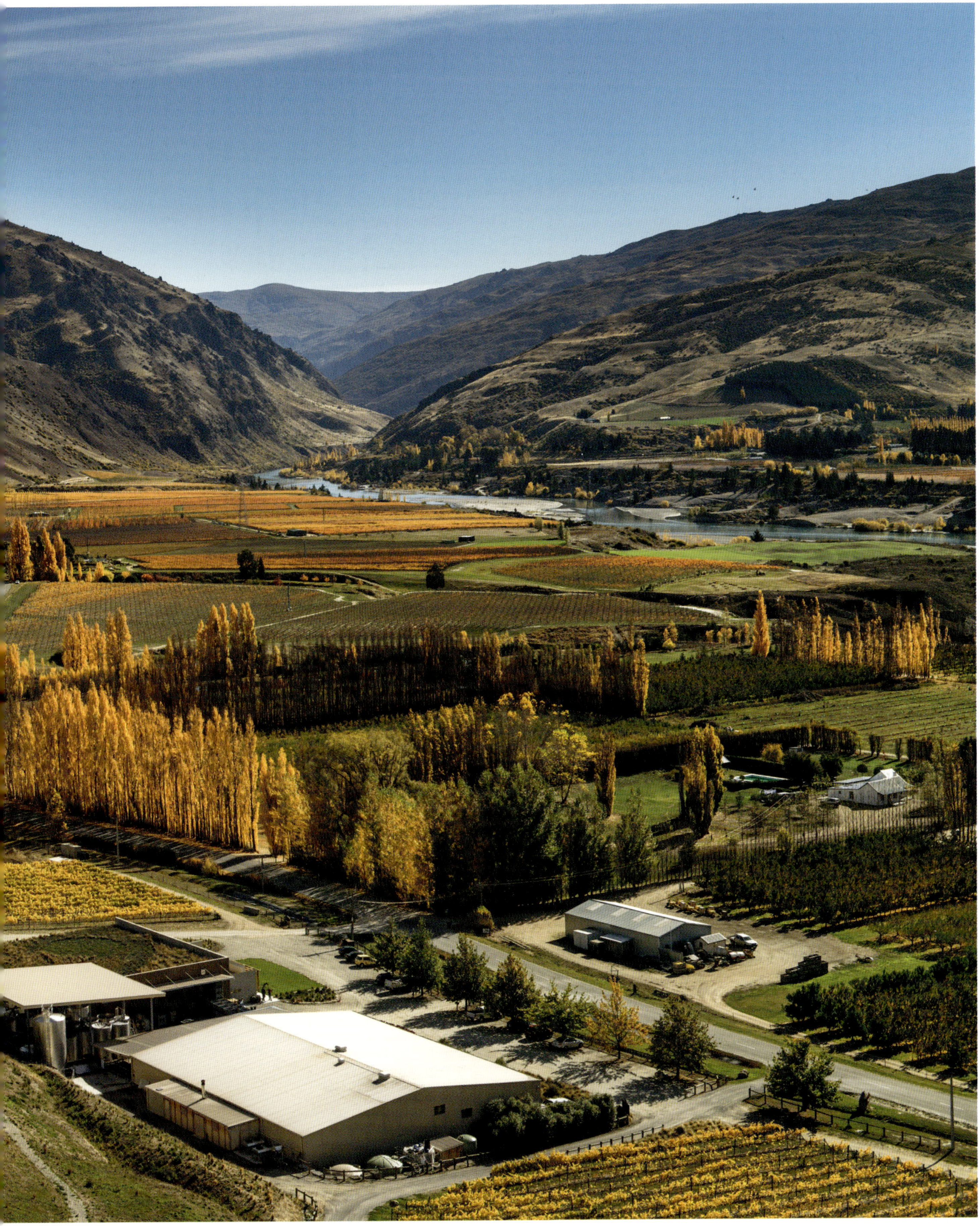

Above Harvest at Templars Hill vineyard. Above right Harvest at Black Rabbit vineyard. Right Workers' briefing at Black Rabbit vineyard.

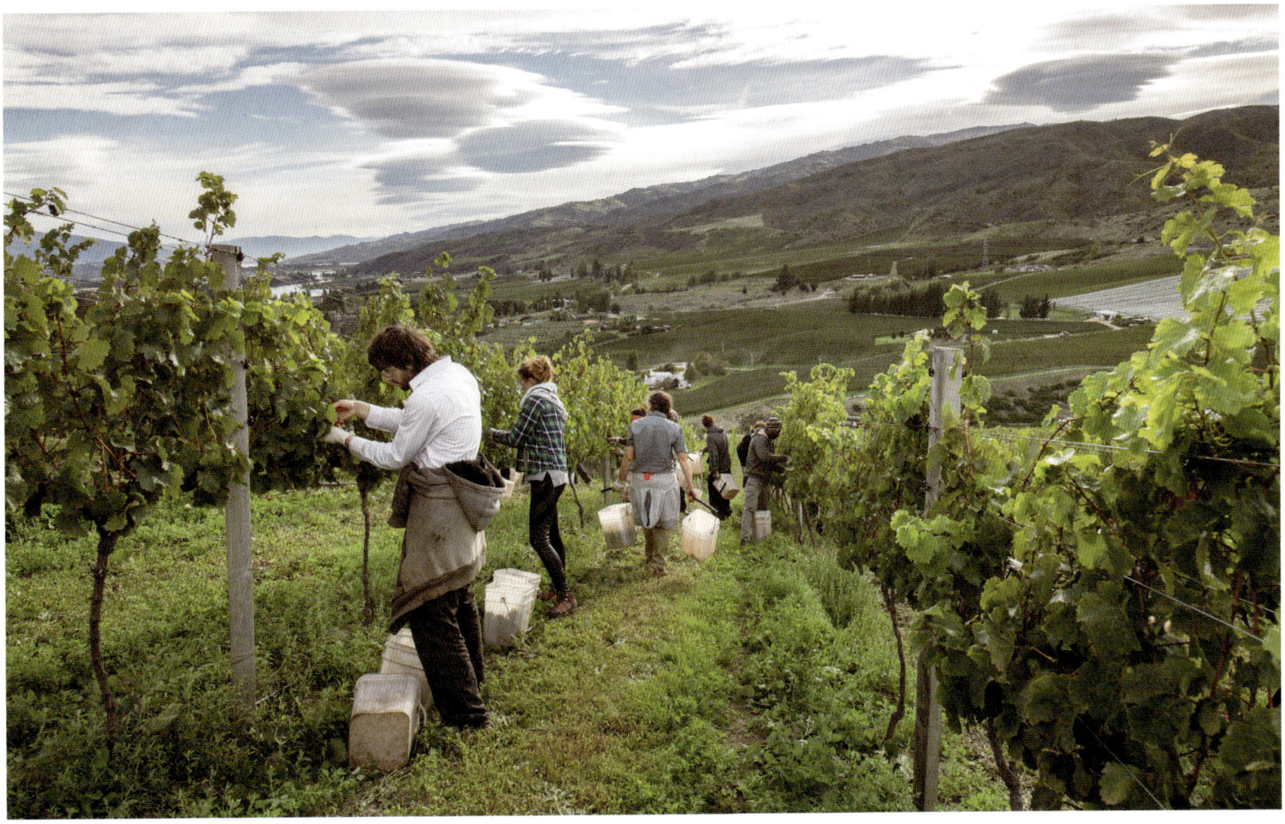

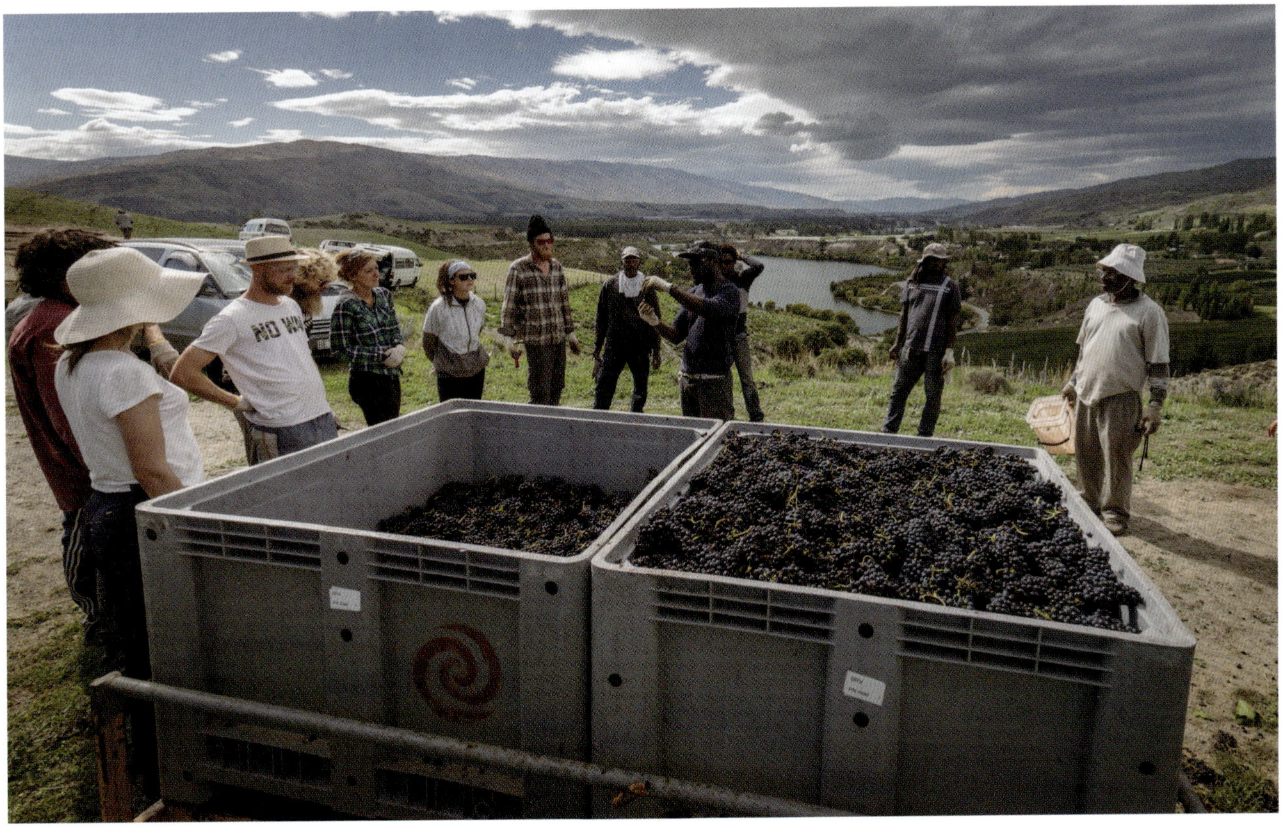

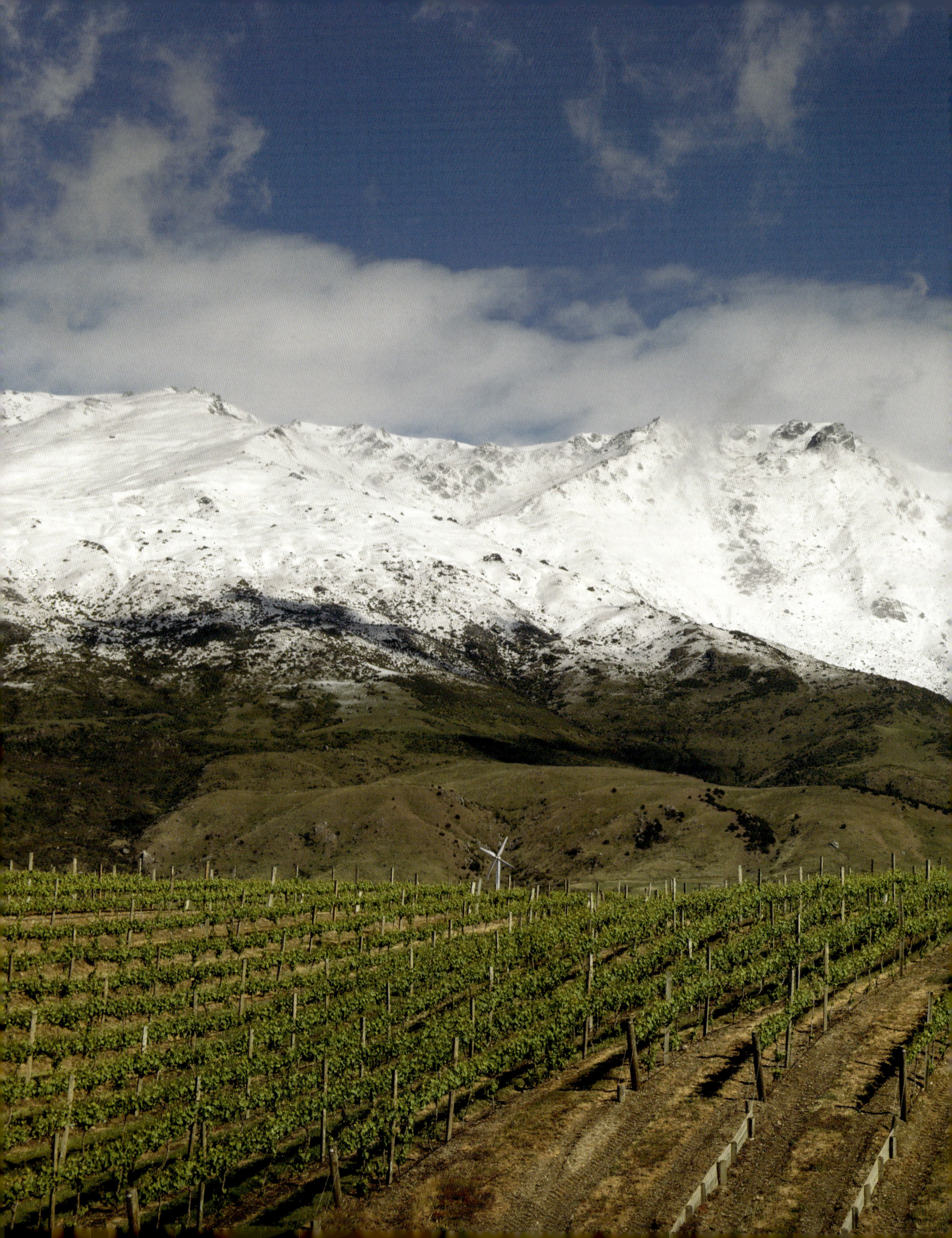

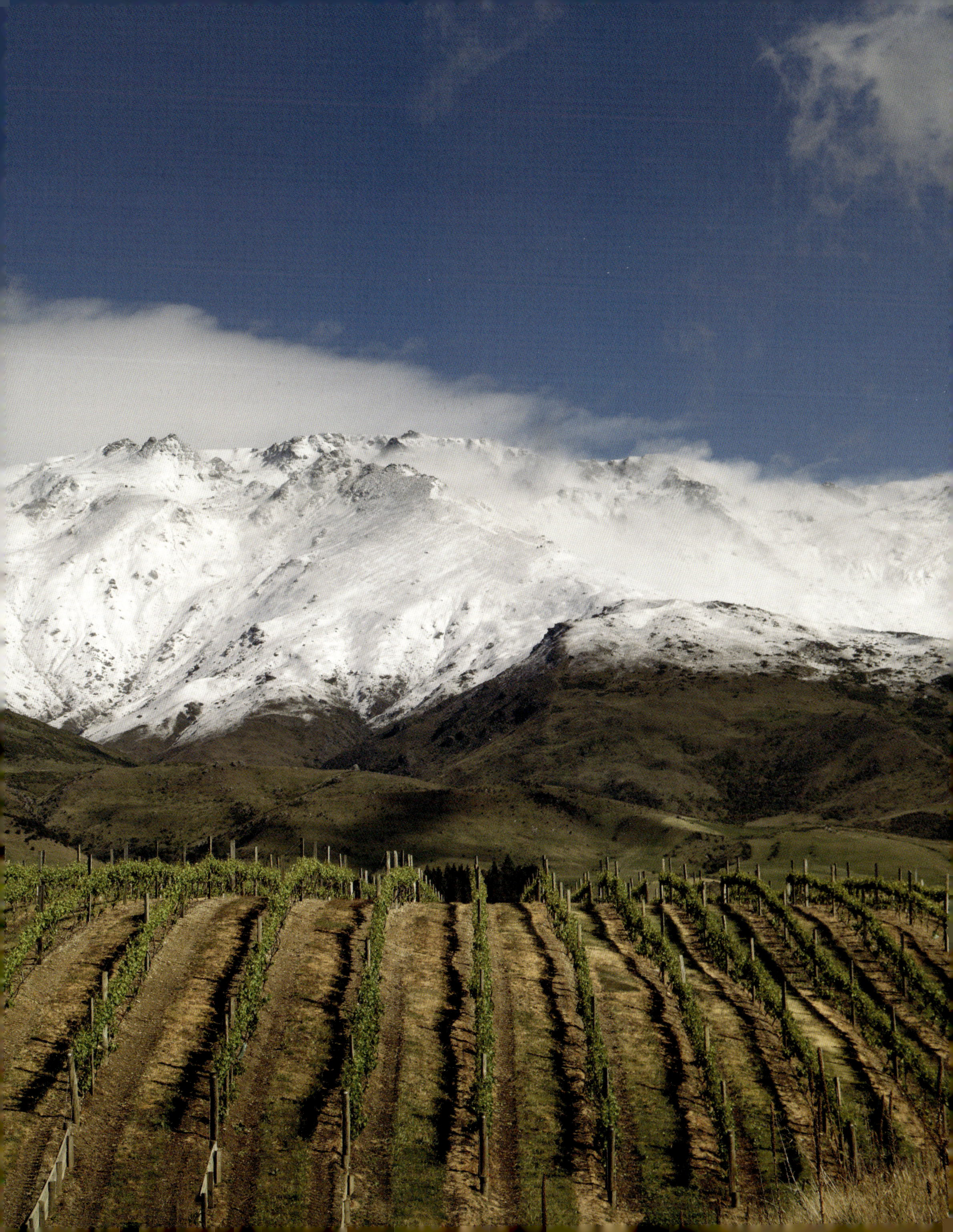

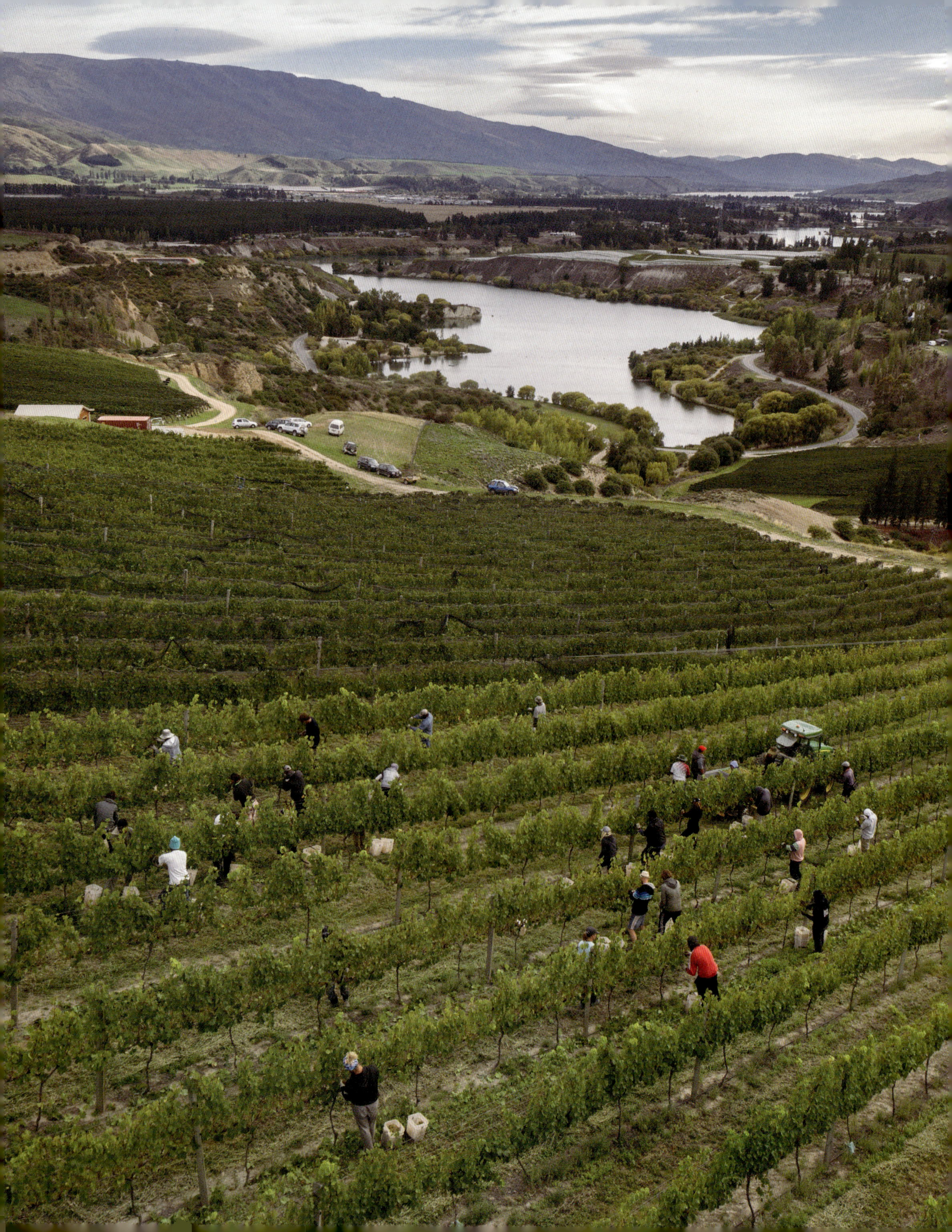

LEFT Harvest at Black Rabbit vineyard, Bannockburn. TOP RIGHT Pinot production line. MIDDLE RIGHT Concrete egg fermenters for Chardonnay. BOTTOM RIGHT Wine cellar.

CARRICK

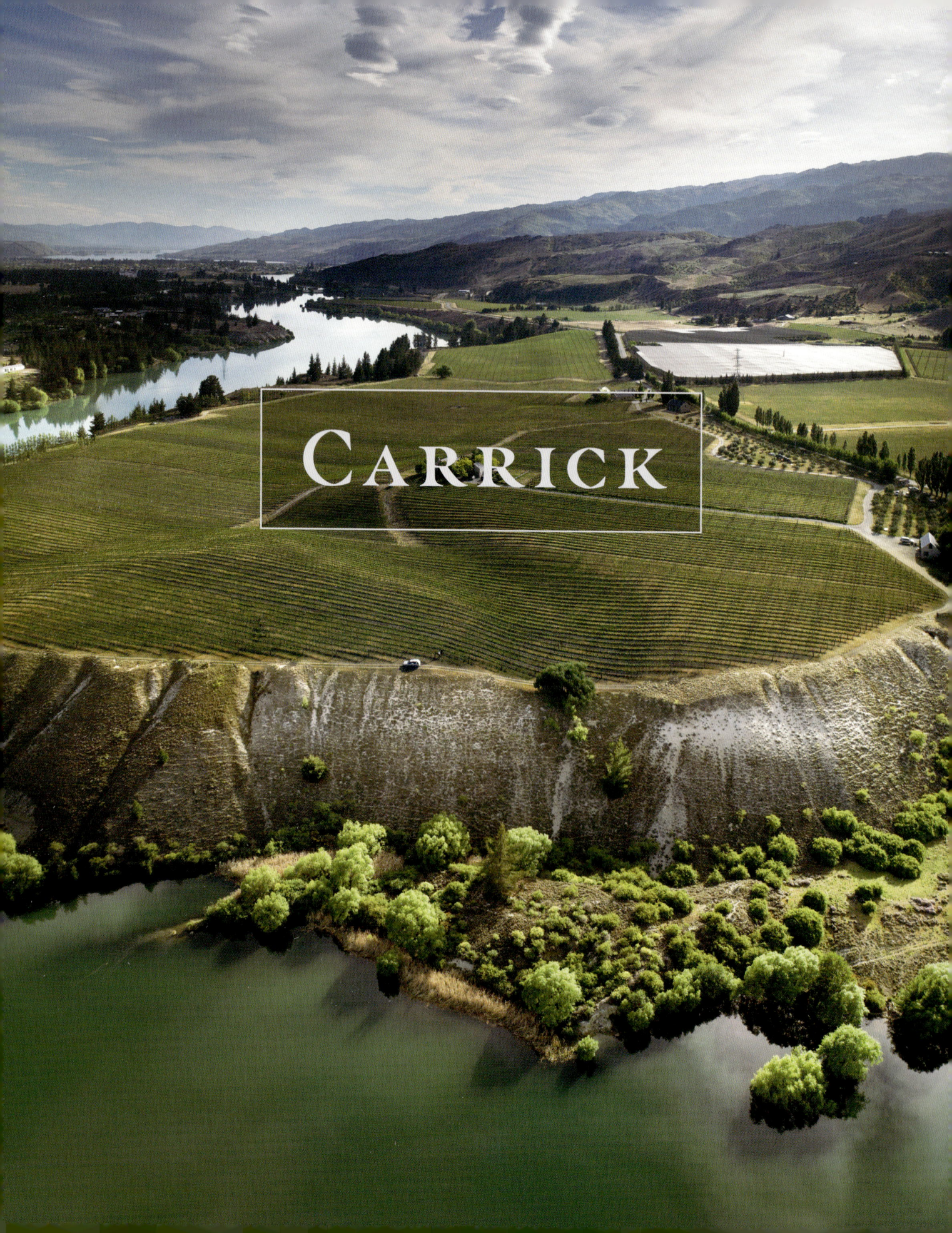

'Working together helped the region establish a global presence in the marketplace.'

Carrick was named for the mountain range to the southwest of Bannockburn, and for the Carrick knot, which symbolises the close connection between the land, the vines and the wine produced.

Originally partners in Mt Difficulty, Steve and Barbara Green decided after two years to set up their own winery and restaurant at their 23.5-hectare vineyard on the Cairnmuir Terraces, overlooking Lake Dunstan in Bannockburn. In 2002 they made the first vintage at their new winery. Green believes there is a big advantage in making your wine on site. 'The relationship between the vineyard and winery is much more symbiotic and satisfying.'

While 70 per cent of its production is Pinot Noir, Carrick also prides itself on its white wines: Chardonnay and Pinot Gris each account for 10 per cent of production, and small quantities of Riesling, Sauvignon Blanc and Pinot Blanc make up the balance.

Carrick started converting to organics over 10 years ago and both the vineyard and winery have been certified organic since 2011. Carrick's viticulturist, Blair Deaker, had come from an organic background and drove the vineyard's conversion, and winemaker Francis Hutt was keen to work in an organic environment. Carrick has also adopted a number of biodynamic practices. This commitment to the environment was rewarded in 2013 when Carrick's Bannockburn Pinot Noir 2011 won the trophies for Best Red Wine and Wine of Show at the Australia and New Zealand Organic Wine Show. Carrick's second-tier Pinot Noir, Carrick Unravelled, has proved popular as well.

Hutt is proud of Carrick's white wines also — the Carrick Chardonnay, like the Pinot, is strongly reflective of its site — and 'natural' wines are another interest. While he is producing fewer than 500 cases, these wines made with minimal intervention in the naturally occurring fermentation process have attracted a small but ardent following among sommeliers from New Zealand and overseas.

Carrick's restaurant, which opened in 2002, at the same time as the winery, has helped create a strong identity and has been important for exposure to the market. Carrick has always made wines that are food-friendly, and the wines on offer in the restaurant are carefully matched with the menu's fresh, seasonal food. As art lovers, the Greens added another dimension to the Carrick identity, displaying works by prominent New Zealand painters on their restaurant walls, and involving their good friend the Central Otago painter Grahame Sydney in the label design for their premium Excelsior Pinot Noir.

Up to 15 per cent of Carrick's wine sales are through the restaurant, cellar door and wine club and another 45 per cent are within New Zealand; the remaining 40 per cent of production is exported. By selling overseas as well as into the domestic market, companies are able to spread their risk. But it is a balancing act too. If more wine is exported and there is less available to supply the local market, popular wines can sell out. Australia has been a really strong market for Central Otago Pinot Noir and there are good sales into the US and the UK, with smaller parcels being sold into Asia and Europe.

Beyond developing and owning the Carrick brand, Green, having previously worked at managerial level in local government, has played a significant role in helping lift the profile of the Central Otago winegrowing industry. He was president of COWA in the late 1990s and was instrumental in setting up COPNL, the company established in 2002 to focus on marketing Central Otago Pinot Noir into overseas

Steve Green.

markets: 'Working together helped the region establish a global presence in the marketplace.' He has also served as chairman of New Zealand Winegrowers, giving Central Otago a voice at a national industry level. 'We're now regarded as one of the top regions in New Zealand, based on our presence and profile in the international scene.'

Barbara Green, like many of the wives and partners in the Central Otago winegrowing industry, played a key role in the development of Carrick. Though often invisible in the past, women like Green have been involved in the industry from the start, working in the vineyard, doing the administration and helping sell the wine. With the growth in the number of qualified female viticulturists, winemakers and managers, though, women are now much more prominent in the industry.

The Greens developed a strong team culture at Carrick: they bring their vineyard and restaurant staff together for a morning tea once a week, and they hold shared wine-tasting sessions. At harvest time, an extra 30 or so staff are taken on, and they, like the permanent team, are well looked after, with many, like the 'grey nomads', returning to help with the vintage year after year. In 2017 the Greens sold Carrick to Kennedy Point Vineyard Ltd. However, it is pretty much business as usual at Carrick. Winemaker Francis Hutt has also taken on the role of general manager, and he and viticulturist Blair Deaker work closely to lead the loyal Carrick team.

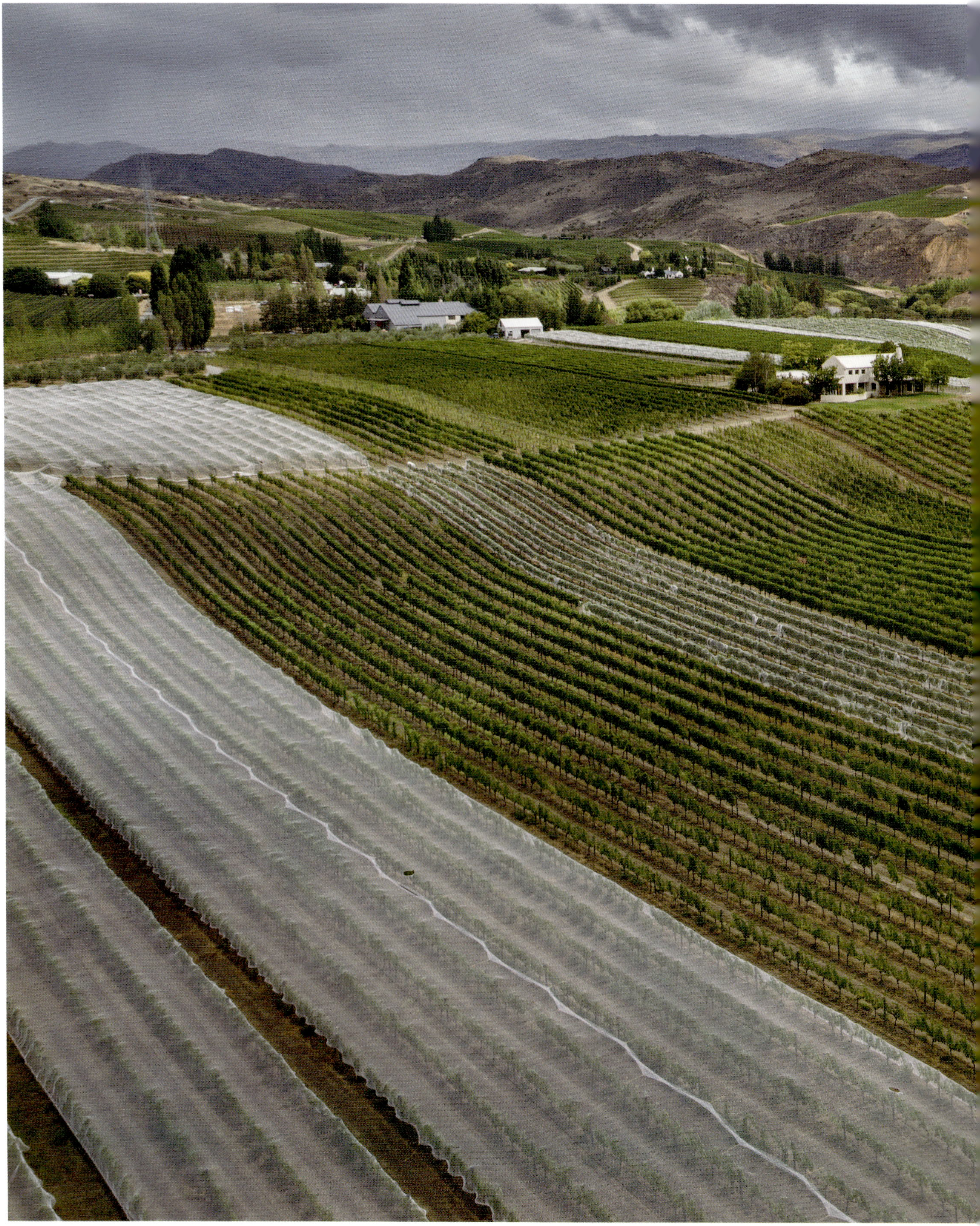

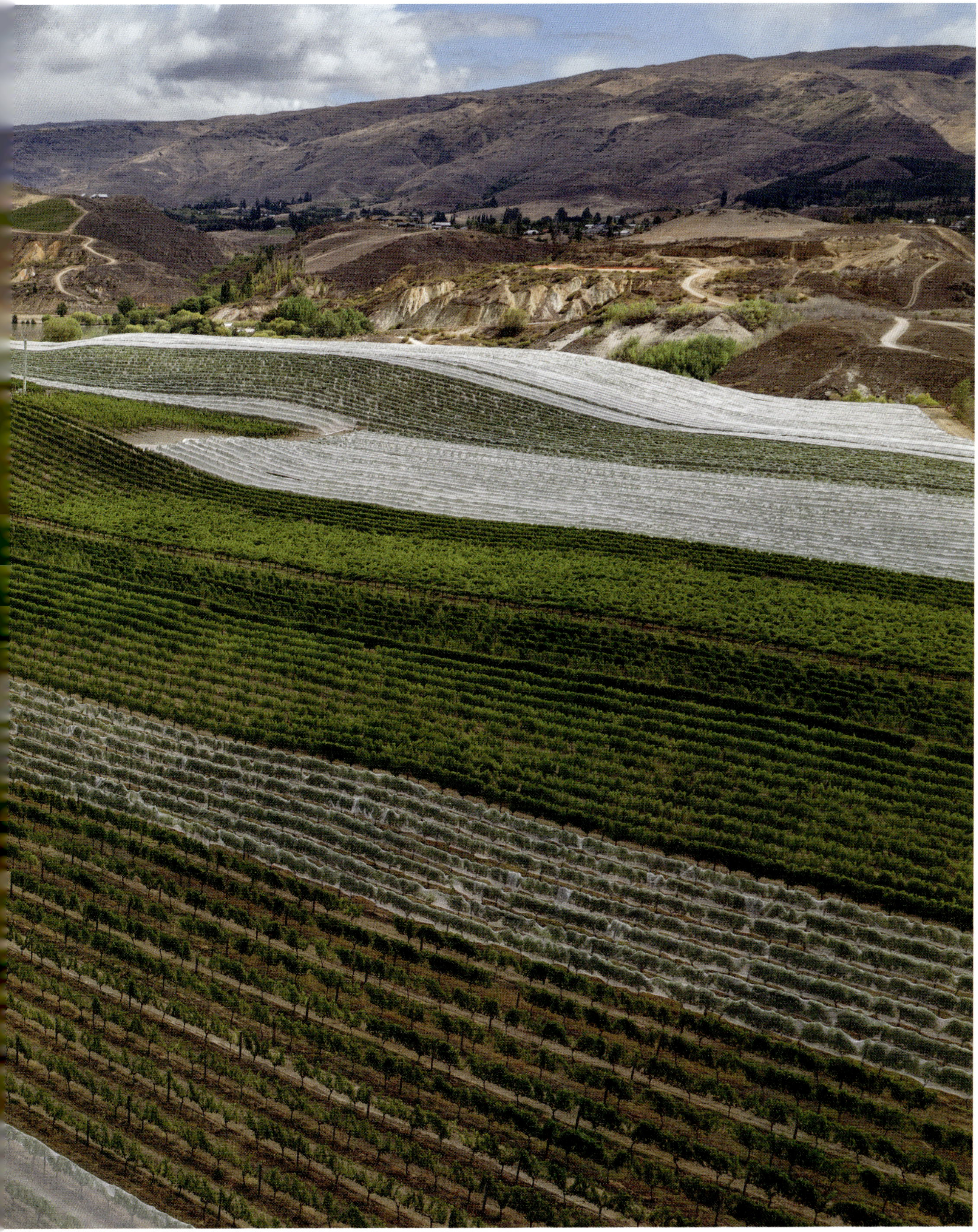

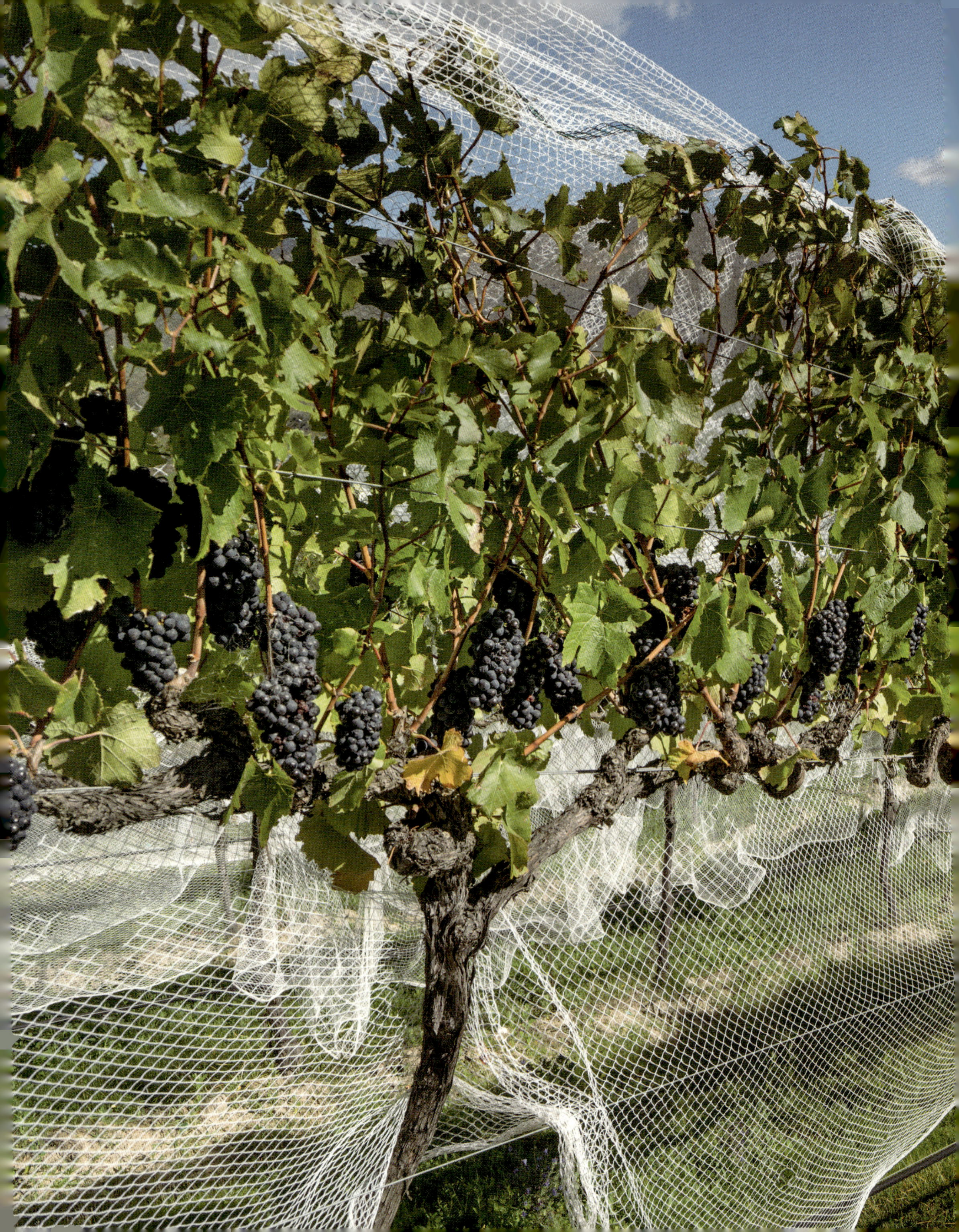

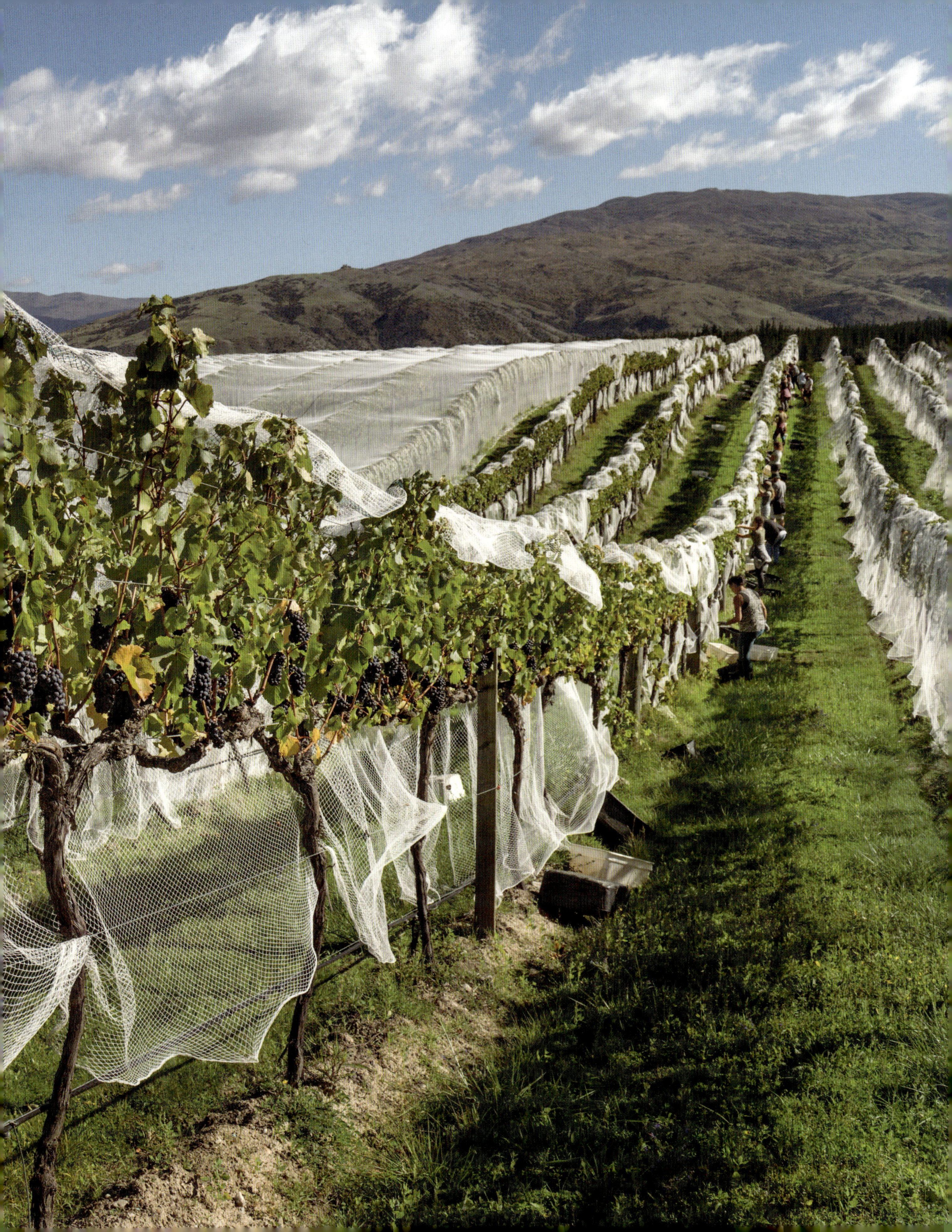

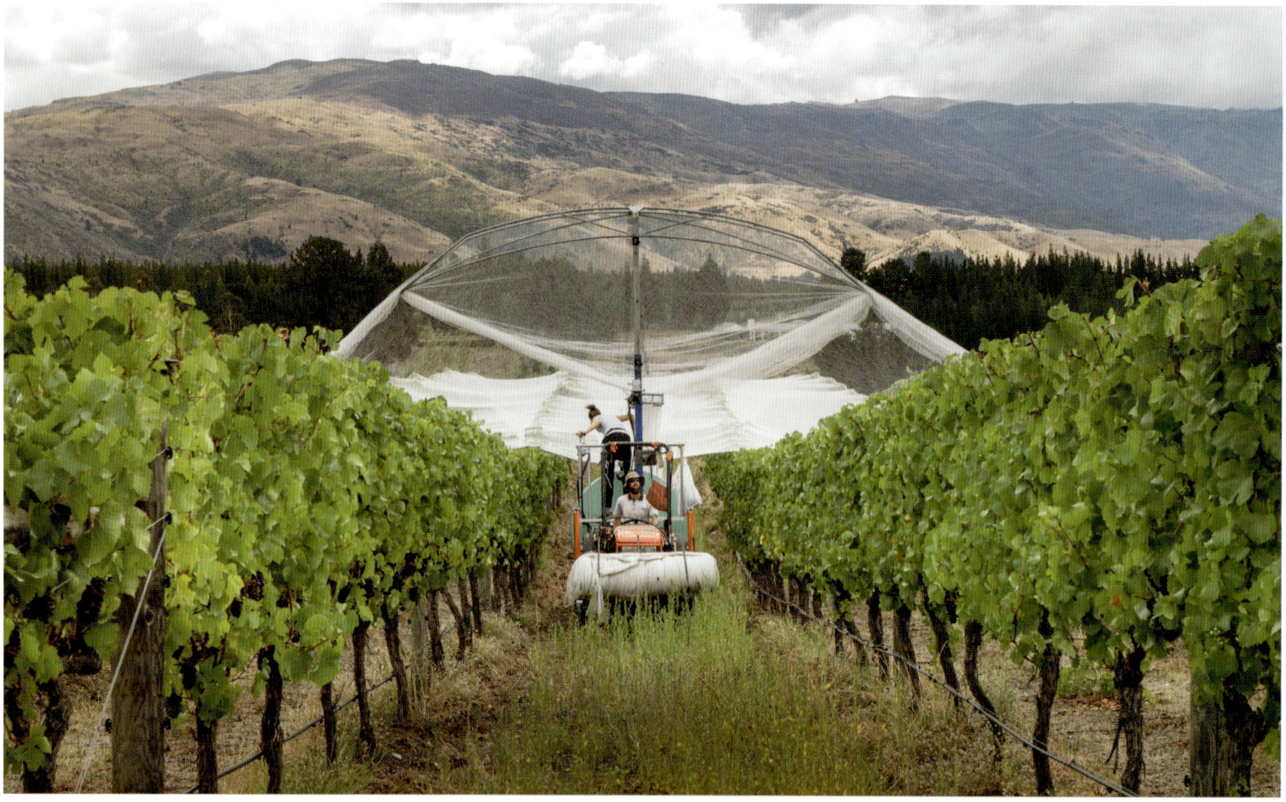
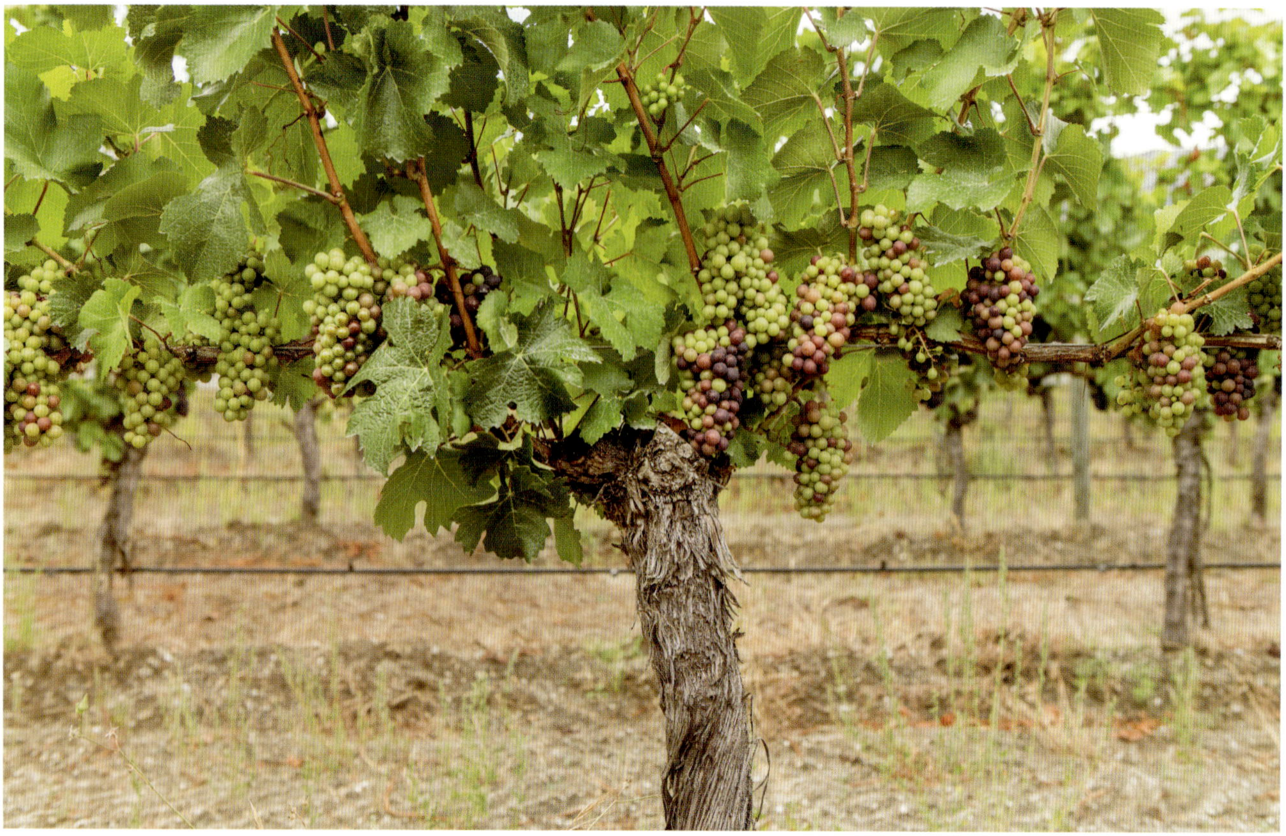

ABOVE LEFT Installing bird nets. LEFT Pinot going through veraison. ABOVE One of the 'grey nomads' harvesting grapes.

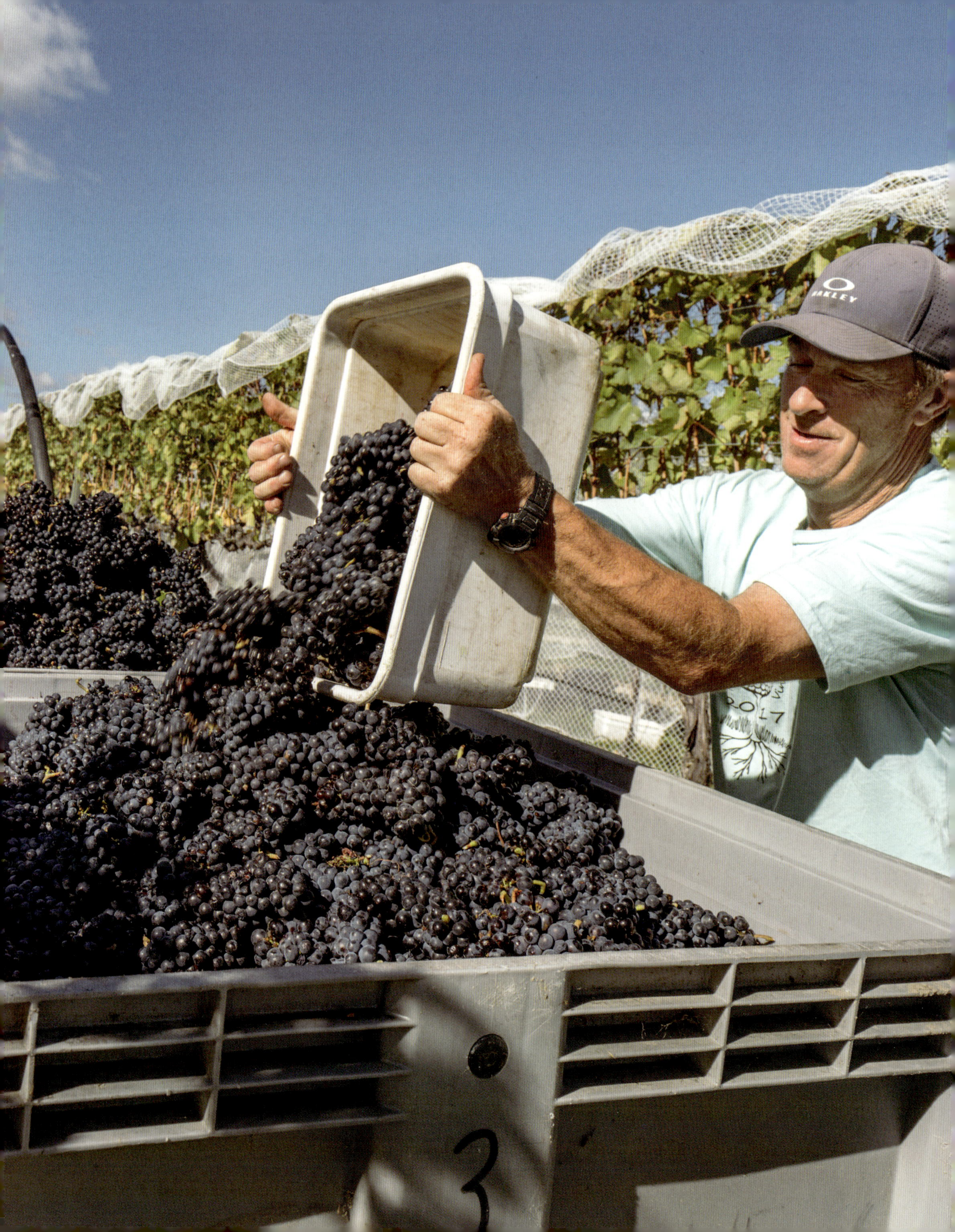
OAKLEY
3

LEFT Viticulturist Blair Deaker. TOP RIGHT Harvested Pinot grapes going into a fermentation vat. MIDDLE RIGHT Winemaker Francis Hutt (right) with Burgundy exchange students. BOTTOM RIGHT Weekly staff morning tea at Carrick.

AKARUA

'While I enjoyed a white wine, I was well aware that we were going to produce "a lot of red shit", but I wouldn't be interested in drinking it.'

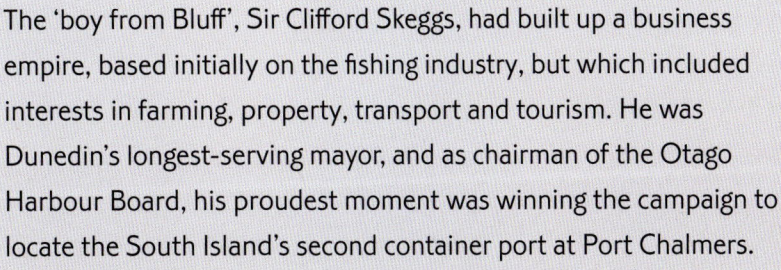

The 'boy from Bluff', Sir Clifford Skeggs, had built up a business empire, based initially on the fishing industry, but which included interests in farming, property, transport and tourism. He was Dunedin's longest-serving mayor, and as chairman of the Otago Harbour Board, his proudest moment was winning the campaign to locate the South Island's second container port at Port Chalmers.

But he had always had a bit of a hankering to own a winery, and in 1996, looking ahead to his retirement, he bought some land in Cairnmuir Road in Bannockburn, and planted his first grapes. He called his new business Akarua which means 'two vines' in Māori. Sir Cliff was never known for thinking 'small' though, and he soon acquired more land, giving him a 50-hectare investment. 'In hindsight,' he says, 'I think I got some of the best land in Central Otago.' Planted in 90 per cent Pinot Noir, with smaller areas of Pinot Gris, Chardonnay and

Australian markets are building momentum. Sweden, and China and other Asian countries are enjoying Akarua wines too, and the US looks like becoming an important market for Akarua Pinot Noir in the near future.

Like other big players in Central Otago, Akarua has developed a second-tier Pinot Noir, and while it may be less expensive, it has proved to be a winner too. In the prestigious *Decanter* World Wine Awards, RUA Pinot Noir 2014 and 2015 both received gold medals. These more affordable wines help to build trust in the marketplace and are where the greatest growth in sales lies.

It might have started out as a retirement project to keep boredom at bay, but Akarua has developed into one of the biggest and most respected brands in Central Otago. Even Sir Cliff now admits, 'I do have the odd glass of Pinot Noir, these days.' He and wife Marie live above the marina at Lake Wanaka, and while Sir Cliff is no longer directly involved in the family's business operations, you get the feeling his binoculars are probably trained on those vineyards down the road at Bannockburn and Lowburn just as often as they are focused on the pleasure boats out on Lake Wanaka.

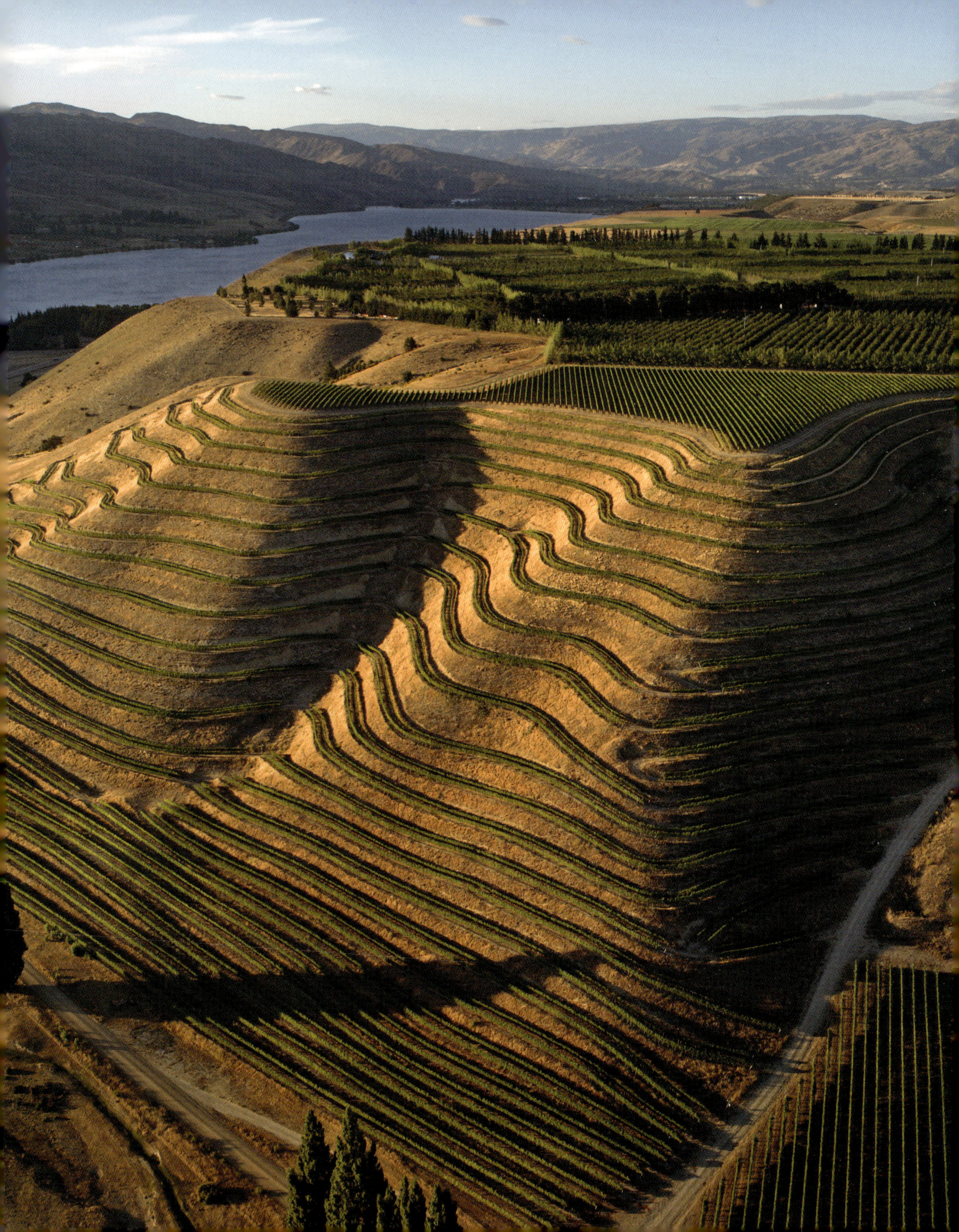

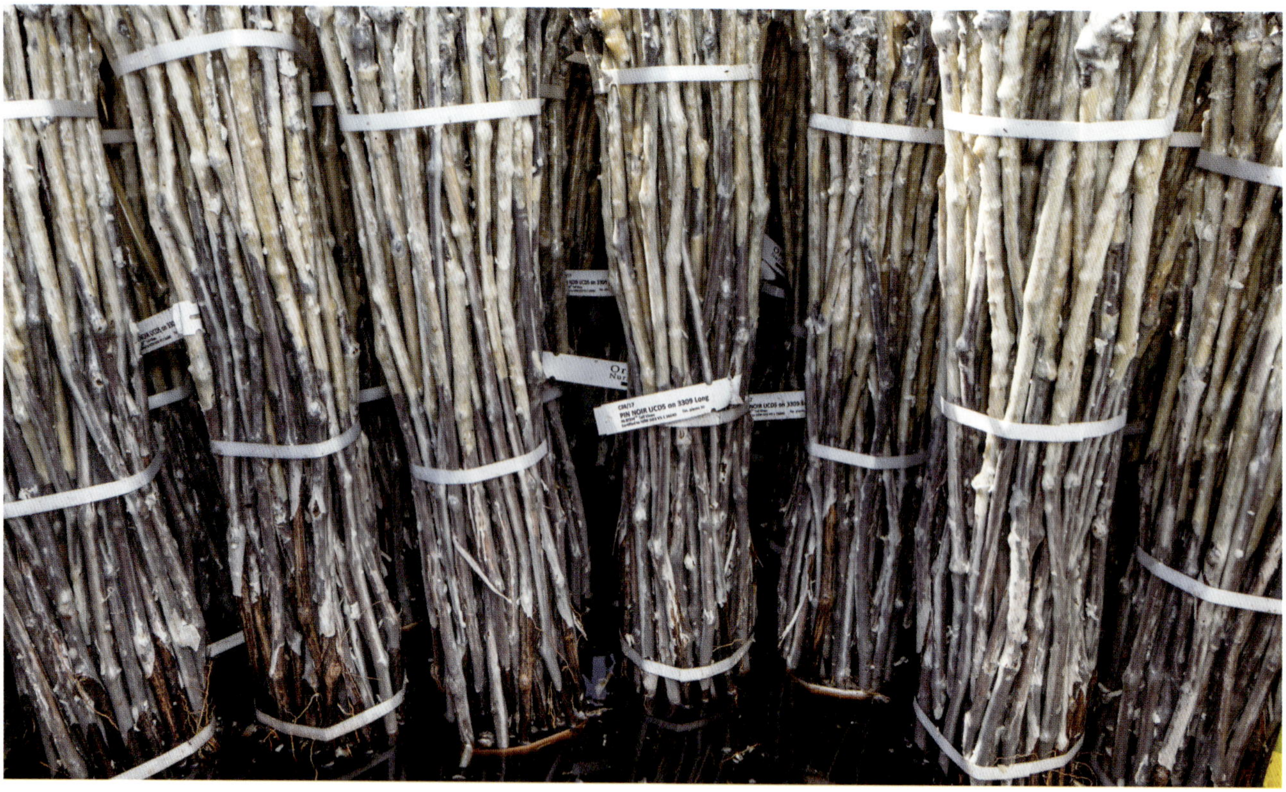
C8/17
PIN NOIR UCD5 on 3309 Long

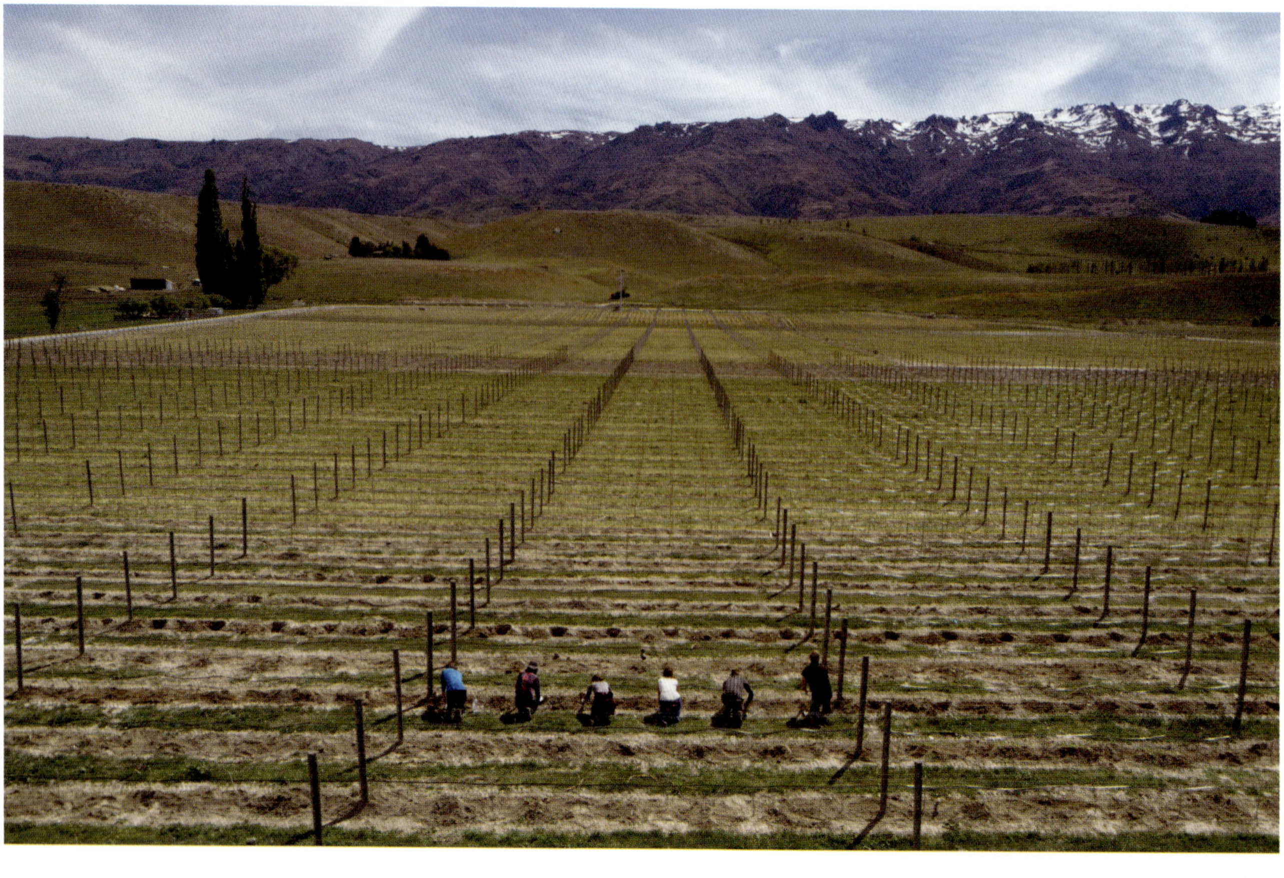

Above left Pinot cuttings ready for planting. **Left and above** Workers planting new Pinot cuttings at Lowburn–Pisa.

TOP Akarua Wines and Kitchen by Artisan. ABOVE Pinot grapes going into stainless steel fermentation vats.

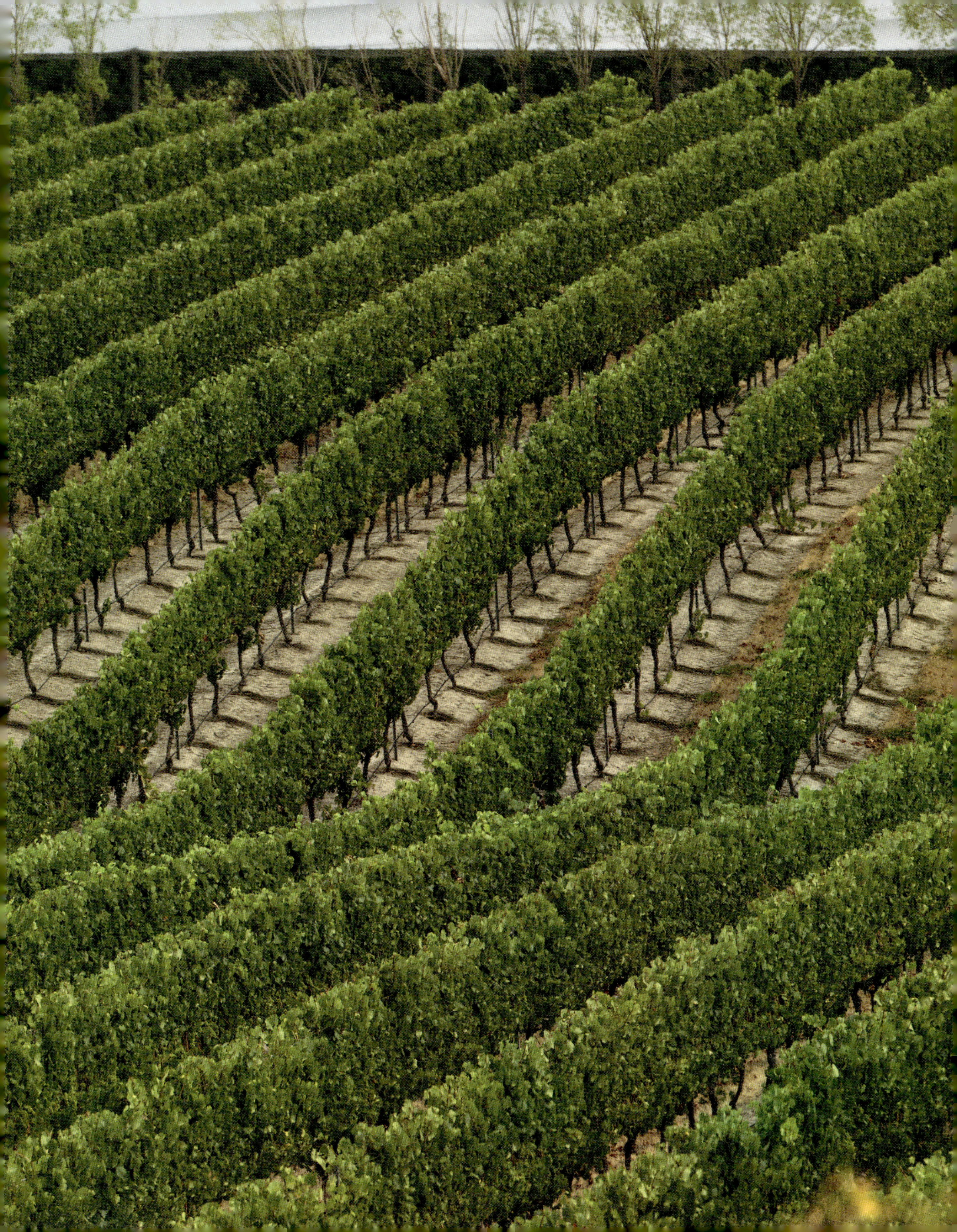

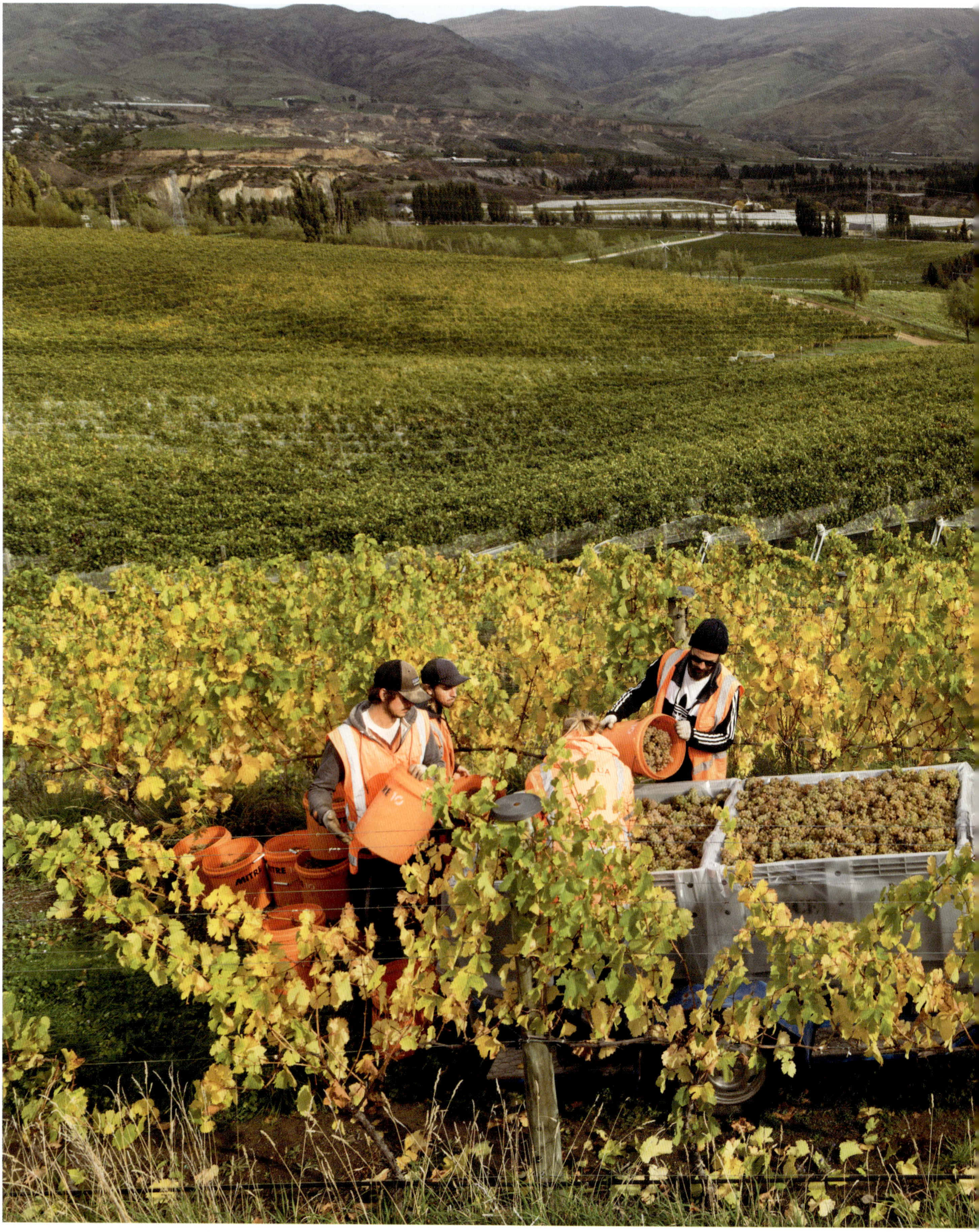

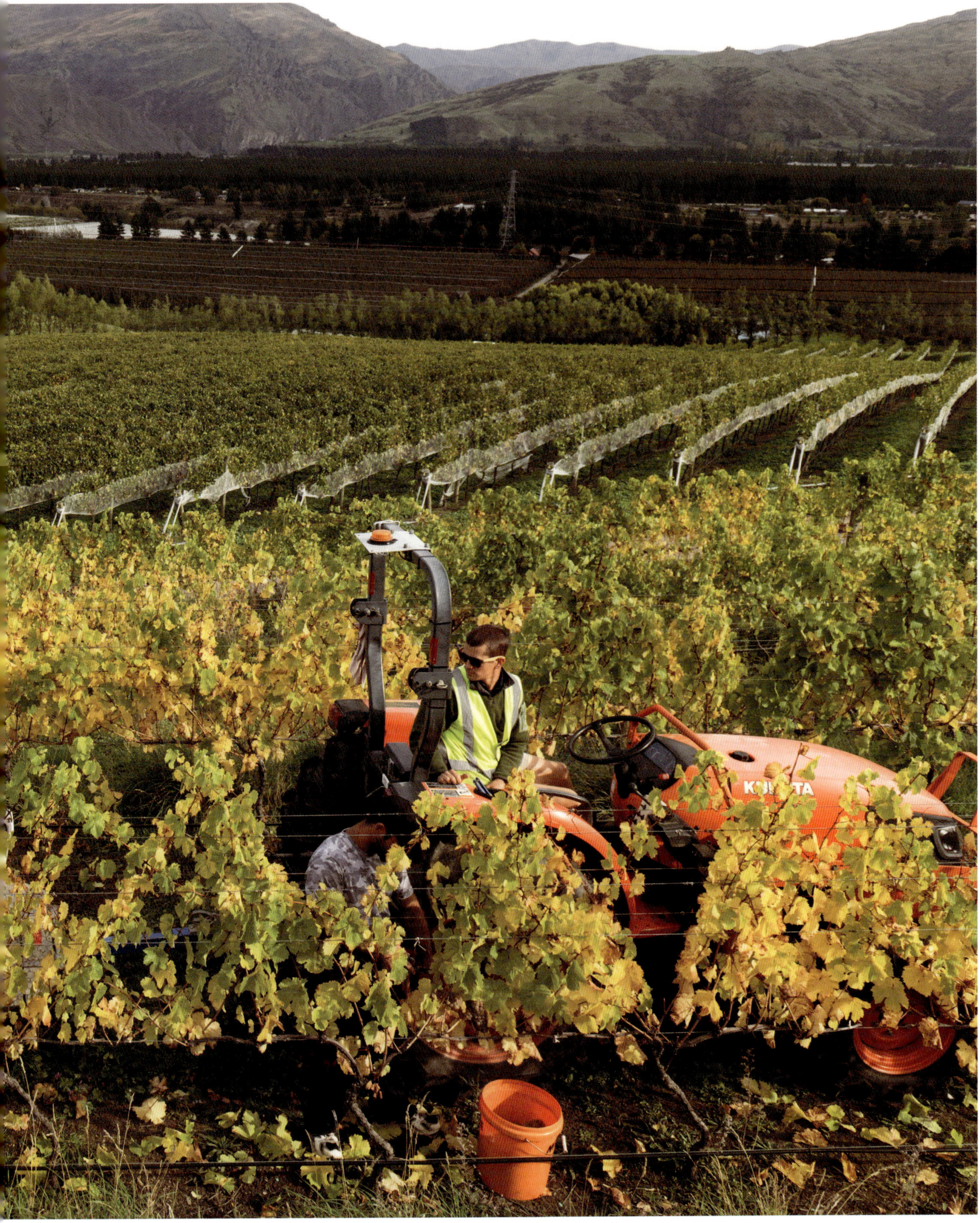

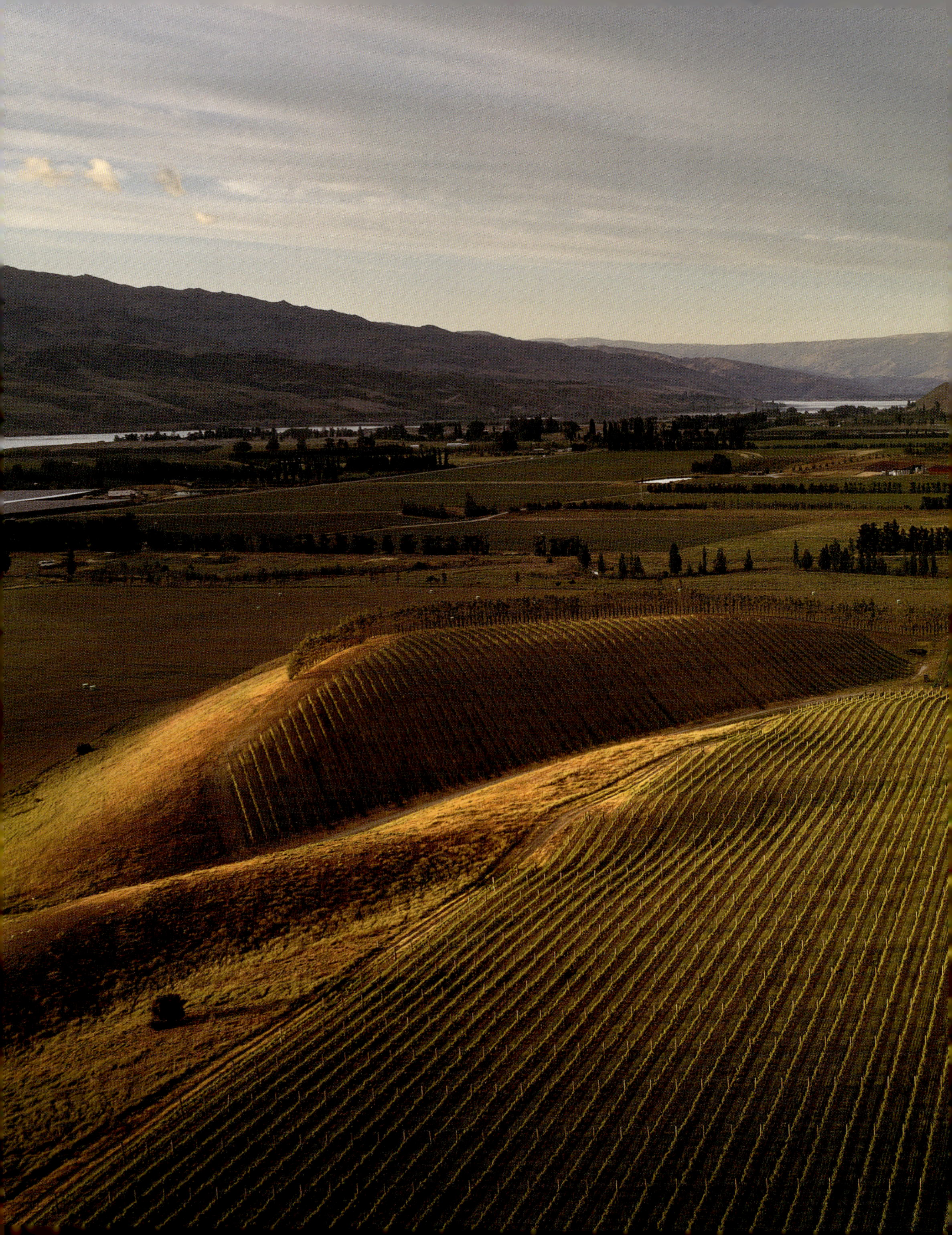

LOWBURN –PISA

Amisfield · Aurum · Burn Cottage

LOWBURN–PISA on the western side of Lake Dunstan is, like the rest of the Cromwell Basin, one of the warmer sub-regions. Diverse, it includes the gullies and lower slopes of the Pisa Range, as well as the extensive flat areas along the Cromwell–Wanaka highway. These areas were easier and cheaper to develop, but because they are flat, they are more frost-prone. There are three main ways to frost-fight in Central Otago's vineyards: water sprinklers, wind machines and helicopters, and while all can be effective, none is cheap.

The first vineyard in this sub-region was Packspur, developed by Laurie McAuley in 1992. A year later, the Kawarau Estate vineyard was planted, becoming the first organic vineyard in Central Otago.

With over 500 hectares of existing vineyards, and with more potential vineyard land available, Lowburn–Pisa is seen as a safe haven by Central Otago grapegrowers and a number of larger vineyards there belong to companies based in either one of the other sub-regions, or outside Central Otago. It is estimated that about 30 per cent of the fruit grown in Central Otago is taken outside the region, mostly to Marlborough to be made into wine by larger companies with established routes to the marketplace.

The Pinot Noirs from all the sub-regions in the Cromwell Basin tend to be more powerful, concentrated and darker coloured, with flavours of plum and darker berries.

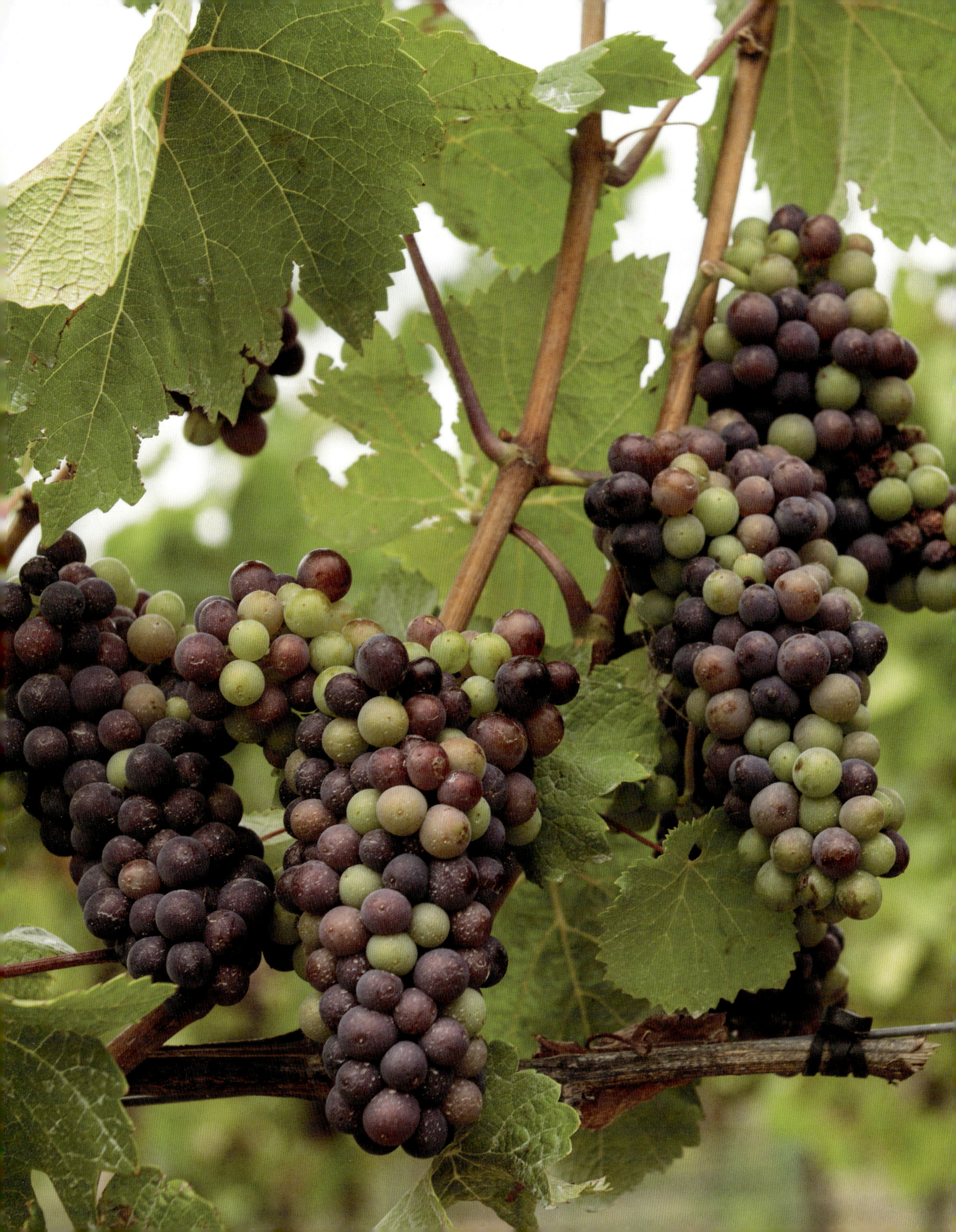

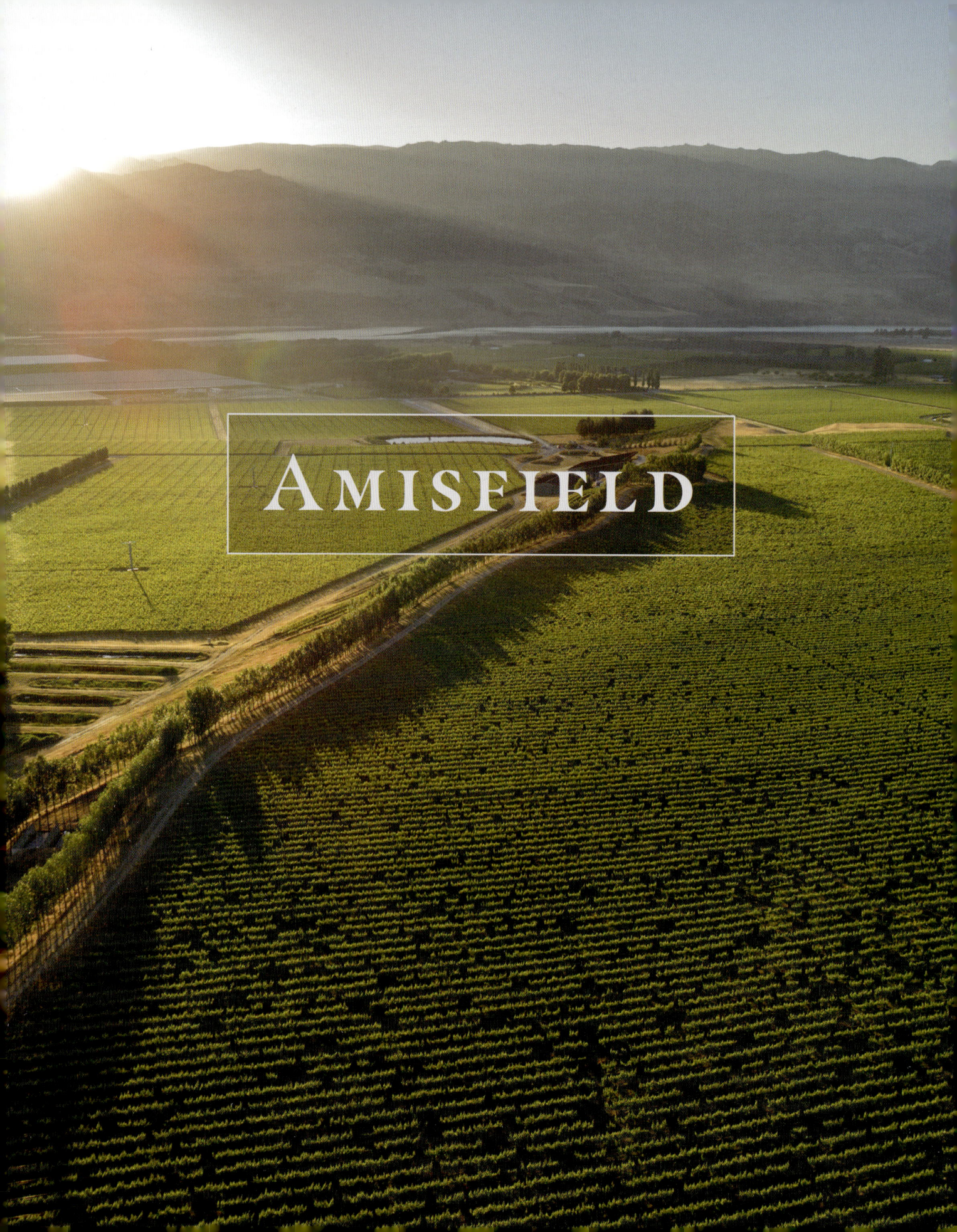

AMISFIELD

'We believe organics help us produce better wine, while being better for our people and the environment.'

The 90-hectare Amisfield vineyard is one of the largest single-vineyard estates in Central Otago. Bought originally in 1998 by John Darby and partners, the 400-hectare Amisfield Farm was one of the first properties to be planted in grapes along the Cromwell–Wanaka highway, in what has become known as the Lowburn–Pisa sub-region of Central Otago. Darby was a Queenstown landscape architect and developer, also qualified in viticulture. His love for the Central Otago landscape went back to childhood days, when he had camped by the nearby Clutha River on family holidays and enjoyed the delicious apricots grown there.

Darby had previously joined forces with Rob and Greg Hay from Chard Farm and Sam Neill to form Lake Hayes Estate. Darby already owned land at Lake Hayes and he and Rob Hay bought more land at Gibbston Valley to plant in grapes. However, several hard harvests convinced Hay and Darby to look further afield for another vineyard site. After extensive research, Amisfield Farm was bought. Half the property was subdivided off, with the partnership retaining

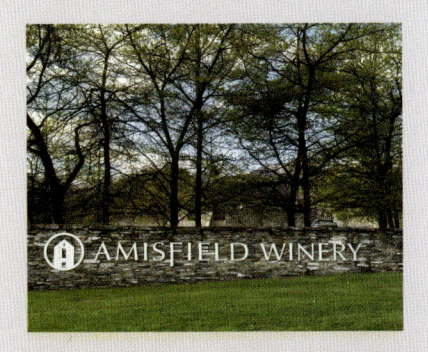

Fifty kilometres away at Lake Hayes, the award-winning bistro and cellar door, built in 2002, is the public face of Amisfield. Reflecting the stark, rugged Central Otago landscape, the imposing stone and recycled timber building has become a local landmark. Popular with tourists and locals alike, the menu is all about fresh, seasonal local produce, and all of the dishes are designed to complement the Amisfield wines on offer.

Craig Erasmus leads the Amisfield team. A qualified accountant, Erasmus studied viticulture and oenology and worked in the Marlborough wine industry before he joined Amisfield in 2012. One of the biggest challenges in the winegrowing industry is selling the wine. Amisfield produces around 30,000 cases of wine annually. Most of this production is accounted for through strong direct sales at the Lake Hayes bistro and cellar door and through distribution partners selling in New Zealand and Australia, but Erasmus says the US, UK and Asian markets are growing too.

With its first Pinot Noir vintage in 2002, Amisfield won the Best Pinot Noir trophy at the 2004 San Francisco International Wine Competition. The 2008 vintage won gold at the 2010 International Wine Challenge, and in the 2013 *Decanter* Asia Wine Awards, Amisfield Pinot Noir 2010 won Best in Show. In the same year, Amisfield was named New Zealand's best winery restaurant in the *Cuisine* magazine New Zealand Good Food Awards.

From the vineyard to the winery, from the winery to the cellar door, from the cellar door to the consumer, the team at Amisfield have together been responsible for growing Amisfield's reputation around the world as one of Central Otago's outstanding wine brands.

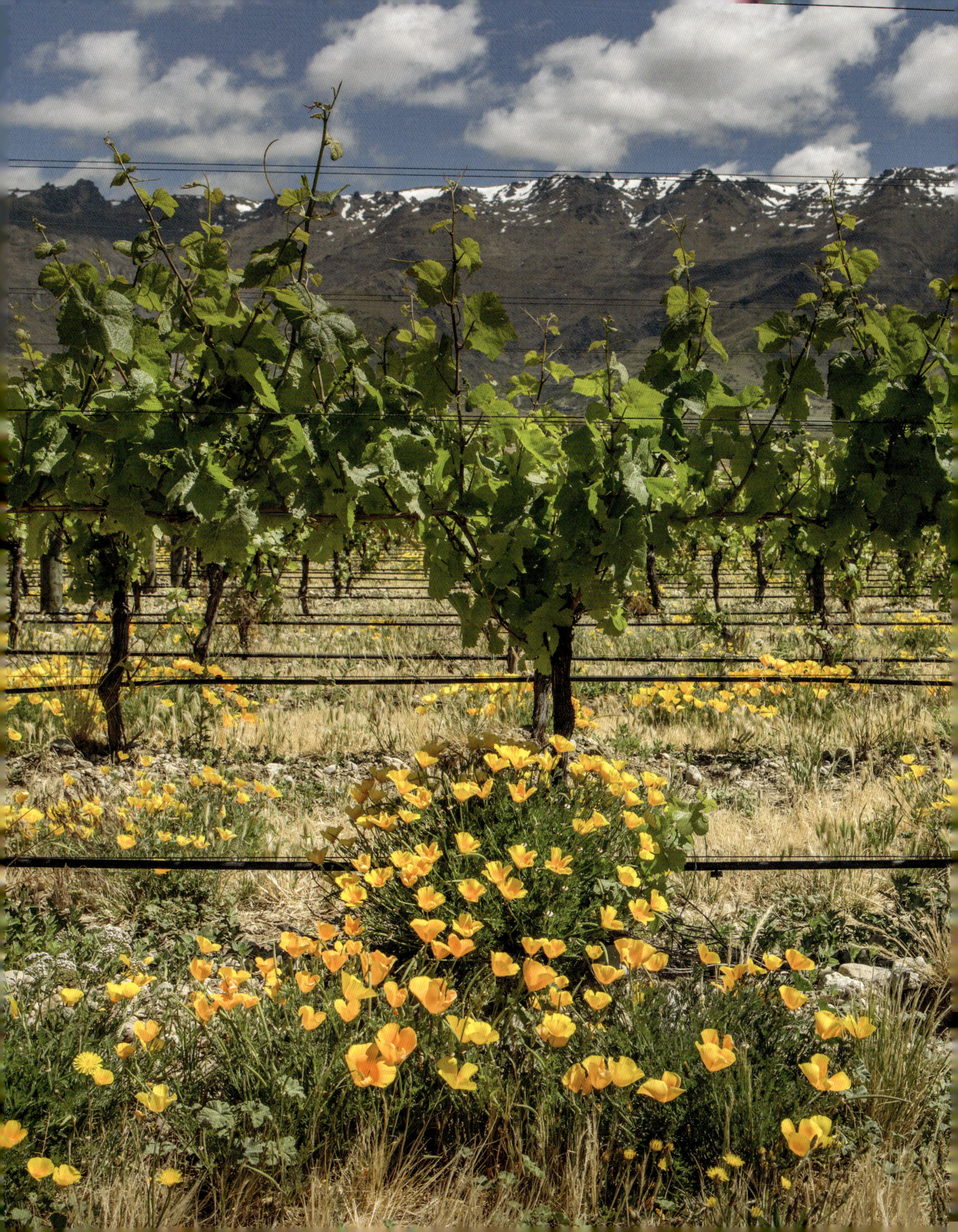

TOP Inflorescence fully developed. ABOVE Wire lifting. RIGHT Spring spraying at Lowburn.

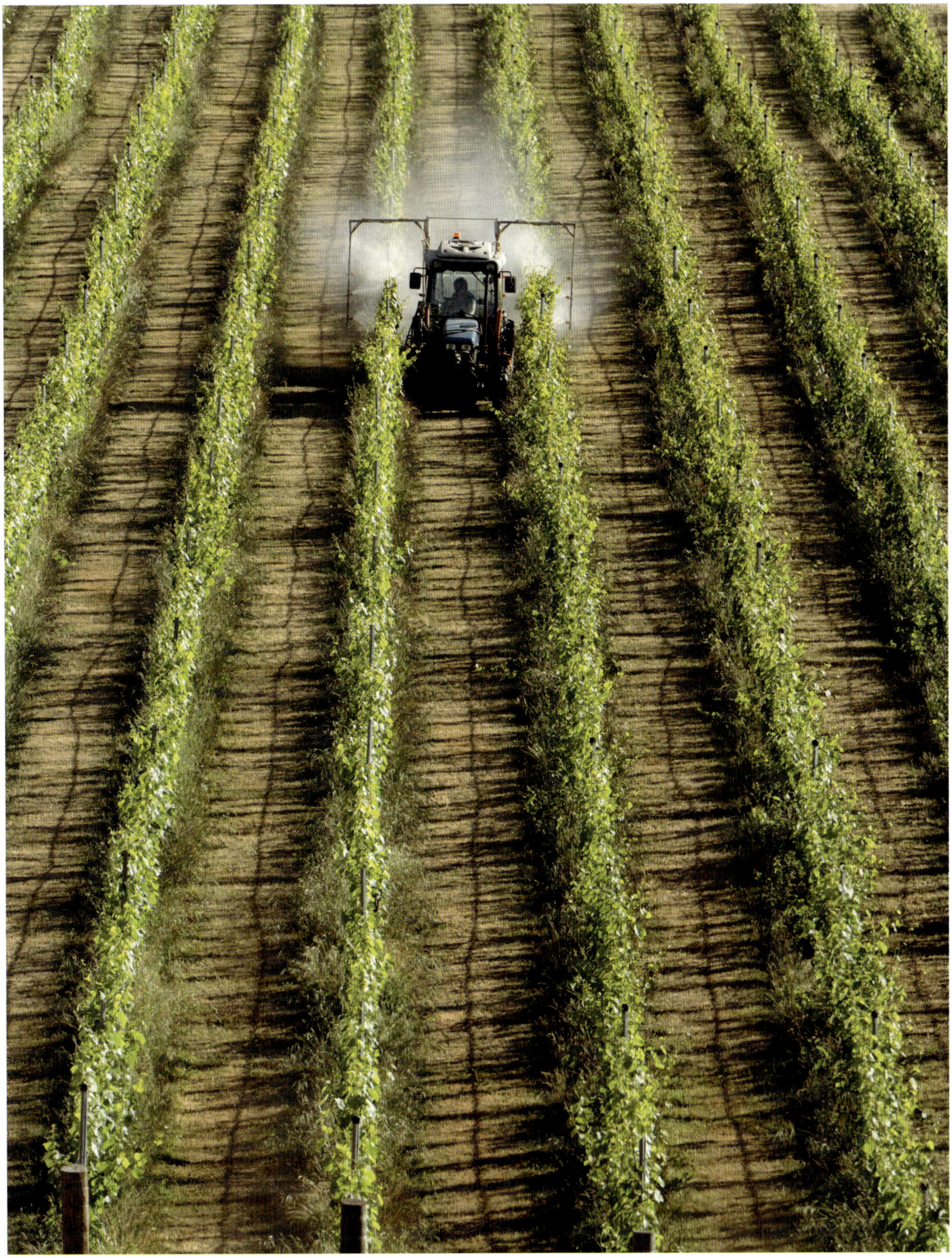

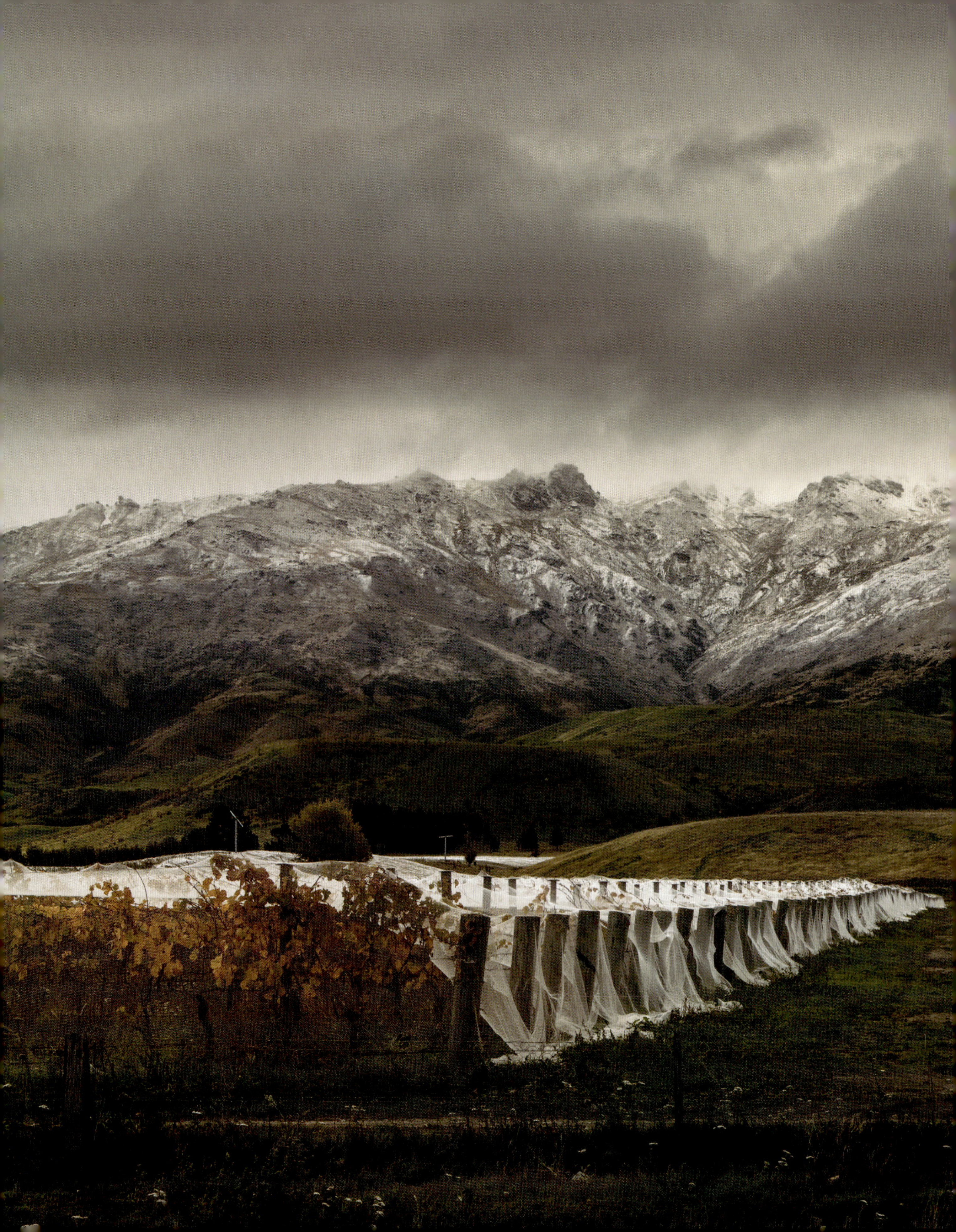

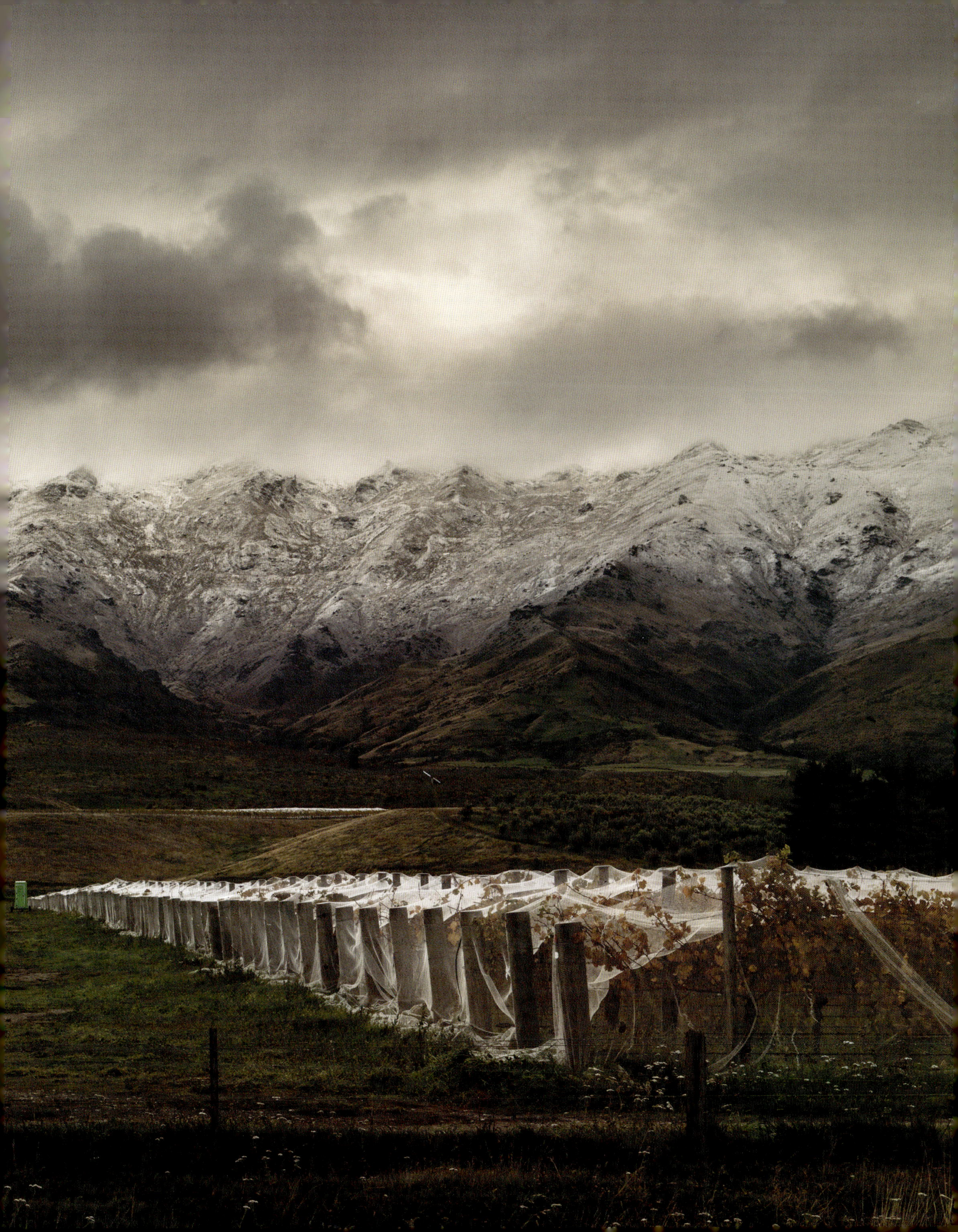

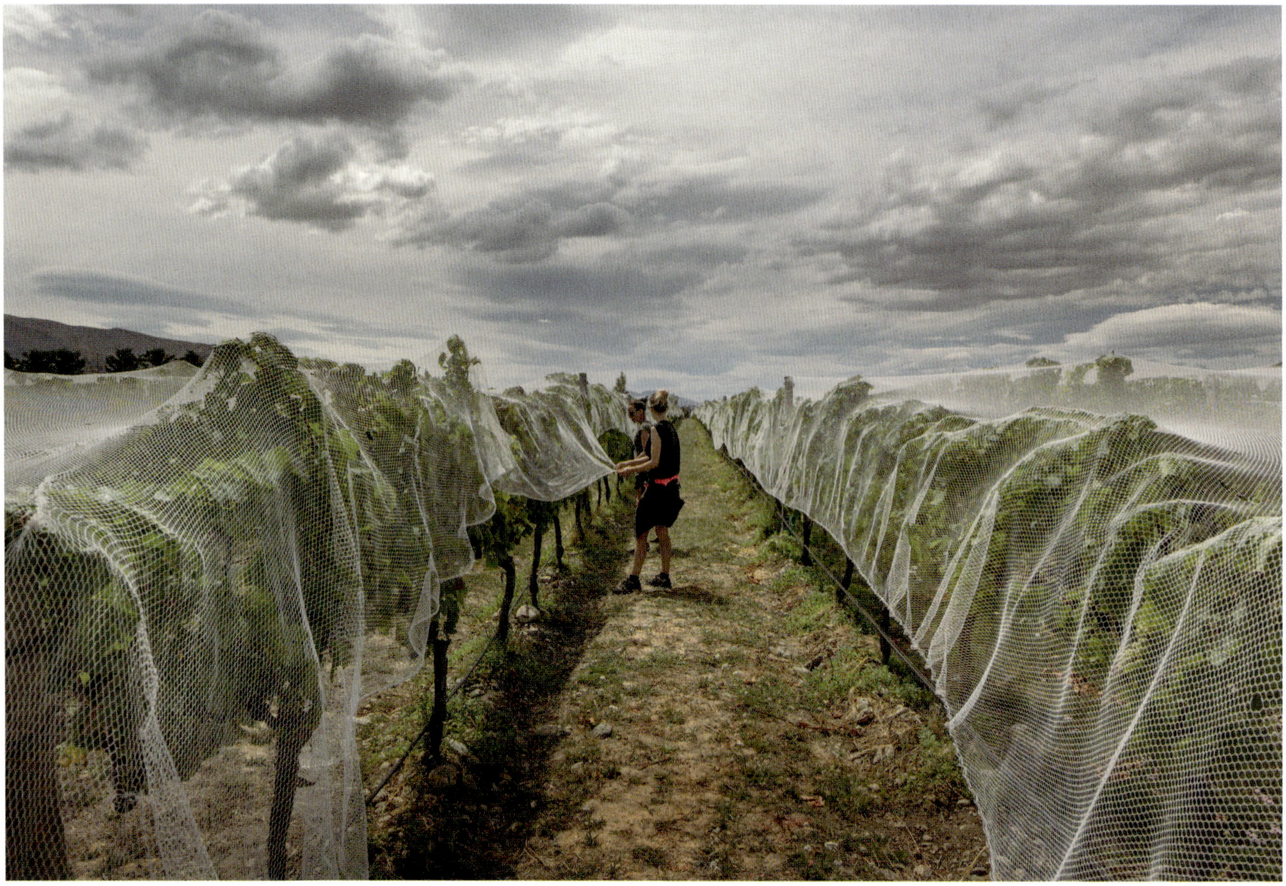

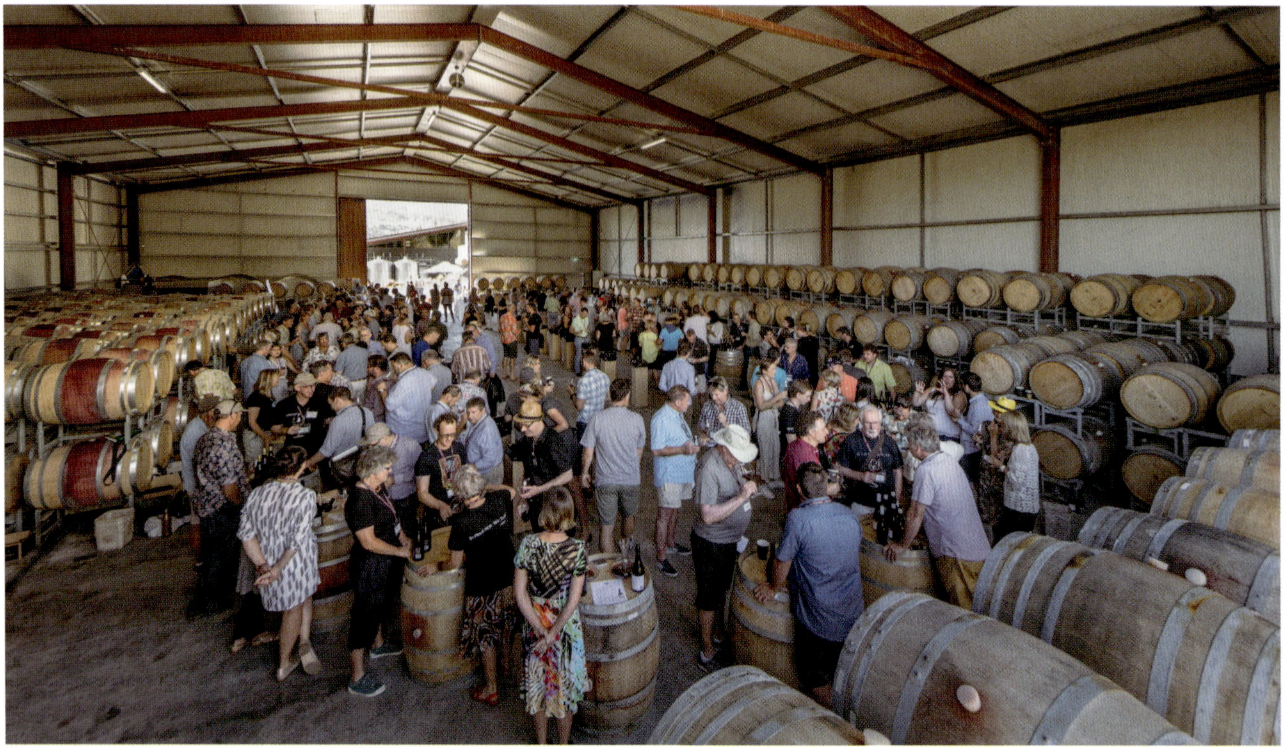

ABOVE LEFT Workers tying down nets. LEFT Grand tasting at Amisfield at Pinot Noir Conference. TOP RIGHT 'Bert the Mechanic'. MIDDLE RIGHT Harvest in full swing. BOTTOM RIGHT Nets ready for bird protection.

Aurum

'We love the same style of wines, so we usually agree, but if we disagree, I win.'

Take a Kiwi bloke who has studied viticulture and winemaking in Australia, send him to France to work at Domaine de l'Arlot in Burgundy and introduce him to Lucie, a young Frenchwoman just starting her studies and working at the same place, and, voilà — you have a winning team.

Brook and Lucie Lawrence met in 2001, and after she finished her studies, they married and moved to Central Otago, where Brook's parents had established the 4-hectare Te Wairere vineyard just north of Cromwell in the Lowburn–Pisa sub-region. In 2005 they opened a cellar door in the quaint, primrose-yellow cottage on site, and in 2006 set up the nearby winery. They have been growing grapes and making organic Aurum wines ever since, as Lucie, a third-generation winemaker, explains. 'This is the French model. You do everything from beginning to end. You have control of every step.' Brook is the viticulturist and makes the wines with Lucie in their winery. She is the chief winemaker and general manager, and looks after the cellar door and marketing.

Sophie Meunier (née Confuron) of Domaine Jean-Jacques Confuron in Burgundy, this student exchange programme between the two wine regions dates back to 2006. In 2017, Aurum was one of 10 Central Otago wineries that took part in the special celebrations in Burgundy, held to mark the tenth anniversary of the programme.

Another important regional event that Aurum gets involved in is the Central Otago Pinot Noir Celebration, which involves tastings and seminars, vineyard lunches and dinners, all promoting the region's wines and wineries to the world. Attending events like these helps to give Lucie ideas and food for thought, and after the very controlled and prescribed wine industry in Burgundy, she has enjoyed the freedom in New Zealand to experiment and develop opportunities.

Working as a tight team, and with all the traditions of winemaking in Burgundy behind them, plus the energy and opportunities of the New World, the Lawrence family have, it seems, struck new gold at Aurum — only this gold is not yellow, it is red and it is white.

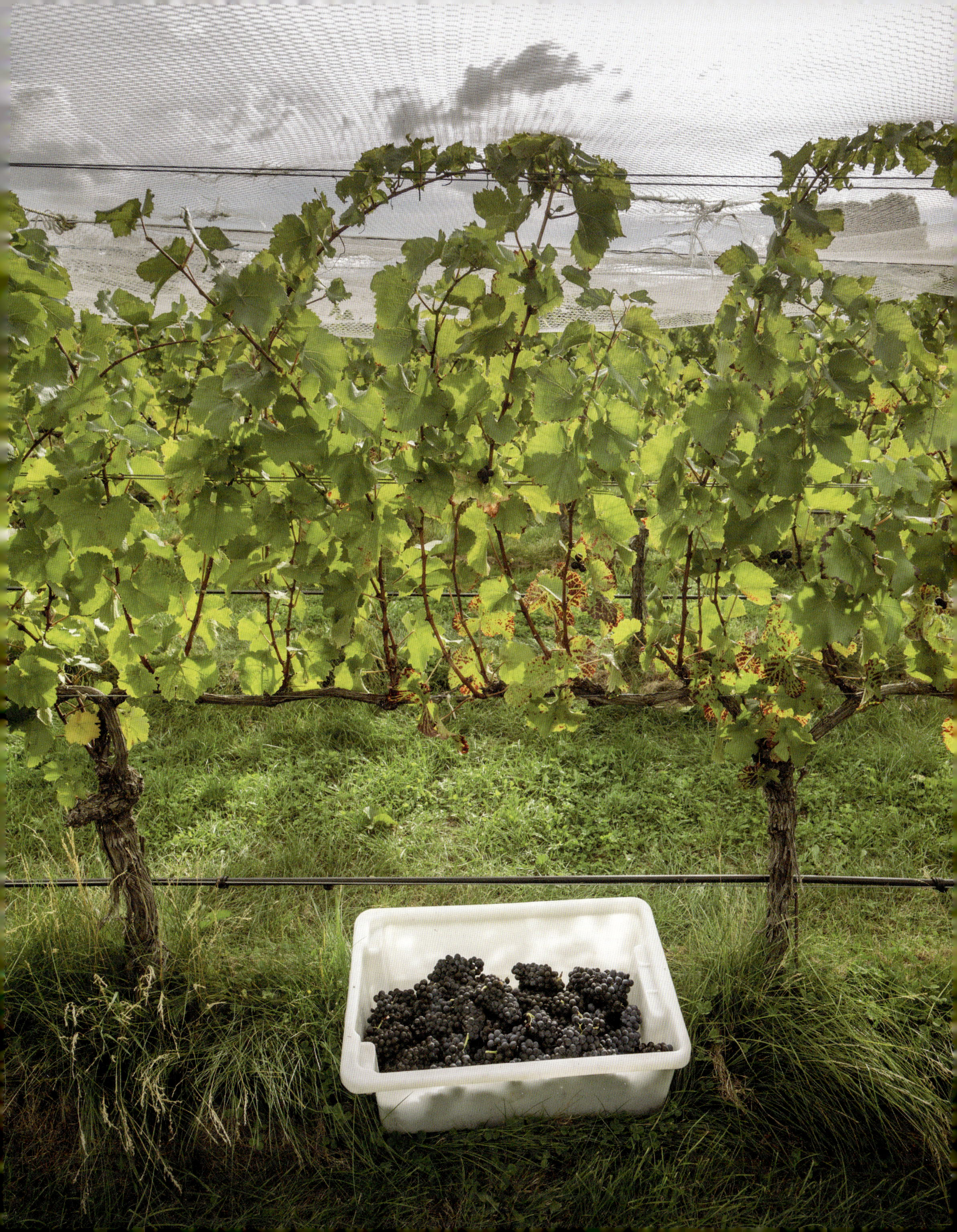

TOP Three leaves unfolded. ABOVE Installing nets. RIGHT Workers bud rubbing.

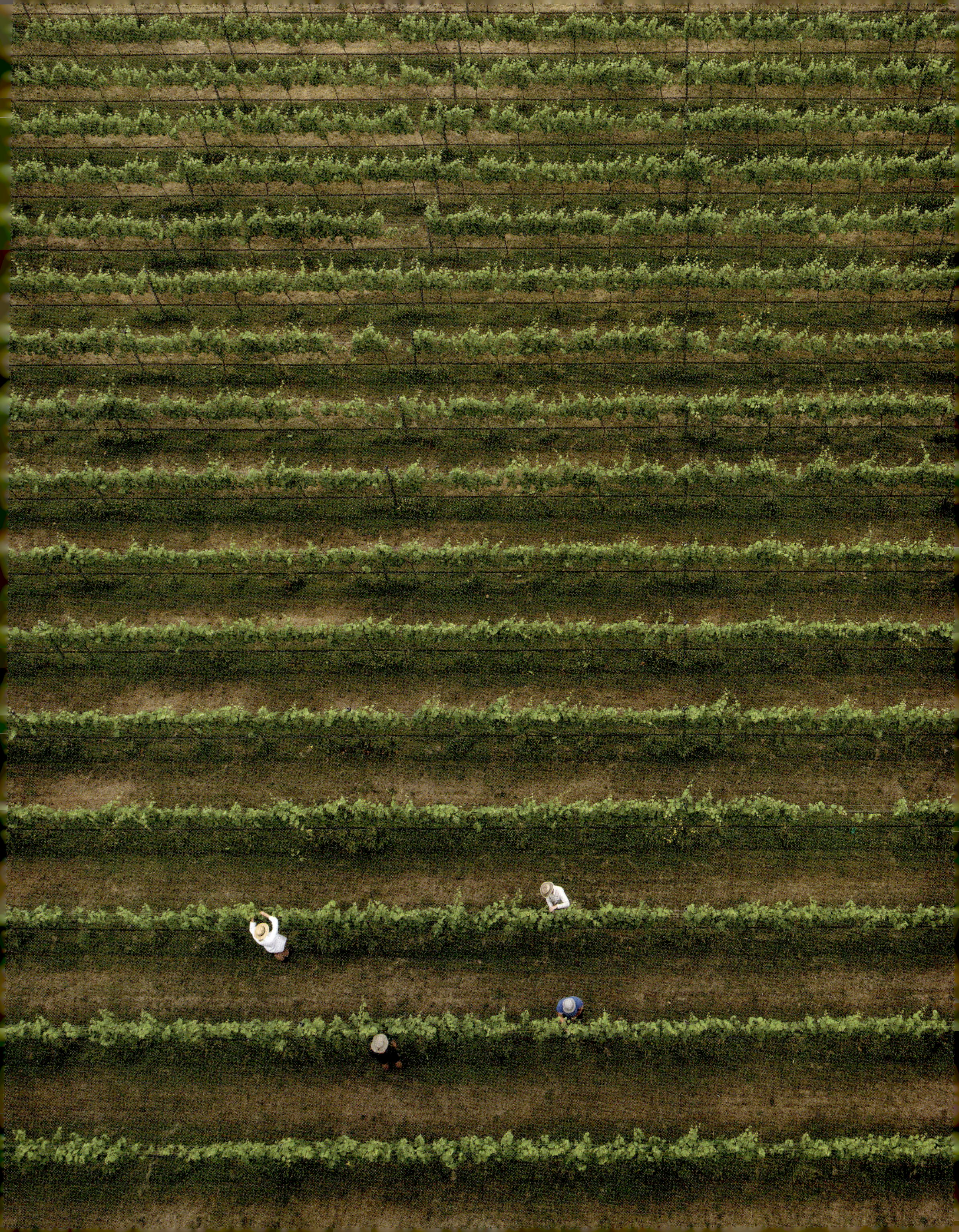

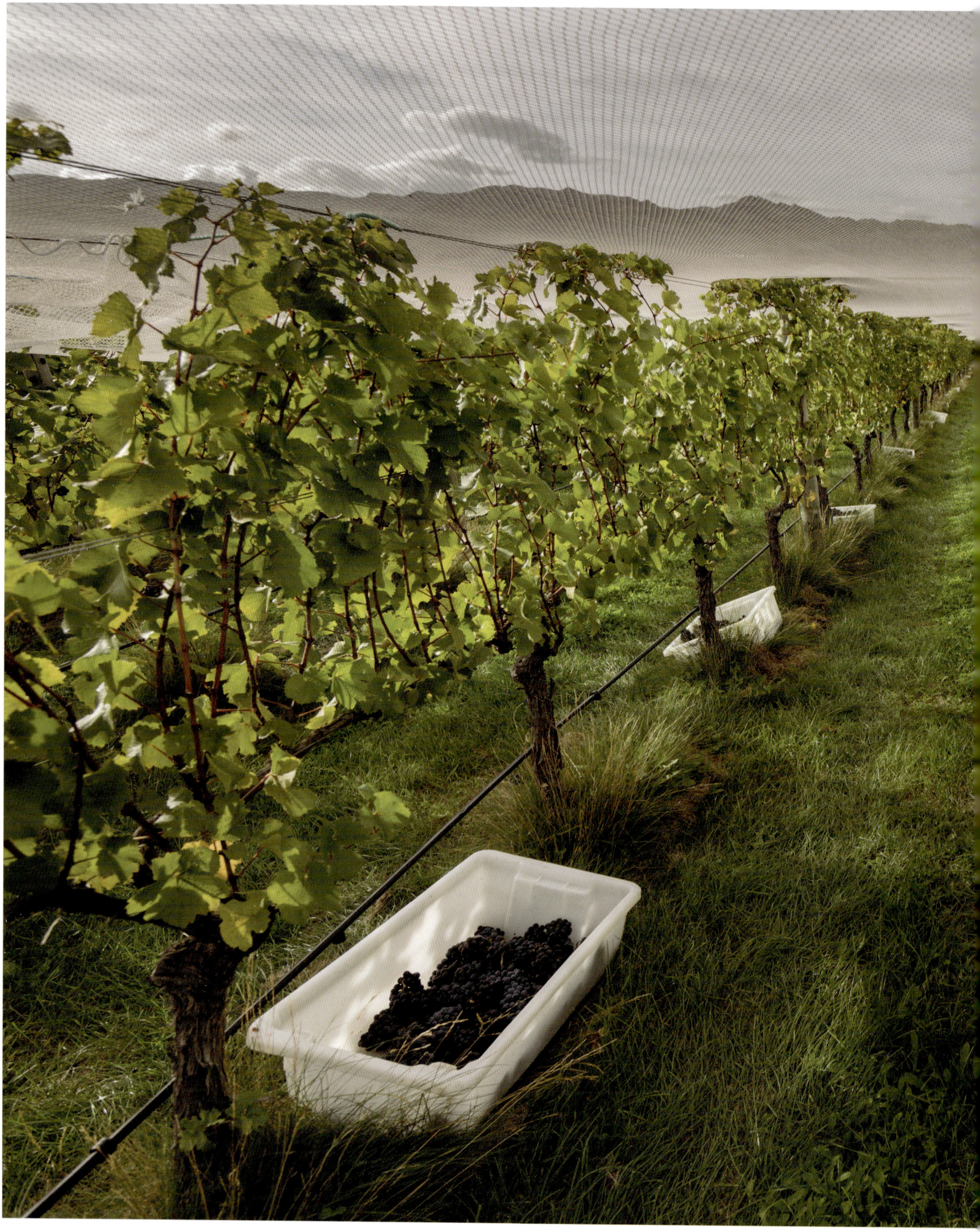

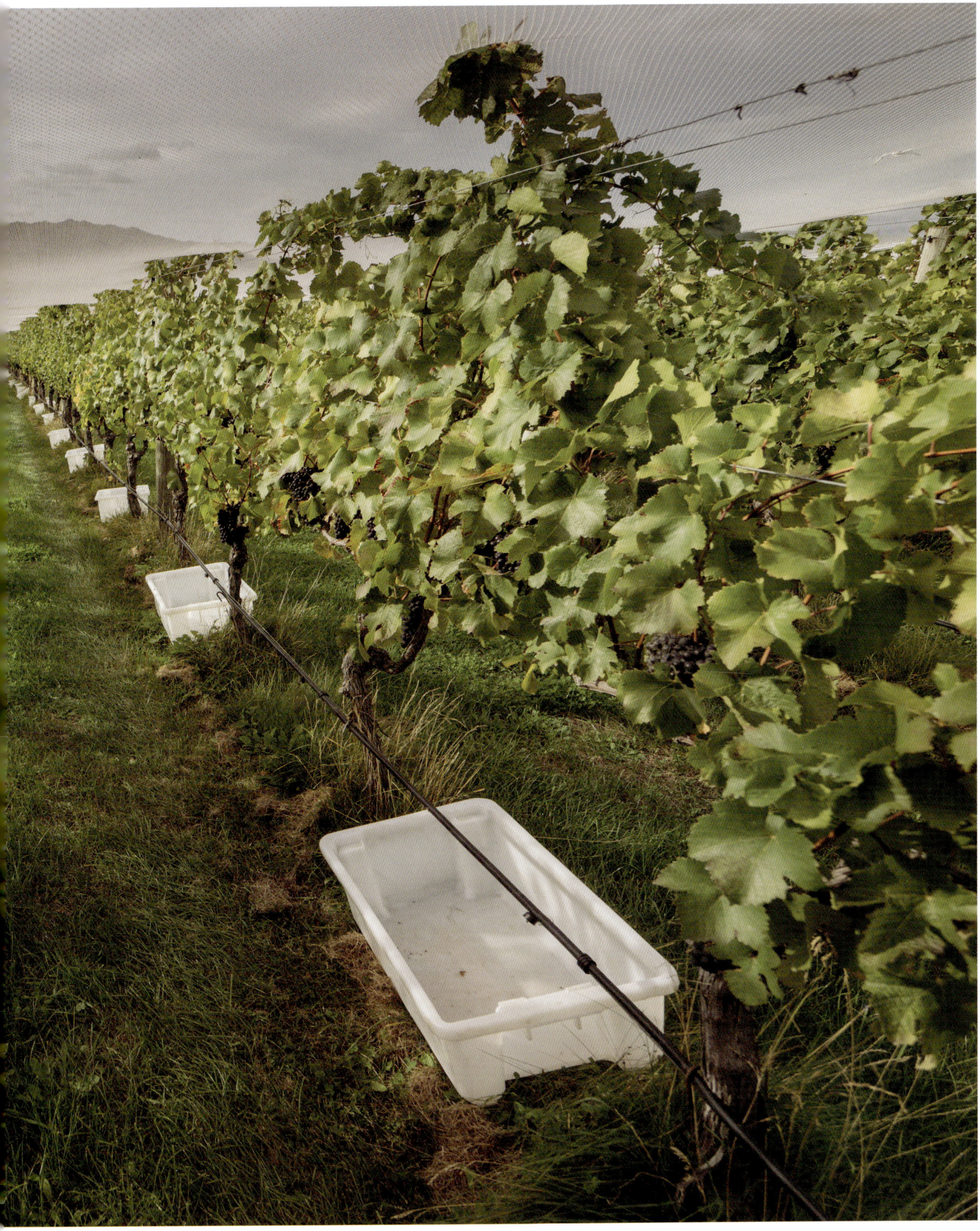

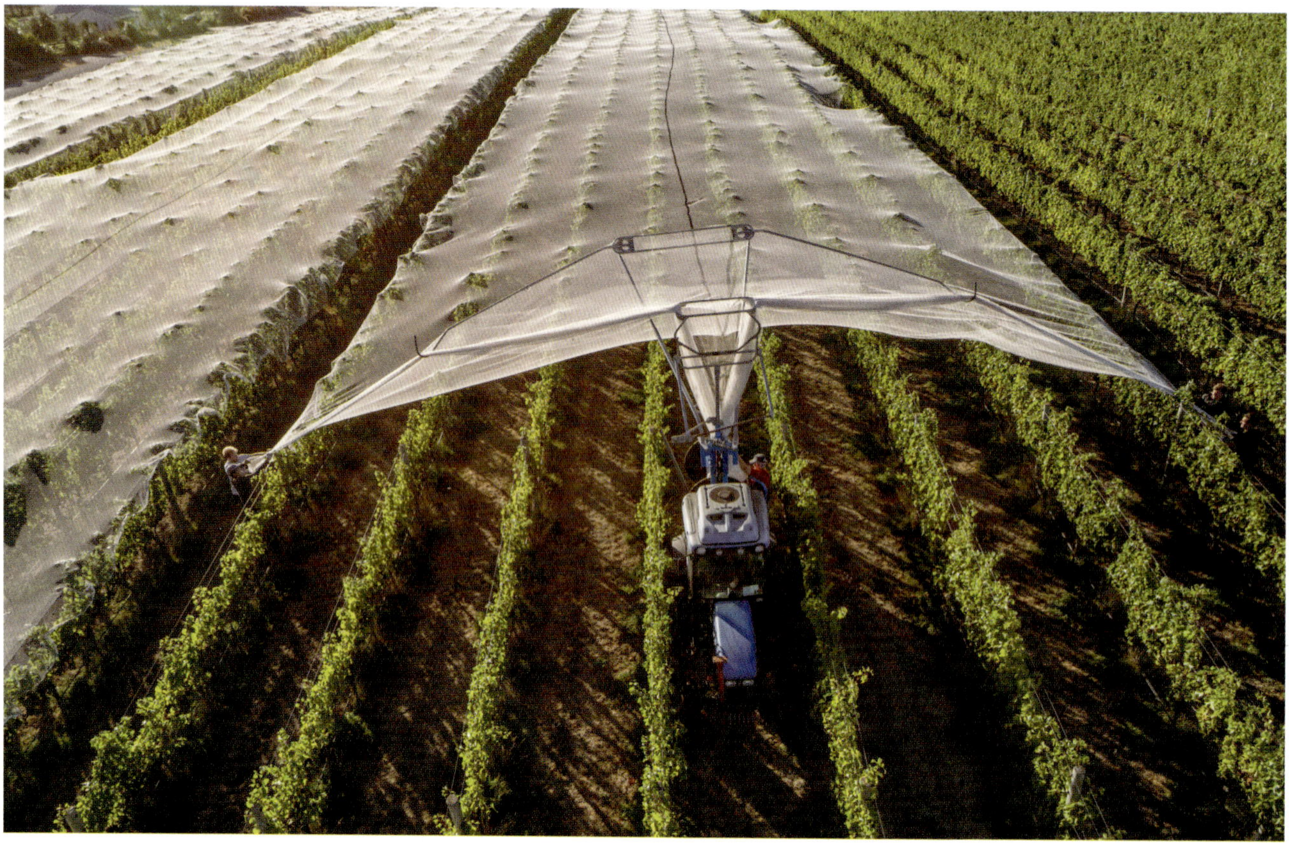

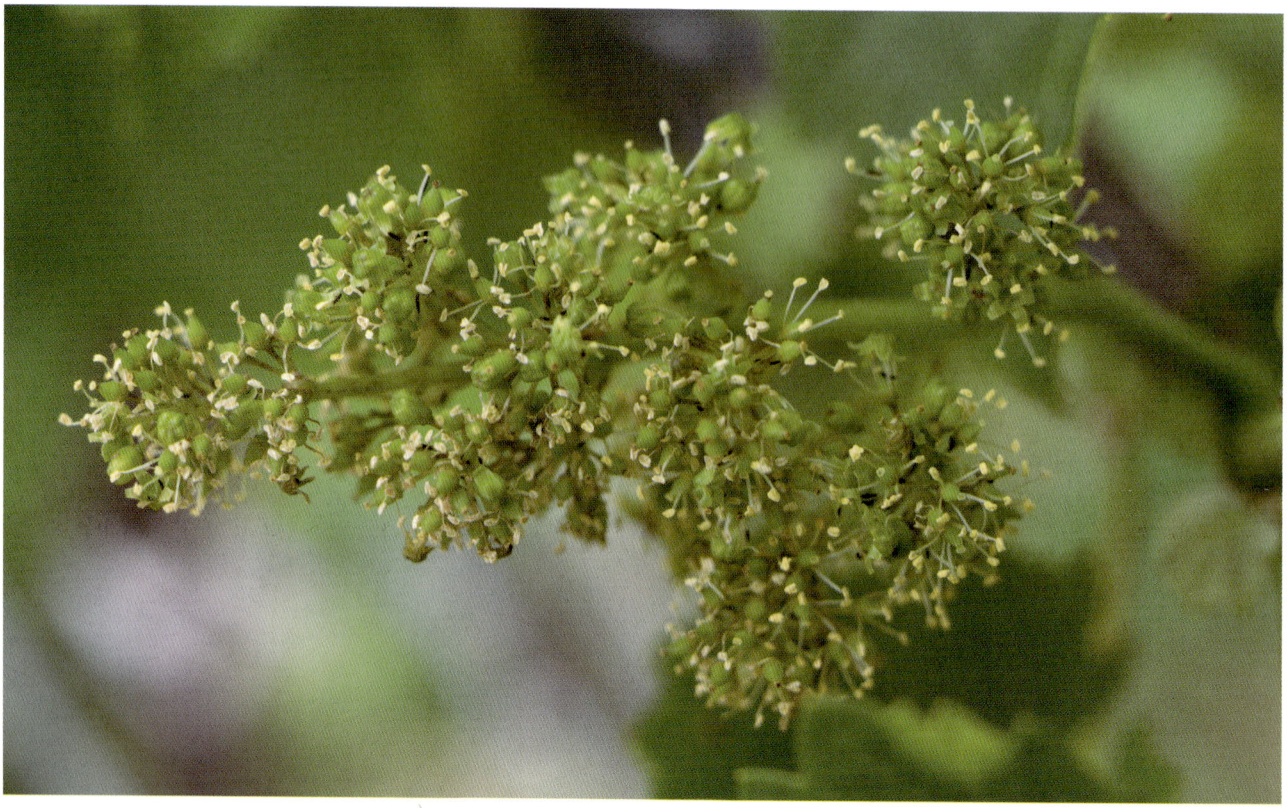

Top left Installing nets. **Left** Grape inflorescence beginning to bloom. **Top** Brook Lawrence tying nets. **Above** Pinot Noir Conference lunch.

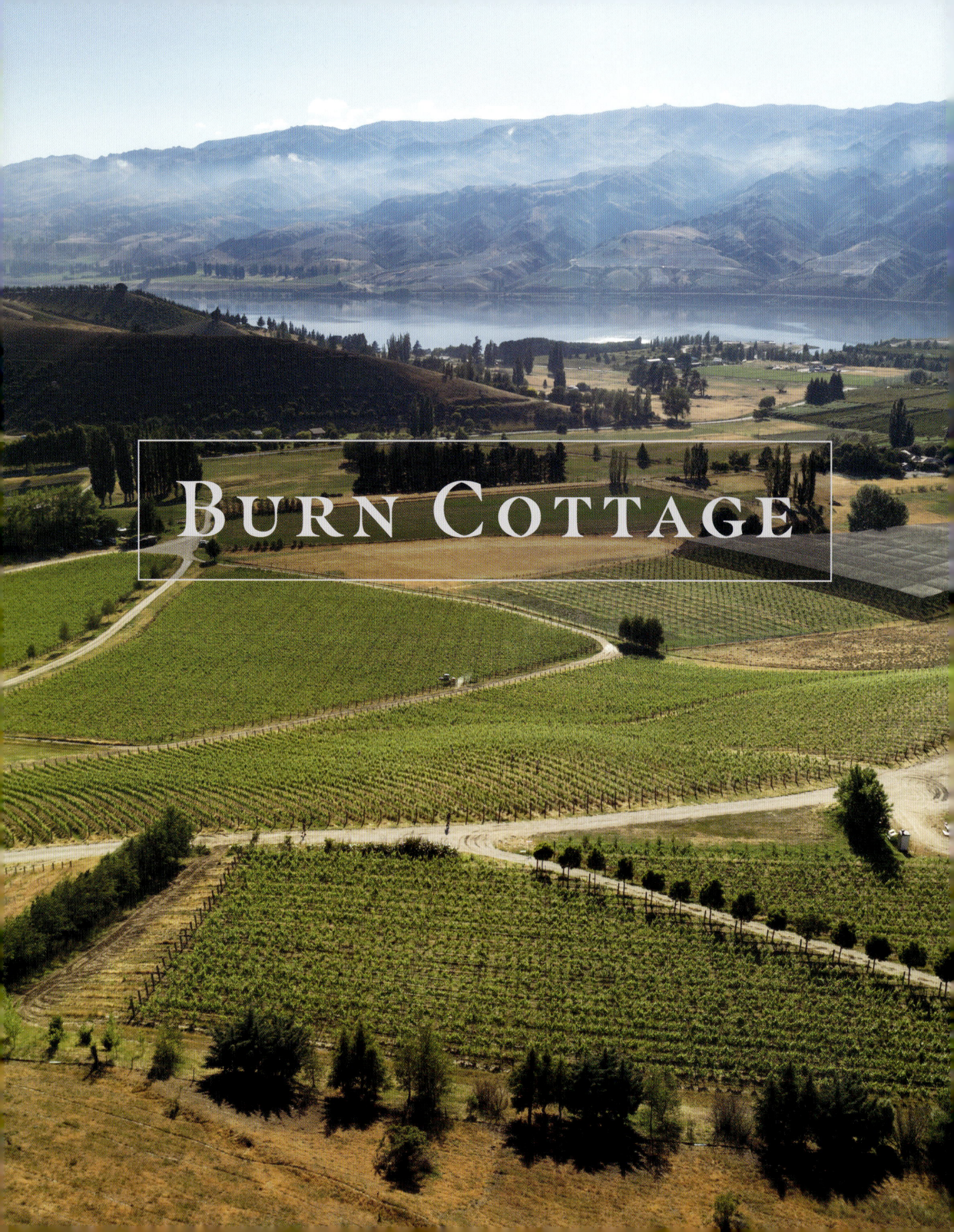

Burn Cottage

'I can't remember when I tasted a first release that was this good.'

From the start, Burn Cottage has been all about making the best wines possible, and its Pinot Noir is one of Central Otago's most sought-after labels. The American Sauvage family already had farming and vineyard interests in Germany, Australia and the US, where they are involved in the wine distribution business, when they bought the Burn Cottage site at auction in 2002. Previously used for grazing sheep, Burn Cottage lies in the foothills of the Pisa Range in the Lowburn–Pisa sub-region and is sheltered from both northerly and southerly winds. They had been looking at vineyard land in Australia, but when they saw Burn Cottage, Marquis and Dianne Sauvage liked the look of the sloping 27-hectare site so much they bought it and began planting their 10.5-hectare vineyard the following year.

Over 93 per cent of the vineyard is Pinot Noir, with small amounts of Riesling and Grüner Veltliner planted on a small upper slope and in a side valley. The climate, with less than 300 millimetres of rainfall, long, warm summer days and cool nights, is ideal for growing Pinot Noir. Early in 2018, after sign-off from the New Zealand Overseas Investment Office (OIO), Sauvage bought another 5.8-hectare vineyard along Felton Road in the Bannockburn sub-region, which they renamed Burn Cottage Sauvage vineyard. The intention is to convert this site, which has 19-year-old vines, to biodynamics and over time release a single-vineyard Pinot Noir. In the meantime, though, the

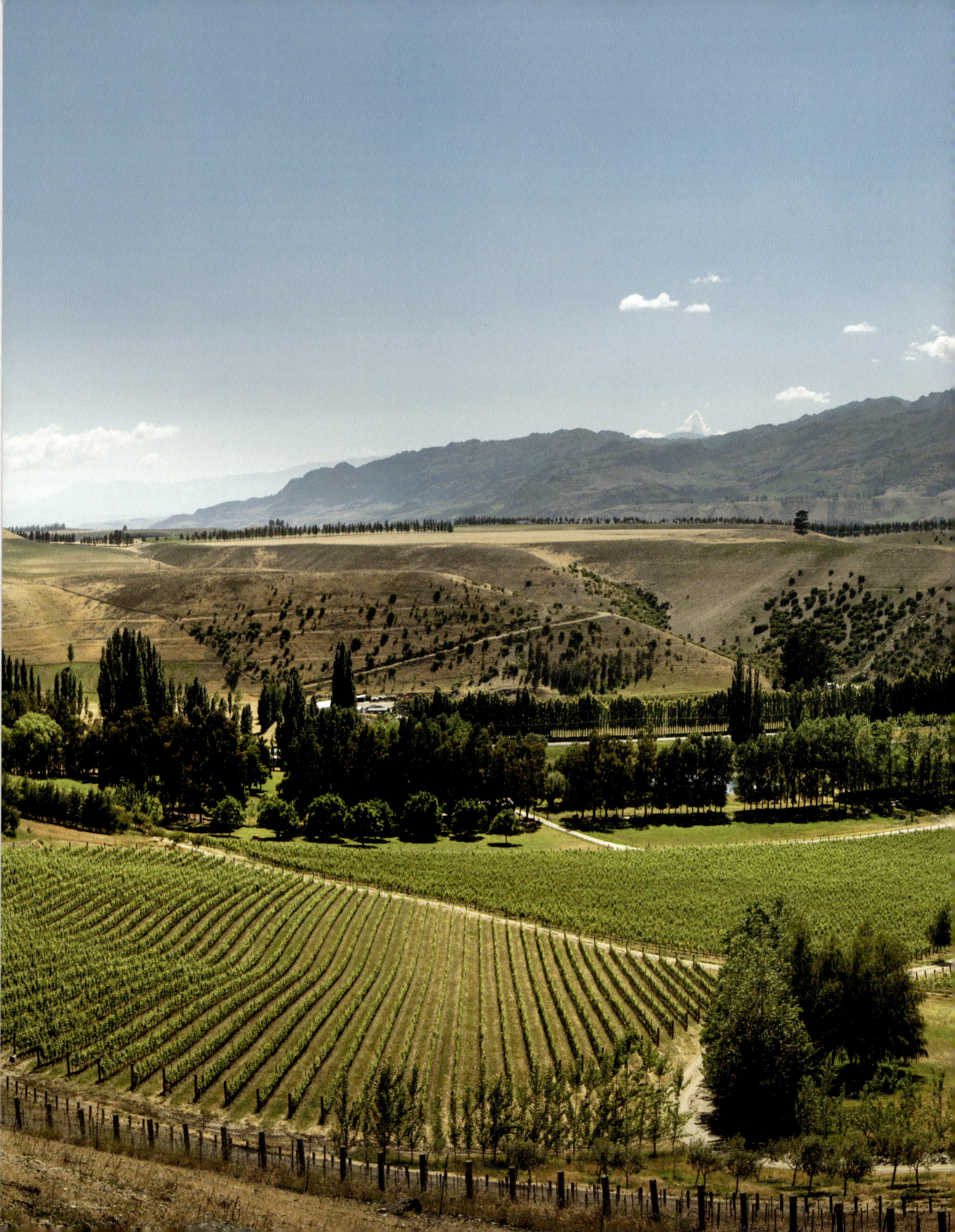

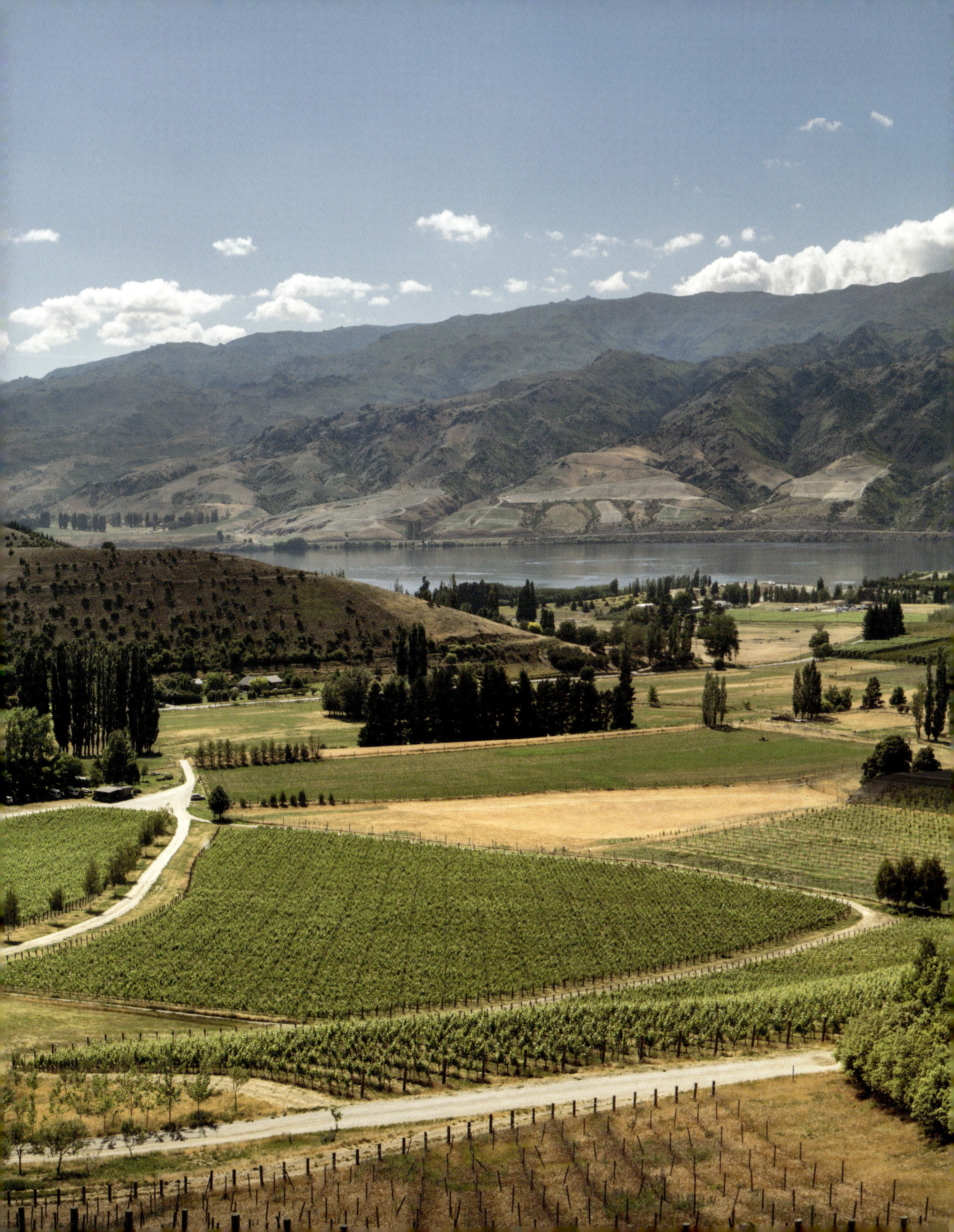

TOP Wire lifting. ABOVE Burn Cottage vineyard manager Shane Livingstone unearthing cow horns for the biodynamic manure 'preparation 500'. RIGHT Leaf thinning.

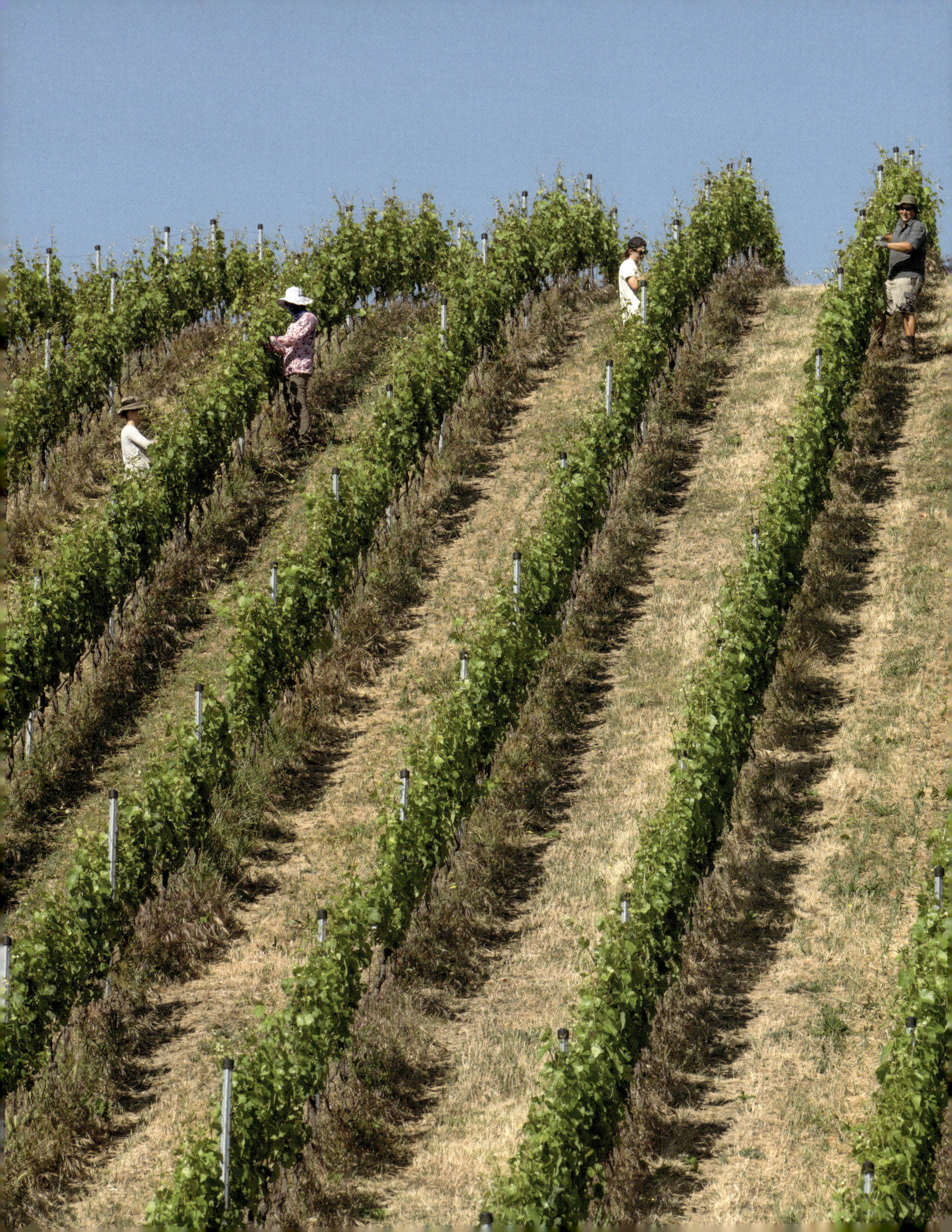

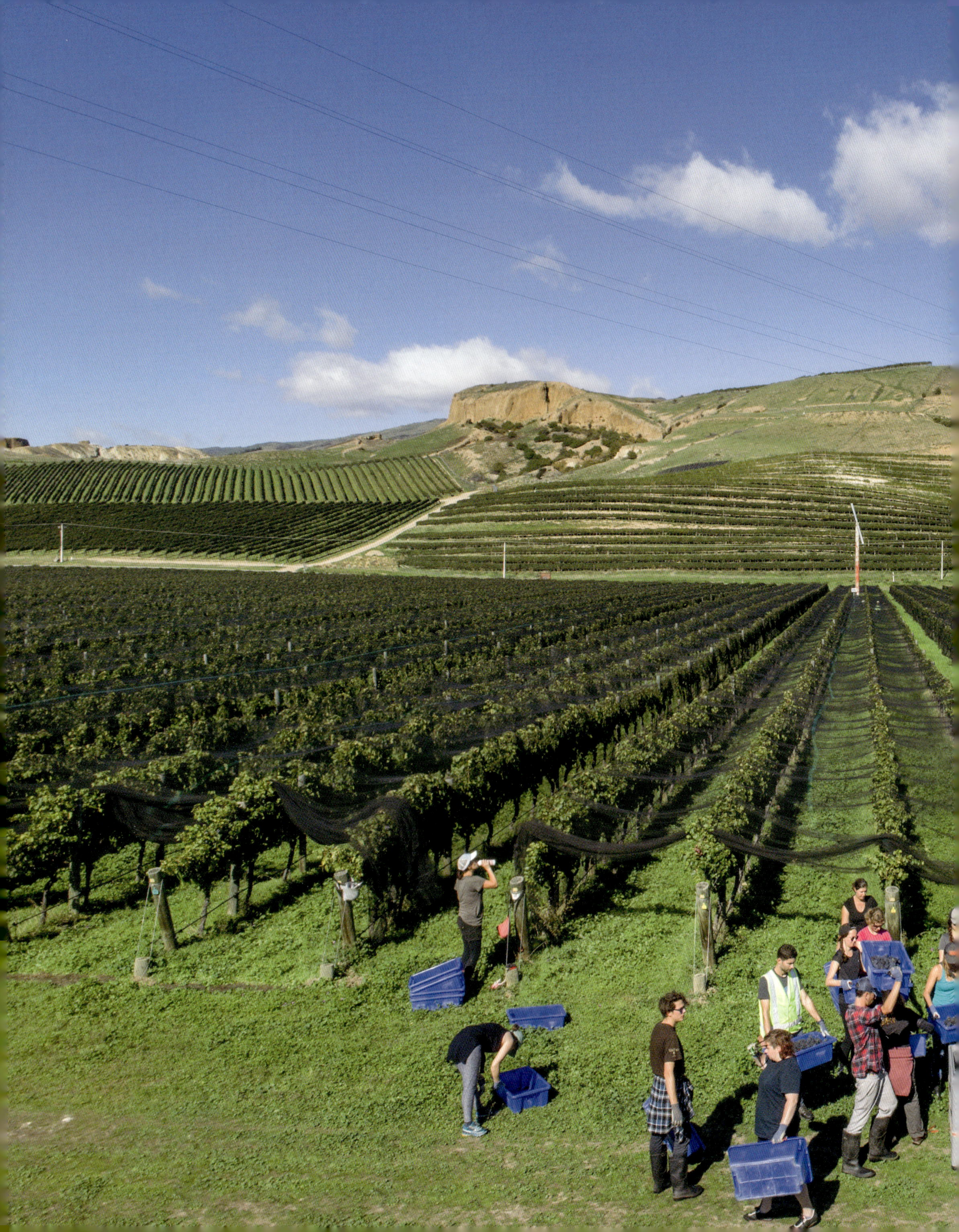

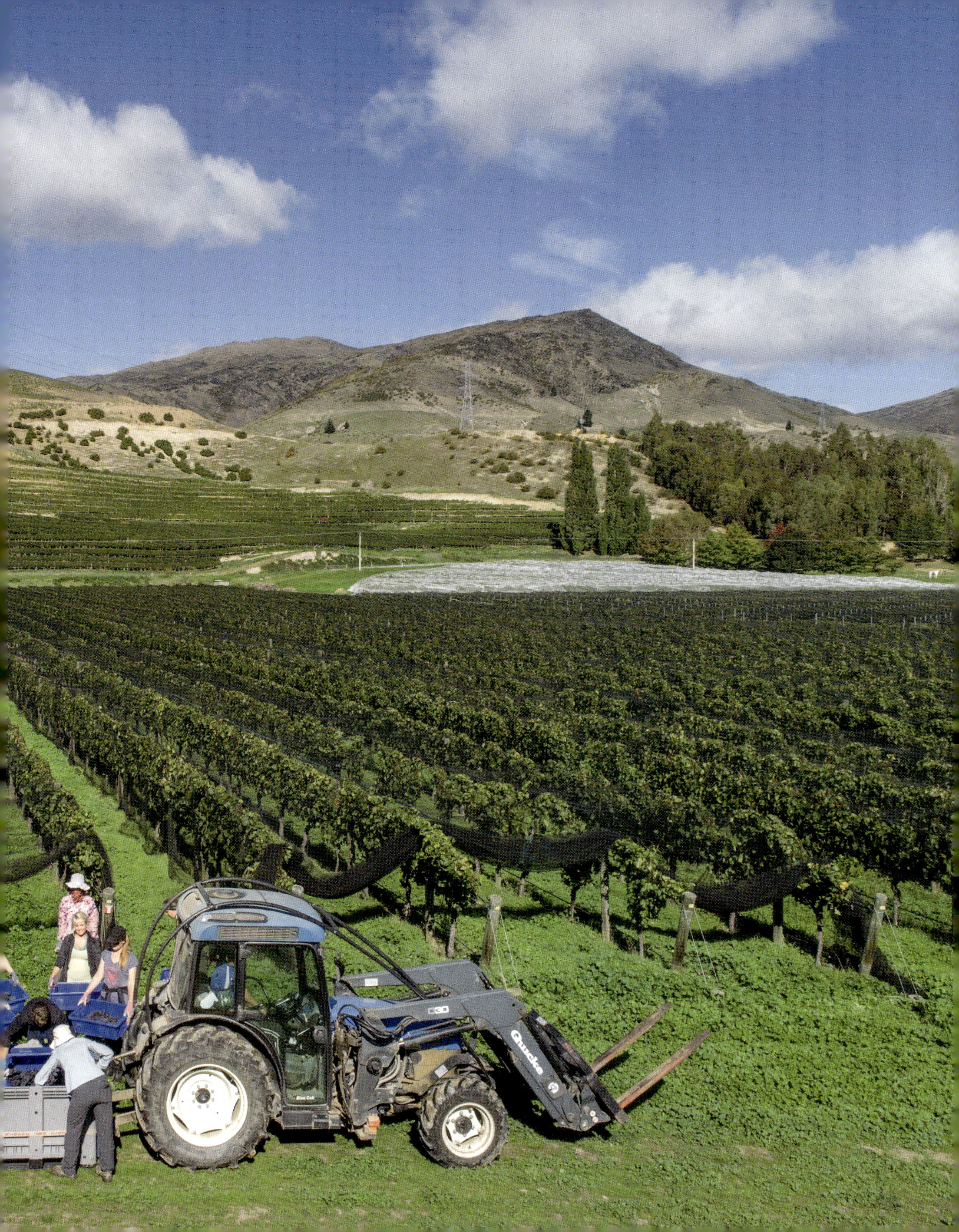
Quicke

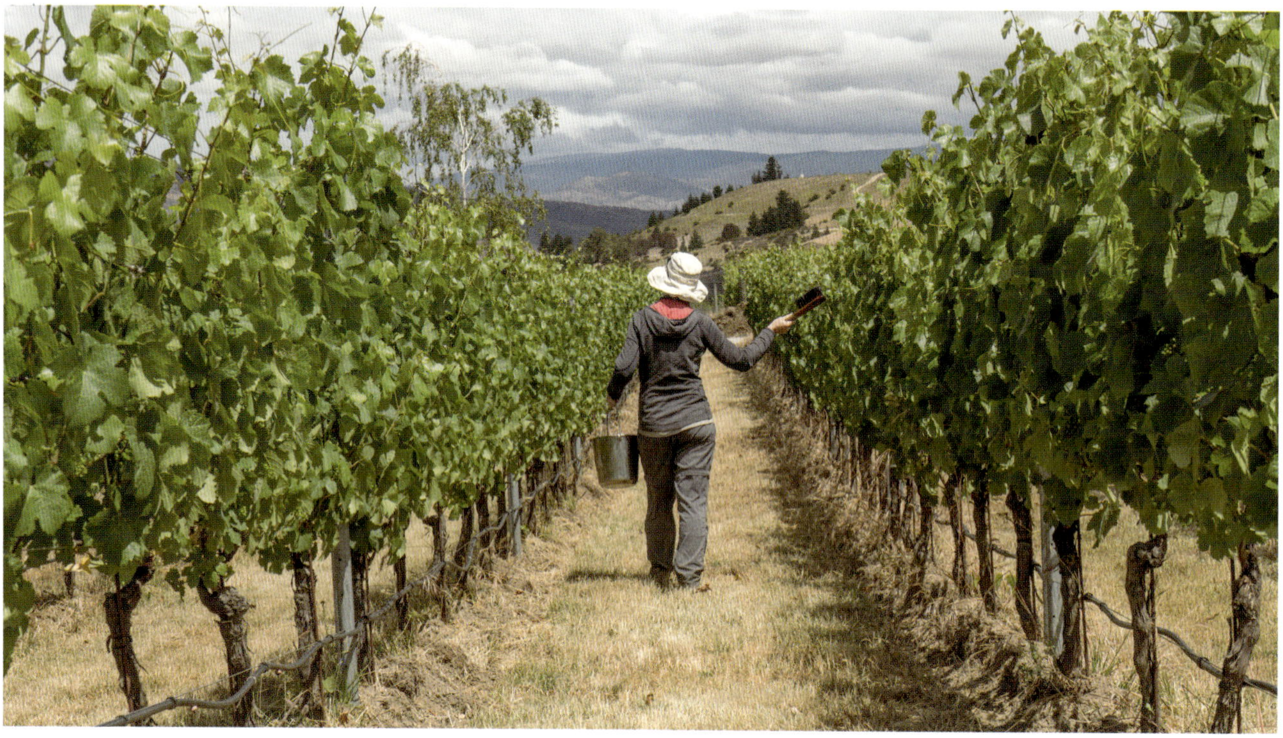

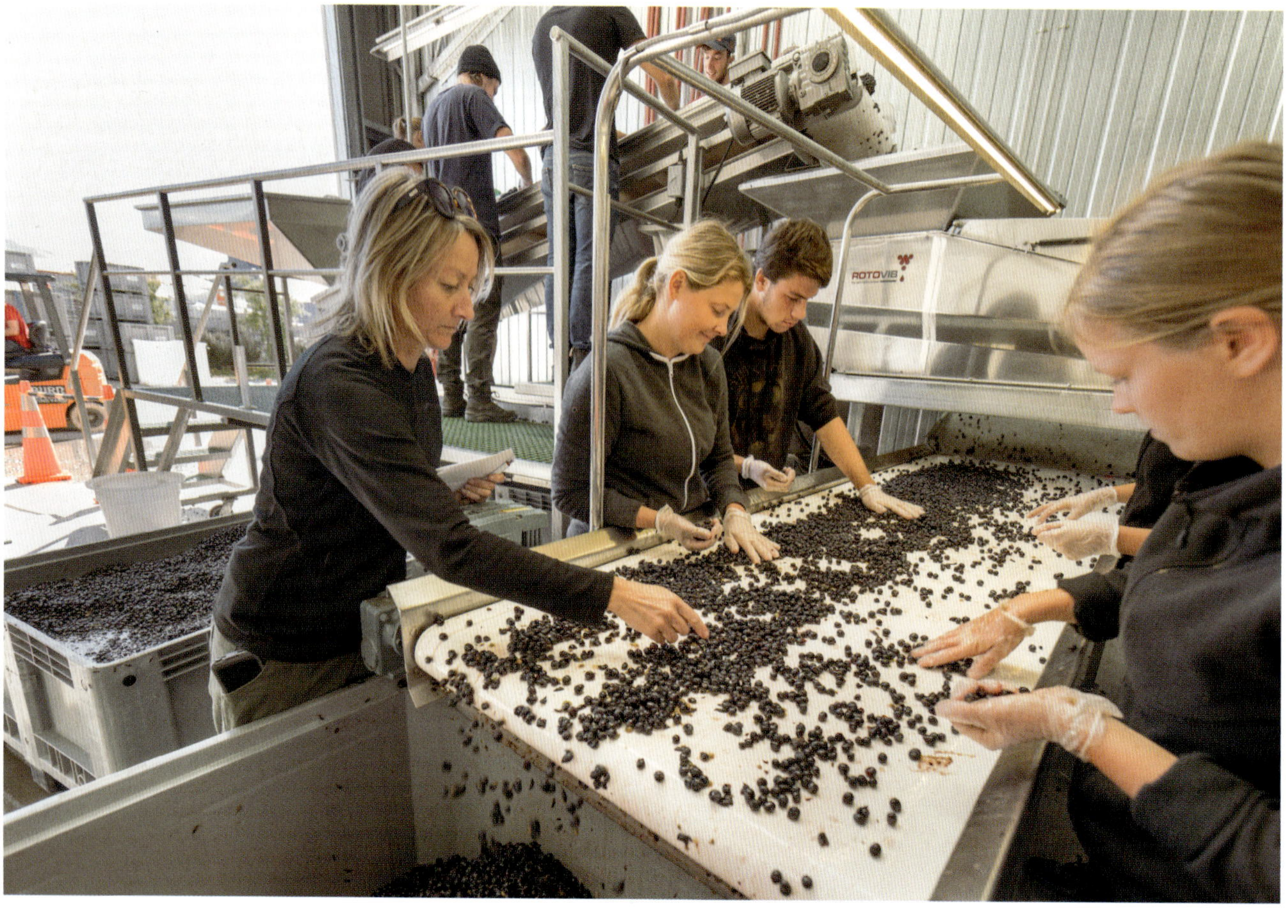
ROTOVIB

Above left Spreading the biodynamic manure 'preparation 500'. **Left** Winemaker Claire Mulholland assisting with hand-sorting grapes. **Right** Sauvage vineyard harvest.

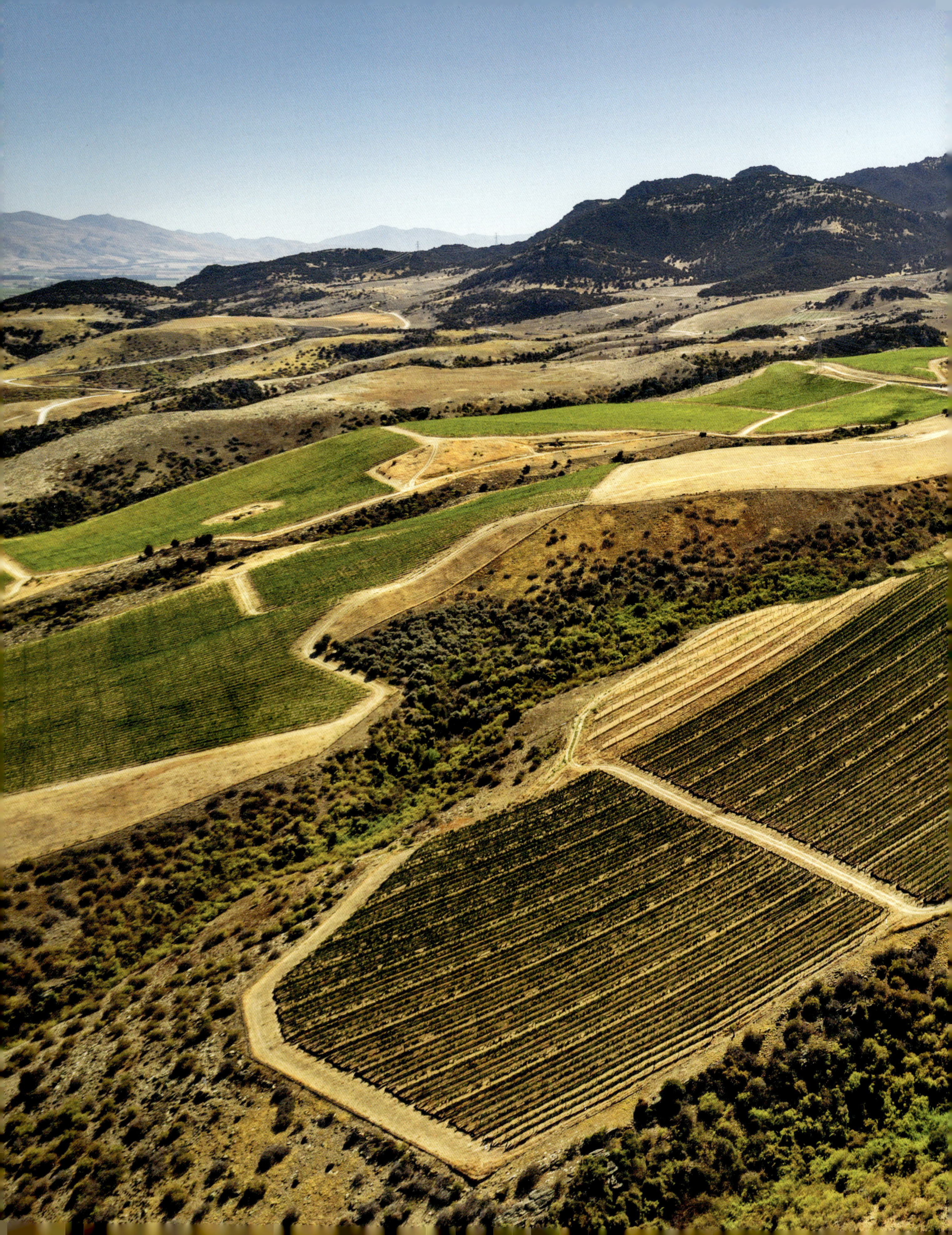

BENDIGO

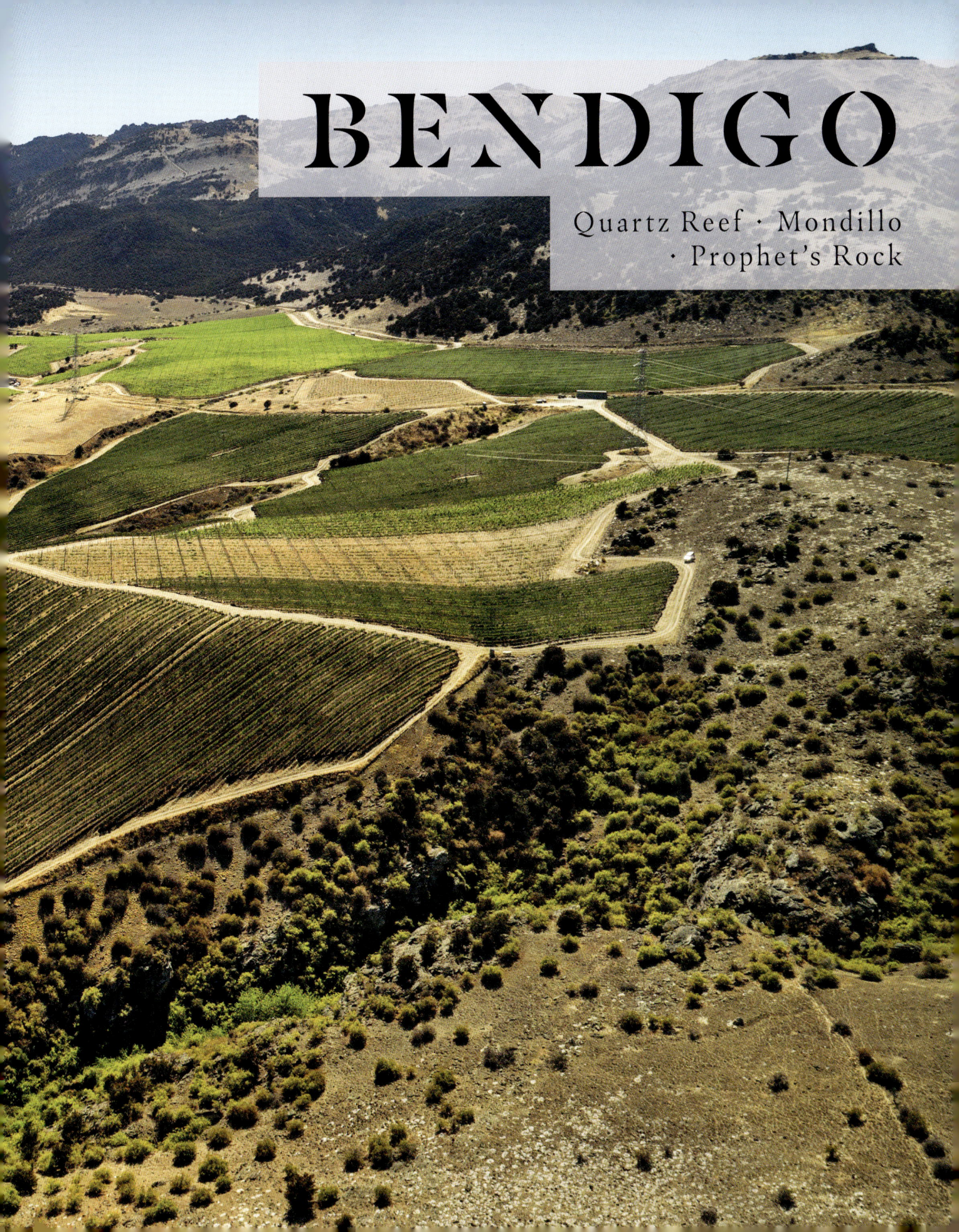

Quartz Reef · Mondillo
· Prophet's Rock

LOCATED on the northeastern side of Lake Dunstan and facing towards the northwest, Bendigo is one of the warmest sub-regions and has longer periods without frosts. It is also the newest of Central Otago's sub-regions — it was not developed until the mid-1990s. Quartz Reef was the first vineyard to be planted on the lower slopes, at 220 metres above sea level, in 1996; and the Gibbston Valley vineyards were among the first to be planted on the higher slopes, at 350 metres.

Bendigo now has around 500 hectares in vineyards; much of the fruit is sold to make wine outside of Central Otago.

Paul Pujol, from Prophet's Rock on the higher slopes of Bendigo, says, 'We get loads of sun, but cool nights. This means good acidity and full fruit flavours in our wines.'

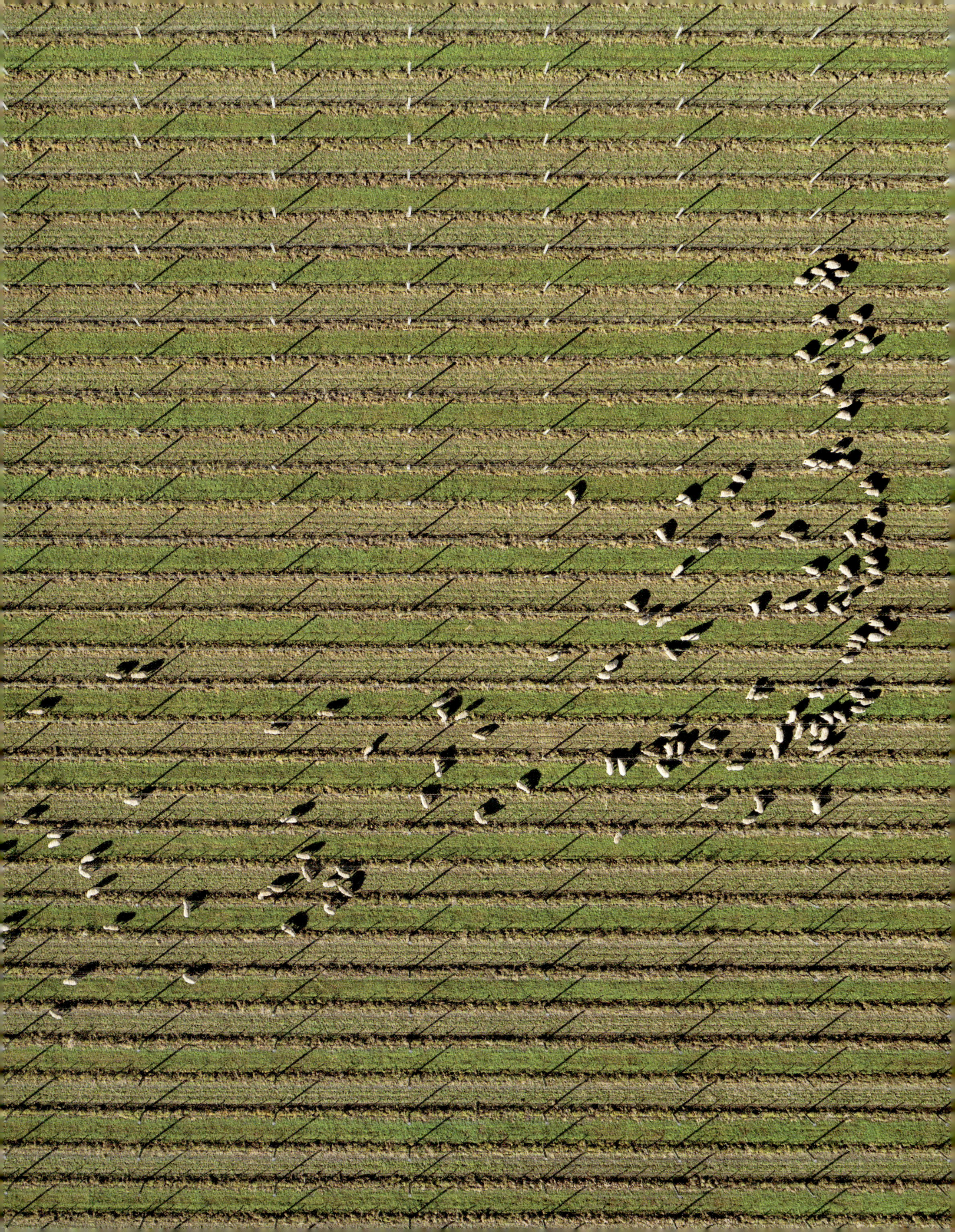

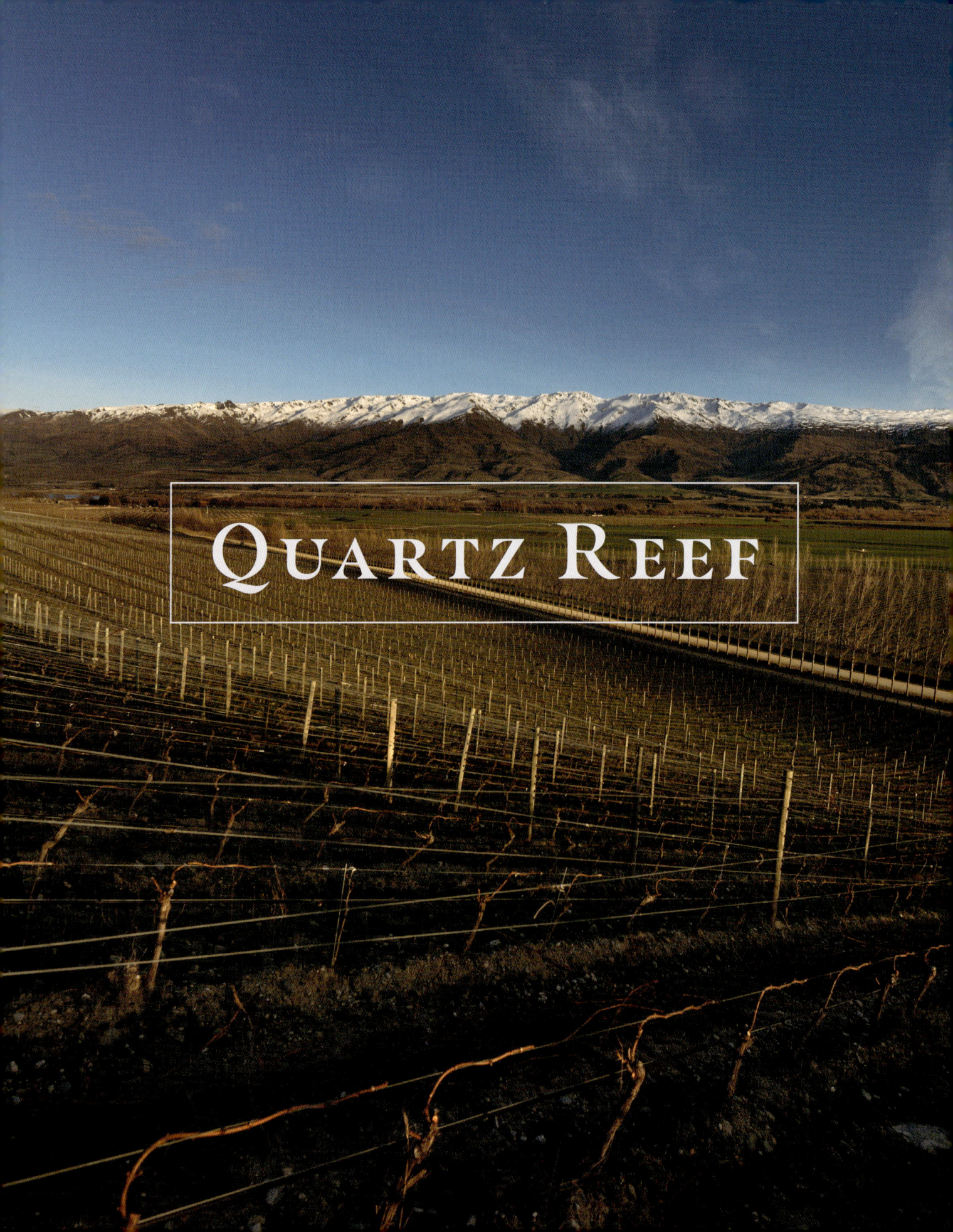

Quartz Reef

'I felt I would be a part of creating history.'

Quartz Reef was established in 1996 by Rudi Bauer, one of a handful of pioneer winemakers who helped put Central Otago on the global wine map. Bauer had grown up on a farm in Austria and trained as a viticulturist and winemaker in Austria and Germany before travelling to work at wineries in New Zealand, California, Oregon and Burgundy. He was 29 years old and already had 10 years' experience in the winegrowing industry when, in 1989, he took on the job of winemaker at Rippon vineyard in Wanaka. With the Central Otago winegrowing industry still in its infancy, Bauer felt he 'would be a part of creating history'.

At Rippon, he was soon making award-winning wines. His Sauvignon Blanc won Central Otago's first gold medal at the 1992 Air New Zealand Wine Awards, and two years later his 1991 Pinot Noir was judged Best Pinot Noir at the Royal Easter Show Wine Awards, and Best Red Wine at the Air New Zealand Wine Awards. 'That vintage was important for the region's credibility as a grape-growing area.'

Bauer left Rippon at the end of 1992 to work first in Burgundy and then in Canterbury, before returning to Central Otago in 1996 to establish Quartz Reef. Having recognised its potential for growing grapes, Bauer joined forces with the owners of Bendigo Station, and Clotilde Chauvet, to develop the Quartz Reef vineyard on the north-facing lower slopes of the high-country station. Quartz Reef takes its name from Bendigo's quartz rock deposit, the largest in New Zealand. It was the first vineyard to be planted in what would later become known as the Bendigo sub-region of Central Otago.

Initially, 15 hectares were planted in Pinot Noir, Pinot Gris and Chardonnay. Bauer had realised in the early 1990s that Central Otago was Pinot Noir country: 'Sparkling wine was Plan B — if Pinot did not work.' Clotilde Chauvet, whom he had worked with at Rippon, came from a French winemaking family which owned the small Champagne house of Marc Chauvet, and Bauer himself had also been working on a Central Otago sparkling wine. Together they developed Quartz Reef Methode Traditionnelle, the sparkling wine which has become a signature wine for the company. So successful was it that, in 2008, when Chauvet returned to France, and Trevor Scott, an Otago businessman, became a majority shareholder in Quartz Reef, an adjacent 15 hectares were bought and planted solely for the production of sparkling wine.

Using Pinot Noir and Chardonnay grapes, Quartz Reef has three sparkling wines in its portfolio: Brut, Vintage and Rosé. Recognised as one of Central Otago's leading sparkling wines, the 2012 vintage of Quartz Reef Methode Traditionnelle was selected as one of the 2017 Air New Zealand Fine Wines of New Zealand. To make it onto this prestigious list, a wine must be considered to display world-class quality and consistency.

In 2007, Quartz Reef started the process of converting to biodynamics, and it became fully certified in 2011. Bauer says that although the initial set-up is expensive, in the long term it is always worth it to look after your land. At Quartz Reef, the aim is to make quality wines with minimal intervention, wines that are a true expression of season and terroir.

Today, 40 per cent of Quartz Reef production is sparkling wine and 40 per cent is Pinot Noir, while Pinot Gris accounts for 10 per cent. Bauer also makes a dry Rosé, and in some years a Noble Riesling (a sweet wine made from grapes affected by botrytis, or 'noble rot').

Rudi Bauer.

In 2015, Bauer also started making a small quantity of Grüner Veltliner, a cool-climate wine from his homeland. Also known as 'Rudi's Grüner', it is a dry white wine with a bouquet of lemon, apricot and white pepper. When it comes to selling its wine, Quartz Reef exports about 40 per cent of its production to Australia, the US, the UK, Asia and Europe, and the other 60 per cent is sold within New Zealand.

Bauer has played a key role in helping to promote Central Otago as a wine region.

Besides being responsible for producing the Quartz Reef portfolio of premium wines, Bauer has played a key role in helping to promote Central Otago as a wine region. While he was at Rippon, Bauer, working with a German company, was responsible for developing a taller than usual wine bottle for Central Otago wines. The slender, distinctive bottle helped get the region's wines noticed in the marketplace and was a popular collector's piece. However, it proved to be impractical and survived for only three years. By then, though, it had served its purpose well, helping to put Central Otago wines on the map.

Along with Gibbston Valley's Alan Brady, Bauer was the driving force behind the first Central Otago Pinot Noir Celebration in 2000, which brought wine writers, critics and Pinot fans from around the world to enjoy the spectacular landscape and sample the region's wines. Bauer says Central Otago is the only place in New Zealand where people in the winegrowing industry have worked so closely together to promote their region. The Pinot Noir Celebration is now held every year, except one year in four, when there is an international Pinot Noir event in Wellington.

In 2013, Bauer was instrumental in helping establish a different connection between Central Otago and his homeland. With Bauer's help, Austrian wine-glass maker Georg Riedel invited 11 Central Otago wineries, including Quartz Reef, to attend a workshop to help determine the design of a special Central Otago Pinot Noir Riedel wine glass. The result has been a distinctive and elegant glass that highlights the aroma and taste of the region's typical fruit-forward and intensely mineral style of Pinot Noir.

As both viticulturist and winemaker at Quartz Reef, Bauer says he is always learning and aiming for more complexity in his wines. These wines have already earned him national and international acclaim. In the 1999 and 2010 Royal Easter Show Wine Awards, Bauer was named Champion Winemaker of the Year, and in 2010 he became the first New Zealander to be nominated for Winemaker of the Year in the prestigious Der Feinschmecker Wine Awards in Germany. Rudi Bauer may be Austrian by birth, but his commitment, innovation and passion for making wine in Central Otago have made him one of the region's most respected viticulturists and winemakers.

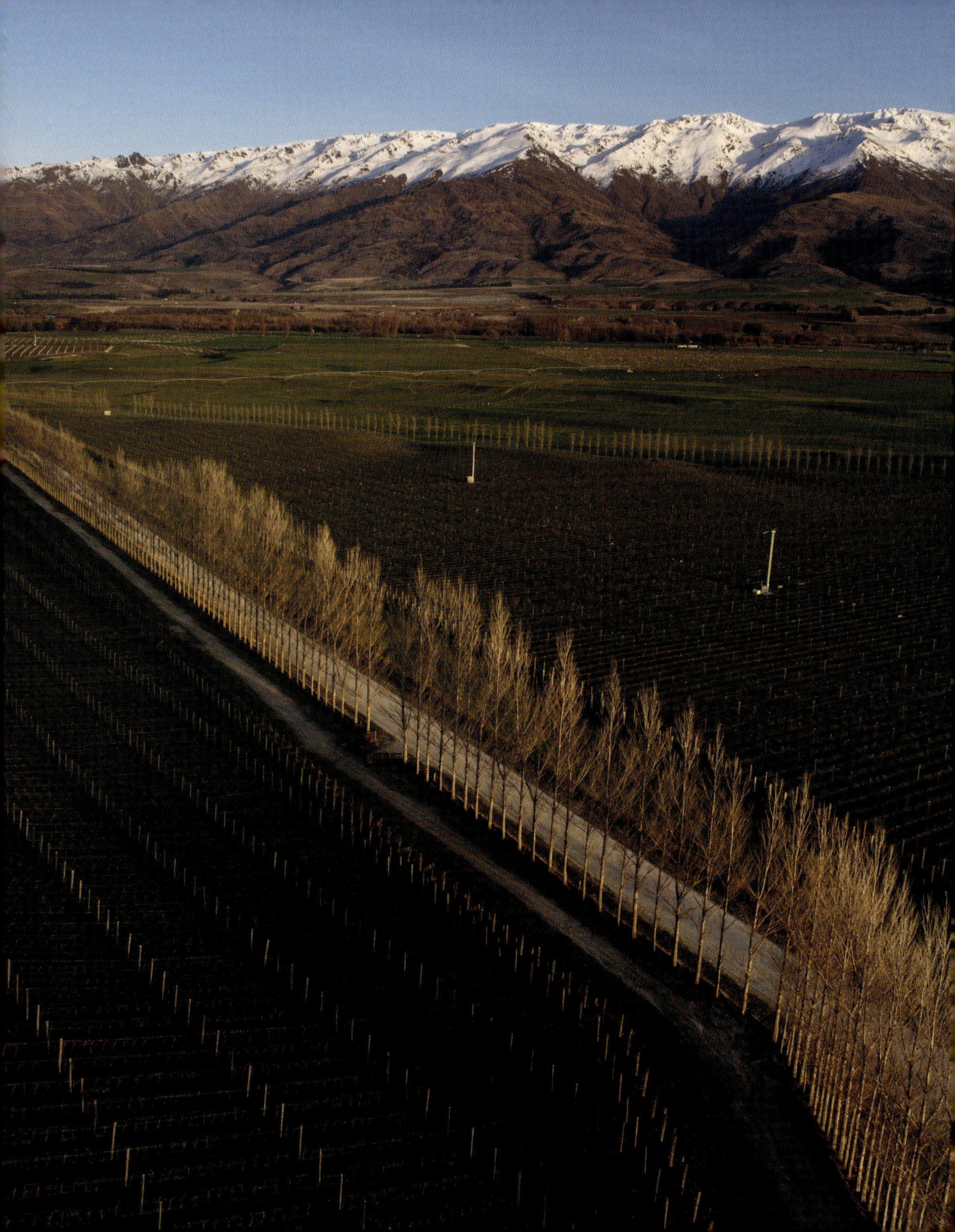

Top Merino sheep at Quartz Reef vineyard. Above Leaf spraying at Quartz Reef. Above right Chardonnay harvest. Right Vineyard in winter.

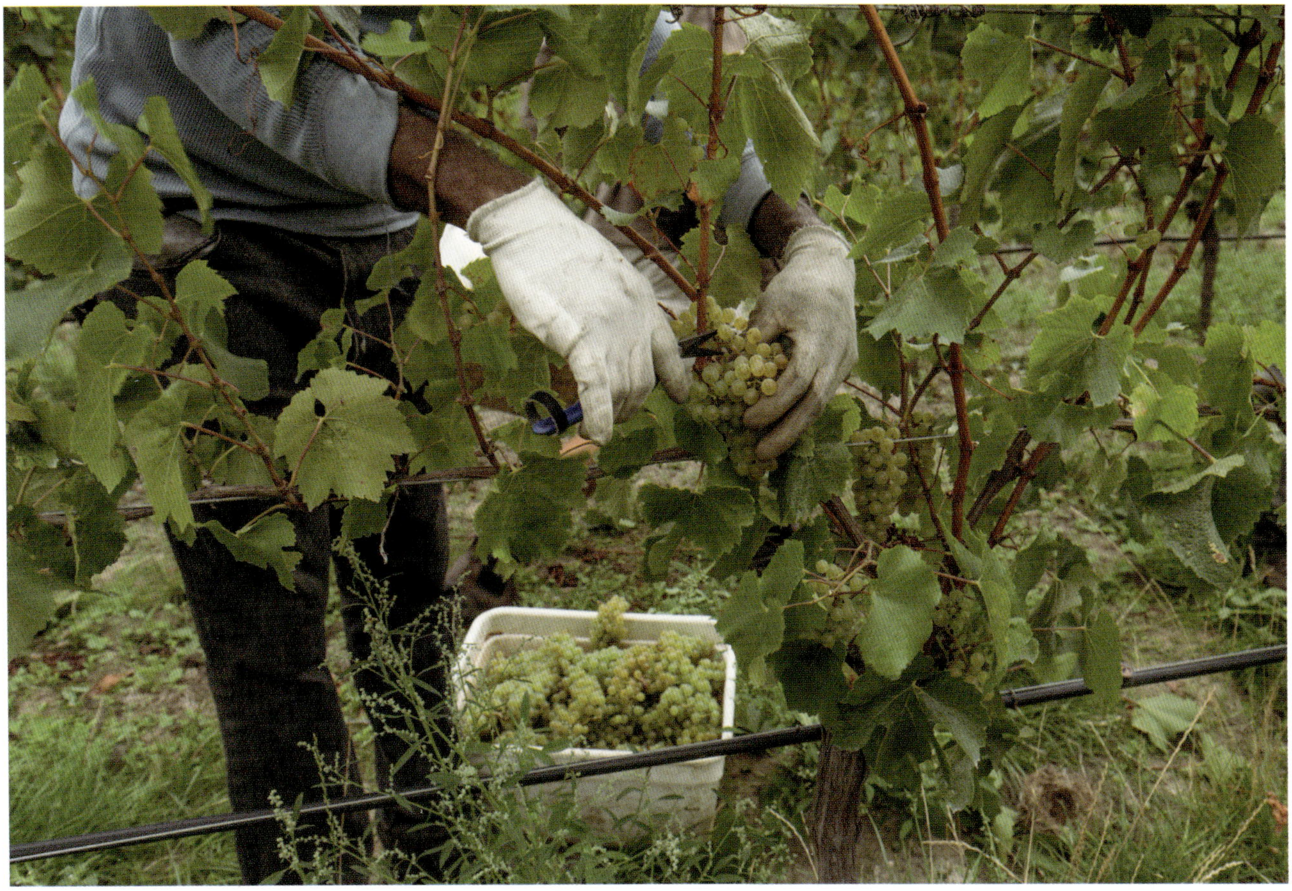

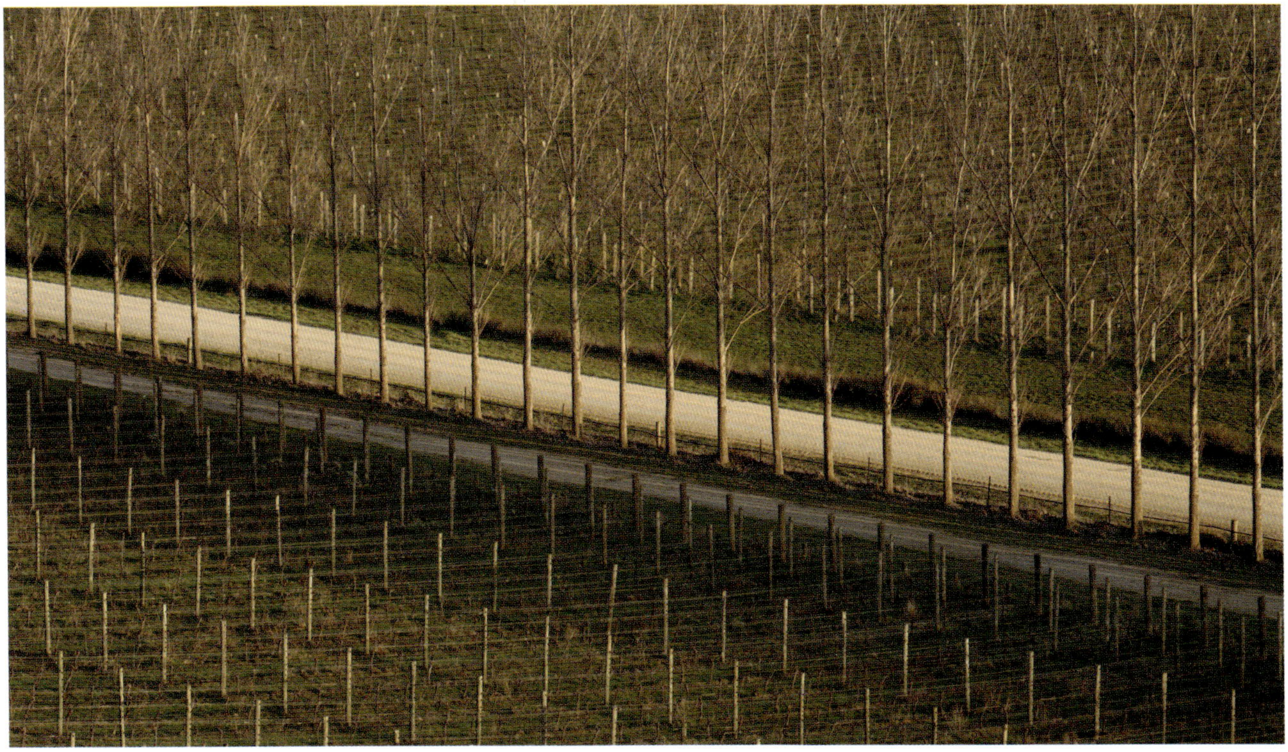

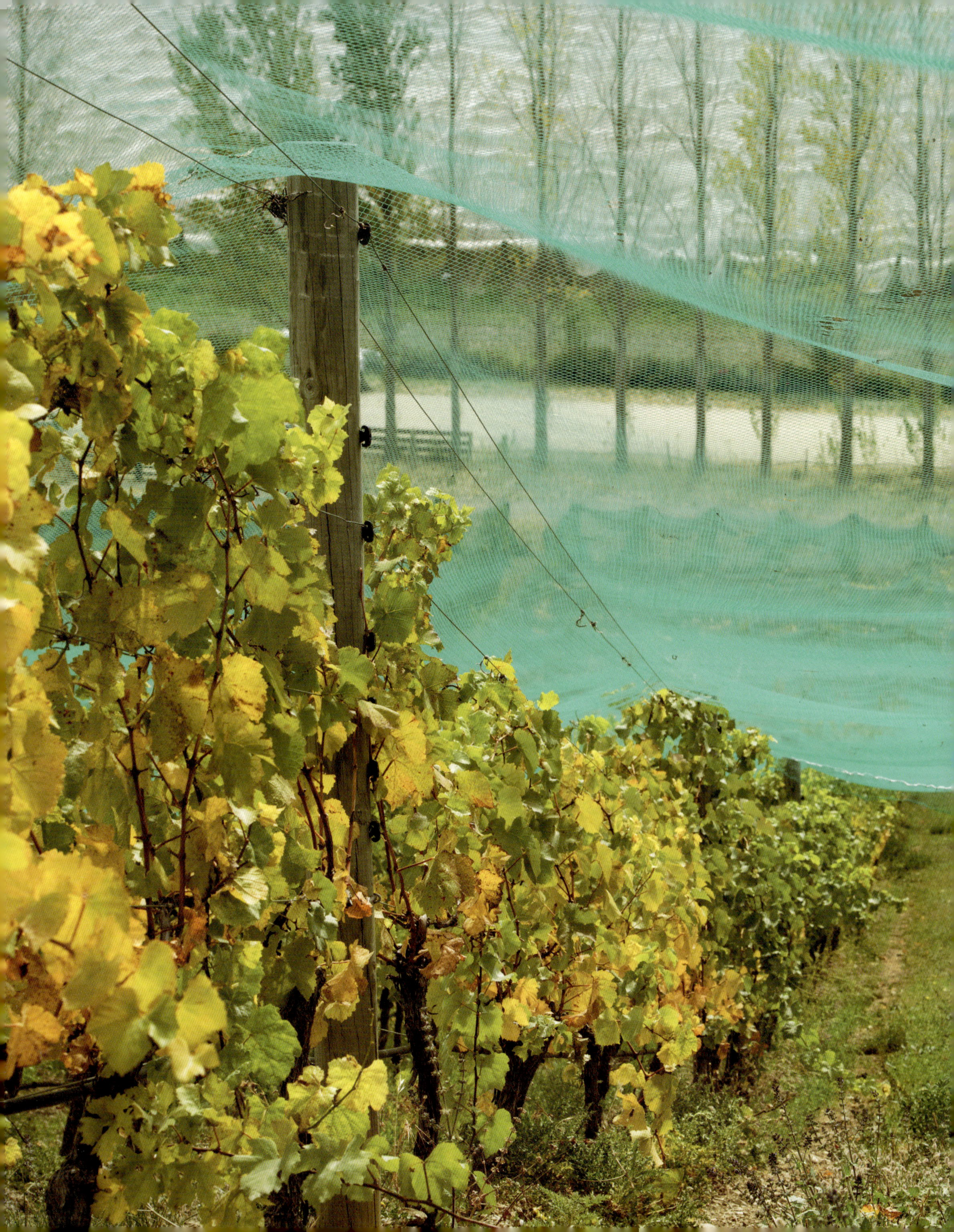

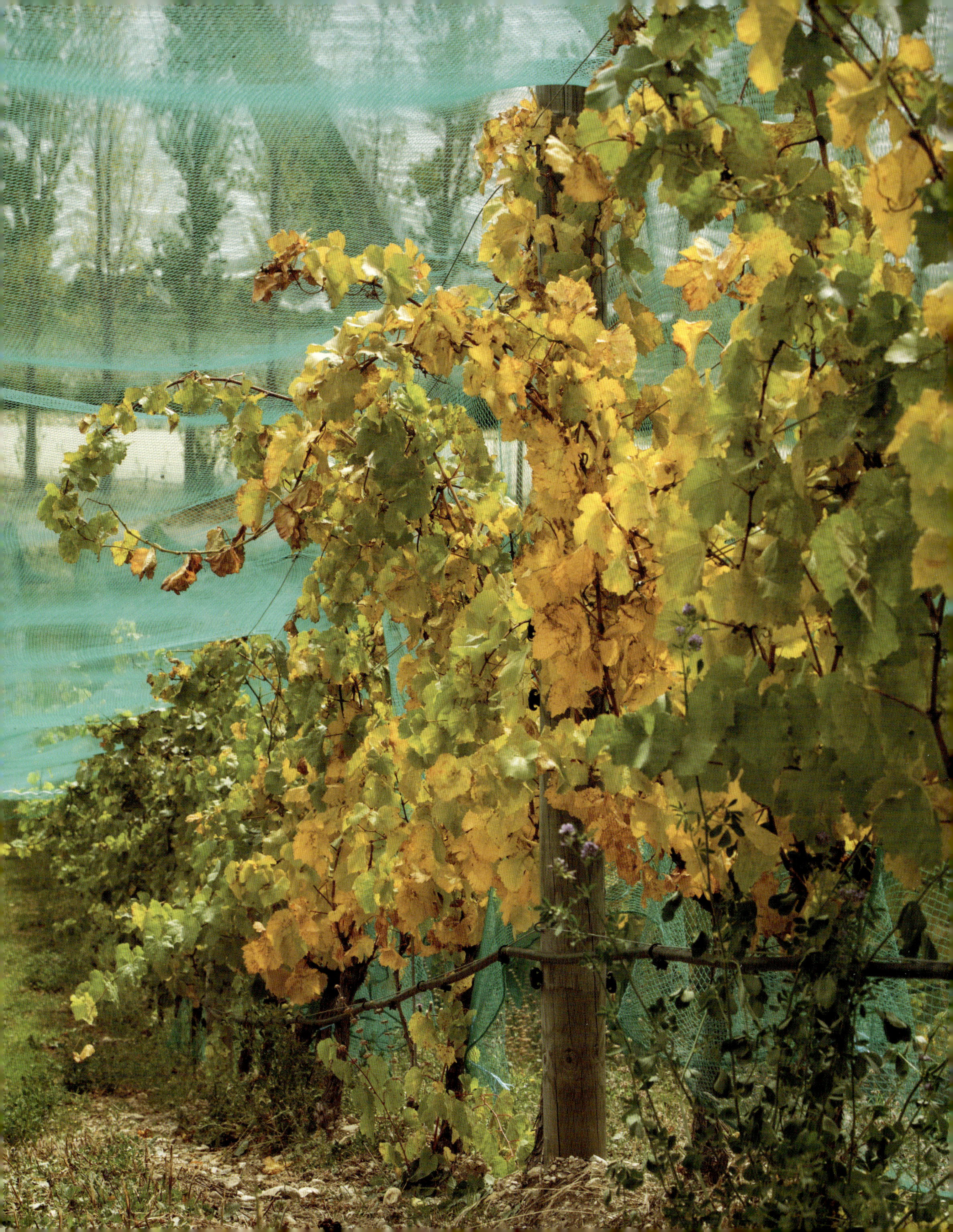

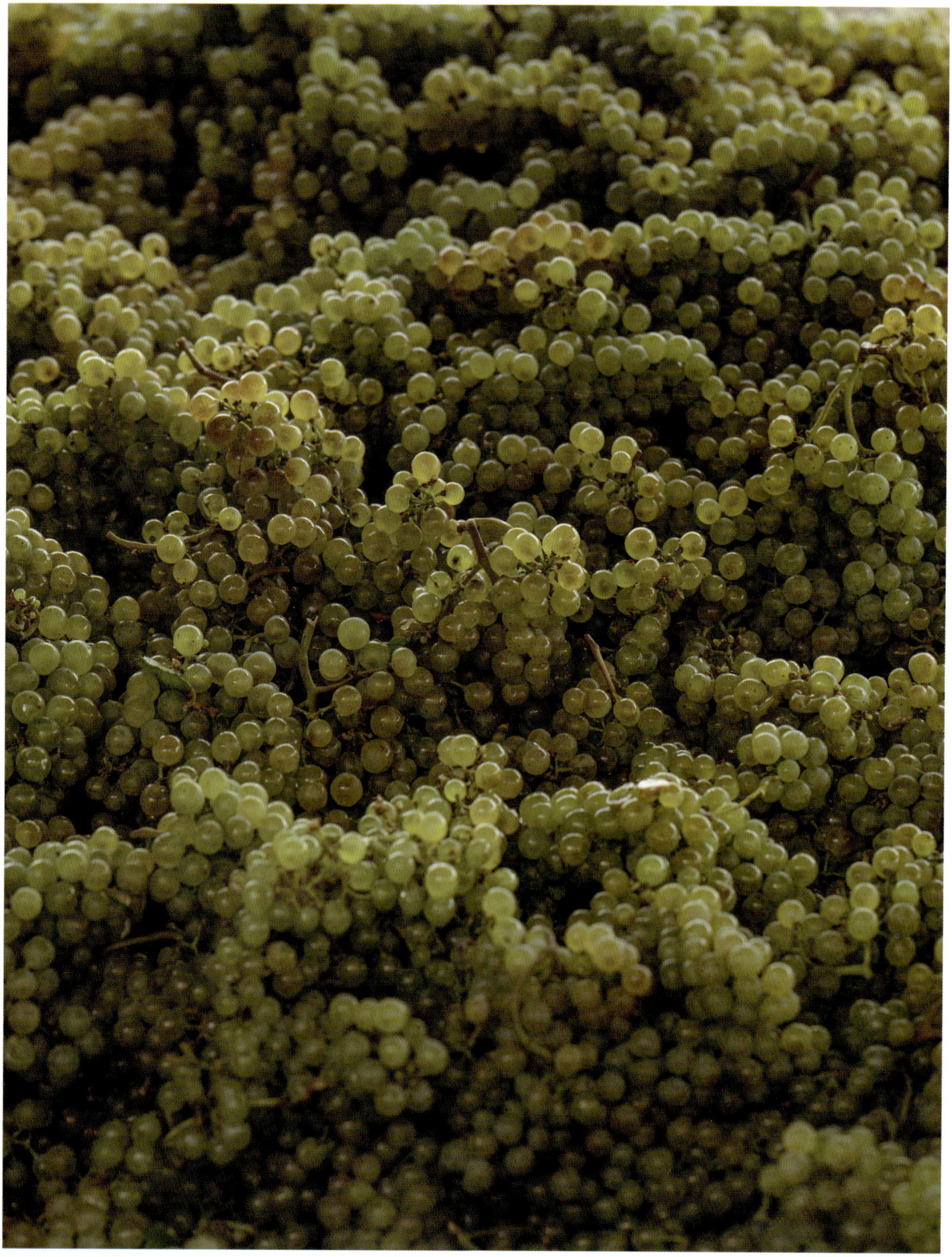

Left Chardonnay grapes ready for pressing. **Top right** Chardonnay harvest at Quartz Reef. **Middle right** Chardonnay grapes ready to go to the winery. **Bottom right** Chardonnay grapes being pressed.

MONDILLO

'While every vintage is different, every vintage is also a quest for the perfect Pinot.'

The grandson of Italian immigrants to the US, Domenic Mondillo grew up with a family heritage of cooking great food and making great wine. From an early age, he learnt to match food with wine, and his Italian grandfather taught him the secrets of making fine wine.

Keeping the family heritage going, Mondillo studied for a degree in restaurant management and culinary arts. Then, in 1981, he moved to Queenstown, where he was executive chef at the two award-winning restaurants he owned. Understanding how wine and food work together and having a good palate are fundamental assets for a good winemaker: the saying in the business is that a winemaker without a palate is like a ship without a rudder. Over the next decade, while running his restaurants, Mondillo got to know different vineyard owners and winemakers, and by helping out in the vineyard and at vintage began his apprenticeship in the winegrowing industry.

In the early 1990s, he sold his restaurants and moved full-time into the world of wine. He gained qualifications in viticulture and winemaking and later worked vintages in Oregon. He then became viticulturist at Gibbston Valley, where he was instrumental in its acquisition of land at Bendigo Station, and developing vineyards there in 1999, first on the lower slopes alongside Quartz Reef, and later on the higher slopes too.

In 2001, Mondillo and his Kiwi wife Ally, having bought their own land at Bendigo, planted their boutique Mondillo vineyard on three carefully selected north-facing terraces. They planted 10 hectares of Pinot Noir and 2 hectares of Riesling. Mondillo says he chose one of the warmest sites in the coolest region — Bendigo in Central Otago. Located at 45 degrees south, Bendigo has an average of 1200 GDD (growing degree days) and the soils are sandy, silty loams over free-draining alluvial gravels — exactly what Pinot Noir enjoys.

Having a 12-hectare vineyard is manageable and works for Mondillo. He and his vineyard manager, James Harcomb, work closely together: 'We both do everything.' As one of the warmest sub-regions, Bendigo is often the first to harvest and Mondillo picks on the slightly riper side. If the tannins are fully ripened, then the wines have more structure, he believes. Pinot clone choice is also important. He has planted 40 per cent Clone 5, a Pommard vine, and Dijon clones 114, 115, 667 and 777 make up the remaining 60 per cent. Each clone has a slightly different flavour profile: the winegrower, through his clone selection, is looking to achieve more depth and complexity in his wines.

Mondillo's first Pinot Noir was made in 2004 and first Riesling in 2007. Originally the winemaker was Rudi Bauer from Quartz Reef, but Matt Connell now makes Mondillo's wines at Hinton Estate in Alexandra. The Mondillo portfolio includes just five wines: two Pinot Noirs, a Rosé, a dry Riesling and a late-harvest Riesling. For Mondillo, it is about quality, not quantity — a good wine is a reflection of place and season: 'While every vintage is different, every vintage is also a quest for the perfect Pinot.'

Mondillo Pinot Noir has been a consistent five-star, gold-medal wine from the start, and the 2013 vintage was selected by Air New Zealand for its first- and business-class flights. Wine writer Bob Campbell MW described the Mondillo Bella Reserve Pinot Noir 2015 in *The Real Review* as 'The best of Bendigo, a flagship Pinot Noir with appealing sweet cherry, plum, raspberry and spice supported by attractive nutty oak. Impressive purity and a strong imprint of place. Silken-textured and very approachable but with potential.' But it is not

Domenic Mondillo.

just Mondillo's Pinot Noir that is right up there. Mondillo Riesling, too, has won gold medals in national and international competitions. The 2013 vintage won gold at the International Aromatic Wine Competition and again in the New Zealand Royal Easter Show Wine Awards. It sold out in the first week of release.

Although his is not an organic vineyard, Mondillo says the best possible sustainable practices are used. Merino sheep keep the grass down before bud-burst and after harvest, and for the most part only sulphur, a 'soft' chemical, is applied. He wants to leave the land better than he found it. The biggest challenge for all Central Otago winegrowers is frost and Mondillo says if it is too cold, nothing will prevent damage to the vines. He has not experienced any significant frost damage at Bendigo, but because it is warmer, bud-burst happens earlier in the season and this means the vines can be more susceptible to spring frosts.

For Mondillo, wine is made in the vineyard. He believes a great winemaker is more of a caretaker, making sure the fermentation process goes smoothly. 'The winemaker should be as gentle as possible, and there should be minimal intervention.'

When it comes to selling his wines, it comes as no surprise to learn that Mondillo does this himself, with Ally's help. He sells direct to his customers through the cellar door and online, and he also distributes his wines personally within New Zealand and into Australia and the US. Like many other smaller producers, he does not use all his own fruit in his wines; he sells 10 to 15 per cent off to other companies. Meanwhile, Ally 'keeps the team together' and is responsible for administration and marketing. A talented graphic designer, she has developed individual barcodes for all their wines. Clever and quirky, they add another dimension to Mondillo's wine labels.

Together Mondillo, Ally and crew make a tight-knit team, a team of which his Italian grandfather would surely be proud.

TOP Mondillo vineyard. ABOVE Vineyard crew tying bird netting. RIGHT Installing bird netting.

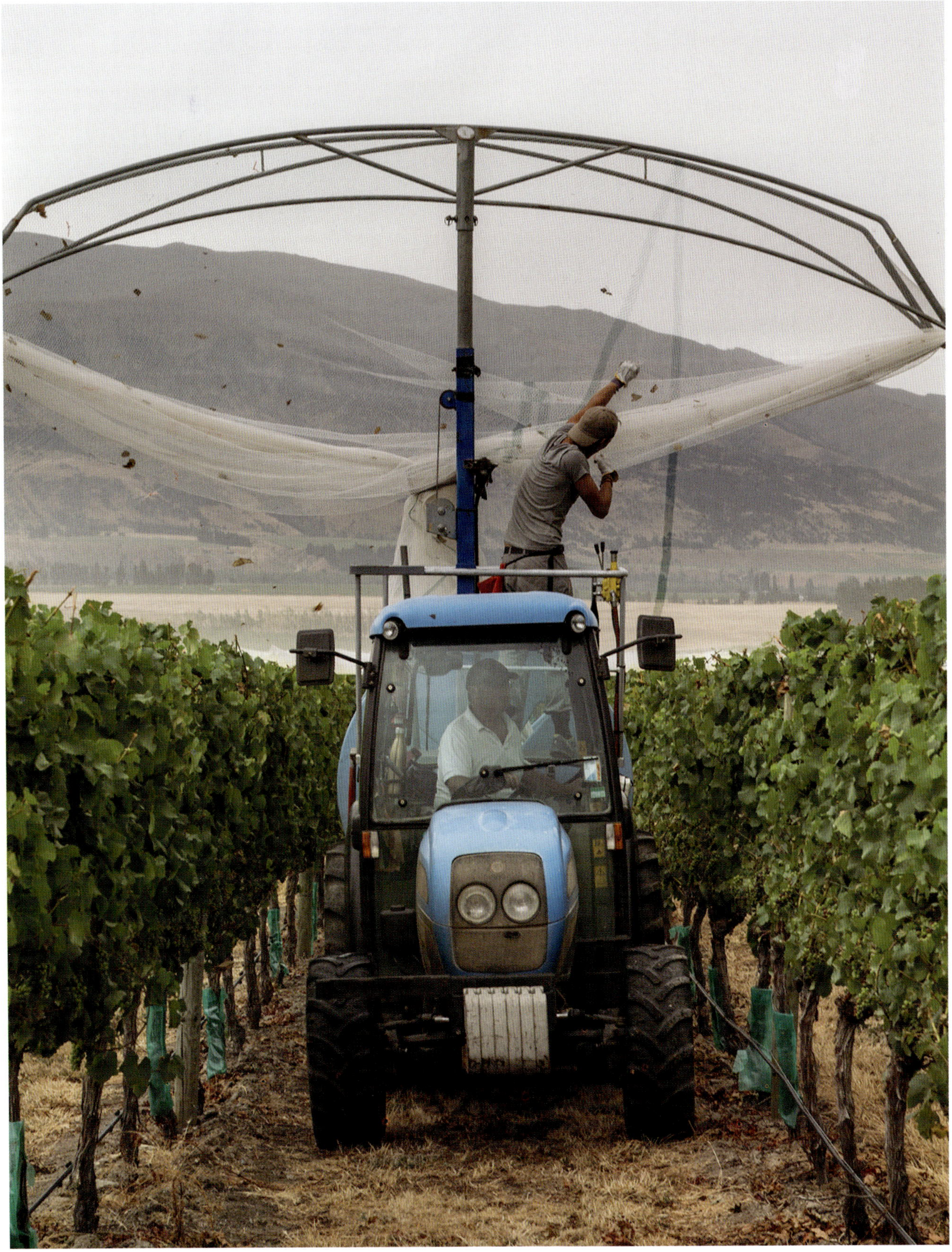

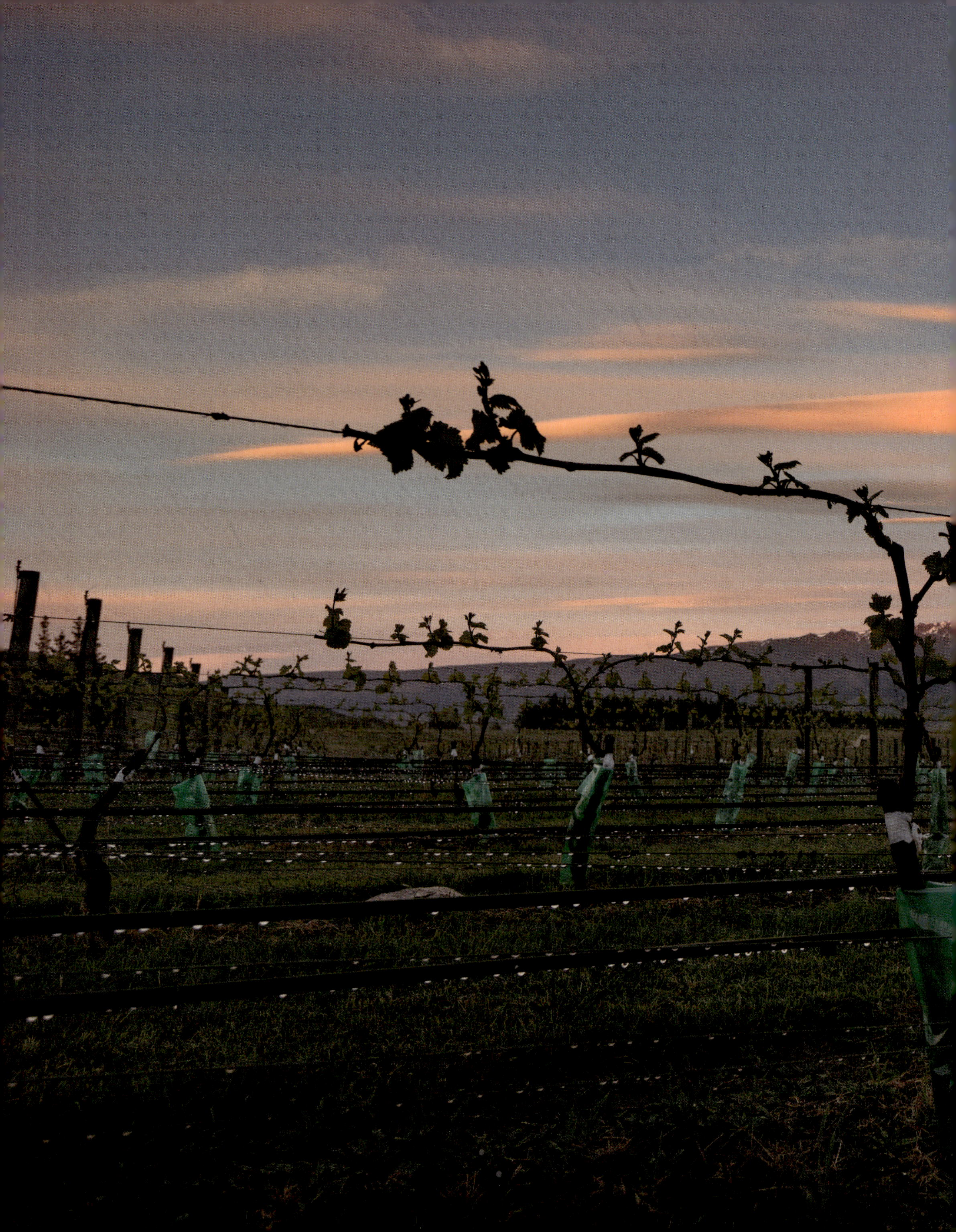

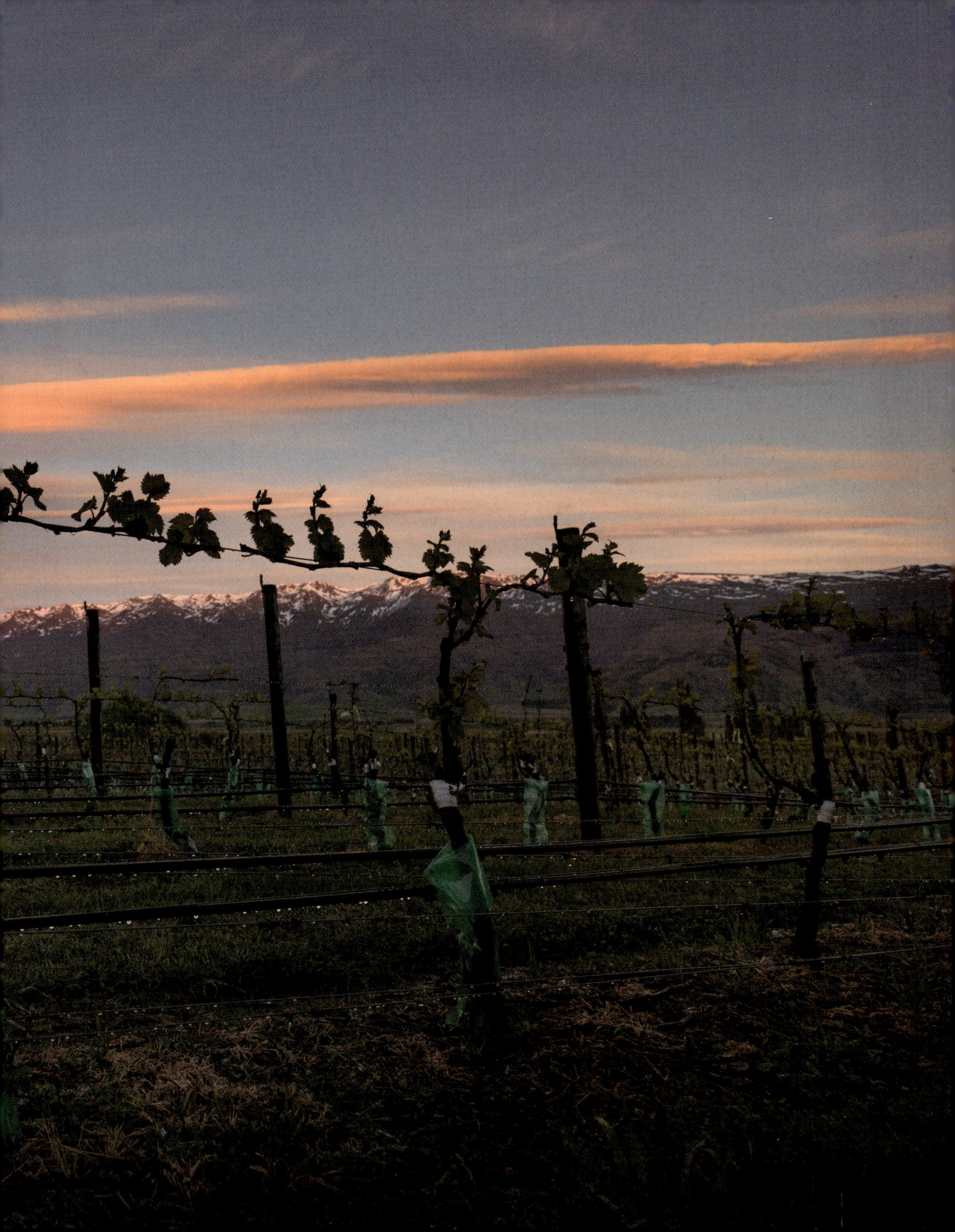

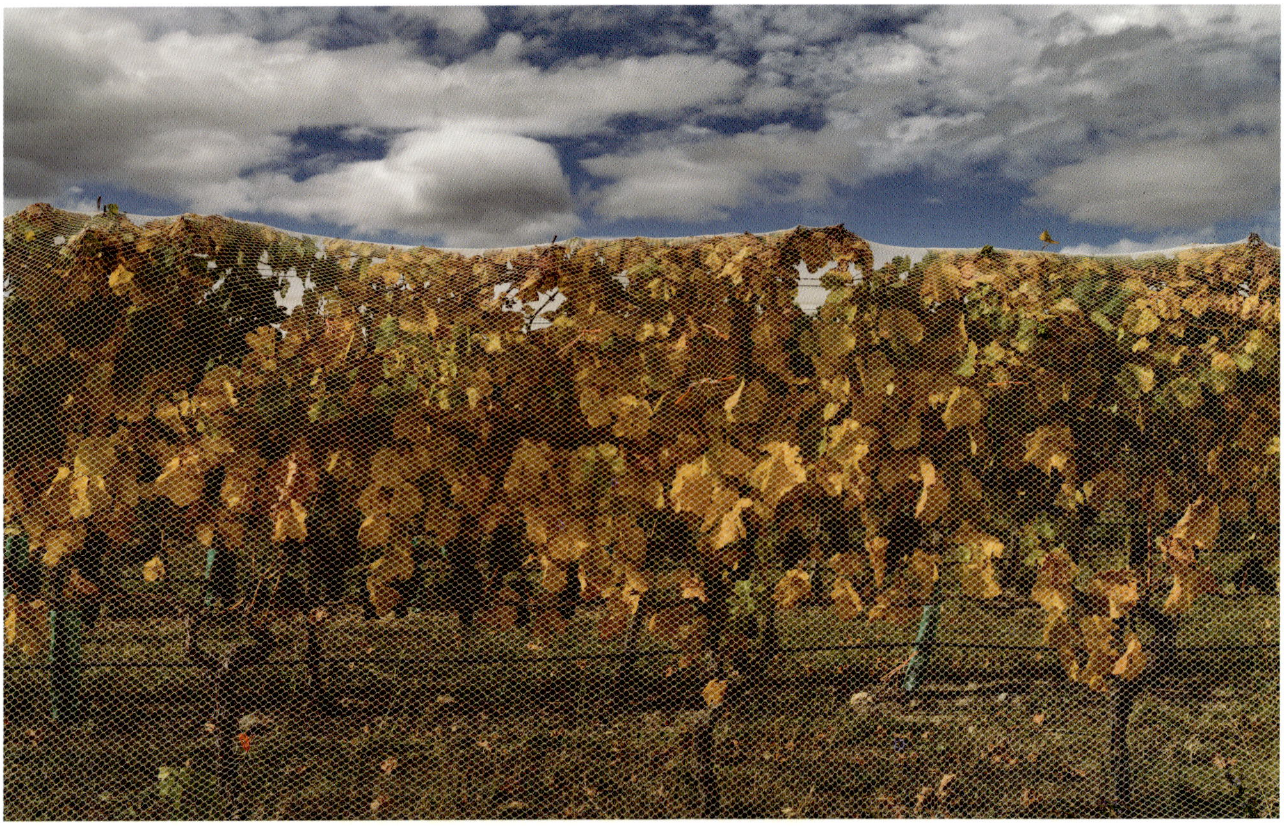

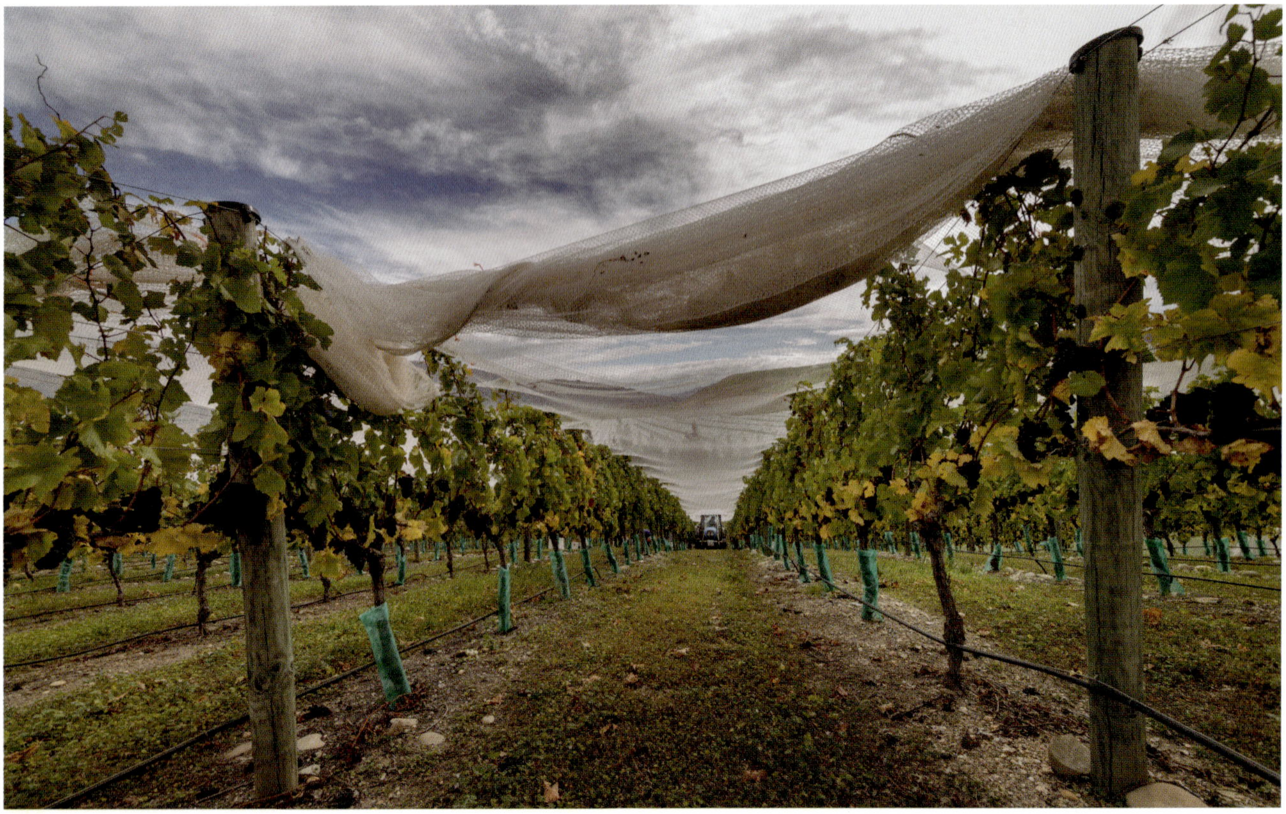

ABOVE LEFT Netted Pinot Noir ready for harvesting. LEFT Pinot harvest in progress. TOP RIGHT Vineyard manager, James Harcomb. MIDDLE RIGHT Domenic Mondillo. BOTTOM RIGHT Full bins at harvest.

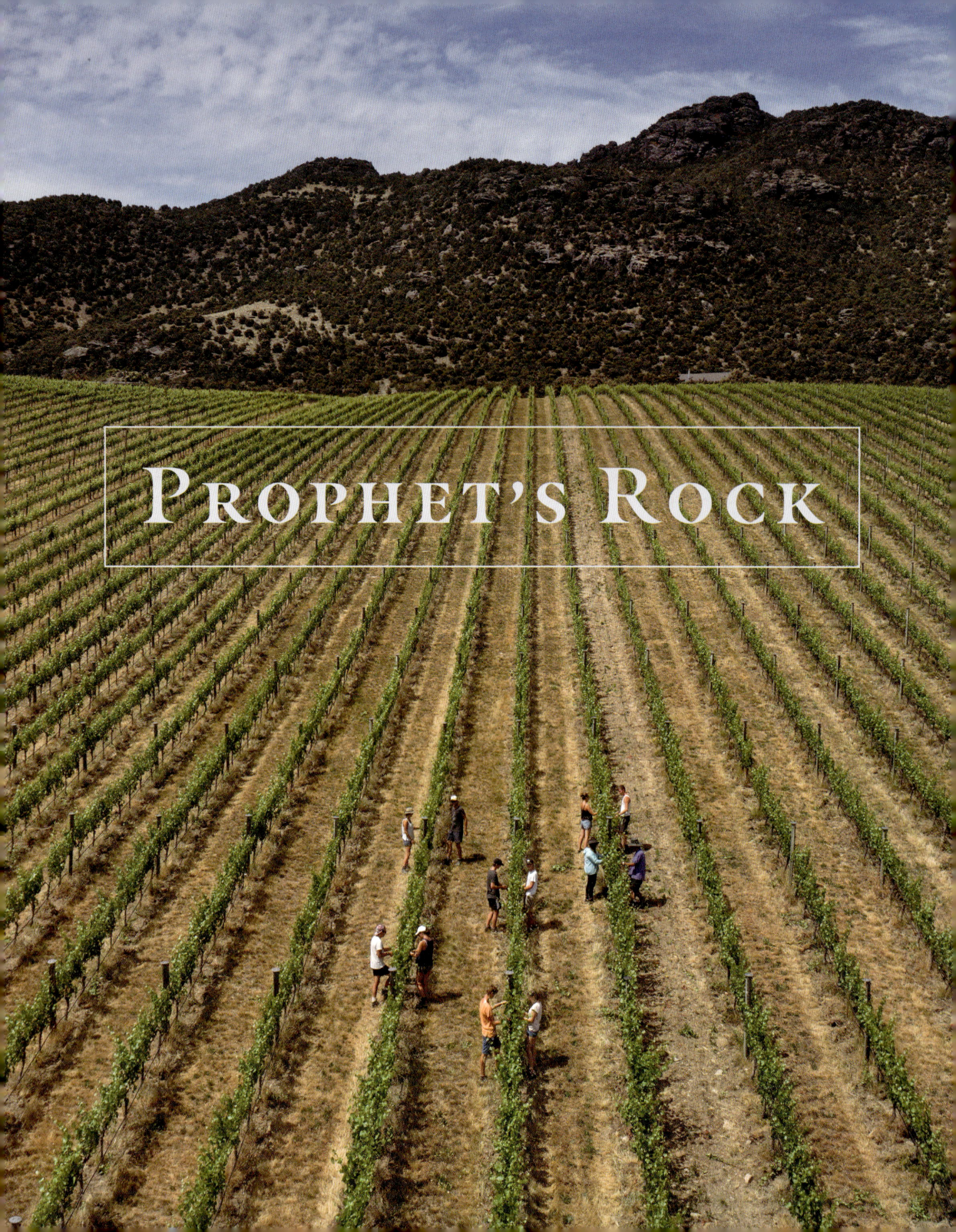

Prophet's Rock

'In Central Otago you win or lose in the vineyard. We focus on quality — we can't ripen big tonnages anyway.'

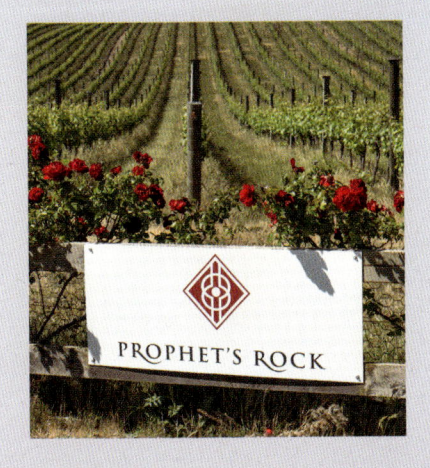

With some of the steepest slopes in Central Otago, the Prophet's Rock Home and Rocky Point vineyards are among the most spectacular in the region. First developed by Mike and Angela Mulvey in 1999, Prophet's Rock Home vineyard rises from 320 metres above sea level to almost 400 metres. The 7.5-hectare vineyard is planted mostly in Pinot Noir, with 0.5 hectares of Pinot Gris. In 2004 a second vineyard, Rocky Point, was planted on very steep slopes overlooking Lake Dunstan. Here there are 10 hectares of Pinot Noir, 4 hectares of Pinot Gris and a small amount of Riesling. In 2012 both vineyards were sold to a group of North Island investors, and in 2017 they bought a further 2.2 hectares beside the Home vineyard for development, bringing the total area to 23 hectares.

Paul Pujol has a minor shareholding in Prophet's Rock and, since 2005, like the classic French vigneron, has overseen all aspects of production. Around 80 per cent of the quality of a wine comes from what happens in the vineyard. The winemaker can direct the style, but the key to quality is the vineyard. 'In Central Otago you win or lose

It's more versatile than a Rosé, and it's got more stuffing and great acidity. It's a great pizza wine,' says Pujol. 'So far it's gone really well.'

Further to his own winemaking, his French connections have enabled Pujol to bring François Millet, the winemaker at one of Burgundy's top domaines, to Central Otago. In 2015, he invited Millet to come here to make wine, using grapes from Prophet's Rock. Millet now comes out several times a year, and makes about 290 cases of Pinot Noir, which he calls Cuvée aux Antipodes. Pujol describes it as 'a massive endorsement of Central Otago and a really important milestone for the region, and for the New Zealand wine industry'.

In 2017, the Central Otago Burgundy Exchange celebrated its tenth anniversary, and as part of the celebrations in Burgundy, 10 Central Otago wineries were invited to pour their wines for French winemakers in the Chambre du Roy in the Hospices de Beaune. Pujol, who was pouring Prophet's Rock Pinot Noir, says the French were really interested and excited and full of compliments for these wines being made on the other side of the world.

Prophet's Rock makes around 6000 cases of wine: half of its production is sold in New Zealand and half is exported. The UK, Australia and Japan are the biggest markets, with small quantities going to the US and Hong Kong. Like many other New Zealand winemakers, Pujol is heavily involved in marketing the wines he grows and makes. 'It's a Kiwi thing, I guess, we just get out there and do it.'

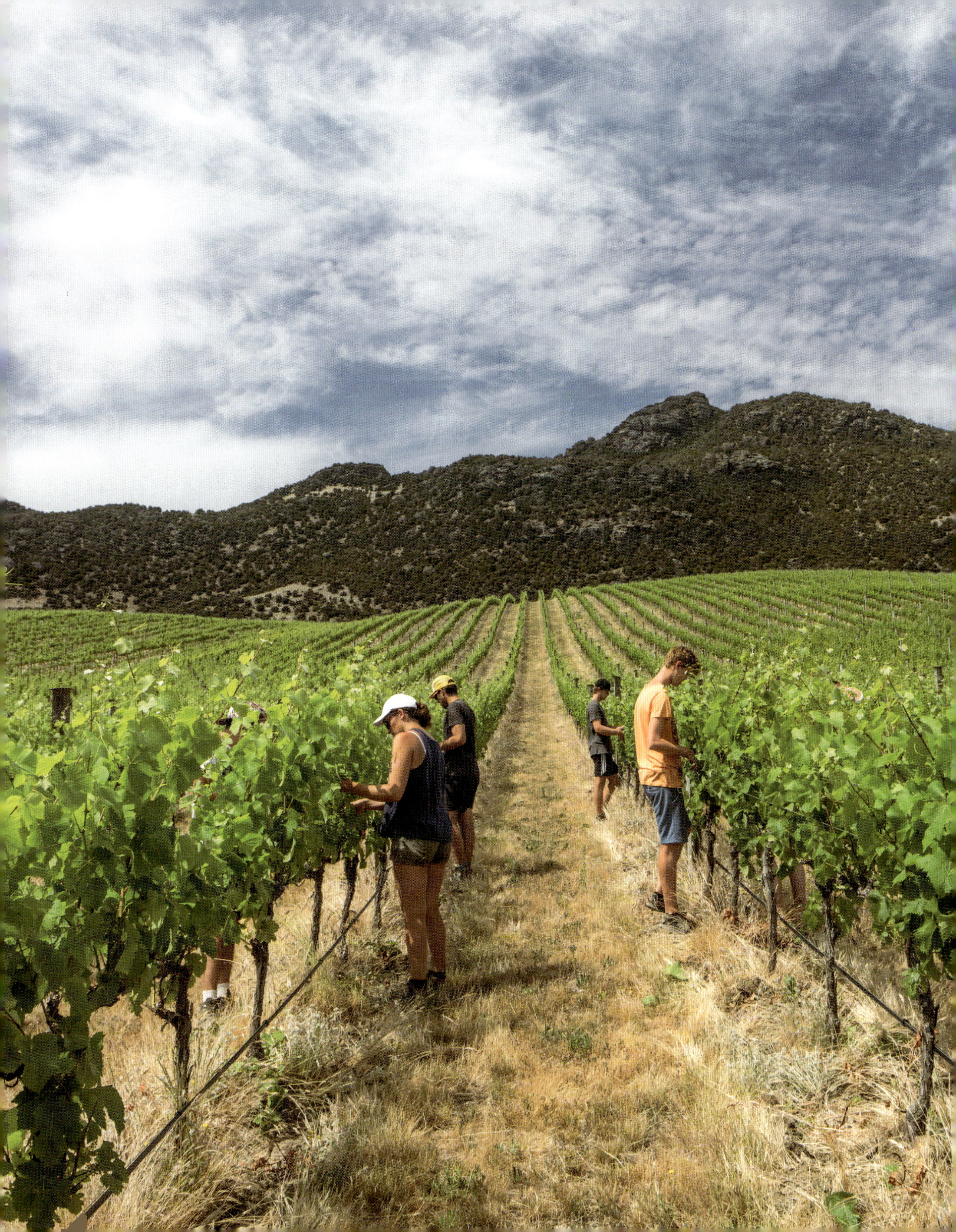

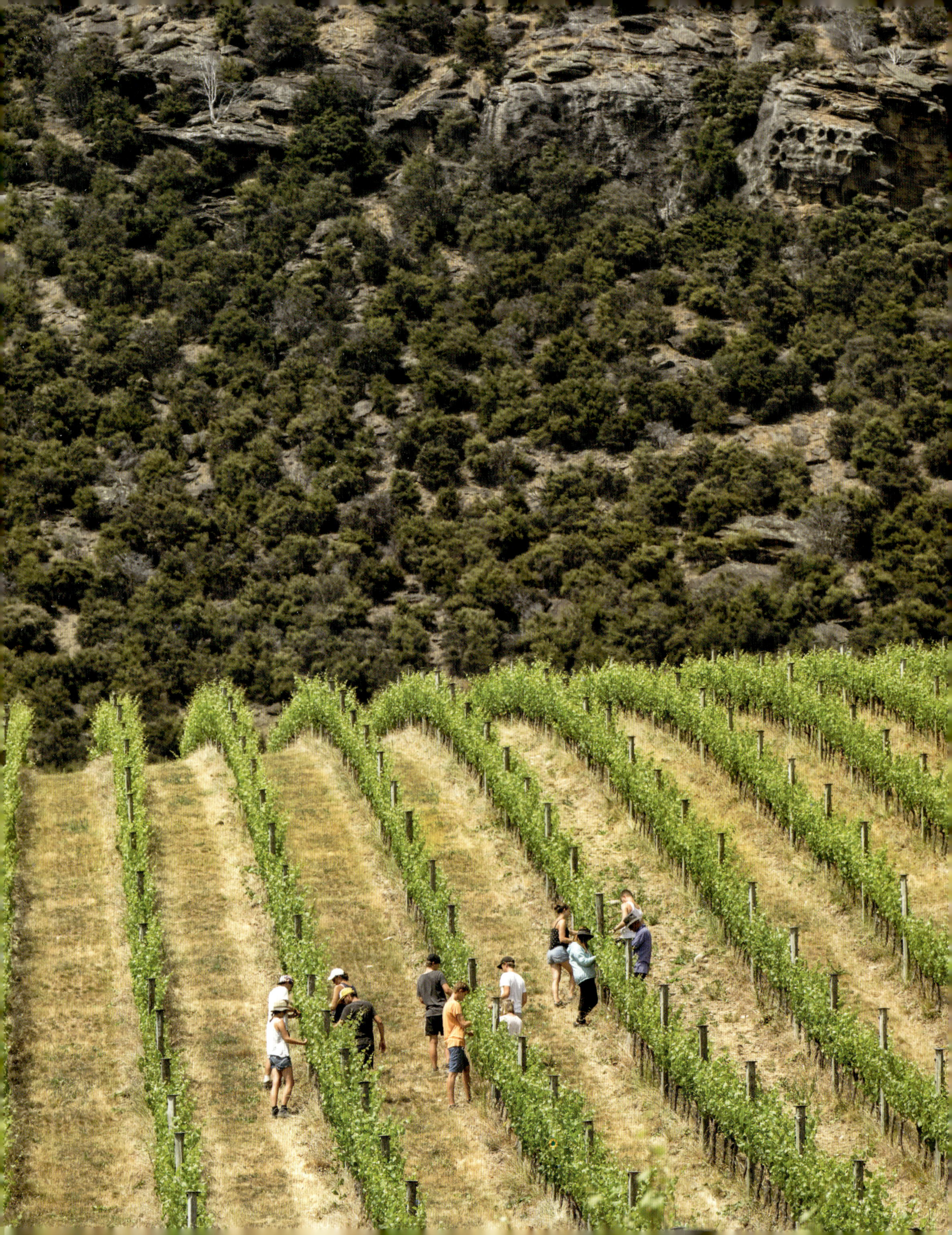

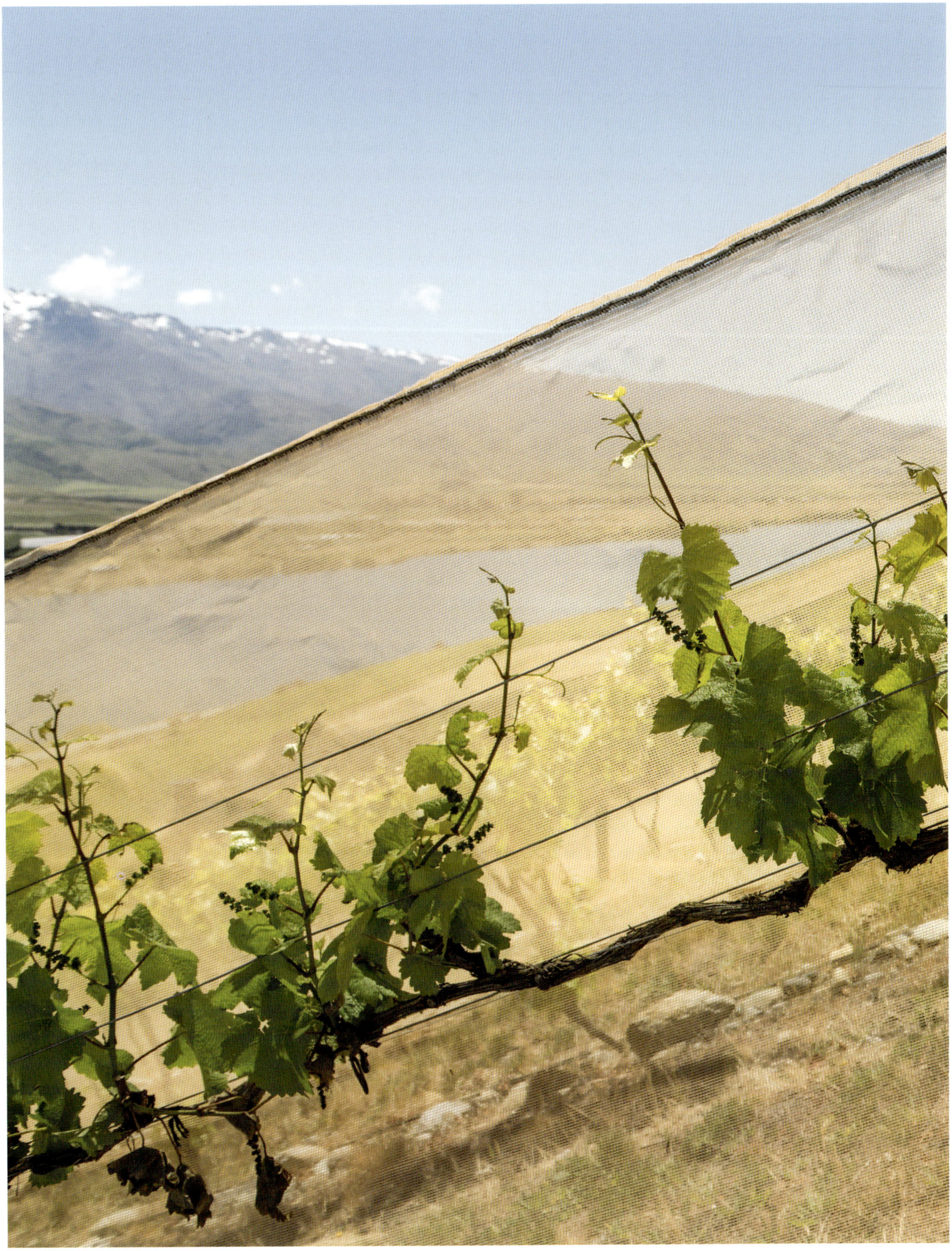

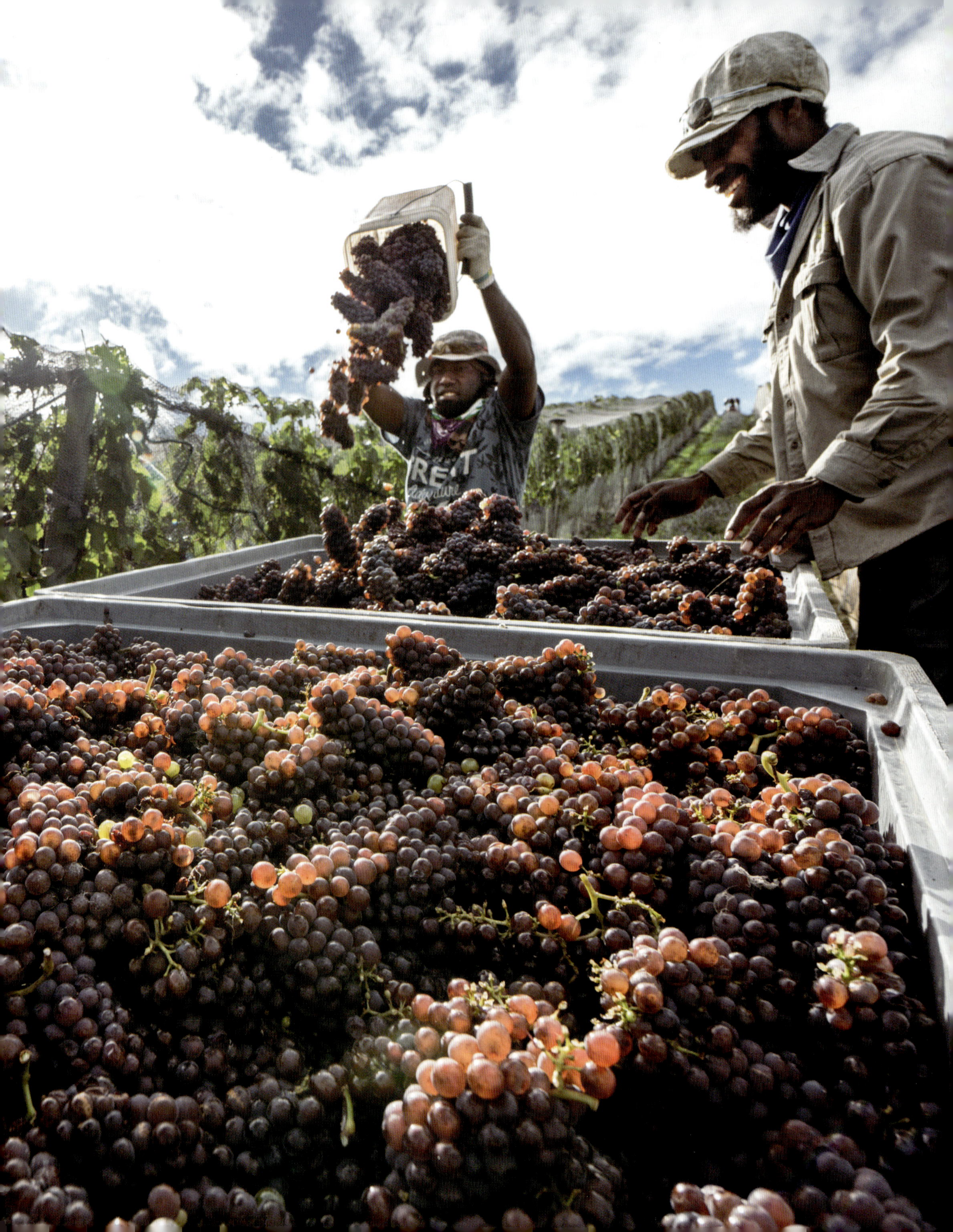

Left, top right, middle right Vanuatuan workers harvesting at Rocky Point vineyard. **Bottom right** Paul Pujol processing Pinot.

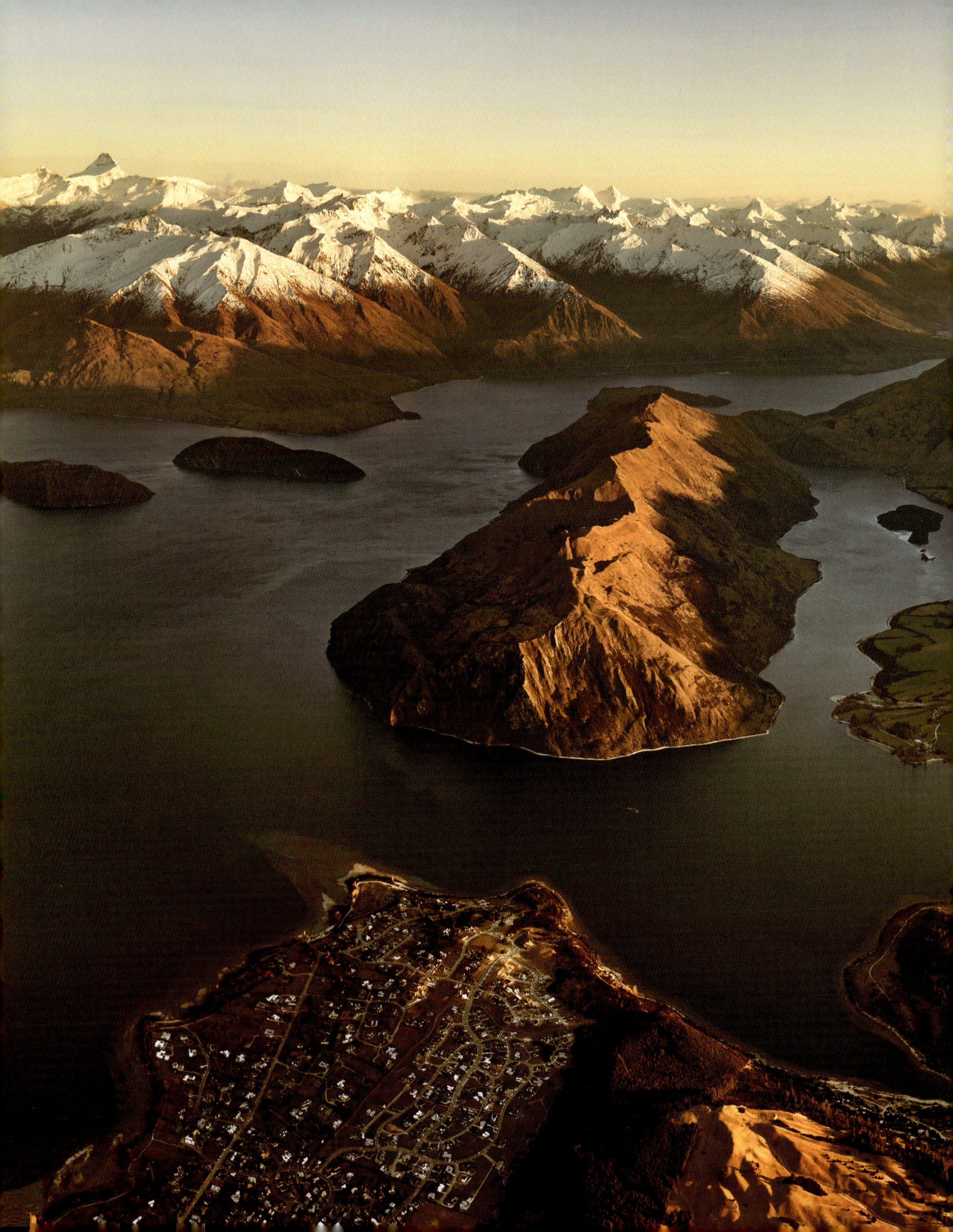

WANAKA

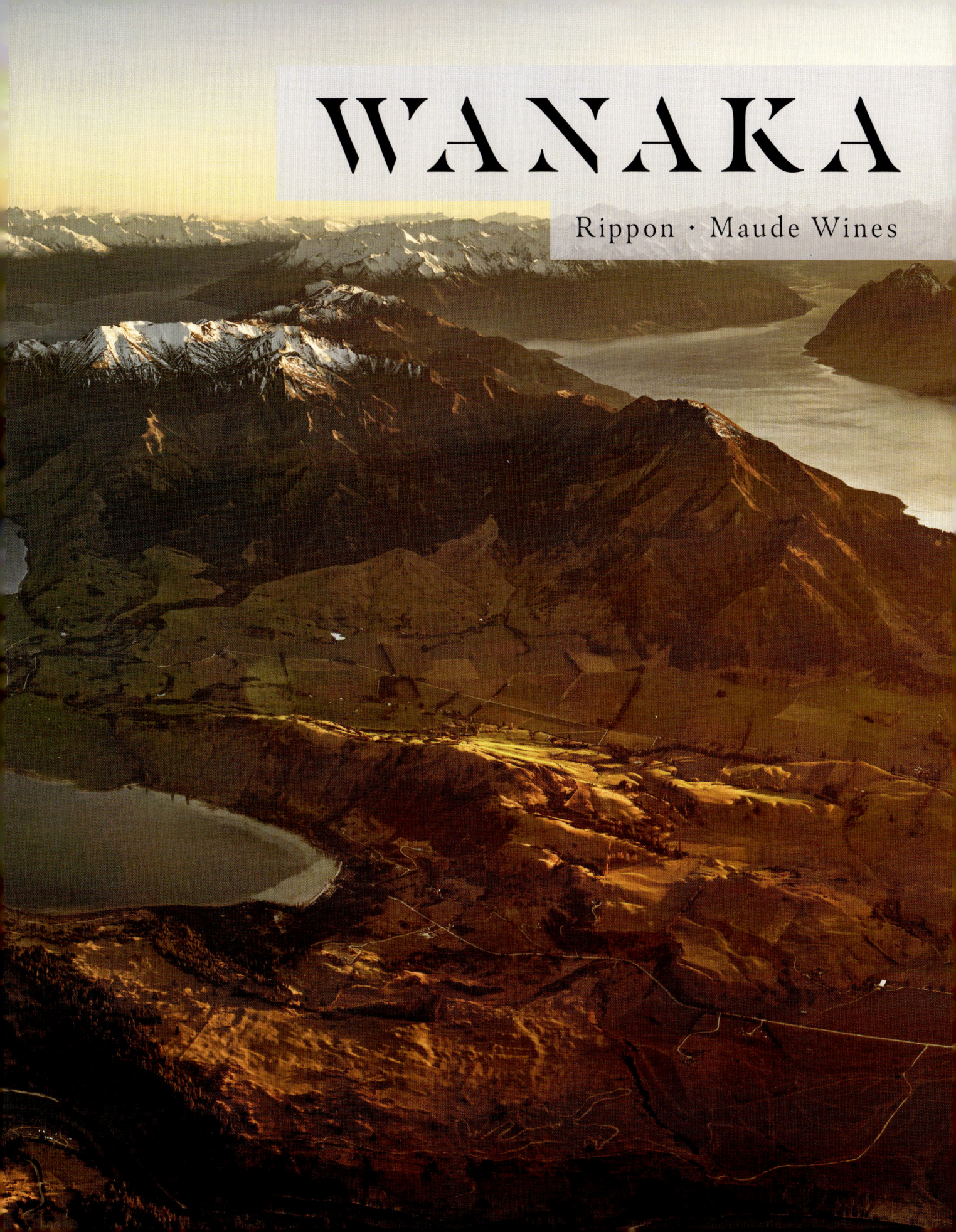

Rippon · Maude Wines

WANAKA is the most northerly sub-region of Central Otago, and while it's slightly warmer than Gibbston, because of its proximity to the Southern Alps, it is cooler and wetter than Alexandra and the Cromwell Basin. Although it is the smallest sub-region, with only about 60 hectares of vines, it enjoys a high profile because of the spectacular Rippon vineyard beside Lake Wanaka.

Site selection is critical in Wanaka — Rippon's north-facing slopes, at 330 metres above sea level, are warmer than other areas. Rolfe Mills started planting experimental vines in 1975, but it was not until 1982 that he planted his first commercial vineyard.

Dan Dineen from Maude Wines says the Pinots coming from Wanaka are 'more elegant wines, suggesting fruits such as blueberries', and as with the other sub-regions, as the vines get more age, the wines are becoming ever more complex.

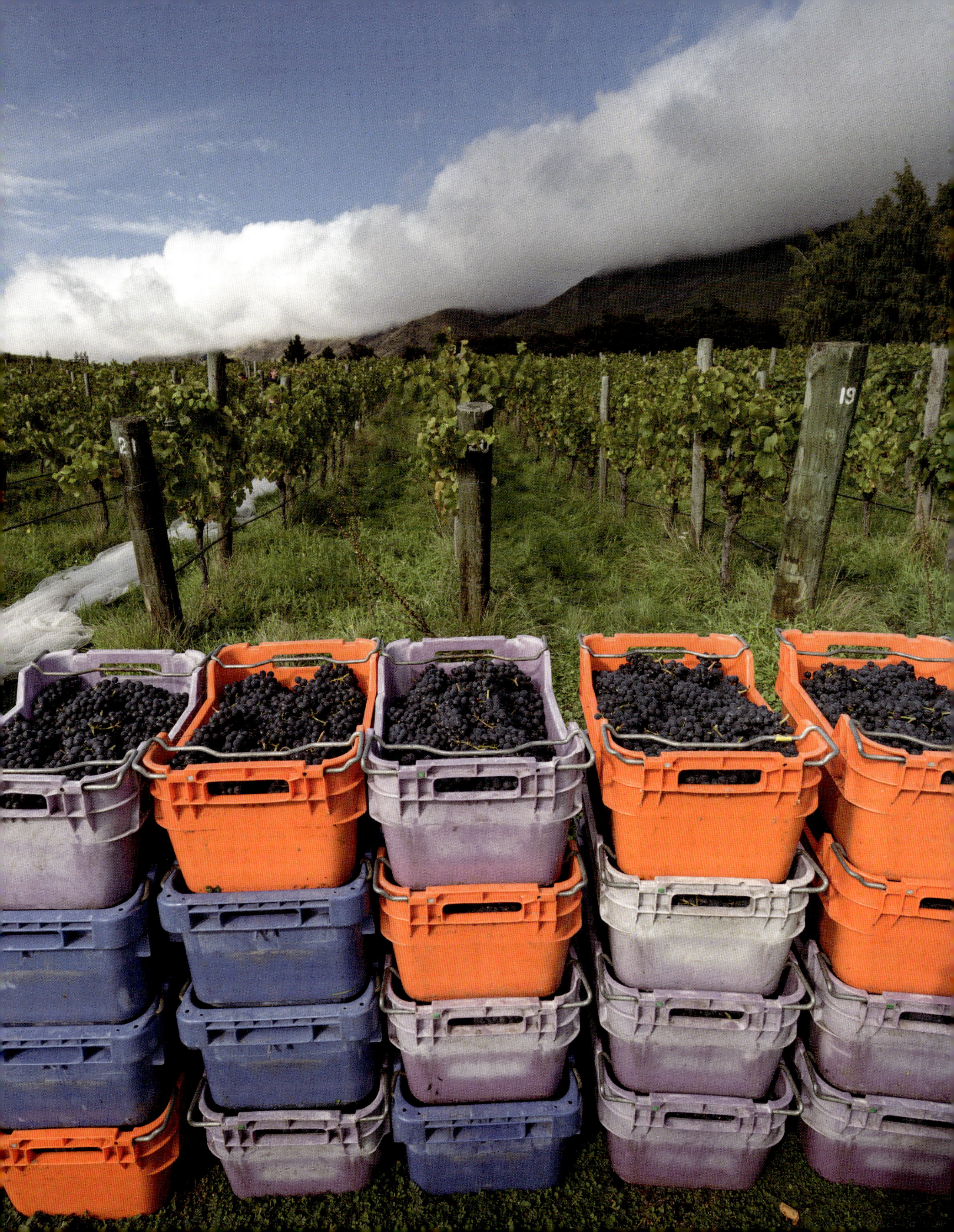
21
19

RIPPON

'He had a strong vision and a great strength of character.'

The Mills family connection to their land at Rippon, on the western shores of Lake Wanaka, goes back over 100 years, when Rippon was part of Wanaka Station and owned by Rolfe Mills's grandfather, Sir Percy Sargood. Most of the property was sold to pay death duties, but the family kept some land to the west of the township, including the 60-hectare lakeside property which Rolfe named after his great-great-grandmother, Emma Rippon, who had married Frederick Sargood, Sir Percy's grandfather.

When Rolfe and his wife Lois moved with their family to live in Wanaka in the early 1970s, Rolfe had a wide knowledge and appreciation of French wines, but no experience in growing grapes or making wine. So, when he and Lois started planting grapes at Rippon Farm in 1975, they planted 30 varieties in 30 rows, experimenting to see what would do well in the free-draining schist soils. At 330 metres above sea level, Rippon is higher than most other Central Otago vineyards, and while frost can be a problem, Lake Wanaka helps to keep the temperature a little warmer in winter and a little cooler in summer. Planting on the sunny north- and northwest-facing slopes above the lake also helped minimise the risk of frost damage.

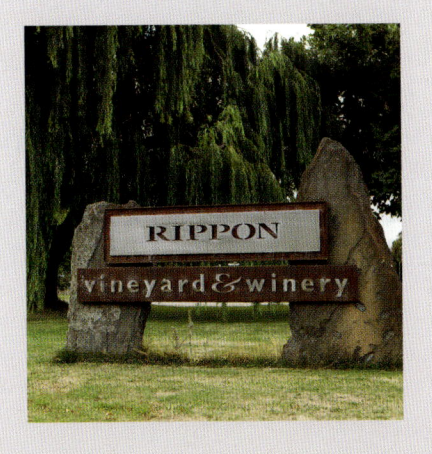

Six years later, in 1981, Rolfe and Lois took their three children to live for nine months in France to find out if developing a vineyard at Rippon was what they wanted for their future. Originally, they planned

time for the next generation to take over. She had travelled to the UK, Europe, the US and Australia developing markets for Rippon wines, and export sales accounted for about half of Rippon's production.

Export sales are still important, but with the opening of Rippon Hall in 2011 and the growth in wine tourism in Central Otago, cellar-door sales have now increased to around 30 per cent of total sales. Lois's dream, Rippon Hall, with its magnificent lake and mountain views, serves as Rippon's cellar door, as well as a wedding venue and a place where the cultural side of wine can be celebrated. Art exhibitions, musical concerts and other arts events are held there, encouraged by Lois's desire to foster the connection between enjoying and appreciating good wine and enjoying and appreciating the arts.

Not surprisingly, that 'good wine' has won accolades around the world. French sommelier Julie Dupouy, writing in *The Taste* in early 2017, enthused: 'From their entry level Pinot Noir to their single vineyard wines, the quality is just outstanding. The schist soil confers a tension, purity and minerality which is simply magical . . . The estate also produces a beautiful dry Riesling, an incredibly digest and food-friendly Gewürztraminer and a seriously good Gamay in a style that reminds me of some of the top producers in Morgon. In summary, whatever you can find from this producer, just buy it!'

One of the most photographed vineyards in the world, Rippon is impossible not to fall in love with at first sight. Or to fall in love with Rippon wines at first taste. Thanks to the vision and dedication of two generations of the Mills family, Rippon's vines and wines should continue to flourish into the next generation and the next . . .

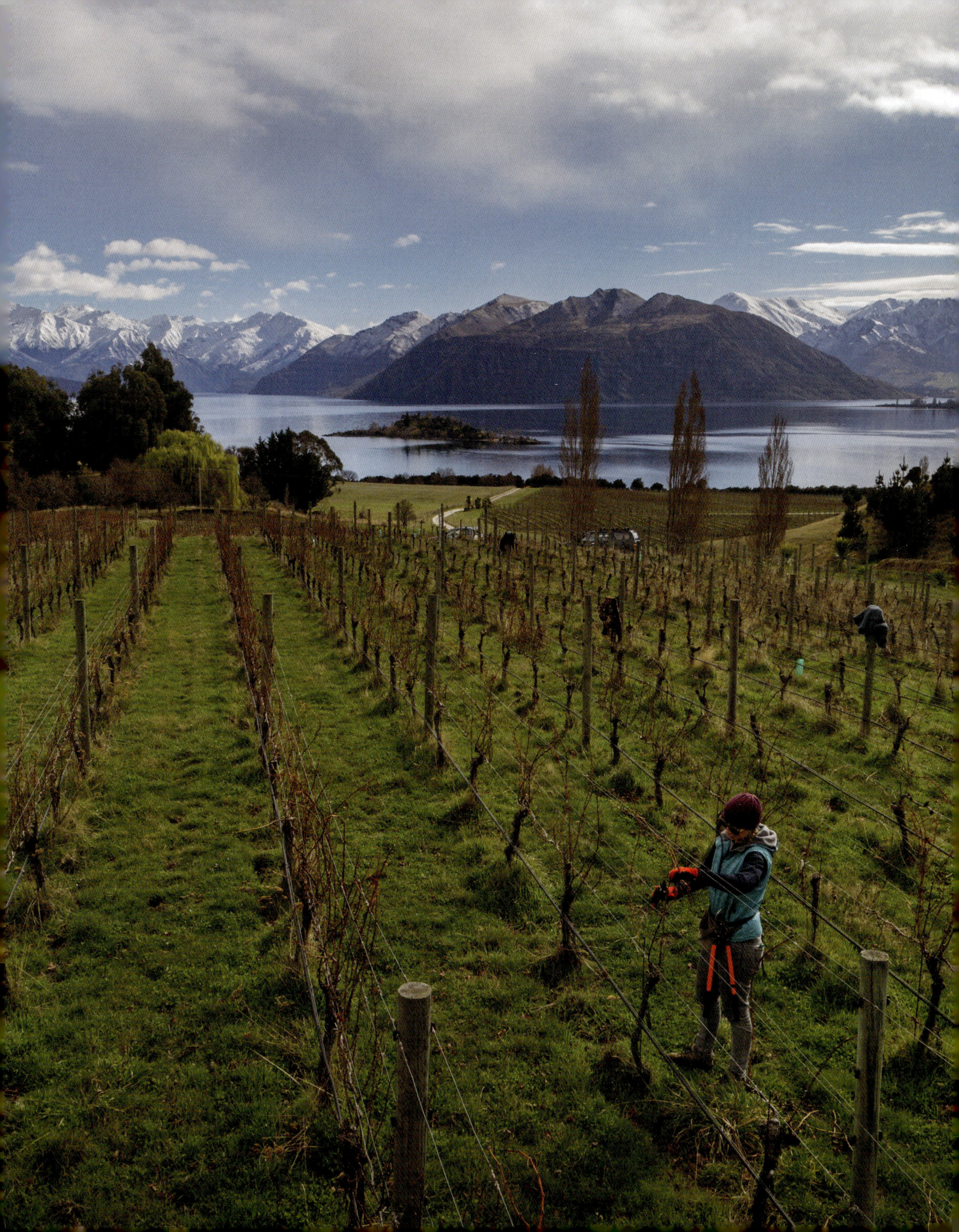

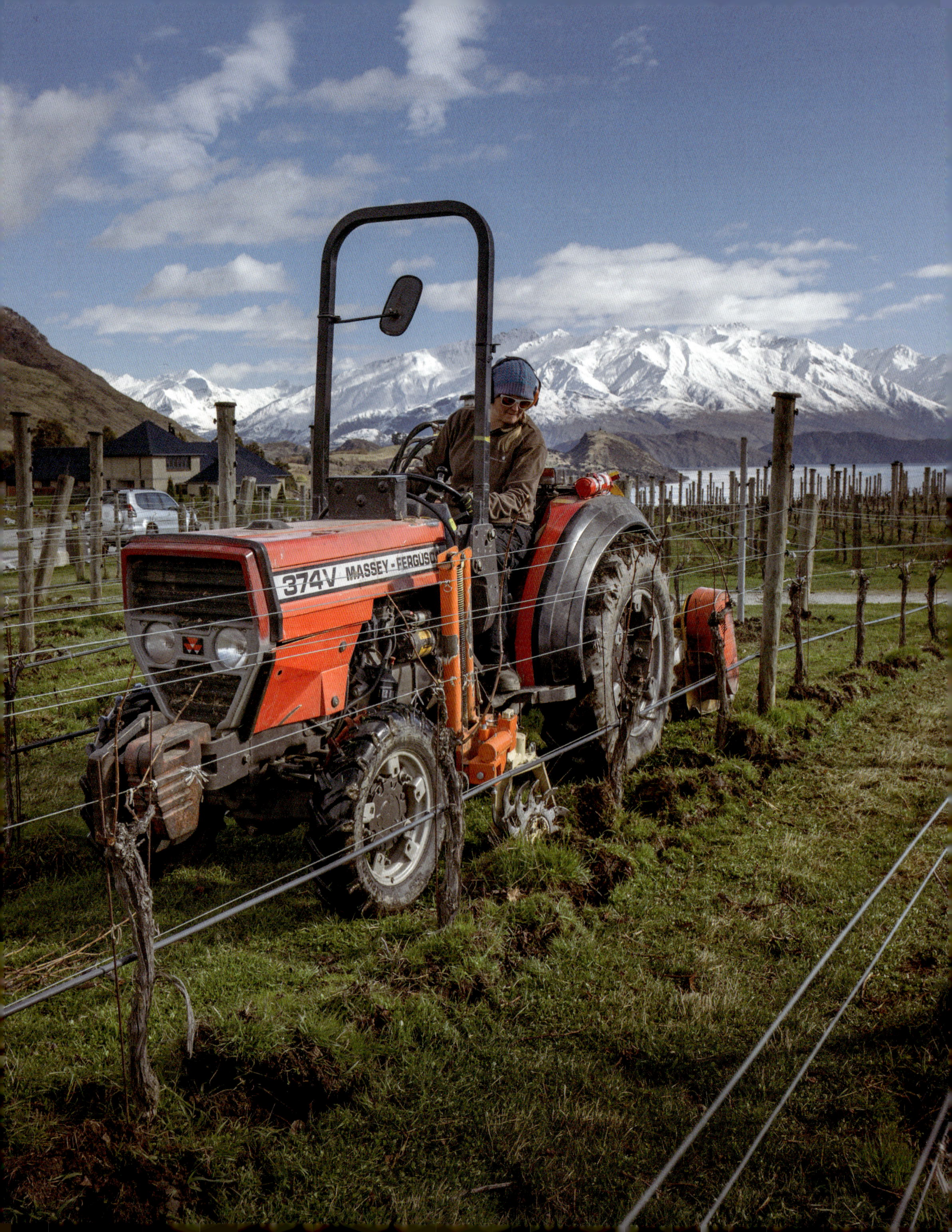
374V

LEFT Vineyard manager Shannon Foley weeding mechanically.
TOP AND MIDDLE RIGHT Winter pruning. BOTTOM
RIGHT Charlie Mills (on right) preparing organic compost.

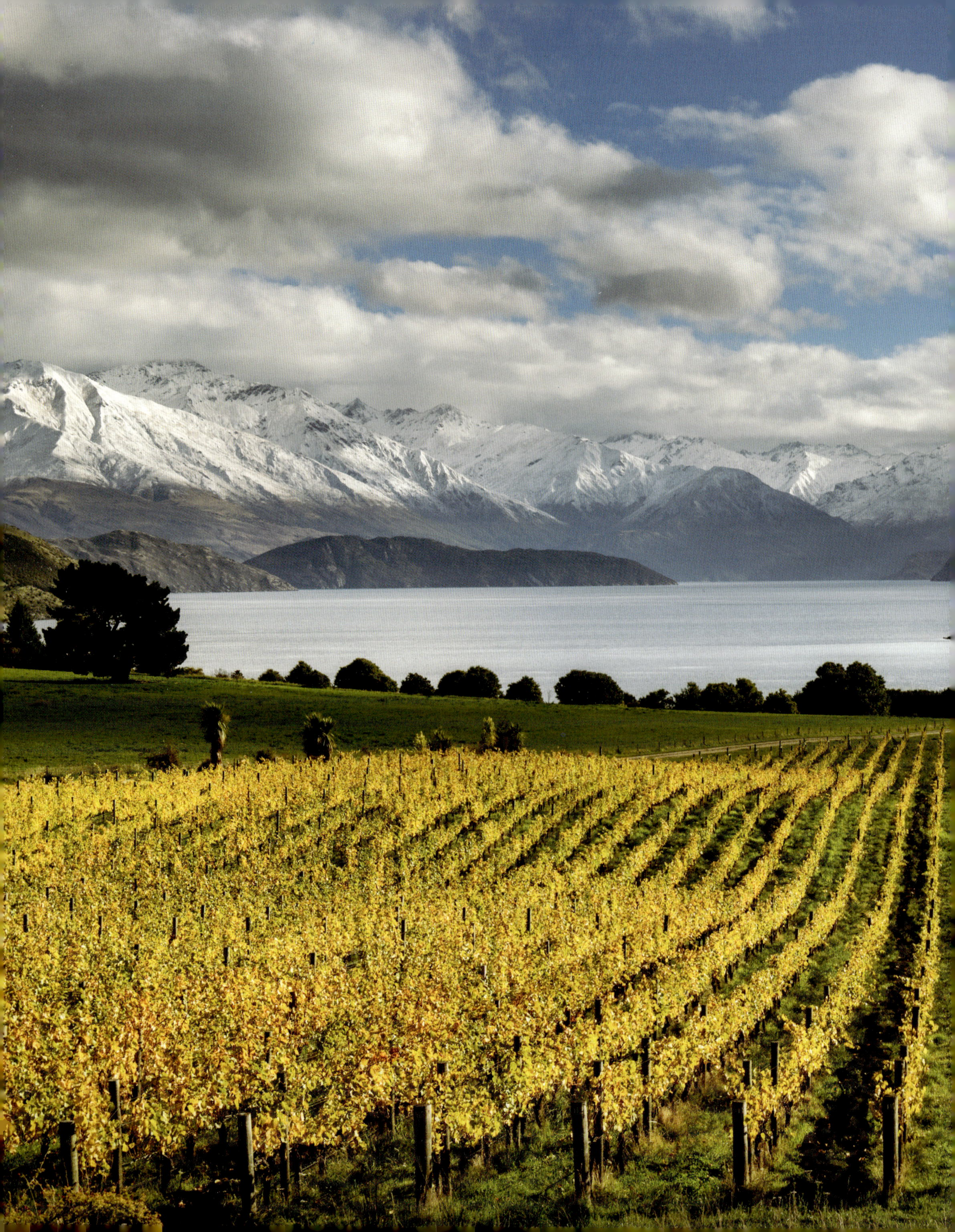

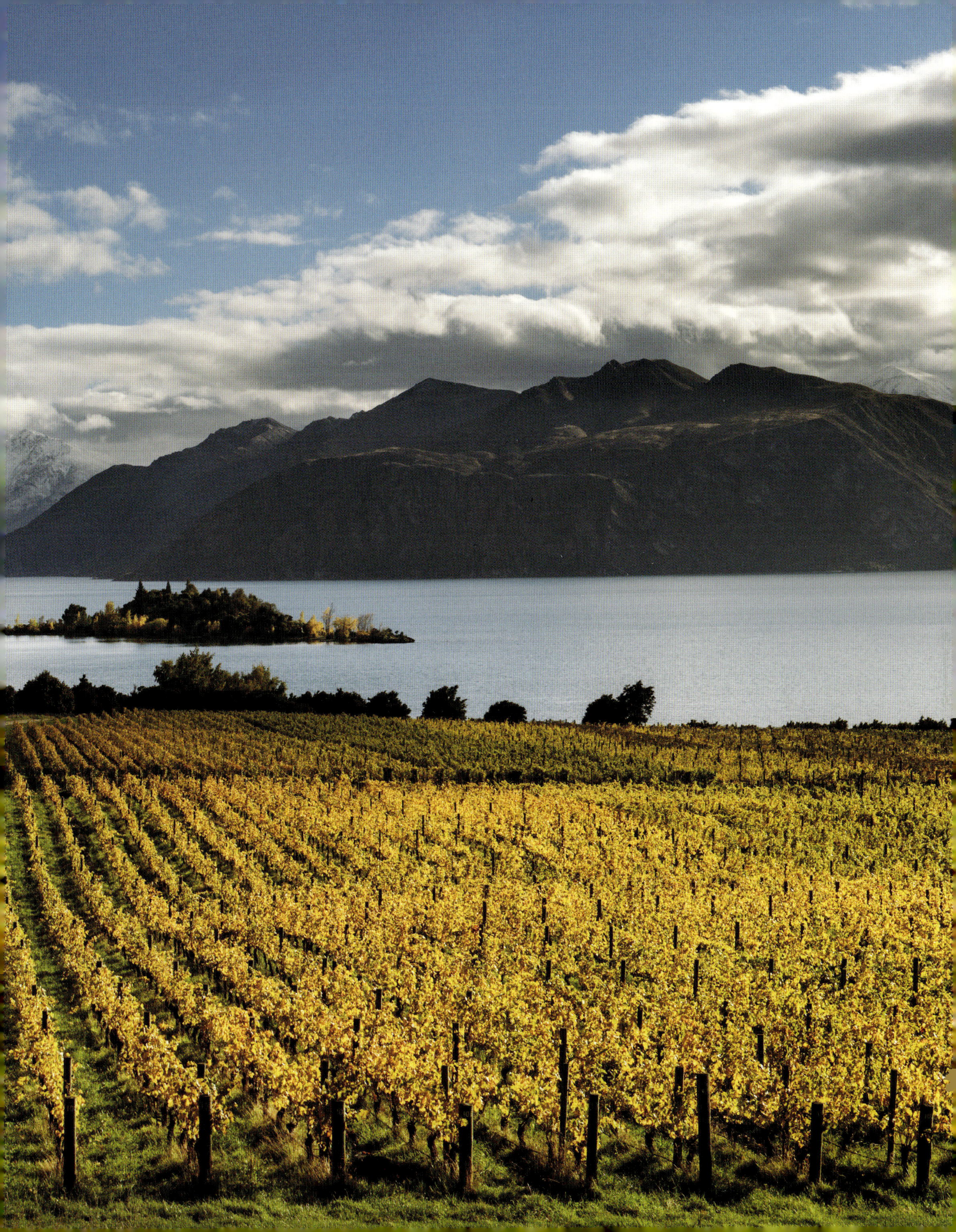

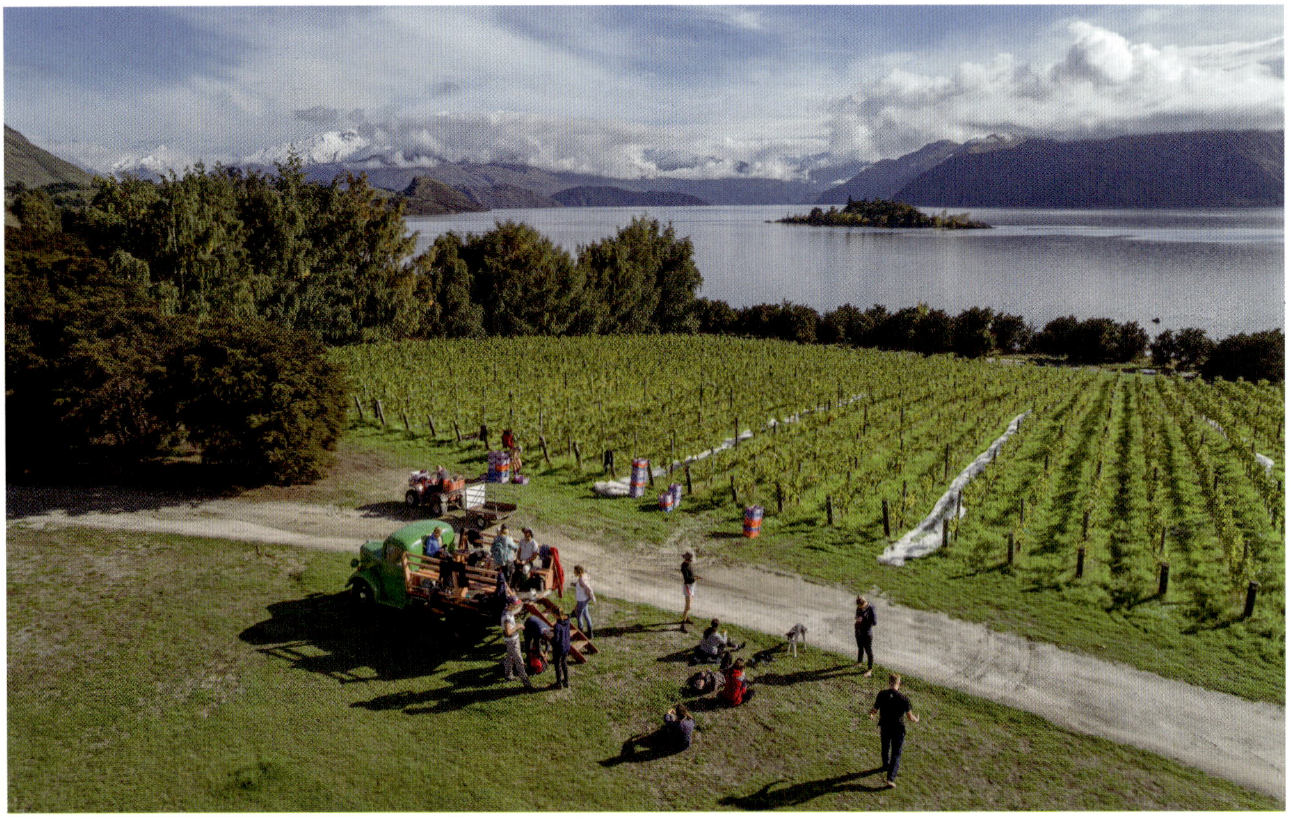

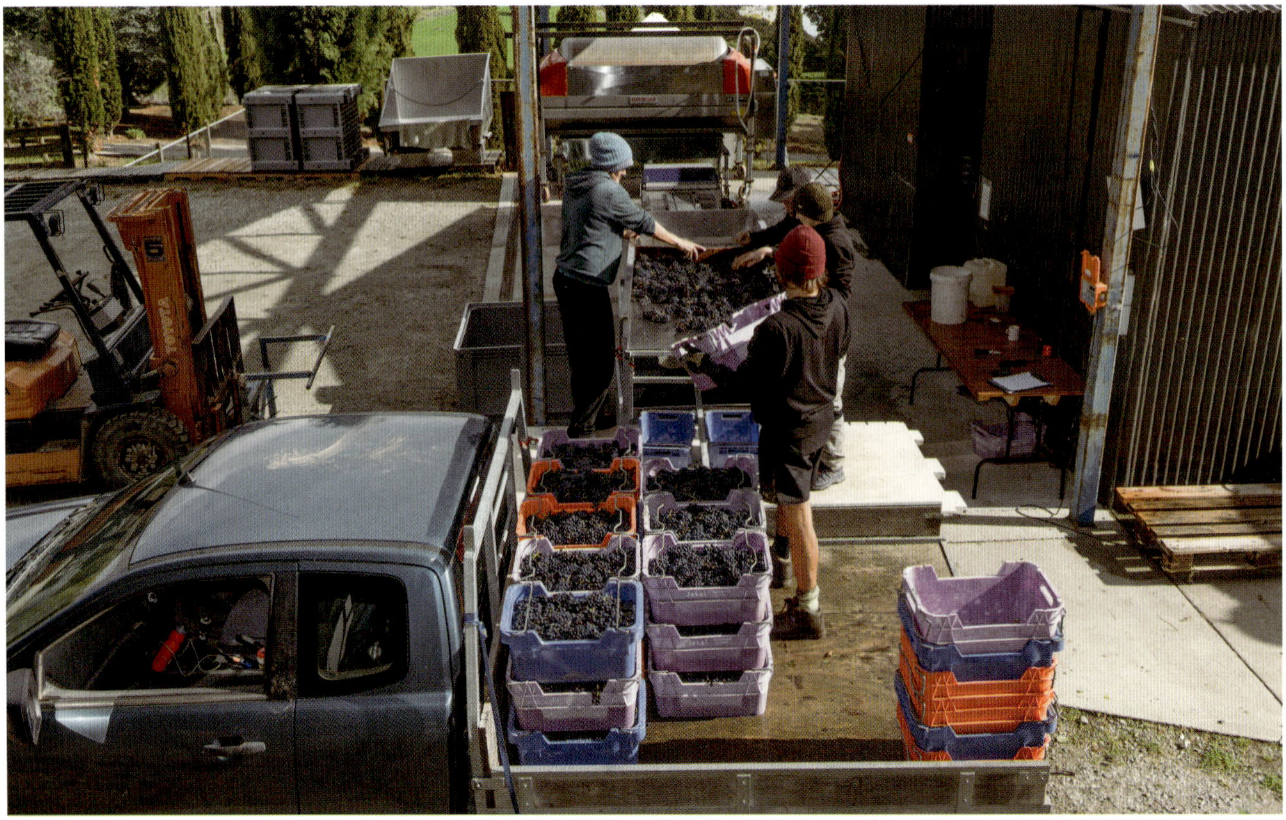

ABOVE LEFT Lunch break during harvest. **LEFT** Shannon Foley and crew processing Pinot Noir. **TOP** Charlie Mills moving crates of Pinot grapes. **ABOVE** Concert at Rippon Hall.

Maude Wines

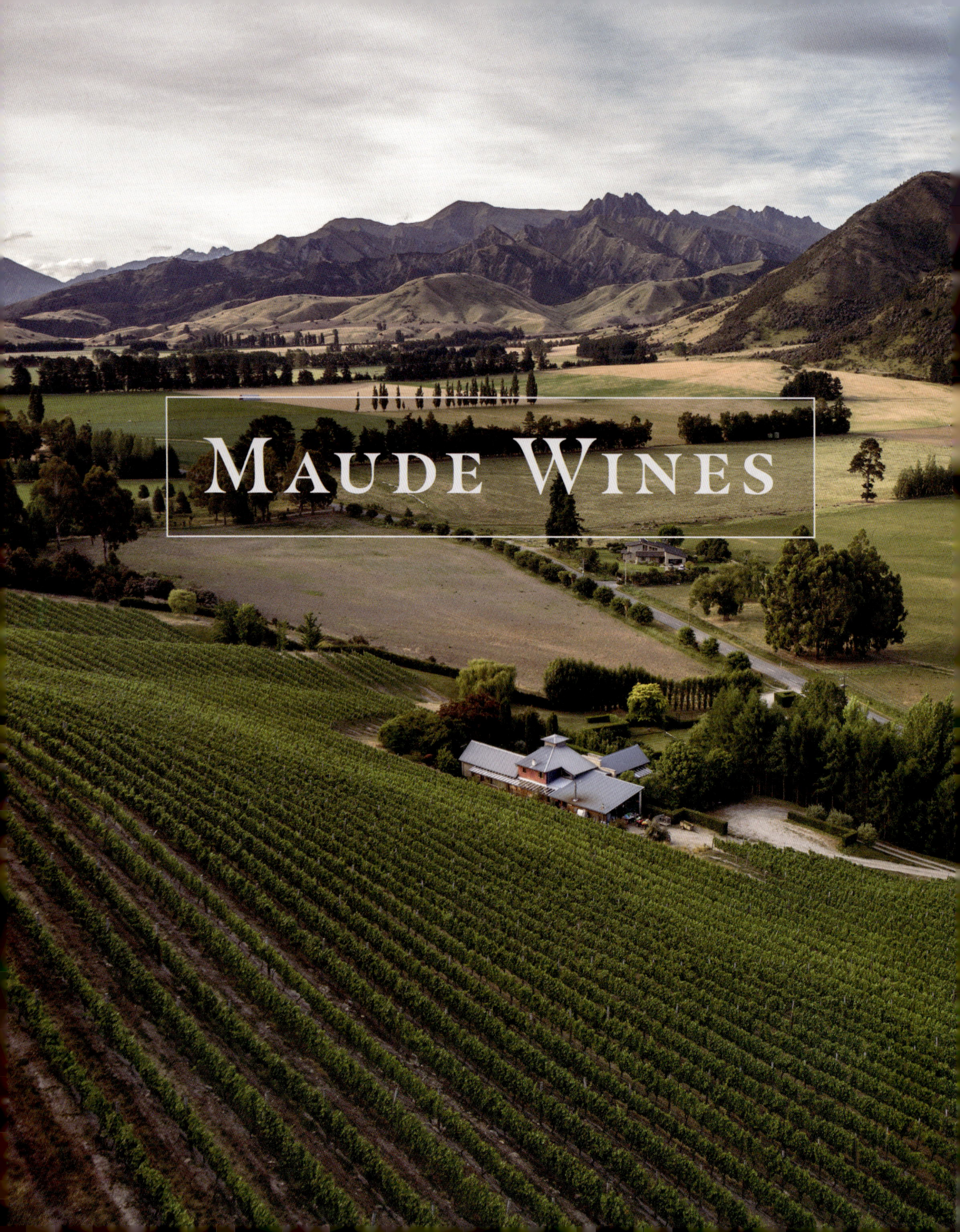

'It will take a lifetime to truly understand the variety and how it performs under different conditions, but SK and I will have a lot of fun learning.'

In 1993, Terry and Dawn Wilson bought 10 hectares in the sheltered Maungawera Valley, between lakes Wanaka and Hawea. Terry had been a medical doctor in Southland and was looking for a retirement project. Well, shall we call that a semi-retirement project? Twenty-five years later, he still does the tractor work at Mt Maude, as well as most of the pruning.

But back to 1994. With the help of family and friends, Terry and Dawn started planting their 4-hectare vineyard on a steep north-facing slope opposite Mt Maude. They planted the vines — 2 hectares of Pinot Noir and 1 hectare each of Riesling and Chardonnay — across the slope, east to west, to help capture all-day sun.

Everything was, and still is, done by hand, and with three generations helping, Mt Maude remains a family affair. Their first vintage was in 1999, and in the early years their wine was made at COWCo. But when their daughter Sarah-Kate returned to Wanaka, would be ideal for growing Pinot Noir grapes too.

SK and Dan at Maude Wines made the first vintage for Two Degrees in 2007, and since then have continued to have a happy and 'fruitful' relationship with Richard and Di. Using about half the crop, they make 800 cases of Pinot Noir and 200 cases of Rosé for Two Degrees, and they take the rest of the crop for blending with other grapes to make their own award-winning Maude Pinot Noir. Two Degrees has not been left out in the cold, though. Their 2009 Pinot Noir won gold in the Air New Zealand Wine Awards in 2011, and in the Royal Easter Show Wine Awards in 2012, 2016 and 2018, Two Degrees Pinots have won the Champion Pinot Noir trophy.

While Richard and Di are not trained in either viticulture or winemaking; they run the business side of Two Degrees and help in the vineyard over harvest. Over half of their production is exported to Australia, a bigger, more affluent market, where there is less competition than in New Zealand, and a tiny amount is sold in the UK. They believe it is important to have a presence in the local market, too, and sell about 30 per cent of their wine in New Zealand.

At the end of the day, whether they are working together at Mt Maude, or in their winery making wine for Mt Maude, Maude or Two Degrees, SK and Dan and their extended family believe in having fun at the same time as they all work hard to produce their award-winning wines and continue their quest for that perfect Pinot.

Top right Sarah-Kate Dineen. **Right** Harvest in full swing on the slopes at Mt Maude.

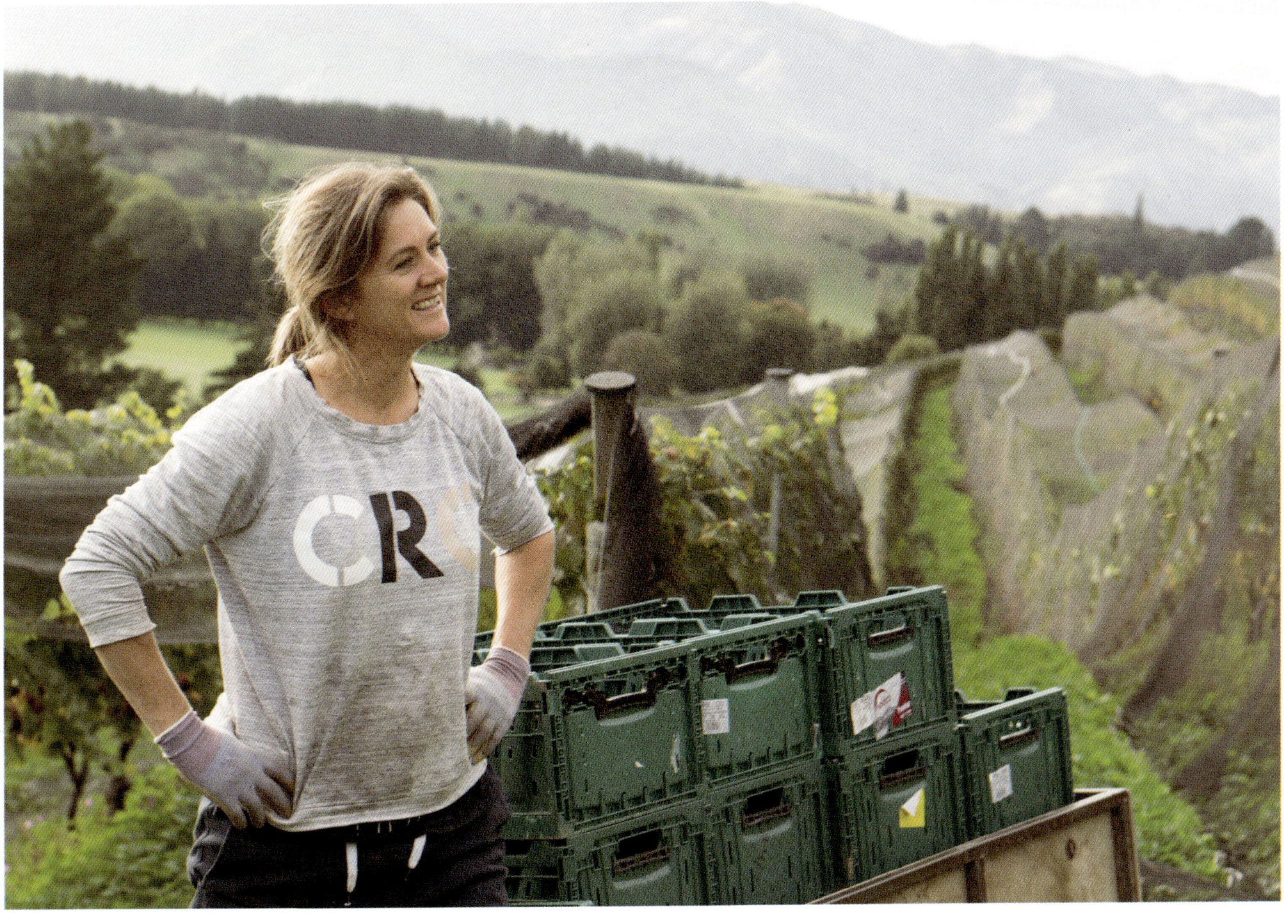
CR

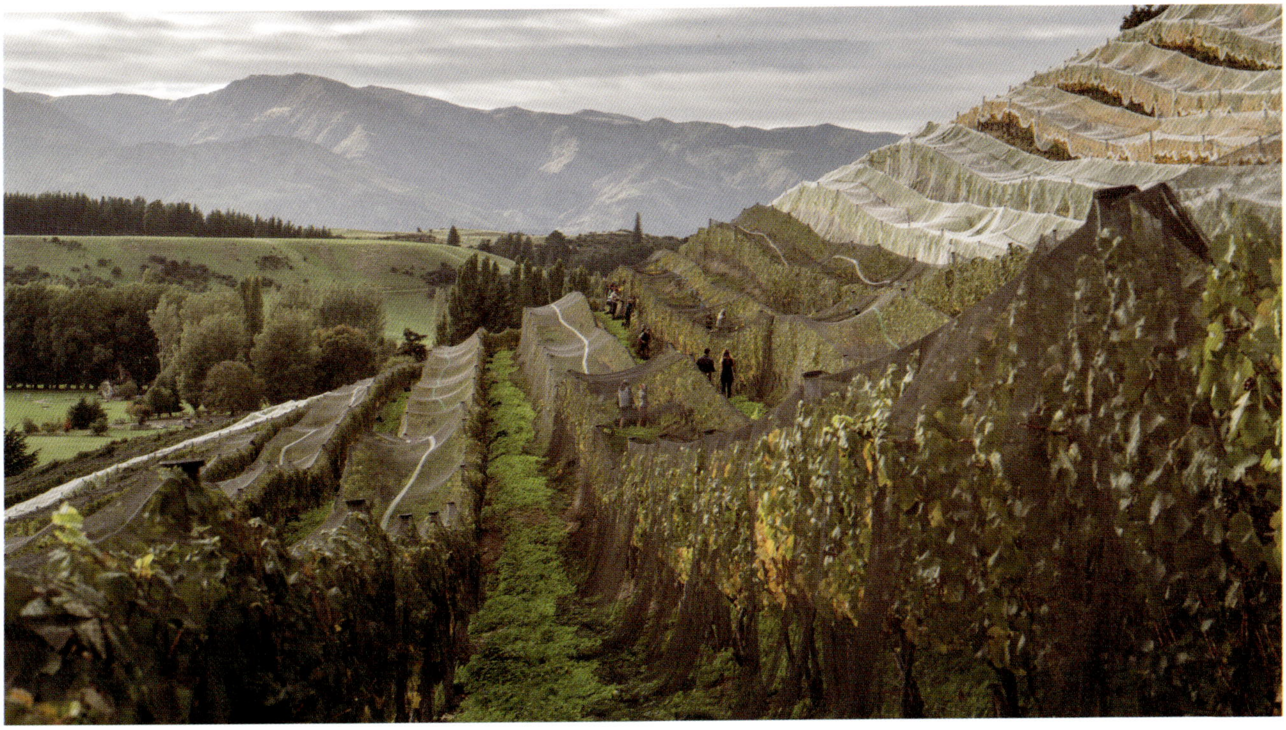

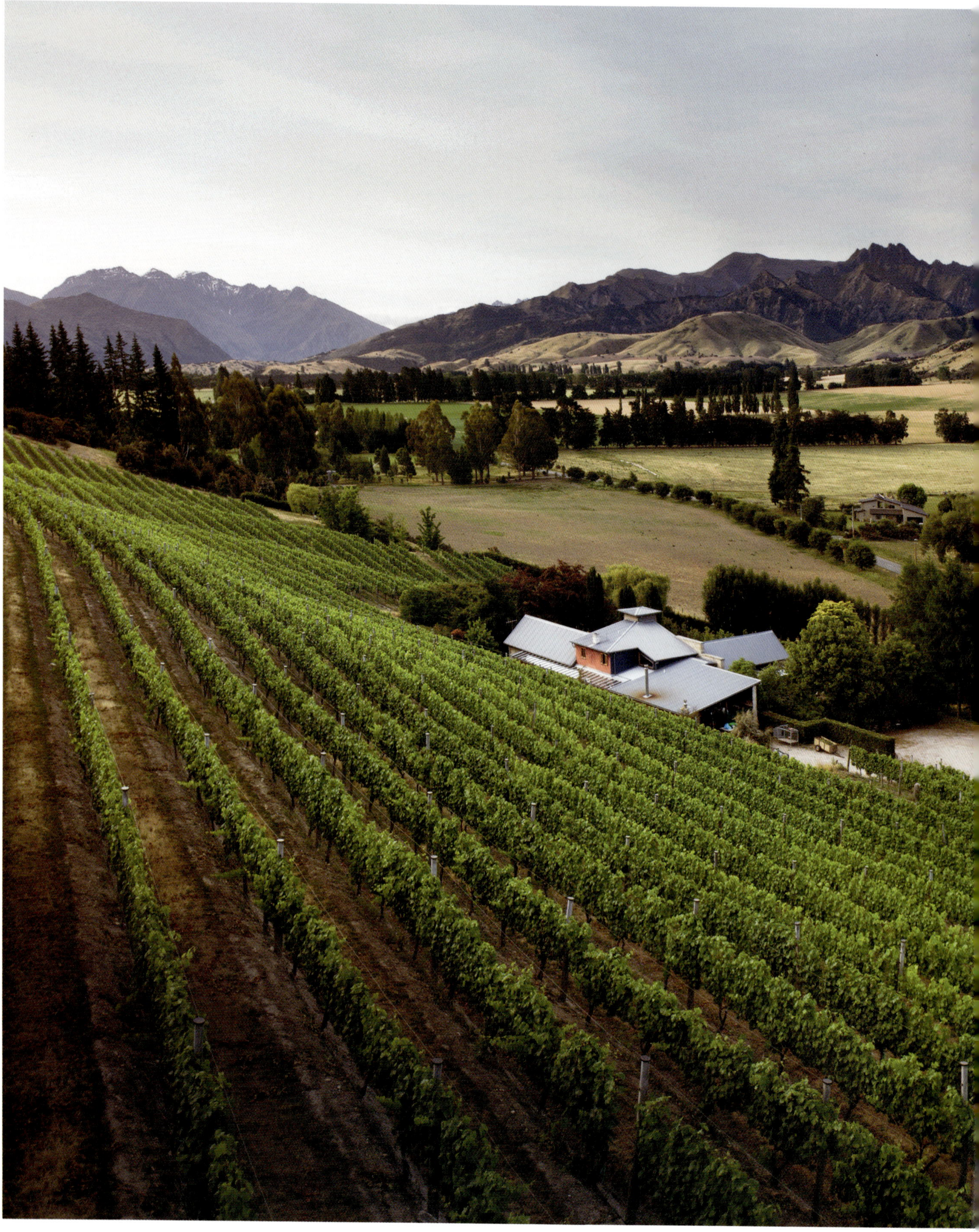

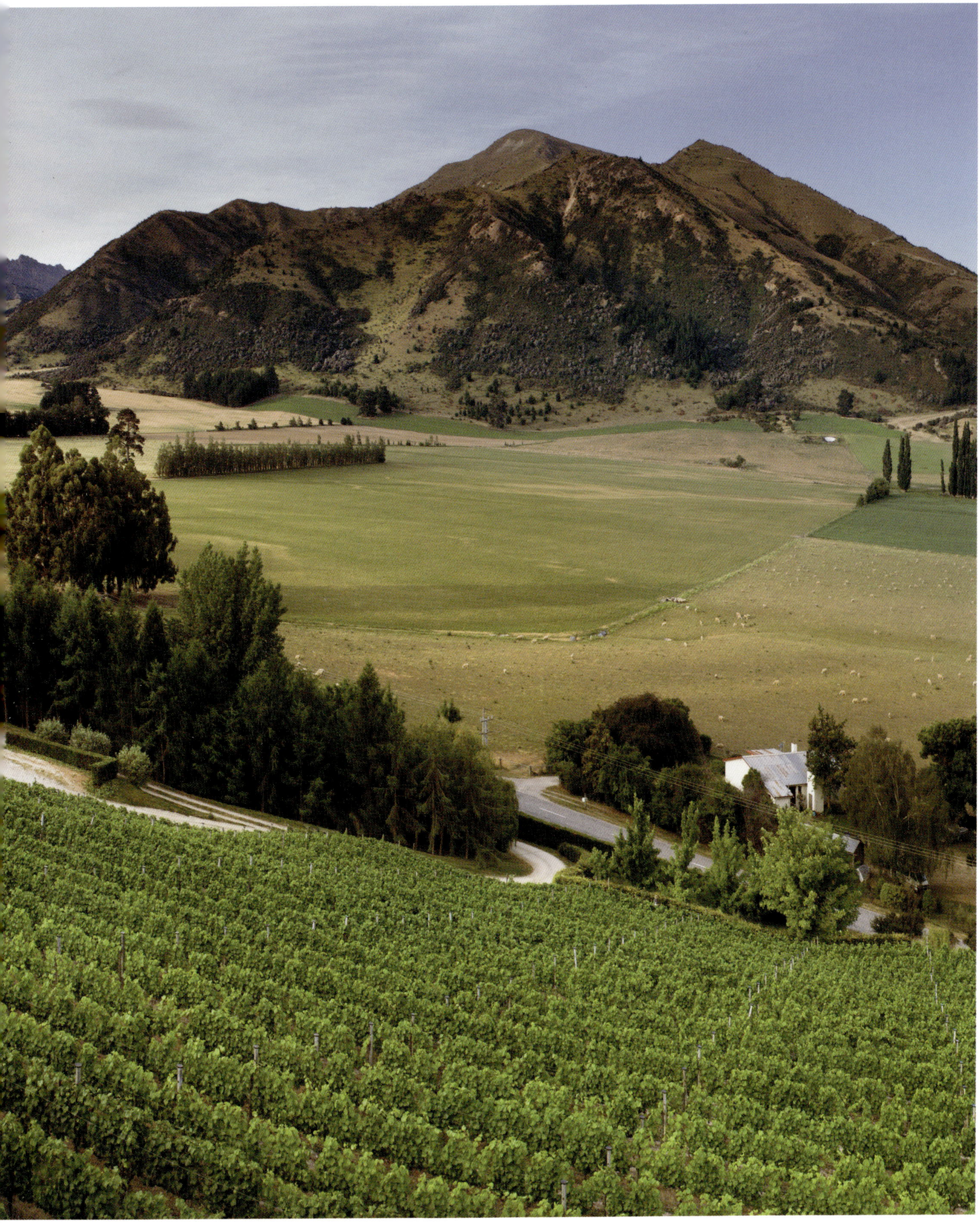

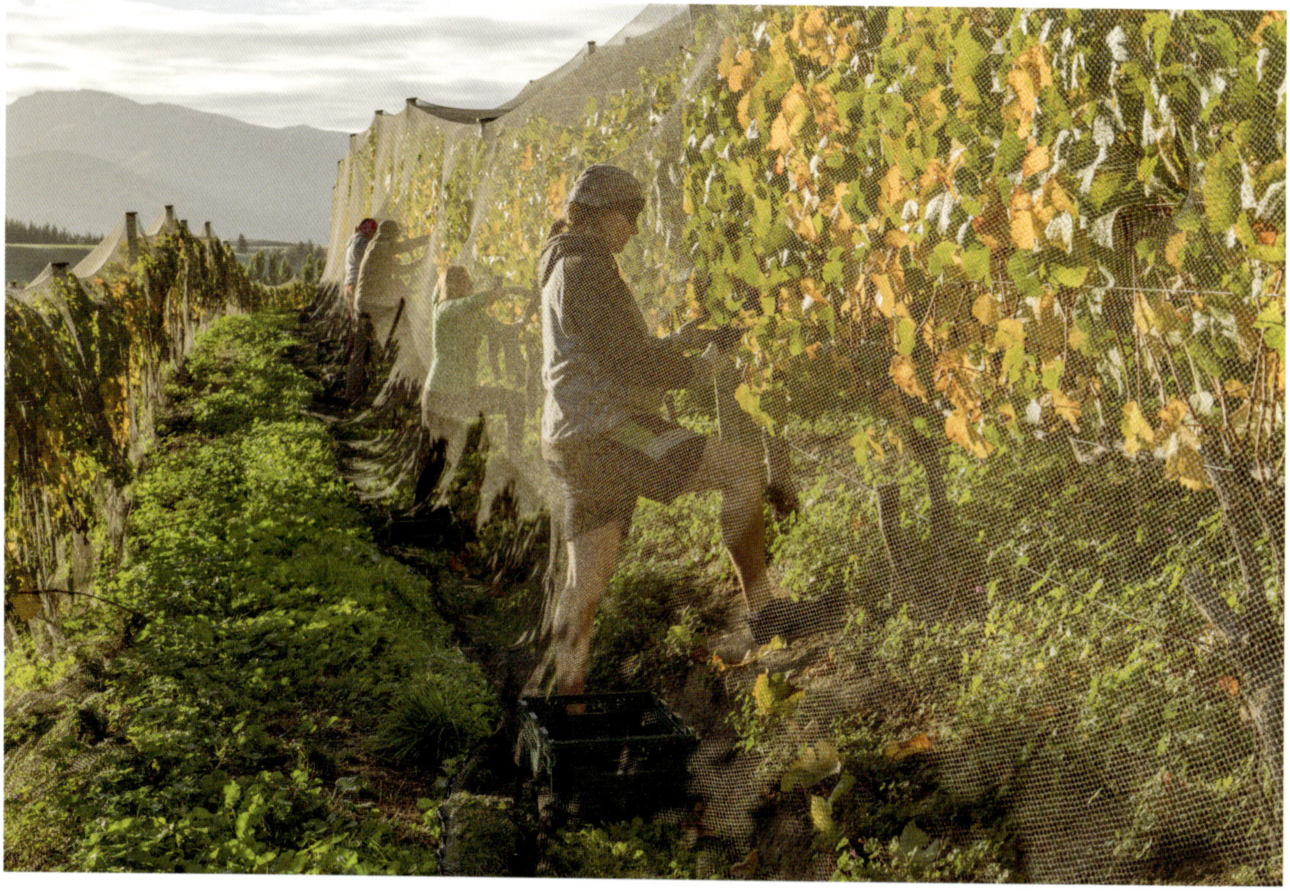

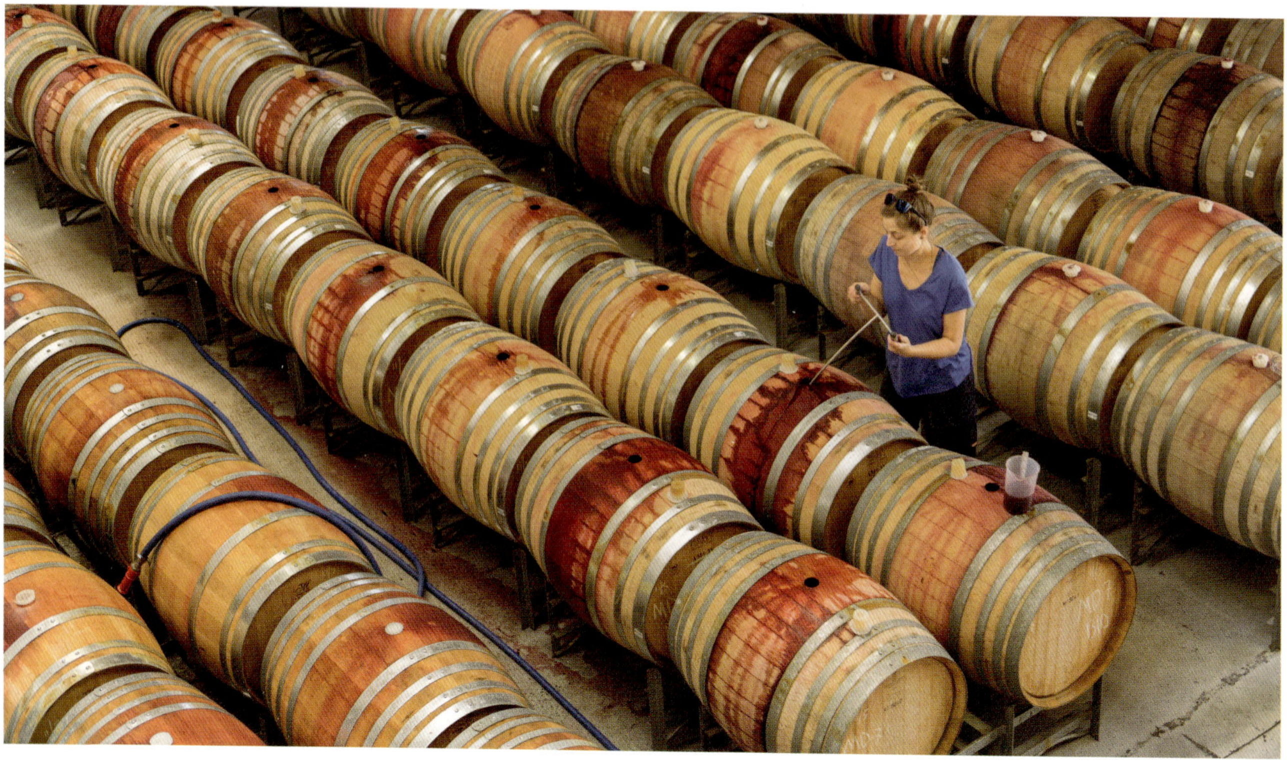

Above left Vineyard workers harvesting under bird nets. **Left** Winemaker Vanessa Robson stirring and topping up Pinot barrels. **Top right** Dan Dineen processing Chardonnay grapes. **Middle right** Winemaker Vanessa Robson 'plunging' the Pinot Noir grapes. **Bottom right** Maude Tasting Room at Bistro Gentil, Wanaka.

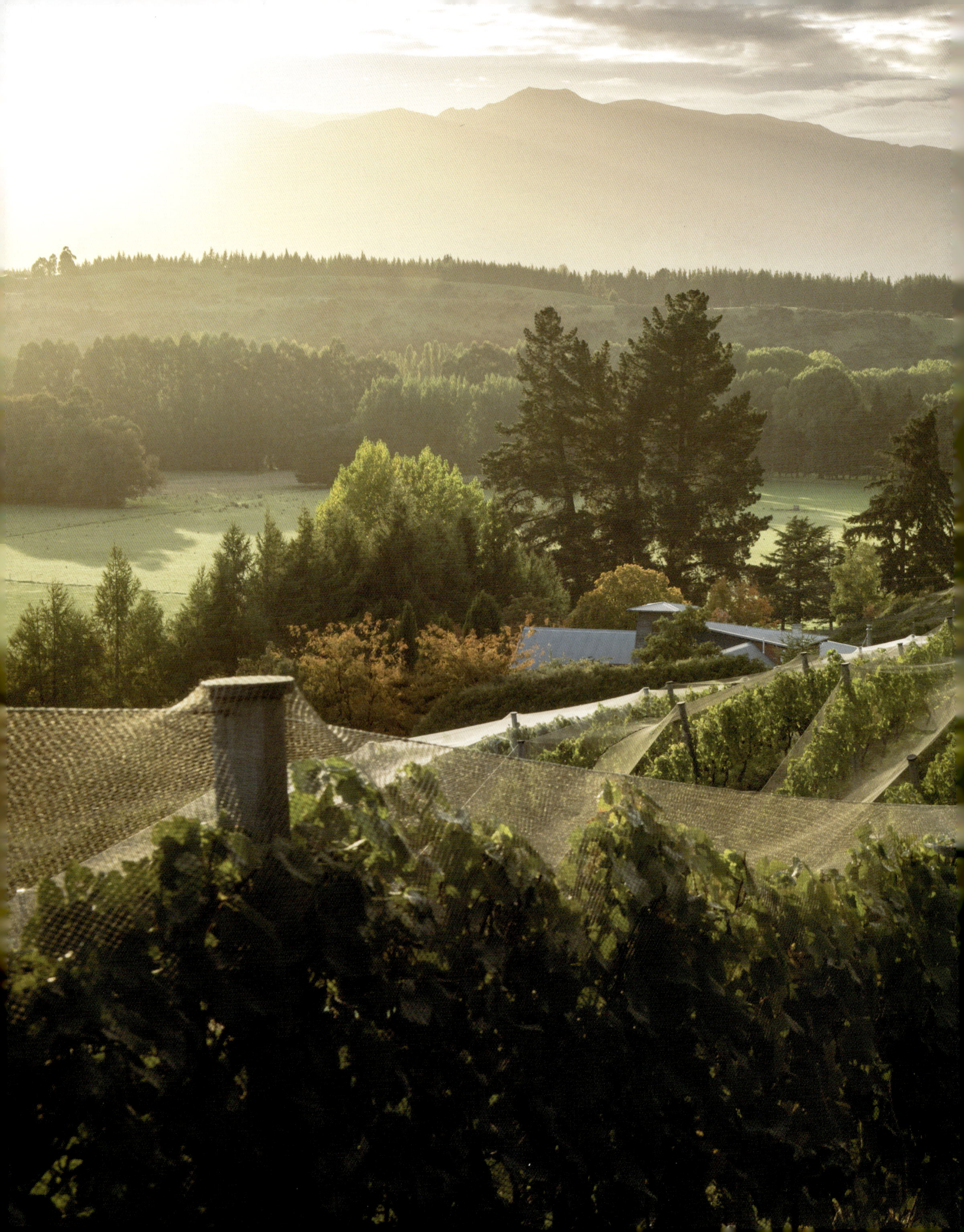

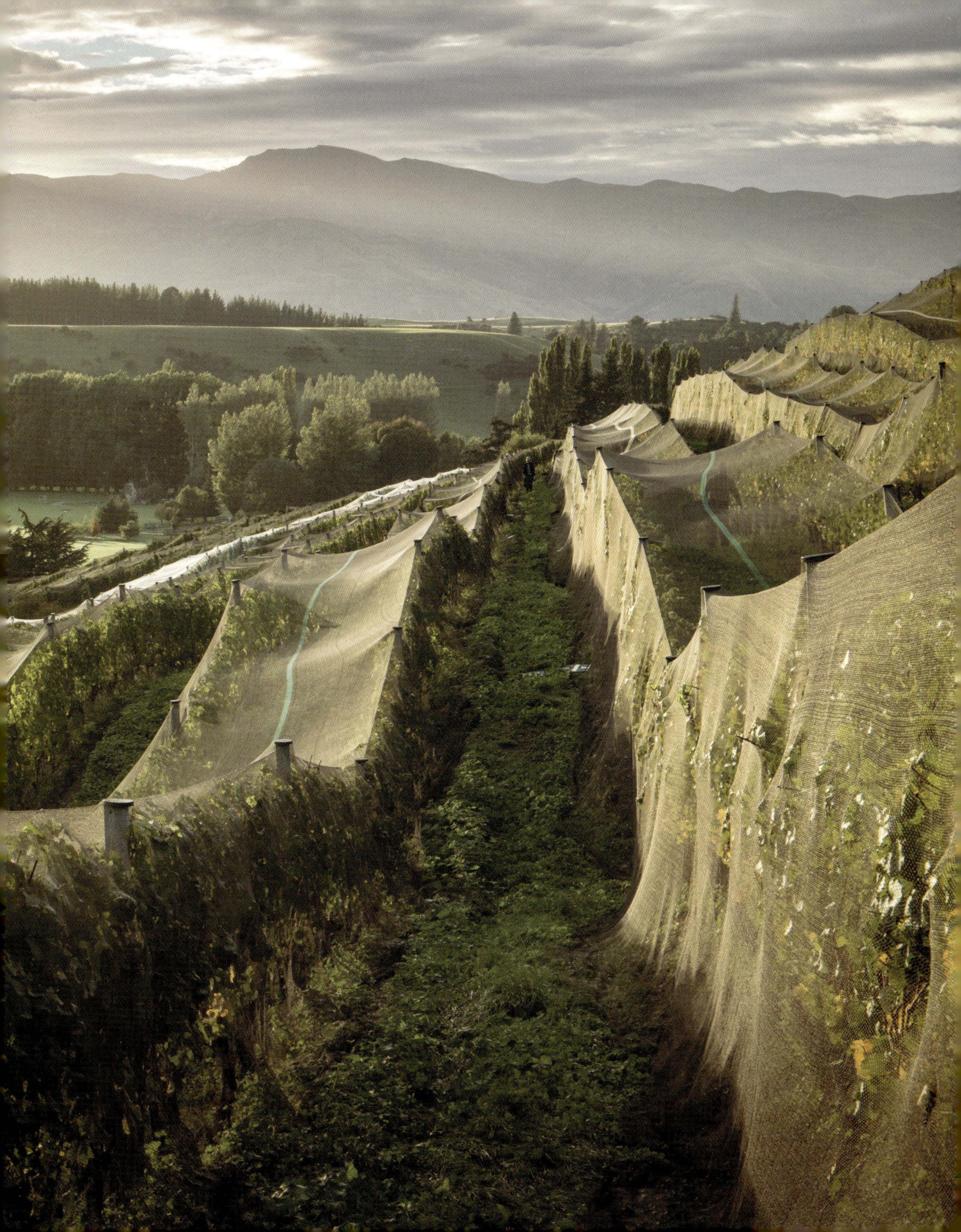

Glossary

alluvial fan — silt, sand, gravel and other sediment deposited where water once flowed

aspect — the outlook or angle of the land and orientation of the vines towards sunlight

biodynamic wine — wine made from biodynamically grown grapes, an alternative form of agriculture based on the holistic philosophies of Rudolf Steiner; see *Demeter certification*

Blanc de Blancs — a sparkling wine made entirely from white grapes, usually Chardonnay

botrytis / noble rot — a sweet wine made from grapes affected by the *Botrytis cinerea* mould, which concentrates the sugars and acidity

Bourgogne — the French name for Burgundy

bud-burst — the period in early spring when the grape vines produce new shoots

clone — genetically identical variety of a grape such as Pinot Noir selected for some specific attribute

COPNL — Central Otago Pinot Noir Limited, established in 2002 to promote and market Central Otago Pinots

COWA — Central Otago Winegrowers Association, established in 1986

COWCo — Central Otago Wine Company, founded in 1997

Demeter certification — a worldwide certification system to verify that a product has been produced by biodynamic methods; the Bio Dynamic Farming and Gardening Association is the New Zealand certifier

diurnal temperature variation — the cycle of temperature variation between day and night

domaine — a wine-producing property (particularly in Burgundy)

Gamay — a red grape variety used for making Beaujolais and other light red wines

GDD — growing degree days, calculated from the daily maximum and minimum air temperature over the growing season. In Central Otago this is 1 October–30 April

Grüner Veltliner — a white-wine grape variety grown primarily in Austria

ice wine — a sweet style of wine traditionally made from grapes that have been frozen while still on the vine, but in the New World more typically from artificially frozen grapes

late-harvest wine — a sweet style of wine, usually white made from very ripe grapes

MS — Master Sommelier qualification issued by the Court of Master Sommeliers in the UK

MW — Master of Wine qualification issued by the Institute of Masters of Wine in the UK

natural wines — wines made with minimal intervention (chemical or technological) in the naturally occurring fermentation process

oenology — the science and practice of making wine

organic wine — wine made from organically grown grapes certified by BioGro NZ; in New Zealand

Osteiner — a white grape hybrid of Riesling and Sylvaner

phylloxera — an aphid of American origin that feeds on vine roots, making grafting onto resistant rootstocks necessary in most wine regions

Pinot Blanc — a white mutation of the Pinot Noir grape

preparation 500 — cow manure that is packed inside a cow horn, buried, and later dug up and mixed with water to be used in biodynamic soil treatment

provenance — geographical origins or source of a wine

rootstock — vine root selected for various attributes including resistance to phylloxera or suitability to particular soil types

Roseworthy Agricultural College — Australia's first agricultural college, established in 1883, specialising in viticulture and oenology, merged with the University of Adelaide's Faculty of Agricultural and Natural Sciences in 1991

sommelier — wine steward or wine service professional

tannins — astringent pigment and flavour compounds from grape skins, stalks and pips

terroir — the 'terrain' or total physical environment of a region or vineyard's landscape and climate

veraison — the onset of ripening of grapes

vigneron — the French term for vine-grower, also involved in the winemaking process

VinPro — Central Otago contract winemaking facility

I would like to thank the following people who have helped and inspired me in the writing of this book: Jeremy Sherlock, my publisher from Penguin Random House; Mike Wilkinson, photographer; Phil Melchior, friend and mentor; Chris Lumsden, Wanaka bookseller; Alex Easton, assistant viticulturist at Ceres Wines; and wine writers Jane Skilton and Elaine Chukan Brown for their forewords.

My thanks also go to those involved in the winegrowing industry in Central Otago who shared their knowledge and stories with me so willingly and generously: Ann Pinckney, old school friend and wine pioneer; Alan Brady; Lois and Nick Mills; Rob Hay; Grant Taylor; Verdun Burgess; Gill Grant; Rudi Bauer; Stewart Elms; Nigel Greening; Blair Walter; Robin, Matt and James Dicey; Steve and Barbara Green; Sir Cliff and David Skeggs; Christopher Keys; Sean Brennan; Lindsay, Jude and Fraser McLachlan; Sam Neill; Dean Shaw; Peter Bartle; Antony Worch; Annie Winmill; Angela Chiaroni and Paul Jacobson; Phil Handford; Mike Moffit; Brook and Lucie Lawrence; Andre Lategan; Dr Stephanie Lambert; Claire Mulholland; Domenic Mondillo; Paul Pujol; Sarah-Kate and Dan Dineen; and Di and Richard Somerville.

— **VIV MILSOM**

A special thank you to all of the vineyards for making me welcome and giving me unrestricted access to the stunning locations, wineries and various activities over the six months it took to compile all these images. Without this help the book would not have been possible. Thanks also to Bill Day, pilot extraordinaire, for helicopter assistance and organising special permission for flying in restricted zones.

— **MIKE WILKINSON**

Penguin
Random House
New Zealand

First published by Penguin
Random House New Zealand, 2018

1 3 5 7 9 10 8 6 4 2

Text © Viv Milsom, 2018
Photography © Mike Wilkinson, 2018

The moral right of the author
has been asserted.

All rights reserved.

Design by Rachel Clark © Penguin
Random House New Zealand
Prepress by Image Centre Group
Printed and bound in China by
Toppan Leefung Printing Limited

A catalogue record for this book
is available from the National
Library of New Zealand.

ISBN 978-0-14-377207-1

penguin.co.nz

MIX
Paper from
responsible sources
FSC® C104723